Creative Industries and Innovation in Europe

In recent years, the study of creativity has shifted from analysis of culture as an end in itself to one of economic enhancement, and its capability to generate wealth and promote economic development. A growing literature is starting to highlight the innovation capacity of cultural and creative industries (CCIs) as they intersect the innovation processes of other manufacturing and services sectors with an innovative and creative output. This book brings together a set of multidisciplinary contributions to investigate the kaleidoscope of European creativity, focusing on CCIs and the innovations connected with them. The two main questions that this volume aims to address are: How can we identify, map and define CCIs in Europe? And how do they contribute to innovation and sustainable growth?

The first part of the book deals with the definition, measurement and mapping of the geography of European CCIs according to a local economic approach, focusing on Italy, Spain, the UK, Austria, Denmark and France.

The second part collects some interesting cases of innovation generated in creative spaces such as cities of art or creative clusters and networks. This entails the study of innovations among creative and non-creative sectors (e.g. laser technologies in conservation of works of art and design networks in Italy) and across European and non-European countries (e.g. Spaghetti Western movies in the US or visual artists in New Zealand). Finally, an innovation capacity of culture that can regenerate mature sectors (e.g. French food supply chain and Swiss watchmaking) or combine the creative and green economics paradigms (e.g. the green creative cities in North Europe) is analyzed.

This book will appeal to academics, scholars and practitioners of urban and regional studies, cultural and creative economics and managerial and organizational studies.

Luciana Lazzeretti is a Professor of Business Economics and Director of the Postgraduate Programme in Economics and Management of Cultural Goods and Museums at the Faculty of Economics, University of Florence, Italy.

Regions and Cities

Series editors: Ron Martin, University of Cambridge, UK
Gernot Grabher, University of Bonn, Germany
Maryann Feldman, University of Georgia, USA
Gillian Bristow, University of Cardiff, UK.

Regions and Cities is an international, interdisciplinary series that provides authoritative analyses of the new significance of regions and cities for economic, social and cultural development, and public policy experimentation. The series seeks to combine theoretical and empirical insights with constructive policy debate and critically engages with formative processes and policies in regional and urban studies.

Creative Industries and Innovation in Europe

Concepts, measures and comparative case studies

Edited by Luciana Lazzeretti

LONDON AND NEW YORK

First published 2013
by Routledge
2 Park Square, Milton Park, Abingdon, Oxfordshire OX14 4RN

Simultaneously published in the USA and Canada
by Routledge
711 Third Avenue, New York, NY 10017

First issued in paperback 2014

Routledge is an imprint of the Taylor & Francis Group, an informa business

British Library Cataloguing in Publication Data
A catalogue record for this book is available from the British Library

Library of Congress Cataloging in Publication Data
Creative industries and innovation in Europe / edited by Luciana Lazzeretti.
    p. cm.
    1. Cultural industries – Europe. 2. Technological innovations – Economic
    aspects – Europe. I. Lazzeretti, Luciana.
    HD9999.C9473C45146 2012
    302.23094–dc23   2011052005

ISBN: 978-0-415-67740-0 (hbk)
ISBN: 978-1-138-79219-7 (pbk)

Typeset in Times New Roman
by HWA Text and Data Management, London

Contents

Figures

Tables

Contributors

Marco Bettiol is Assistant Professor at the Department of Economics and Management, University of Padua. He was visiting scholar (2002) at the School of Information Management and Systems, University of California, Berkeley. His research is focused on two main areas: ICT, and creativity and industrial design. He also analyzed the models of adoption of ICT by small and medium firms in Italy.

Rafael Boix is Lecturer at the Department of Economic Structure, Universitat de València. He previously held an academic position at the Universitat Autònoma de Barcelona and has been an external advisor for the Organisation of Economic Co-operation and Development (OECD), the Spanish Ministry of Industry, Barcelona's provincial government, and Barcelona City Hall.

Francesco Capone PhD is Research Fellow and Lecturer of Economics and Management of Enterprises, Faculty of Economics, University of Florence. He is the author of several papers and articles on creative industries and creative cities, tourism and innovation.

Gino Cattani is Associate Professor of Strategy and Organizations at the Stern School of Business, New York University. He received an MA in Management Science and Applied Economics (2001) and a PhD in Management (2004) from the Wharton School, University of Pennsylvania. His research focuses primarily on creativity, innovation and micro-determinants of industry dynamics.

Tommaso Cinti PhD is Research Fellow and Lecturer of Economics and Management of Enterprises in the Department of Business and Social Studies, University of Siena. His research interests deal with cultural clusters, cultural districts, local development and innovation.

Philip Cooke is Research Professor in Regional Economic Development and Founding Director of the Centre for Advanced Studies, at the University of Wales, Cardiff, as well as adjunct professor in Development Studies at Aalborg University, Denmark and Toulouse University, France. His research interests lie in studies of eco-innovation, biotechnology, regional innovation systems, knowledge economies, entrepreneurship, clusters and networks.

Pedro Costa is Assistant Professor at the Political Economy Department of ISCTEIUL (Higher Institute of Business and Labour Sciences of Lisbon University) and Vice President of Dinâmia-CET (Research Centre on Socioeconomic Change and Territory), at Lisbon University Institute. His research activity is mainly focused on territorial and urban economics, cultural economics, territorial planning and research methodologies.

Olivier Crevoisier is Professor of Territorial Economy at the Institute of Sociology and Director of the Research Group on Territorial Economy (GRET) at the University of Neuchâtel. He is also a member of the European Research Group on Innovative Milieux (GREMI). Research interests: innovative milieus, finance industry and cultural resources.

Lisa De Propris is Senior Lecturer in Industrial Economics at the Birmingham Business School. Her main research interests are: competitiveness in clusters and industrial districts, innovation, knowledge economy and clusters, and creative and cultural industries. In parallel, she has been concerned with the role of the government and institutions, and has looked at policy implications.

C. Moritz B. Fliescher is a PhD candidate in Management at the Stern School of Business, New York University. He earned a BS in business from Georgetown University (2006) and has worked as a management consultant. His research interest lies in organizational change and organizational learning.

Hugues Jeannerat is Research Associate at the Institute of Sociology, and Member of the Research Group on Territorial Economy (GRET) at the University of Neuchâtel. He focuses his research on industrial clusters, cultural and creative industries, and experience economy.

Leïla Kebir is a Visiting Scholar at the Proximity team, UMR SADAPT (National Institute for Agronomic Research) at the National Institute for Agricultural Research (INRA) in Paris (Swiss National Science Foundation Fellowship). She is a member of the European Research Group on Innovative Milieux (GREMI) and focuses in her research on regional development, innovation and resource development issues. She currently works on food production systems.

Luciana Lazzeretti is a Professor of Business Economics and Director of the Postgraduate Programme in Economics and Management of Cultural Goods and Museums at the Faculty of Economics, University of Florence, Italy. She is also Associate Professor at the Institute of Applied Physics 'Nello Carrara' CNR-IFAC (National Centre of Research – Institute of Applied Physics), Florence. Her current research interests are focused on industrial districts, cultural clusters and cities of art, creative and cultural industries, innovation and creativity.

Anne Lorentzen PhD is Professor of Geography at Aalborg University, Denmark. She is co-founder and board member of the Centre of Regional Development at Aalborg University, and member of the National Bibliometrical Committee. Her research interests lie in experience and knowledge economy, regional, urban and local development, innovation and technology, and economics of transition.

Daniel Sánchez is a PhD candidate at the Universitat Autònoma de Barcelona. His research focuses on the determinants that drive knowledge and creative concentration within local labour systems in Europe.

Masayuki Sasaki is Director of Urban Research Plaza and Professor of Urban and Cultural Economics at the Graduate School for Creative Cities, Osaka City University, Japan. He is President of the Japan Association of Cultural Economics and Editor-in-Chief of *City, Culture & Society*, published by Elsevier. He has been dean of the Graduate School for Creative Cities.

René Schuldner is Research Assistant at the Institute for Regional Development and Environment at the Vienna University of Economics and Business.

Silvia Rita Sedita PhD is presently Assistant Professor of Economics and Management of Enterprises, Faculty of Political Science, University of Padua. Main research interests: industrial districts, clusters, creative networks, communities of practice and inter-organizational learning.

Udo Staber is Professor and Chair of Organization Studies at the University of Canterbury, New Zealand. He has led a number of research projects funded by agencies such as the US National Science Foundation, Social Science and Humanities Research Council of Canada, and the German Research Foundation. His research interests focus on organizational evolution and social and inter-organizational networks, with special reference to networks in business clusters, entrepreneurship and regional development.

Franz Tödtling is Professor and Head of the Institute for Regional Development and Environment at the Vienna University of Economics and Business. He has been involved in many international research projects and collaborations funded by the European Science Foundation, the European Framework Program and the US National Science Foundation. His main research areas are regional development, innovation systems and policy, and the knowledge economy from a spatial perspective.

André Torre is Research Director at the National Institute of Agricultural Research (INRA) and AgroParisTech in Paris. He teaches in several French universities, and is currently the chairman of the French-speaking section of ERSA (European Regional Science Association). His main research fields are the analysis of proximity and coordination relations in the process of innovation, regional development and in land use and neighbourhood conflict solving.

Michaela Trippl is Associate Professor at the Institute of Regional Development and Environment at the Vienna University of Economics and Business. Her main areas of research comprise spatial aspects of knowledge-intensive industries, regional innovation processes and clustering, and new forms of political governance.

Cultural and creative industries

An introduction

Luciana Lazzeretti

The cultural and creative industries: a successful paradigm

The issues of culture and creativity have long been at the centre of a multidisciplinary scientific debate, which emphasizes the relationship among culture, creativity, local development and innovation (Jeffcutt and Pratt 2009). Many scholars from different disciplines, ranging from the economics of culture (Throsby 2010), and of local development (Cooke and Lazzeretti 2008) to managerial and organizational studies (DeFillippi *et al.* 2007) have been involved in this field of studies.

While at first the subject was tackled emphasizing culture, more recently there has been a shift of focus from preservation to economic enhancement, and to culture's capability of generating wealth and promote economic development, so attention has been drawn to creativity and innovation.

The economics of creativity, which has now become the major paradigm in research, was first associated with the knowledge economy, information and communications technologies (ICTs) (Howkins 2001) and the creative cities (Scott 2006), and later with Florida's (2002) creative class. Only recently, Cultural and Creative Industries (CCIs) have been considered as a relevant economic proxy for measuring creativity (UNCTAD 2010), thanks also to the acknowledgment of their impact on innovation within the wider economy (Bakhshi *et al.* 2008).

The new concept of creative class has not only contributed to shift the attention from cultural economics to the economics of creativity, from the artistic and cultural heritage to the human capital, but it has also generated an important number of empirical studies in the US, Canada, Australia (Hartley and Cunningham 2001; Stolarick and Florida 2006), China (Qian 2010) and East Asia (Yusuf and Nabeshima 2005). In Europe, these were mainly led by Northern European countries (Asheim and Hansen 2009), and have often produced comparative surveys of the US (Clifton and Cooke 2009). The research is presently spreading to the East European countries, but not so much in Central and Southern Europe. Countries like Italy, Spain, France and Switzerland were less interested in this perspective, probably because they are more concerned with their huge artistic, architectural and cultural heritage. The analyses carried out have been most often related to the cultural industries, drawn on national reports and statistics, and addressed mainly the preservation and economic enhancement of cultural and artistic resources (Greffe 2003), whereas the creative economy has entered the scientific debate only more recently. At present, the main strategic resource is human capital, and the attention of scholars has progressively turned from the creative contexts to the dynamics of the creative processes and innovation.

The CCIs traditionally associated with the paradigm of cultural economics have grown in importance within the domain of creative economy, in parallel with the criticisms aroused against the creative class approach (Glaeser 2005).

Some authors, although following this approach, complain about its practical application (Comunian *et al.* 2010), while others are especially critical about the ways it connects with the issues of growth and urban regeneration. Pratt (2008) suggested that policy makers may achieve more successful outcomes in terms of economic renewal if they look upon the cultural industry as an entity that links production and consumption, manufacturing and service. Storper and Scott (2009) argue that the economic geography of production must explicitly deal with the complex recursive interactions between the location of firms and the movements of labour.

CCIs are now considered as core activities of the new 'cognitive cultural capitalism' (Scott 2008), as well as offering an excellent opportunity to support the exiting of the current economic crisis (KEA European Affairs 2009a). The interest in these issues was raised in conjunction with the resurgence of the city as a focus of the development policies, and it was fed by the examination not only of American and Asian metropolitan areas, but also of European small towns and rural areas (Lorentzen and van Heur 2011).

A growing literature has now started to highlight the innovation capacity of CCIs as they intersect the innovation processes of other manufacturing/services activities, and the innovative and creative outputs of arts and cultural organizations (Bakhshi and Throsby 2010).

Although established as a successful paradigm, CCIs have been constantly redefined – and still are being redefined – taking up different meanings over time (O'Connor 2008). Initially, in line with the English *Mapping Document* (DCMS 2001) the industries that had been traditionally classified as cultural were included among the creative industries (Garhnam 2005). More recently, the classification system tends, on the one hand, to adopt a broader approach and, on the other hand, to distinguish between the cultural and the creative industries. The field has also been extended to include activities that are interdependent with CCIs, for instance leisure, experience and tourism, recognizing their basic contribution to the transition to a green economy and a new sustainable development model (European Commission 2010a).

However, while revealing the variety and heterogeneity of CCIs, the widening of the concept has certainly not smoothed the implementation of suitable measurement and evaluation tools (DCMS 2010). Consequently, our knowledge of the different types and levels of creativity in the northern, central and southern regions of Europe cannot be said to be satisfactory. Likewise, the policies needed for supporting creativity have not been implemented yet. Even though the *Green Paper*[1] proves a good understanding of the impact of CCIs, as part of the 'Europe

2020' agenda for a smart Europe (European Commission 2010b), there is still a lack of commitment towards this industry sector (Cooke and De Propris 2011).

In short, if a 'resurgence of cultural and creative industries' seems to be underway, which assigns them a primary role if compared to the creative class approach's viewpoint, the debate on their definition, measurement and evaluation still represents an open issue.

Measuring creativity: a cultural and creative industries approach

Creativity is a fuzzy concept of permeable and hardly identifiable boundaries (Markusen *et al.* 2008). For example, creative workers are considered by some as those employed in cultural industries, and by others as those devoted to cultural occupations, even if many cultural industries employ people whose work does not involve creative tasks. Allen Scott says that creativity is connected with learning and innovation. At a rough approximation, learning offers an important informative and practical basis for creative action; *creativity* especially concerns thought and action (of individuals and groups) that generate new insights and perceptions, whatever their tangible significance is; *innovation* derives from these insights and perceptions but is particularly focused on their implementation in various application fields (Scott 2010: 119).

Likewise, CCIs also constitute a rather 'fuzzy' concept, which, however, represents an important standard of measurement deeply rooted in cultural studies and in the economics of culture (Caves 2000; Hesmondhalgh 2002).

Starting from the introduction of the creative industries' classification drawn up by the British government in the *Mapping Document* (DCMS 1998, 2001), there has been a rise in the creative sector at the expense of the cultural sector. The traditional cultural industries, such as publishing, have been gradually included in the creative ones, favoured by the establishment of the new technologies (ICTs). These have a significant impact on cultural productions and on the forms of their fruition, not only because they advance new products, but also because they change consumption behaviours (Bakhshi and Throsby 2010). The creative sector is more and more often taking on the features of a Schumpeterian 'disruptive innovation' (Chesbrough 2003). At the same time, the economic activities typical of the cultural economy, such as the 'visual and performing arts', were at first classified among multimedia or entertainment, and were later included in the typology of creative industry. As mentioned earlier, the boundaries of the sector are currently widening, with the inclusion of leisure, experience economy and cultural tourism: one of the most comprehensive taxonomy of creative industries, the one proposed by UNCTAD (2010), even includes sectors belonging to manufacturing, despite most of it constituting services, especially of knowledge-intensive services (Gallouj and Savona 2009).

The creative one has became a 'priority sector' in the European agenda (Power and Nielsén 2010), and its evaluation employs not only sectoral, but also territorial approaches that emphasize the tight connection with the cultural diversity of places (De Propris *et al.* 2009). What is crucial in this field is the relationship between creativity, diversity and space (Baycan-Levent and Nijkamp 2010). In fact, creative industries as well as creative classes are clustered according to different typologies and spatial patterns (Lazzeretti *et al.* 2008). This is not all: the studies using a territorial approach are also enriched by an organizational and managerial perspective, which is able to investigate the individual creative process of both the artists and the creative networks (Belussi and Staber 2012).

As a first geographical view of the creativity studies led in Europe, we might say that in the various countries that undertook them two main paths were followed: on the one hand, the 'technology-driven' way, mostly followed in Northern Europe and mainly referred to as the creative class/industries approach; and on the other hand, the 'heritage-driven' way, preferred in central and southern European countries and more directly related to studies on cultural economics and to cultural industries.

The second approach was not extensively investigated: this is why the first aim of this volume is to identify, map and define the creative industries in Europe, including the heritage-driven countries, and also presenting some comparative models of analysis.

Yet, creativity remains a fuzzy concept, whose richness cannot be exhausted by merely codifying it in terms of a 'creative class' versus 'creative–cultural industries' standpoint. Creativity is a cross-sectional phenomenon that spreads and develops 'across industries'; it also concerns the 'individual creativity' of peculiar managerial approaches (Perry-Smith and Shalley 2003), which are able to rejuvenate sectors as well as products, as in the case of the US film industry (Cattani and Ferriani 2008). Creativity is the 'creative capacity' (Lazzeretti 2009), what can give life to radical and incremental innovation of both products and processes through cross-fertilization. An emblematic case is that of design, once a cultural industry mainly related to new technologies and fashion (Aage and Belussi 2008), and now an officially recognized transversal technology capable of reviving mature products and sectors, or advancing new ones. Design requires the combination of a wide range of knowledge resources, which are of fundamental importance for industrial renovation, e.g. in the industries of food (Santagata 2003) or construction (i.e. building design). In fact, it can be employed by hotel and restaurant enterprises, as well as by museums and theatres.

Furthermore, the innovation power of creativity is enforced by emerging paradigms deriving from the experience economy (Pine and Gilmore 1999) and the green economy (Cooke 2009), and it will take new shapes whose identification and codification are beyond imagination.

The second aim of the present volume is to investigate how CCIs contribute to innovation and local development, and bring to light uncodified, tacit and embedded creativeness, so as to provide a kaleidoscopic view of creativity in Europe.

Finally, a last and complementary aim is to collect interesting cases and experiences from European as well as non-European countries. By encouraging the undertaking of comparative and benchmarking studies, it is possible to supply a helpful tool and recommend a 'creativity policy' for Europe, which is presently still unclearly defined (KEA European Affairs 2009b).

The spatial and social dimension of creativity: a multidisciplinary approach

In social sciences, studies on creativity have been conducted by scholars of several disciplines, but the recent trend seems to privilege a more explicitly multidisciplinary approach. An example may come from the recent studies on creative cities by Andersson *et al.* (2011) that combine the contributions coming from the creative class approach with those of psychologists and urban sociologists. Belussi and Staber (2012), in their volume on creative networks, have collected contributions from the areas of organizational and management studies, whilst the DCMS (2010) report includes a multidisciplinary literature review of the methods used to measure the value of culture. The complexity itself of creativity requires a plurality of investigative instruments. Following this direction, this book gathers the contributions of scholars belonging to the culture, experience and creative economy fields alongside experts of regional sciences, organization and innovation studies. The result will be the start of an 'open conversation'[2] centred on the measurement and evaluation of CCIs and related innovations according to a shared concept of the 'spatial and social dimension of creativity'.

There is a strong relation between creativity, space and society, and it recurs across the various approaches adopted: while in the first part of the book the main focus is on the spatial dimension of creativity, the second part discusses more broadly its social side, examining the relation between CCIs and innovation.

The cultural and the economic systems co-evolve, whilst in managerial studies the debate revolves around managing 'situated' creativity in cultural industries (Belussi and Sedita 2011). In order to understand and appreciate creativity it should be contextualized not only in space, but also in time, as Törnqvist (2004) argues.

Study after study on economic development, from Marshall onwards, has discussed this relationship and explored the advantages produced by co-localization of specialized firms in terms of agglomeration economies and knowledge spillovers that can involve the creative dimension. It is also possible to have creative knowledge spillovers connected with the creative industries and the creative class, or to observe further diffusive effects in adjacent sectors also due to a 'creative use' of knowledge spillovers (Bille and Schulze 2006).

Creative economies are those external agglomeration economies that can be explained in terms of both diversity and specialization. Feldman and Audretsch (1999) link them to innovation, while Lorenzen and Frederiksen (2008) underline the co-existence of creative cities and knowledge. Clustering also affects creative industries (Maskell and Lorenzen 2004) and it is important to understand the reasons behind it, and to single out the appropriate methods for the identification and mapping of clusters.

But the spatial dimension of creativity also concerns the innovation processes, and involves the social dimension of creativity. One of the most important forerunners of this branch of study can be traced in the French *milieu innovateur* school (Camagni and Maillat 2006), whose concept can be understood from this new viewpoint as 'creative milieu' (Becattini 2004). The theories of geographical proximity (Torre and Gilly 2000) are reinterpreted from a perspective that considers the creative and cultural dimension (see Chapter 10), alongside those on cognitive proximity/distance (Nooteboom 2000; Boschma 2005), which are fundamental for the development of creative thinking (De Bono 1971). New innovation paths are searched not only within the boundaries of the firm, but also in different contexts (networks, clusters, etc.) and in society as a whole. The boundaries of firms have become porous, and creative people no longer interact only inside but also outside their firms (places of employment), at inter-firm level. As the importance of the local context grows, the 'open innovation' paradigm (Chesbrough 2003) is established, assigning a strategic role to informal environments and public spaces, such as the 'traditional' industrial districts and the new social communities (Lester and Piore 2004). Public creative spaces are capable of absorbing, transforming and recombining new and old experiences with new and diverse resources and capabilities. The role of creative industries becomes paradigmatic, as confirmed by the way the open innovation paradigm was first suggested by Chesbrough (2003). In fact, he examined the innovation processes of the Hollywood movie industry, based on partnership and alliance networks among production studios, directors, talent agencies, actors, scriptwriters, independent producers and specialized subcontractors. In the future, the new paradigm will expand due to new technologies, in areas such as computer science, telecommunications and life sciences.

Innovations are increasingly transversal, cross-sectoral and path dependent, representing the result of a neo-Schumpeterian combinatory capacity that connects mature and emerging sectors, and seems to find in the Jacobian clusters of the European cities and regions a favourable context for cross-fertilization (Cooke 2010). The evolutionary approach establishes itself together with key concepts like 'absorptive capacity' (Cohen and Levinthal 1990) – i.e. the ability of a firm to understand and absorb external knowledge depending on its own knowledge base – which is typical of managerial studies and is now developed in regional sciences. Giuliani (2005) proposes the concept of 'cluster absorptive capacity', and the new evolutionary geography connects it to the related variety approach (Frenken *et al.* 2007), thus broadening this perspective to cities and regions. Lazzeretti links this aspect to the creative approach by introducing the concept of 'creative capacity' and then applies it to the case of the cultural cluster of restoration (see Chapter 9).

Therefore, the spatial and social dimensions of creativity must be taken into account when measuring and evaluating its impact on the innovation processes. The contributions collected in this book provide interesting arguments about this point.

Research questions

It seems useful to recall the two main questions that guided our discussion on creative industries and innovation in Europe:

- How can we identify, map and define CCIs industries in Europe?
- How do they contribute to innovation and growth?

In other words, our open conversation resulted in a collection of contributions that, aside from their differences, finally define two interconnected axes of discussion, which form the basis of the two-part volume.

The first part ('Cultural and creative industries in Europe') deals with the definition, measurement and mapping of the geography of European CCIs according to a local economic development approach, which combines the different perspectives used in the comparative case studies. The authors refer to the areas of regional sciences, cultural economics, creative and experience economy. This part investigates what is meant by CCIs, which theories are used to define them, and which statistical methodologies are applied to identify, measure and map creative industries, and to analyze the determinant of their clustering. The English *Mapping Document* (DCMS 2001) constitutes a reference model for benchmarking with the most widespread taxonomy, where a distinction is made between the traditional creative industries (i.e. cultural) and the non-traditional creative industries (i.e. creative). A survey is made of the different industrial typologies and spatial patterns, which underlines a significant dissimilarity between the north and the south of Europe, mainly due to the differences between heritage-driven (e.g. Italy) and technology-driven (e.g. the UK) countries. The main policy implications for creative industries are investigated, both in cities and in the periphery, the geography of culture, leisure and experience economy is examined (especially in the Danish case) and, finally, a comparison is made with the case of the cultural policy for creativity in Japan.

The main questions discussed in this part are:

- How are cultural and creative industries defined?
- What are the methods for identifying and measuring CCIs?
- What are their main spatial patterns and the determinants of clustering?
- What are the main policy implications for urban and rural creativity?

The second part ('Innovation, creative space and symbolic value') collects some interesting case studies of innovations generated by cross-fertilization and renewal processes in creative spaces (cities, clusters, firms, networks and so on). The principal object of analysis is the 'embedded creativity', which is not exhausted in a list of CCIs, but rather oversteps the boundaries of the codified creative sector.

The innovation capacity of CCIs is investigated through the link between creative contexts, innovations and symbolic values (identity, authenticity and reputation) according to an evolutionary approach tackled by scholars of organization and management studies. It entails the study of innovation and transversality among creative and non-creative sectors (such as the laser technologies used in the conservation of artworks) and across countries (Spaghetti Western movies) with particular reference to cross-fertilization and economic renewal processes. In particular, the capacity of culture to regenerate mature sectors (food supply chain) or to combine the creative and green economics paradigms (green creative cities) is analyzed. Emerging among the key value-added factors of creative processes are those based on the place identity of artists, or the reputation-building processes in cities, places or industries related to authenticity and legitimation (e.g. Swiss watchmaking).

The first four chapters in this part present cases of innovation through cross-fertilization and renewal among creative and non-creative sectors. The last three chapters focus on creative spaces and on processes favouring innovations.

The main questions discussed are:

- How do CCIs stimulate innovation inside and across industries/countries?
- How do CCIs stimulate the renewal of mature products, professions, sectors and chains?
- How do creative spaces affect innovation in the CCIs?
- What is the role of the symbolic factors in creative processes?

Chapter organization

Following this introduction, the volume is divided into two parts and fifteen chapters.

The first part comprises seven chapters. Chapter 1 provides a starting point, which is elaborated in the subsequent contributions in this part. Rafael Boix, Luciana Lazzeretti, Francesco Capone, Lisa De Propris and Daniel Sánchez present an inter-country analysis of the geographical distribution of creative industries measured in terms of employment across four European countries: France, Great Britain, Italy and Spain. The spatial agglomerations of creative industries are identified by calculating for each local labour market the location quotient of its creative activities; the taxonomy utilized is that of traditional and non-traditional CCIs. The results show that France, Italy and Spain specialize more in the traditional creative industries, while Great Britain specializes more in the non-traditional ones. Creative industries show diverse patterns of spatial distributions, such as mono-polar, bi-polar or more diffused. This chapter contributes to the ongoing debate by empirically confirming that creative industries do cluster, giving rise to local production systems around medium and large cities.

Starting from this observation, in Chapter 2 Luciana Lazzeretti, Rafael Boix and Francesco Capone analyze the determinants for the clustering of creative industries. They address a review of the theories about the reasons behind this process of territorial concentration, following a multidisciplinary approach based on cultural and creative economics, evolutionary geography and urban economics. The main results of a comparative analysis performed for Italy and Spain show the existence of some common determinants of creative industry clustering, of which the most important are the human capital, the creative class and the agglomeration economies. Urbanization economies are particularly important in Spain, where creative industries cluster in the heart of the largest metropolitan areas. In Italy, where they are more distributed across the territory, forming networks of medium-sized cities, not only urbanization economies but also district-based localization economies are especially important, together with the presence of a cultural and artistic heritage. The aims of this chapter are to operationalize in an econometric model the main founding theories of CCIs and to show how these are not equally effectual in countries that have different space typologies and patterns.

In Chapter 3, Rafael Boix goes into the analysis of the printing and publishing sectors in Spain, providing an overview of this country's creative industries. Printing and publishing are the most important creative industries in Spain but, despite the size of the linguistic domain (400 million people), the advantages of scale associated with the language are still underused. The analysis highlights the rise of powerful spatial economies of scale that generate huge levels of concentration with the co-localization of printing and publishing in two large metropolitan areas, Madrid and Barcelona.

In Chapter 4 Michaela Trippl, Franz Tödtling and René Schuldner provide a quantitative study of the creative and cultural industries in Austria according to the benchmarking model presented in this first part of the book. These authors underline that creative and cultural industries have been regarded in Austria as dynamically grown key sectors in the past years – just as in many other countries – but that due to a lack of empirical analyses, the tendencies of spatial clustering of the Austrian CCIs are not well understood so far. The chapter seeks to investigate their location pattern in the country, and to examine to what extent these sectors are clustering in the core of large urban areas. By the analysis of the location quotients of employment, the authors find surprisingly high values for the districts surrounding the large cities, particularly Vienna, Linz and Salzburg.

In Chapter 5 Lisa De Propris reconstructs the state of the art in the main definitions of creative economy, cultural economics and CCIs, including the recent tendency to include the leisure, experience and tourism economies, and presents an interesting research agenda for the English case. The author thoroughly investigates the UK's CCI clusters, and geographically identifies their main concentrations, underlining that although the English government has been the most active in supporting CCIs, now it is not clear how it will take the creative economy agenda forward.

Chapter 6 by Anne Lorentzen focuses on the trio 'culture, leisure and experience economy' and on the recent attention it has received, particularly in the strategies of local development in peripheral areas, in view of job creation, attraction of educated labour and industrial diversification. The chapter combines the theories of experience economy, creative industries and local development in a new, diversified approach to discuss the viability of these strategies. By empirically investigating the territorial patterns of experience economy and the role of creative industries in a region like North Denmark, the analysis reveals a pattern of peripheralization and raises the question of whether experience-based strategies can lead to a new 'industrial lock-in'.

The chapter by Masayuki Sasaki concludes this first part, presenting a non-European case. His analysis of the recent policy trends for creative industries in

Japanese cities like Tokyo, Kanazawa and Yokohama constitutes an interesting benchmark against which to measure the European cases and a reminder of the global level of our object of study. The author underlines that as a result of urban and regional policies, the disparity between large cities, small cities and rural areas has increased, with almost all cities except Tokyo facing serious economic and fiscal problems. Since creative industries show very strong trends towards a concentration in Tokyo, the issue of creative cities and urban regeneration through cultural creativity deserves special, increased attention. The work first analyzes the reasons for this concentration of creative industries in Tokyo and second clarifies the achievements and limits of the policies on creative cities specifically adopted by the Kanazawa and Yokohama municipalities.

The second part comprises eight chapters. In Chapter 8, Philip Cooke discusses how the recent developments in complexity theory assist with explaining the combinative evolution that characterizes innovation in ways not yet explored by innovation theorists. This allows for the consideration of processes by which economic activities may become 'strange attractors'. Two such industries are creative industries and ecological industries. The chapter shows how these two segments of the economy have had almost no interactive qualities outside their own systems. The one exception is architecture. Much time is devoted to exploring ways in which the 'sustainable city' could evolve a green aesthetic. Real green design examples from waterfronts in the UK, Denmark and Sweden are analyzed and, in the final section of the chapter, a complexity model of 'relatedness' and 'transversality' is evolved based on actual practice, for implementation of the green creative city.

Chapter 9 by Luciana Lazzeretti and Tommaso Cinti deals with a creative capacity of culture that can identify an unusual relatedness between apparently distant sectors and develop innovations by cross-fertilization. The issue is exemplified by the use of laser in the art restoration sector of Florence. In this field, laser technologies were first employed for the cataloguing of works of art, while they are presently used for the cleaning of materials degraded by environmental pollution. The recombination that brings about innovation occurs between the two sectors of health diagnostics and cultural goods. In particular, the study describes the factors liable to transform a cultural cluster like that of restoration into a creative cluster, and tries to understand whether the cities of arts can be considered as examples of public creative places.

In Chapter 10, Leïla Kebir and André Torre maintain that the issue of geographical proximity comes back into force today, notably in relation to one of the basic functions of our society: food. Based on the literature on short supply food chains and on the works on proximity relations, this chapter aims to understand the roles, content and meaning of different types of proximities in terms of creativity, innovation and regional development dynamics. It presents an interesting case of cultural rejuvenation of mature products in the food market, also connected with the 'place property right' and the Appellation d'Origine Contrôlée (AOC) – applied for instance to oil and wine – as well as with the relation between traceability and authenticity. It also presents an instance of rejuvenation of the traditional models of local development (like the *milieu innovateur*). These had always assigned a primary role to physical proximity and the industrial *filière* (a chain of economic activities from raw materials to final products), while the innovation in this case is rather that of an organizational kind, induced by consumption behaviours respectful of sustainability and green economy.

The rejuvenation of mature products in the film industry sector is dealt with in Chapter 11 by Gino Cattani and C. Moritz B. Fliescher with the example of a renewal of the Western genre that benefited from the inter-country connections between Italy and the US. Building on the cognitive psychology research on the hierarchical structure of categories, they argue that a cognitive relationship between categories enhances the chances of their interaction but without eliciting the creation of a new category – as suggested by extant research on category dynamics. Specifically, categories that share the same basic-level category can evolve their meaning by absorbing elements from other vertically related categories, while maintaining their label. Empirically, the authors look at the influence of Spaghetti Westerns on the Western movies produced in the US from the 1960s onwards. The conditions and mechanisms underlying this evolution are discussed.

The significance of the symbolic value of culture comes to light in the analysis proposed in Chapter 12 by Hugues Jeannerat and Olivier Crevoisier on the revitalization of the Swiss watchmaking industry, a case where two creative and cultural (profit and non-profit) enterprises participate in the promotion of Swiss watches. This contribution proposes not restricting cultural activities to the question of production and of commodification of culture but addressing the broader question of culture in market construction. The first case emphasizes how a traditional Swiss media company seeks to exploit its proximity to traditional watchmaking companies to develop a new market niche dedicated to luxury multimedia services. The second case relates to the creation by several luxury watch brands of a foundation whose mission is to promote, legitimate and diffuse the specific cultural and technical value of *haute horlogerie* towards increasingly knowledgeable consumers. Away from a restrictive comparison of these two cases, the authors' proposition is that both enterprises participate in a common process of cultural co-production, diffusion and legitimation of Swiss watchmaking at local and international scales.

The strategic role of places and of their meanings, whether they are clusters, networks or cities, is the issue developed in the last three chapters. In Chapter 13, Udo Staber argues that the research on artists has often taken on an essentialist perspective about the position of 'place' in their identity, suggesting that it provides a single surface against which the artist constructs a sense of his self. In this study, the author adopts an ecological and practice perspective to examine differences and similarities in the meaning of place. Using interview data from the self-employed visual artists in two urban creative clusters in Germany and New Zealand, he explores the meanings of place in the mutual constitution of identity attributes and practices. The analysis shows that the identity of creative workers is place-based but not place-bound.

In Chapter 14 Marco Bettiol and Silvia Rita Sedita analyze the first Italian design community, located in Turin. The interwoven effect of territorial embeddedness, social ties and business networks in shaping creative projects within a community of practice is amply examined. The authors investigate the main factors that favoured the development of the Turin community of practice, which is for the most part composed of members who attended the same schools and lived in the same area. Concepts like community of practice, territorial embeddedness and social network are then delineated with reference to the design sector. The original data from a survey conducted by the authors are analyzed using social network analysis tools and statistical methods.

The last chapter by Pedro Costa deals with many of the issues already discussed in the previous contributions, introducing an international comparison and the dimension of policy. This chapter explores a specific set of conditions that enable the success of creativity-led territorial dynamics, specifically those related to reputation-building mechanisms and gatekeeping processes, which play a fundamental role in the development and sustainability of cultural and creative activities. Departing from a conceptual exploration of symbolic aspects in the development of creative milieu situations, the author provides an empirical illustration by drawing on ten case studies in Lisbon, Barcelona and São Paulo. Each experience is briefly described, including the key aspects of the role of gatekeeping processes and mediation mechanisms in their development, and evidence of the importance for their success of symbolic aspects and reputation building. After a systematization of these issues, the chapter concludes with some comments on policy-making orientations.

Conclusions and research agenda

We would like to close this introduction by identifying some future perspectives for CCIs and with a research agenda departing from the different contributions collected in the present volume.

The constitution of CCIs certainly represents a fertile field of study that deserves monitoring, especially given the opportunities they may offer to exit the present economic crisis. The most of the contributions in this book provide interesting views in this direction, but further studies and research will be needed to find evidence supporting the observations.

Without doubt, many good points are made. However, in the course of this debate a 'dark side of creativity' turned up that signals – although not always directly or explicitly – the presence of some risks for CCIs associated with 'excessive economic enhancement' of artistic, cultural and natural resources.

In conclusion, our research agenda seems to indicate proceeding in two directions: in one a more proactive attitude for delving further into the work done so far, investigating the characteristics and innovation capacity of CCIs; in the other more critical direction, the prospect of questioning the role played by these industries in the shift from a stage of economic enhancement to one of social valorization of culture and creativity.[3]

In particular, there are three priority questions that must be addressed.

The first question is still the definition of the boundaries of the creative sector, which is considered by many as already mature, but is presently still in progress. Consequently, we think it appropriate to reach a shared codification that can legitimize the sector's features on a permanent basis, in order to decide the required policies in support of innovation and at an industrial level.

The second question concerns a closer scrutiny of innovation trajectories associated to CCIs. This is an emergent issue that has disclosed only a few paths, like that of the rejuvenation of mature sectors/products, or the creation of new sectors linked to the green economy. Many others may yet come to light.

The third question touches the dark side of creativity, and implies an analysis of the risks that CCIs might face because of 'excessive creativity' or excessive economic enhancement, bearing effects that may even lead to the revision of current economic and social development models.

The definition of cultural and creative industries

With regard to the first question above, we can say that the issue concerning the definition, identification and measurement of CCIs still remains an open matter, although dealt with over and over again, even in the present volume. The boundaries of the sector are constantly evolving. Notwithstanding the aid offered by the guidelines of the 2010 EU *Green Paper* (European Commission 2010a), there still seems to be no exhaustive reference model that is representative of European variety and appropriate for the different contexts. Staying with the EU, the core activities of CCIs are those of the traditional art sector and of the new creative one. The separation of cultural and creative industries that initially seemed obsolete is thus restored. The first sector includes performing arts, visual arts and cultural heritage (also including the public sector), while the second includes architecture and design, integrating creative elements into wider processes, as well as subsectors like graphic design, fashion design and advertising. At a more peripheral level, many other industries rely on content production for their development and so are to some extent interdependent with CCIs. They include, among others, tourism and the new technologies. These types of specifications are quite important, but to really overcome the current definition problems what seems desirable is a more radical top-down plan, fine-tuning the multifarious policies that must be followed to support and advance the sector.

CCIs are now being taken into greater account, because they represent, as Scott (2010) recently wrote for the US, the core activities of the 'creative fields' in the 'emerging cities of the third wave'. Their presence is also significant in Europe, and has even spread to rural and more peripheral areas. A second noteworthy issue for our research agenda might be to distinguish rural and urban CCIs, which would constitute a further investigation aimed at drawing up a European geography of creativity. It must be recalled that a recent tendency is to incorporate more nature-related assets into the analysis of the economic enhancement of artistic and cultural heritage, and that there is now a significant branch of study on landscape, developed by agronomists and foresters.

Another aspect needing explanation is the relation between CCIs and leisure, experience and cultural tourism. The latter has long been regarded as the most direct form of economic enhancement of culture (e.g. the tourism in cities of art). Today a different interpretation is given due to the relevance of the so-called 'economy of events', interlinking tourism and experience economy. Striking evidence of this phenomenon can be found in the upsurge of traditional festivals related to popular customs and practices, as well as in events such as the Olympic Games, expos and myriad festivals, exhibitions and fairs that in recent times have been organized one after another. These events that were formerly unique have now become routine, resulting in that incessant search of experiences and emotions dominating the present consumption behaviours. The cultural and 'experiential' sides of many products and services have turned into strategic components of the marketing mix, diffusely applied at a place-marketing level in big cities, small towns and even in the most traditional cultural organizations (experience museums).

However, this is not all that can be said on the matter of the widening of the sector's boundaries. It poses further problems related to classification and measurement, a common case for other sectors typical of the new millennium and born out of the recombination of old and new sectors. An emblematic case is mechatronics, growing out of a combination of mechanical engineering and electronics. The same problem is particularly evident for CCIs because of their innovation and recombining capability – just think of bio-architecture, green design or the green creative city.

We would like to conclude this first question with an observation about methodology. Given the evolution of cultural statistics, we can say that CCIs constitute an area still needing codification. The geography of European creativity is an ongoing patchwork whose pattern might be enriched with benchmarking models, inter-country and cross-sector analyses, as well as with longitudinal studies that can bring to light its evolution. It is not only the inner nature of this in-progress sector that demands this work, but also the evaluation of its different time and intensity impacts in all the EU countries, especially those that have recently joined.

Cultural and creative industries: innovation trajectories

Confronting the issue of innovation, a wide field of study has just taken shape, opening up interesting prospects for regional sciences as well as for organization and business studies. As already mentioned, the creative sectors can offer space and applicability to the emerging model of open innovation, giving birth to innovations that may be incremental or radical, cross- or intra-sectors and chains, lateral, horizontal or path dependent.

A first topic deserving careful consideration concerns the relation between creative and innovative processes. While the 'close innovation' paradigm focused the attention primarily on the final stages of the innovation process and on technology transfers, now the initial stages are privileged. This is the time to look for ideas. European creativity can find in its heritage of variety and difference, new and diverse combinations to use as competitive advantages. Thus it can position itself in the global value chain as the European *filière* of collective creativity and knowledge.

At the moment, we can say that in this volume two basic axes have emerged. The first axis concerns the study of the creative process of rejuvenation for mature products and sectors, while the second looks upon the processes of cross-fertilization between creative and non-creative sectors (such as agriculture, energy, environment and health diagnostics).

This is not all the innovation capacity CCIs have to offer. There is at least a third axis that deserves consideration, resulting only indirectly from this debate: the digitalization of artistic and knowledge heritages. This development path is particularly important because it can determine considerable changes in cultural demand and artwork consumption (see the virtual museum fruition of historical and photographic archives). A literal industrialization process of cultural activities involving various typologies of CCIs and ICTs is about to begin. This can lead to a rapid globalization process of the product 'culture'. The results of this process must be investigated in detail.

There is ample space for experimentation, and the potential development paths we have pointed out here are but a few among many. These new combinations may touch on the creative and cultural sector or others, like manufacturing or service sectors, with the opportunity for cross-fertilization and relationships as wide as creative thinking can develop. However, on the other hand, many risks can arise. The problem is therefore not so much to promote creativity in its general meaning, but to support a 'goal-oriented creativity'. That alone can generate successful and result-oriented ideas. To this end, creative industries can change from a sector interesting to monitor, into a laboratory of innovations and discoveries to be selected and weighed up in favour of other sectors.

The development of cultural and creative industries: some critical aspects

A third and last question is that of the critical points regarding the development of CCIs. The second part of this volume repeatedly recalls the strategic role assumed by the concepts of authenticity, legitimation and reputation. Consumers of cultural products and services are now seeking reassurance about the risks involved in the economic exploitation of culture and in the experience economy. The answers always come to them from the local contexts and communities. The idiosyncratic features of places have become a strategic competitive advantage even for companies, and the safeguard of their authenticity today is not only an ethical, but also an economic problem, as it is under the attack from international counterfeiting. Yet this is not the only risk: another one is involved in the excessive aestheticization to which small and big centres are exposed when they happen to be the object of urban regeneration programmes developed by the globalized system of archistars.

It has been written many times that the creative sector is a 'priority sector'. The question now is what the future will be like for CCIs if excessive creative economy nullifies its ability to incorporate many of the previous paradigms (such as the culture economy, the knowledge economy or the experience economy) and thus changes it from a disruptive innovation into a creative bubble.

To find ways for uncovering the traps laid out in the economy of events and in the 'Disneyfication' of culture, the 'tourismification' of historical centres is but one of the challenges that CCIs will have to face in the future. The front line is there, together with the proliferation of causes for criticism against the creative economy in general, and the concept of 'creative city' in particular. On the one hand, culture and creativity can constitute one of the foundations for growth models in the new millennium. On the other hand, they must also be the basis of a 'new beginning', after which culture will no longer be just an asset or a source for innovation and economic development, but a 'shared value' sustaining social development.

Acknowledgements

The starting point for this volume was the seminar 'Creative Industries and Cities of Art: An International Perspective', organized by the Master in Economics and Management of Cultural Goods and Museums, University of Florence, 26 March 2010; and the session 'Creative regions in a creative economy' of the Regional Studies International Conference, Pecs, 24–26 May 2010.

I would like to thank all the contributors to this book, and also the publisher Routledge in the person of Robert Langham, who encouraged me to make it a reality.

This volume would not have been possible without the financial support of the project PRIN 2008 'Creative local system and urban cluster in metropolis. An analysis of determinants of clustering of creative industries for the governance of creative local systems', and the organization and editing assistance of Francesco Capone, Alessandra Pini and Andrea Sartori.

Notes

1 The *Green Paper* adopts a broad approach. The 'cultural industries' are identified with the traditional art sectors (performing arts, visual arts, cultural heritage – including the public sector), and also comprise those of film, DVD and video, television and radio, videogames, new media, music, books and press. 'Creative industries' include architecture and design, which integrate creative elements into wider processes, as well as subsectors such as graphic design, fashion design and advertising. At a more peripheral level, many other industries rely on content production for their own development and are therefore to some extent interdependent with CCIs. They include among others tourism and the new technologies sector (European Commission 2010a).

2 The following are some of the theories followed by the authors: industrial district and cluster approach; innovative milieu and proximity approach; related variety approach and new evolutionary geography; cultural, creative and experience economy; social networks approach and organization studies; and evolutionary approach and innovation studies.

3 This tendency also emerged during the Cost Strategic Workshop on 'Safeguard of Cultural Heritage' (Various authors 2011) in the session devoted to the 'Societal function of cultural heritage'. Some results will be collected in a special issue published in the journal *City, Culture and Society*.

References

Aage, T. and Belussi, F. (2008) 'From fashion to design: Creative networks in industrial districts', *Industry and Innovation*, 15(5): 475–91.

Andersson, D.E., Andersson, Å.E. and Mellander, C. (eds) (2011) *Handbook of Creative Cities*, Cheltenham: Edward Elgar.

Asheim, B.T. and Hansen, H.K. (2009) 'Knowledge bases, talents, and contexts: On the usefulness of the creative class approach in Sweden', *Economic Geography*, 8(5): 425–42.

Bakhshi, H. and Throsby, D. (2010) *Culture of Innovation: An Economic Analysis of Innovation in Arts and Cultural Organizations*, London: NESTA.

Bakhshi, H., McVittie, E. and Simmie, J. (2008) *Creating Innovation: Do the Creative Industries Support Innovation in the Wider Economy?* London: NESTA.

Baycan-Levent, T. and Nijkamp, P. (2010) 'Diversity and creativity as a research and policy challenge', *European Planning Studies*, 18(4): 501–14.

Becattini, G. (2004) 'The industrial district as a creative milieu', in G. Becattini (ed.), *Industrial District. A New Approach to Industrial Change*, Cheltenham: Edward Elgar, pp. 34–47.

Belussi, F. and Sedita, S. (2011) *Managing Situated Creativity in Cultural Industries*, London and New York: Routledge.

Belussi, F. and Staber, U. (2012) *Managing Networks of Creativity*, London and New York: Routledge.

Bille, T. and Schulze, G. (2006) 'Culture in urban and regional development', in V.A. Ginsburh and D. Throsby (eds) *Handbook of the Economics of Art and Culture*, Amsterdam: Elsevier, pp. 1051–93.

Boschma, R.A (2005) 'Proximity and innovation: A critical assessment', *Regional Studies*, 39(1): 61–74.

Camagni, R. and Maillat, D. (2006) *Milieux innovateurs. Théorie et politiques*, Paris: Economica Anthropos.

Cattani, G. and Ferriani, S. (2008) 'A core/periphery perspective on individual creative performance: Social networks and cinematic achievements in the Hollywood film industry', *Organization Science*, 19(6): 824–44.

Caves, R.E. (2000) *Creative Industries*, Cambridge, MA: Harvard University Press.

Chesbrough, H.W. (2003) 'The era of open innovation', *Sloan Management Review*, 44(3): 35–41.

Clifton, N. and Cooke, P. (2009) 'Creative knowledge workers and location in Europe and North America: A comparative review', *Creative Industries Journal*, 2(1): 73–89.

Cohen, W. and Levinthal, D. (1990) 'Absorptive capacity: A new perspective on learning and innovation', *Administrative Science Quarterly*, 35(1): 128–52.

Comunian, R., Faggian, A. and Li, Q.C. (2010) 'Unrewarded careers in the creative class: The strange case of bohemian graduates', *Papers in Regional Science*, 89(2): 389–410.

Cooke, P. (2009) 'Transition regions: Green innovation and economic development', paper presented at the DRUID Summer Conference, Frederiksberg, Denmark, 17–19 June.

Cooke, P. (2010) *Transversality and Transition: Branching to New Regional Path Dependence*, Papers in Evolutionary Economic Geography, no. 10.10, Utrech University.

Cooke, P. and Lazzeretti, L. (eds) (2008) *Creative Cities, Cultural Clusters and Local Economic Development*, Cheltenham, UK: Edward Elgar.

Cooke, P. and De Propris, L. (2011) 'A policy agenda for EU smart growth: The role of creative and cultural industries', *Policy Studies*, 32(4): 365–75.

DCMS – Department for Culture, Media and Sport (1998) *The Creative Industries Mapping Document*, London: DCMS.

DCMS – Department for Culture, Media and Sport (2001) *Creative Industries Mapping Document 2001*, London: DCMS.

DCMS – Department for Culture, Media and Sport (2010) *Measuring the Value of Culture: A Report to the Department for Culture Media and Sport*, London: DCMS.

De Bono, E. (1971) *The Use of Lateral Thinking*, 1st edn 1967, Middlesex: Penguin Books.

De Propris, L., Chapain, C., Cooke, P., MacNeil, S. and Mateos-Garcia, J. (2009) *The Geography of Creativity*, Interim report, London: NESTA.

DeFillippi, R., Grabher, G. and Jones, C. (2007) 'Introduction to paradoxes of creativity: Managerial and organizational challenges in the cultural economy', *Journal of Organizational Behavior*, 28(5): 511–21.

European Commission (2010a) *Green Paper on Cultural and Creative Industries: Unlocking the Potential of Cultural and Creative Industries*, Brussels: EU Commission, COM(2010) 183.

European Commission (2010b) *Europe 2020. A Strategy for Smart, Sustainable and Inclusive Growth*, Brussels: EU Commission, COM(2010).

Feldman, M.P. and Audretsch, D.B. (1999) 'Innovation in cities: Science-based diversity, specialization, and localized competition', *European Economic Review*, 43(2): 409–29.

Florida, R. (2002) *The Rise of the Creative Class: And how it's Transforming Work, Leisure, Community and Everyday Life*, New York: Basic Books.

Frenken, K., van Oort, F.G. and Verburg, T. (2007) 'Related variety, unrelated variety and regional economic growth', *Regional Studies*, 41(5): 685–97.

Gallouj, F. and Savona, M. (2009) 'Innovation in services. A review of the debate and a research agenda', *Journal of Evolutionary Economics*, 19(2): 149–72.

Garnham, N. (2005) 'From cultural to creative industries', *International Journal of Cultural Policy*, 11(1): S15–29.

Giuliani, E. (2005) 'Cluster absorptive capacity. Why do some clusters forge ahead and others lag behind?', *European Urban and Regional Studies*, 12(3): 269–88.

Glaeser, E. (2005) 'Review of Richard Florida's *The Rise of the Creative Class*', *Regional Sciences and Urban Economics*, 35(5): 593–96.

Greffe, X. (2003) *La valorisation économique du patrimoine*, Paris: La Documentation Française.

Hartley, J. and Cunningham, S. (2001) 'Creative industries: From blue poles to fat pipes', in M. Gillies (ed.) *The National Humanities and Social Sciences Summit: Position Papers*, Canberra: Department of Education Science and Training, pp. 1–10.

Hesmondhalgh, D. (2002) *The Cultural Industries*, London: Sage.

Howkins, J. (2001) *The Creative Economy: How People Make Money from Ideas*, London: Allen Lane.

Jeffcutt, P. and Pratt, A. (eds) (2009) *Creativity and Innovation in the Cultural Economy*, London: Routledge.

KEA European Affairs (2009a) *The Creative Economy in Europe. EU Policies and Creative Urban Hubs*, Brussels: KEA European Affairs.

KEA European Affairs (2009b) *The Impact of Culture on Creativity*, Brussels: KEA European Affairs.

Lazzeretti, L. (2009) 'The creative capacity of culture and the new creative milieu', in G. Becattini, M. Bellandi and L. De Propris (eds) *The Handbook of Industrial Districts*, Cheltenham, UK: Edward Elgar, pp. 281–94.

Lazzeretti, L., Boix, R. and Capone, F. (2008) 'Do creative industries cluster? Mapping creative local production systems in Italy and Spain', *Industry and Innovation*, 15(5): 549–67.

Lester, R.K. and Piore, M.J. (2004) *Innovation. The Missing Dimension*, Cambridge, MA: Harvard University Press.

Lorentzen, A. and van Heur, B. (2011) *Cultural Political Economy of Small Cities*, London and New York: Routledge.

Lorenzen, M. and Frederiksen, L. (2008) 'Why do cultural industries cluster? Localization, urbanization, products and projects', in P. Cooke and L. Lazzeretti (eds) *Creative Cities, Cultural Clusters and Local Economic Development*, Cheltenham, UK: Edward Elgar, pp. 155–79.

Markusen, A., Wassall, G., De Natale, D. and Cohen, R. (2008) 'Defining the creative economy: Industry and occupational approaches', *Economic Development Quarterly*, 24(1): 24–45.

Maskell, P. and Lorenzen, M. (2004) 'The cluster as market organization', *Urban Studies*, 41(5–6): 991–1009.

Nooteboom, B. (2000) *Learning and Innovation in Organizations and Economics*, Oxford: Oxford University Press.

O'Connor, J. (2008) *The Cultural and Creative Industries: A Review of the Literature*, London: Creative Partnerships.

Perry-Smith, J.E. and Shalley, C.E. (2003) 'The social side of creativity: A static and dynamic social network perspective', *Academy of Management Review*, 28(1): 89–106.

Pine, J.B. II and Gilmore, J.H. (1999) *The Experience Economy. Work is Theatre and Every Business is a Stage*, Boston, MA: Harvard Business School Press.

Power, D. and Nielsén, T. (2010) *Priority Sector Report: Creative and Cultural Industries*, Stockholm: Europe Innova, European Cluster Observatory.

Pratt, A.C. (2008) 'Creative cities: The cultural industries and the creative class', *Geografiska Annaler*, Series B, Human Geography, 90(2): 107–17.

Qian, H. (2010) 'Talent, creativity and regional economic performance: The case of China', *The Annals of Regional Science*, 45(1): 133–56.

Santagata, W. (2003) 'Cultural districts, property rights and sustainable economic growth', *International Journal of Urban and Regional Research*, 1(26): 9–23.

Scott, A.J. (2006) 'Creative cities: Conceptual issues and policy questions', *Journal of Urban Affairs*, 28(1): 1–17.

Scott, A.J. (2008) *Social Economy of the Metropolis: Cognitive-Cultural Capitalism and the Global Resurgence of Cities*, Oxford: Oxford University Press.

Scott, A.J. (2010) 'Cultural economy and the creative field of the city', *Geografiska Annaler*, Series B, Human Geography, 92(2): 115–30.

Stolarick, K. and Florida, R. (2006) 'Creativity, connections and innovation: A study of linkages in the Montréal Region', *Environment and Planning A*, 38(10): 1799–1817.

Storper, M. and Scott, A.J. (2009) 'Rethinking human capital, creativity and urban growth', *Journal of Economic Geography*, 9(2): 147–67.

Throsby, D. (2010) *The Economics of Cultural Policy*, Cambridge: Cambridge University Press.

Törnqvist, G. (2004): 'Creativity in time and space', *Geografiska Annaler*, Series B, Human Geography, 86(4): 227–43.

Torre, A. and Gilly, J.P. (2000) 'On the analytical dimension of proximity dynamic', *Regional Studies*, 34(2): 169–80.

UNCTAD – United Nations Conference on Trade and Development (2010) *Creative Economy. Report 2010*, Geneva and New York: UNDP and UNCTAD.

Various authors (2011) *Safeguard of Cultural Heritage. A Challenge from the Past for the Europe of Tomorrow*, Proceedings of the Cost Strategic Workshop, Florence, 11–13 July, University of Florence.

Yusuf, S. and Nabeshima, K. (2005) 'Creative industries in East Asia', *Cities*, 22(2): 109–22.

Part I

Cultural and creative industries in Europe

1 The geography of creative industries in Europe

Comparing France, Great Britain, Italy and Spain

Rafael Boix, Luciana Lazzeretti,
Francesco Capone, Lisa De Propris and
Daniel Sánchez

Introduction

Creative industries and creative people tend to concentrate spatially. The spatial patterns of distribution of creativity highlight the importance of the *place* for the economic creative process. In this chapter we analyze the geographical distribution of creative industries drawing upon a sector-based approach to the phenomenon of creativity. Despite the importance of space in the creative process, there is little research on the geography of the creative industries. Studies on how such activities are unevenly distributed geographically are still at an early stage. The methodology is also evolving and is heavily constrained by the best data available in various countries. In particular, there is a lack of inter-country comparative studies, making it difficult to assess the particularities of each model of creativity.

The main novelty of this research is to compare the geography of creative industries across four European countries: France, Great Britain, Italy and Spain. In addition, the research introduces two particularities: first, the use local labour markets (LLMs) as territorial units of analysis allows problems of regional heterogeneity across the four countries to be overcome, as well as local creative systems (LCSs) to be more rigorously mapped. Second, creative industries are divided in traditional and non-traditional, in order to better understand the type of creativity embedded in each country and LCS.

Our measurements show that France, Italy and Spain are more specialized in traditional creative industries, whereas Great Britain stands out because of the relative importance of non-traditional creative industries. A second result is that creative industries are much more spatially concentrated than other industries; in particular, they are attracted by the main LCSs in each of the countries. Indeed, the spatial distributions of creative industries show different patterns such as mono-polar, bi-polar or more diffused in the four countries.

Creative industries and local creative systems: a review of the literature in France, Great Britain, Italy and Spain

This section focuses on the contextualization of the research in the literature on creative industries as empirical and quantitative studies on the spatial distribution of creative industries across countries. To do this, the two basic dimensions of our analysis –namely industry and territory – are defined drawing on the current scholarly debate on creative industries across the countries under analysis.

The term 'creative industry' is increasingly used in the context of policy making across developed countries (OECD 2007; UNCTAD 2008, 2010). The term originated in Australia with the report *Creative Nation: Commonwealth Cultural Policy* (DCA 1994) although it was popularized by the Department for Culture, Media and Sport in the UK (DCMS 1998) and extended by the *United Nations Conference on Trade and Development* (UNCTAD 2004; 2008), Leadership Group on Quality Eurostat (LEG Eurostat 2000) and KEA European Affairs (2006).

DCMS (2001: 5) defines creative industries as 'industries which have their origin in individual creativity, skill and talent and which have a potential for wealth and job creation through the generation and exploitation of intellectual property'. Alternatively, the United Nations Conference on Trade and Development defines creative industries as

> cycles of creation, production and distribution of goods and services that use creativity and intellectual capital as primary inputs; constitute a set of knowledge-based activities, focused on but not limited to arts, potentially generating revenues from trade and intellectual property rights; comprise tangible products and intangible intellectual or artistic services with creative content, economic value and market objectives; are at the cross-road among the artisan, services and industrial sectors; and constitute a new dynamic sector in the world trade.
>
> (UNCTAD 2008: 4)

Both definitions refer to 'creative industries' as a set of economic activities that extend well beyond the cultural sector as it also includes media and information and communication technologies (ICTs) reflecting the shift in the technological platform that digitalization has brought.

The second dimension in the definition of the unit of analysis is the territorial one. Studies on the creative industries have often focused at country-level analysis or specific case studies such as in the UK (De Propris *et al.* 2009), in Australia (DCITA 2002), the US (Brinkhoff 2006; Markusen *et al.* 2008), East Asia (Yusuf and Nabeshima 2005), or Arabic countries (Morocco, Tunisia, Egypt, Jordan and Lebanon) (Harabi 2009). On Europe, LEG Eurostat (2000) and KEA European Affairs (2006) have carried out more aggregate studies on creative industries, and recently Power and Nielsén (2010) explicitly analyzed the spatial patterns of geography of creative and cultural industries.

Power and Nielsén (2010) use regional data (at the NUTS (Nomenclature of Units for Territorial Statistics) 2 level when available) and a definition of creative industries that includes advertising, architecture, broadcast media, design and fashion design, gaming software and new media, film, the 'finer' arts, heritage, music, photography, print media and *object d'art*. Their findings suggest that the largest concentration of employees in creative industries is found in the regions of Île-de-France (301,000), Inner London (235,000, plus another 80,000 in Outer London), Lombardy (195,000), West Nederland (195,000), Madrid (172,000), Catalonia (153,000), Denmark/Copenhagen (124,000) and Lazio (118,000).

The different administrative borders of European regions, as well as their size and internal diversity, tend to constraint their ability to define a geography of their creative industries and for this we suggest focusing on smaller and better defined units of analysis. On the other hand, Pratt (1997; 2004) is quite critical of the concept of 'creative cluster' because, he argues, it 'fails to capture the broader spatial, temporal and organizational dynamics of production across the creative industries', and proposes the concept of creative industries production system (Pratt 2004). In the same way, Lazzeretti *et al.* (2008) propose the similar concept of LCS as a socio-territorial entity characterized by a high concentration of creative industries and by specific features that facilitate the generation and diffusion of creativity. The LCS is an analytical concept that advances our understanding of the creative processes from the point of view of the place and, in this sense, creativity can be understood as a localized and locally embedded process. In the LCS, creative industries benefit from local external economies and the rules, conventions and local institutions that nourish the creation and diffusion of creativity (see Chapter 2 in this volume). Pratt (2004) argues that this notion is a suitable point of departure for the analysis of creative industries and an appropriate tool for the governance of the creative industries.

Forms of LCS have been mapped for the UK (De Propris *et al.* 2009), Italy and Spain (Lazzeretti, Boix and Capone 2008). For this study, we put together these three countries and add France to form a continuous neighbourhood of countries. These countries are four of the five largest producers of creative industries in the EU. Methodological similarities across these three previous mapping studies enable a comparison that suggests that the spatial distribution of creative activities varies across countries. This endorses the possibility of a more structured comparative analysis.

France

The geography of creative industries in France is still incomplete. Existing studies have mainly focused on culture, the most traditional part of creative industries.

At the national level, the main contributions have come from the French Ministry of Culture (Ministère de la Culture 2005, 2006a). These reports present studies of traditional creative sectors such as publishing, film and video activities, performing arts, architecture, museums, archives, libraries and trade of cultural products. Their key finding was that in France these sectors employ more than

400,000 employees, accounting for about 2 per cent of total employment. Cultural industries are particularly important in services, where they represent 8.5 per cent of total production and 4 per cent of employment. Another report by the French Ministry of Culture (Ministère de la Culture 2006b) analyzes the creation of cultural enterprises across French regions between 1998 and 2004 and found that one third of French new cultural industries (33.7 per cent) was concentrated in the Île-de-France, in particular, specializing in publishing and audiovisual. Other relevant concentrations are found in Provence-Alpes-Côte d'Ázur (11.5 per cent), Rhône-Alpes (7.9 per cent) and Languedoc-Roussillon (5 per cent).

On the other hand, Lacour and Puissant (2008) focus on the analysis of creative services in the functional urban areas of France, including: art, banking, insurance, producer services, trade, management, information technology, data processing in industry, research, telecommunications and transport. Their main results show that the urban area of Paris tends to mainly specialize in the information technology and producer service sectors. More generally, large urban areas are found to specialize in research, while the medium-size urban areas specialize in management, telecommunications, trade, banking, insurance and art.

Baumont and Boiteux-Orain (2005) analyze, in particular, cultural employment in the Île-de-France, and finds that it accounts for 2.8 per cent of the total employment. They observe that around 67 per cent of the cultural employment of the whole region is concentrated in the city of Paris. In the same way, Scott (1997, 2000) analyzes the cultural economy of metropolitan Paris, focusing on media, clothing industries, newspaper publishing, advertising, architectural services and recreation, cultural and sporting activities. His findings are that about 100,000 employees in cultural industries are concentrated Paris, but these appear to be quite dispersed across the city.

Great Britain

The debate on creative industries in Great Britain has been led by the Department for Culture, Media and Sport: its mapping documents unearthed a sector that was not only growing in terms of employment, but also performing very well in terms of exports, as well as positively impacting on the innovation capability of other sectors (DCMS 1998, 2001; HM Treasury 2005).

The work of think tanks such as *National Endowment for Science, Technology and the Arts* (NESTA) and the government-funded 'Creative Economy Programme' are keeping these themes at the top of the policy agenda and they have since trickled down to the regional and local levels, with initiatives such as 'Manchester Digital' or '01Zero-One' in London.

It can be argued that the definition of creative industries in the UK has privileged those that are more technology-intensive rather than the more traditional ones. This means that policy and scholarly attention has focused on those creative industries that tend to revolve around technology platforms, such as digital, design and software. The consequence of this is that the 'creative economy' has been mostly perceived as an urban phenomenon that for instance can spin out from around centres of excellence – such as universities.

The scholarly debate has explored a wealth of case studies, with the view of reaching a better and clearer understanding of the linkages, spillover effects and inter-sector synergies that creative industries are generating – see for instance Turok (2003) on the Scottish film industry; Grabher (2002) and Pratt (2006) on the advertising sector; GLA (2004) and Freeman (2007) on creative industries in London more broadly; Knell and Oakley (2007) on creative occupation; Cooke (2006) on Wales; Crewe (1996) on the Nottingham Lace Market; Nachum and Keeble (2003) on the London media cluster; and Sunley *et al.* (2008) on fashion design.

More recently, De Propris *et al.* (2009) have carried out an extensive mapping analysis of UK creative industries using both the DCMS and the Frontier Economics classifications – i.e. with a fine-grained analysis at the five-digit standard industrial classification (SIC) sectors. This analysis has utilized LLMs as well as much more minute geographical units of analysis at the super-output area level. The findings are that creative industries are spatially unevenly distributed and some sectors are more thinly spread than others, for instance arts and antiques, as opposed to architecture, which is extremely concentrated. Another finding confirms that creative industries benefit from urbanization economies as they tend to concentrate in cities, especially London, followed by Brighton, Manchester, Birmingham, Bath, Oxford and Cambridge, and Cardiff (see also Cooke 2006).

Italy

In Italy, studies on creative industries have primarily focused on cultural industries due to their importance. Creative industries are usually analyzed as extensions of the cultural sector (Bodo and Spada 2004) or as exceptionally fast-growing industries, such as ICT services (Sforzi and Lasagni 2008).

The Tagliacarne Institute (2007) proposes defining and measuring cultural and creative industries by looking at the link and the involvement of economic activities with the cultural and environmental heritage together with its exploitation and enhancement. They therefore classify cultural and creative as including: cultural heritage, cultural industry, food and wine, industrial and artisan production, architecture and construction.

The first analysis of creative industries in Italy was presented in the *White Paper on Creativity* (Santagata 2009). According to the report, the macro-sector of cultural and creative industries exceeds 9 per cent of the gross domestic product (GDP) and accounts for 2.5 million jobs. The report deals with all activities based on creative contents and culture as factors of production, intellectual property protection and new communication technologies. Three main types of creative industries are recognized: those related to the material culture (fashion, design, handicrafts, industry of food and taste), those to ICT and information (software, publishing, TV and radio, advertising and cinema) and those to cultural heritage (music and performing arts, architecture, artistic and cultural heritage, contemporary art). Fashion is the most important economic sector in Italy and together with related activities (fashion, design, handicrafts, and food and taste industries), it accounts for more than 50 per cent of the total sector employment.

Other authors have focused on specific cities like Turin (Amadasi and Salvemini 2005) or Florence (Lazzeretti 2007) analyzing the degree and the percentage of employees and firms in the different creative industries. Sedita and Paiola (2008) focus on creativity in relation to the physical and cognitive aspects of places, with specific attention on cultural industries. Tappi (2005) explores the internal and external factors that determined the evolution of the Marche's musical instrument district. Capone (2008) carries out a country-wide mapping analysis of LCSs, which then set the scene for other studies on the presence of creative clusters in Italy and Spain (Lazzeretti *et al.* 2008).

Spain

As in France and Italy, in Spain integrated research on creative industries is anecdotal. The dominant approach in Spain is still to look at the 'economics of culture'. The Spanish Ministry of Culture (Ministerio de Cultura 2008) differentiates between cultural industries (heritage, archives, libraries, printing and publishing, performing arts, film and video) and intellectual property intensive industries (printing and publishing, performing arts, film and video, software, and advertising). The recent overview by Boix and Lazzeretti (2012) is an exception. The authors use UNCTAD (2008) classification and find that Spain is the fifth largest European producer in creative industries, although the share of these industries in Spanish production (5.7 per cent) is below the EU average.

A policy strategy to support creative industries has not yet been put in place at country level; however, there are several policy initiatives focusing on cultural industries, such as the 'Plan for the Promotion of Cultural Industries' (2008). In relation to specific policy schemes, the printing and publishing sector benefits from initiatives to encourage the publication, translation and dissemination of books and cultural magazines in the Spanish language. Books also benefit from specific price subsidies. For instance, support aimed at the film and video sector coincides with the creation of a protection fund and a reciprocal guarantee company (in order to improve companies' access to funding) as well as a compulsory quote of share for movie theatres and televisions and funding to Spanish and European productions (25/1994 Act). Policy support for the music industry, however, includes intellectual property (IP) protection with the introduction of the Information Society Directive (34/2002 Act) and amendments to the Intellectual Property Act (23/2006 Act). On the other hand, the 'Plan for the Promotion of Cultural Industries' introduces incentives for firms in the design, fashion, architecture, ICT and digital cultural contents sectors; supports small and medium enterprises in these sectors; and fosters their internationalization by providing new funds and financial instruments to access credit.

Some regional governments and cities have been quite active in designing policies for creative industries. Catalonia has created the Catalan Institute for Creative Industries (20/2000 Act). The Basque Country has introduced the II Basque Culture Plan 2009–12 and the creation of the Basque Institute for Arts and Cultural Industries. Andalusia has created the General Directorate for Cultural and Performing Arts Industries. Galicia has created the Galician Agency for Cultural Industries. Asturias has developed a *White Paper on Cultural Industries*. In particular, Barcelona has been one of the most active Spanish cities in supporting creative cities thanks to the development of the 'Plan for the Culture Sector' (2004) and the setting up of the public agency 'Barcelona Activa', dedicated to foster creative industries.

Methodology

Operational definition of creative industries: traditional and non-traditional

Inter-country comparisons are subject to several limitations. First, there is not a commonly accepted list of 'creative industries', indeed even the scope and criteria for considering an activity as creative or not tend to differ across countries. However, there is a group of creative industries accepted as such across the main current contributions:[1] we start from these to come to a meaningful and robust definition of creative industries for the current study.

We acknowledge that some places might be more specialized in more traditional cultural activities as a result of their historical evolution, whereas a rapid development of non-traditional creative industries could take place in other locations. We suggest therefore distinguishing between *traditional creative industries* (publishing; architecture and engineering studies; music, film and performing arts) and *non-traditional creative industries* (Research and Development (R&D); software and computer services; advertising). We operationalize such classifications by referring to NACE (Nomenclature générale des Activités économiques dans les Communautés Européennes [General Classification of Economic Activities in the European Community]) sector 2 digit codes as detailed in Table 1.1.[2]

Selection of countries

The research focuses on France, Great Britain, Italy and Spain. The reason for this choice is twofold. First, the academic debate and the related policy discourse in these European countries differs in some significant aspects regarding the definition of creative industries, with Britain having favoured technology-intensive creative industries, whereas France, Italy and Spain having appreciated the role of cultural industries and tourism. Second, the four countries also differ in the way policy making has placed creative industries more or less at the centre of a general framework to promote innovation and competitiveness. The four countries form a continuum covering two Mediterranean countries (Italy and Spain), an Anglo-Saxon Atlantic country (Great Britain), and France, which is located in the middle and contains the creative agglomeration of Paris.

Table 1.1 Traditional creative and non-traditional creative industries

Traditional creative industries	Non-traditional creative industries
Publishing	*R&D*
22.1 Publishing	73.1 R&D experimentation in the field of natural sciences and engineering
22.2 Publishing and other activities related to publishing	
	73.2 R&D experimenting in the field of social and humanistic sciences
Film, video, performing arts	*Software and computer services*
22.3 Reproductions from original sound registrations	72.2 Production of software and information consulting
92.1 Production and distribution of videos and films; film projection;	72.6 Other activities related to computer services
92.2 Radio and television activities, excluding the management of the radio and television transmission networks	
92.3 Other entertainment activities	
Architecture and engineering studios	*Advertising*
74.2 Architectural and engineering activities and related technical consultancy	74.4 Advertising

Sources: Our elaboration on data from DCMS (2001); OECD (2005); Gordon and Beilby-Orrin (2006); UNCTAD (2008); NACE Rev. 1.1 codes

Territorial level of analysis

The decision to refer to LLMs as a territorial unit of analysis is consistent with our main interest in the place, more than in the simple concentration of activity. Indeed, other units (such as regions, provinces or municipalities) would be too large or too small to capture the socio-economic processes of creativity over space. Second, each LLM contains an area where the population lives and works, creating therefore an overlap between the agglomeration of firms and the community of people. The latter coincide with what the literature calls 'local production system' (Sforzi 2009). LLMs have already been used as territorial units for the analysis of creative industries in Italy and Spain (Lazzeretti *et al.* 2008) and Great Britain (De Propris *et al.* 2009).

LLMs are based on daily commuting flows. The procedures to identify them are not homogeneous across the four countries, although their basis is the same, in the sense that they are self-contained areas where people live and work. In Italy and Spain, LLMs have been identified by Sforzi (ISTAT 1997) and Boix and Galletto (2006) using the same procedure, which is very similar to the UK Travel-To-Work areas defined by the Office for National Statistics (ONS; Bond and Coombes 2007).[3] In France, they are called *zones d'emploi* and are defined by the Institut National de la Statistique et des Études Économiques (INSEE 1994, 1999). There are 384 LLMs in France (in 1999, metropolitan France), 243 in Great Britain (2001), 686 in Italy (2001) and 806 in Spain (2001).

Data sources

The data used in this research have been extracted from the national census of population and activity in the four countries, and provided by the respective national statistical offices. We use the more recent homogeneous data available for each data set, which is 1999 for France, 2001 for Italy and Spain, and 2007 for Great Britain.[4]

We use employment data for the inter-country comparison and to measure sector specialization concentration. There are several reasons for this choice. First, employment is an appropriate measure to study industrial patterns (or groups of industries) since the human cognitive activity is particularly important in the form of human capital or creative class. Second, in the absence of comparable regional GDP or turnover data across the four countries, employment provides a good proxy for economic activity. Finally, we consider it more appropriate to draw our inter-country comparison on employment data rather than on the number of firms because: (a) the organizational structures are different across countries producing very different average firm sizes that will favour countries with many small firms; and (b) using the number of firms might have resulted in an excess of small LLMs registering high value of concentration but nonetheless having an (absolute) low value of employment.

Identification of local creative systems

The spatial agglomerations of creative industries are identified by calculating for each LLM the location quotients (LQs) of its creative activities. The picture that emerges for each country forms a pattern of LCSs (LLMs where there is a high concentration of employment in specific creative industries). LQs have been used to map 'traditional' creative industries and cultural industries in Italy, Spain and the UK (Pratt 1997; Bassett *et al.* 2002; García *et al.* 2003; Lazzeretti *et al.* 2008; De Propris *et al.* 2009).

The basic LQ provides a measure of spatial specialization that combined with other criteria (such as the lowest number of employees per LCS) simultaneously assures specialization and concentration, and makes such information comparable across countries.[5] LQs are calculated as follows:

$$LQ_{ij} = \frac{L_{ij}}{L_i} \bigg/ \frac{L_j}{L}$$

where L_{ij} is the number of employees in the creative industry i in a LLM j, L_i is the total number of employees in the creative industry i, L_j is the number of employees in a LLM j, and L is the total employment in the country. A LQ above 1 indicates that the agglomeration of creative industry i in place j is greater than the national average, suggesting therefore that such a LLM is specialized in that specific creative industry, and is therefore a LCS.

Each LCS can specialize in traditional or non-traditional creative industries, or a combination of both. In order to clarify the specialization of the LLM, we consider three criteria:

1   *Traditional LCSs* are those LLMs with a LQ above than 1 and a minimum of 250 jobs in traditional creative industries.
2   *Non-traditional LCSs* are those LLMs with a LQ above 1 and a minimum of 250 jobs in non-traditional creative industries.
3   *Diversified LCSs* are those for which the criteria 1 and 2 occur simultaneously, namely where the LLM presents a LQ that is greater than one and there is a minimum of 250 jobs in traditional and non-traditional creative sectors.

The geography of the creative industries in Great Britain, France, Italy and Spain

General trends

The first two findings of our research are that creative industries are important for the productive structure of the countries under analysis, and that the profiles of specialization differ across the countries.

Using the classification of traditional and non-traditional creative industries suggested in this chapter, we find that Great Britain has about 1.49 million jobs in creative industries, France has 983,000, Italy 878,000 and Spain 673,000 (Table 1.2). Creative industries account for a significant share of these countries' employment: the largest is found for Great Britain with 5.66 per cent and Italy with 5.60 per cent, whereas the share is significantly smaller for France (4.46 per cent) and Spain (4.10 per cent).

Looking at the type of creativity dominating in each of the countries, traditional creative industries account for the largest share across the four countries. However, these are more relevant in France, Italy and Spain where they account for about 66 per cent of the overall employment in creative industries. By contrast, Great Britain presents the smaller share of non-traditional creative industries across the four countries, with around 42 per cent of employment in these sectors (Table 1.2).

Thus, Great Britain emerges not only as the economy with the largest number and share of employees in creative industries but also as the one that is characterized by the importance of non-traditional creative activities.

In particular, we find that the four countries under analysis tend to specialize in different creative industries. Printing and publishing are especially important for Spain (29 per cent of the overall creative industry employment) (Table 1.2). Architecture and engineering are particularly relevant for Italy (33.6 per cent) and tend to be associated with history and heritage. Film, video and performing arts (21.2 per cent) as well as R&D (14.3 per cent) are significant in France. Finally, Great Britain is characterized by large shares of employment in printing and publishing, architecture and engineering, and advertising, which overall account for three quarters of overall creative employment.

Concentration

Creative industries show a highly concentrated spatial pattern, both in absolute terms and in comparison with the rest of the economy.

Table 1.2 Employment in creative industries, 2001

	Employment				Percentage on total employment				Percentage on creative industries			
	France	Great Britain	Italy	Spain	France	Great Britain	Italy	Spain	France	Great Britain	Italy	Spain
Traditional	649,694	868,071	579,855	457,864	2.98	3.29	3.70	2.80	66.80	58.05	66.00	68.00
Printing and publishing	224,206	287,491	173,391	196,951	1.03	1.09	1.10	1.20	23.05	19.23	19.70	29.20
Architecture and engineering	218,620	366,407	295,289	142,459	1.00	1.39	1.90	0.90	22.48	24.50	33.60	21.20
Film, video and performing arts	206,868	214,173	111,175	118,454	0.95	0.81	0.70	0.70	21.27	14.32	12.60	17.60
Non-traditional	322,967	627,324	299,107	215,499	1.48	2.37	1.90	1.30	33.20	41.95	34.00	32.00
Software and computer services	88,058	437,643	223,771	144,785	0.40	0.32	0.30	0.40	9.05	5.57	5.90	9.20
Advertising	95,824	83,350	52,240	61,949	0.44	1.66	1.40	0.90	9.85	29.27	25.50	21.50
R&D	139,085	106,331	23,096	8,765	0.64	0.40	0.20	0.10	14.30	7.11	2.60	1.30
Total creative industries	972,661	1,495,395	878,962	673,363	4.46	5.66	5.60	4.10	100.00	100.00	100.00	100.00

Sources: Our elaboration on data from ISTAT (Census 2001); INE (Census 2001); INSEE (Census 1999); ONS (Census 2007)

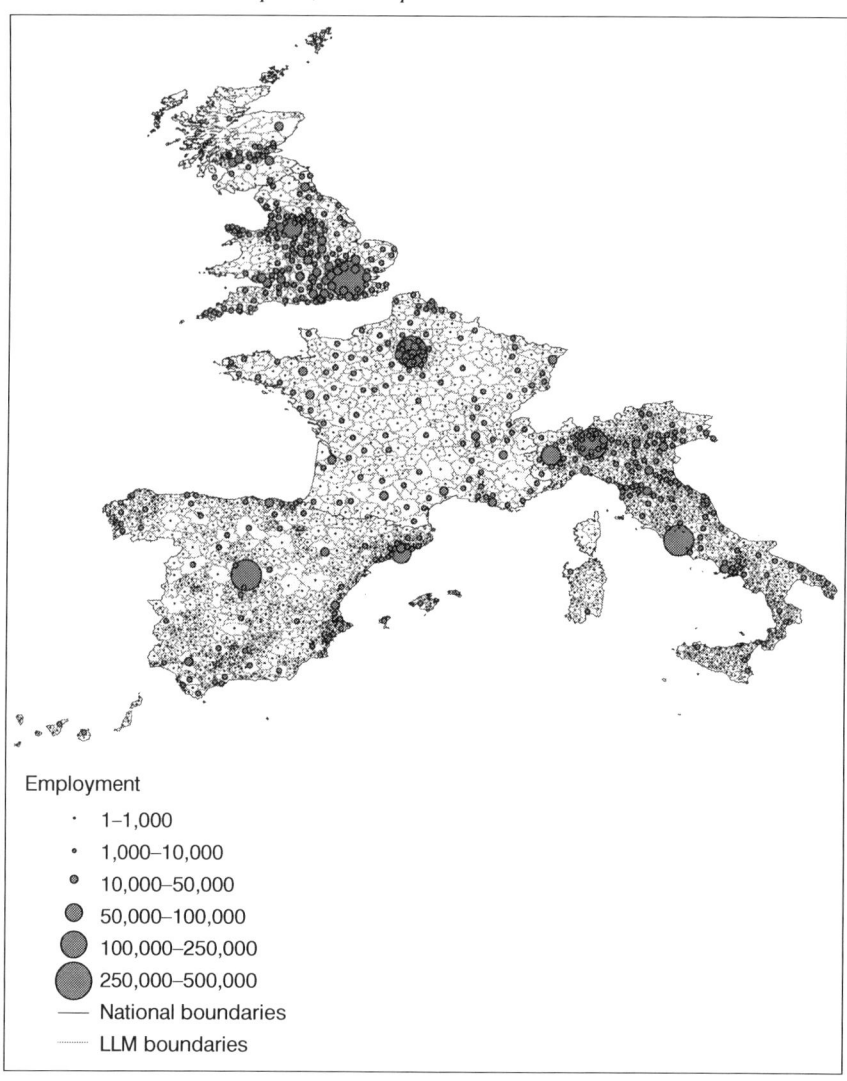

Figure 1.1 Employment in creative industries by local labour market: Great Britain, France, Italy and Spain

Sources: Our elaboration from ISTAT (Census 2001); INE (Census 2001); INSEE (Census 1999); ONS (Census 2007)

Figure 1.1 shows the maps with the distribution of LLMs in the four countries as determined by the LQ calculations. It is immediately evident that different spatial patterns emerge across countries. In France, there is a big concentration of creative employment around Paris with the remainder thinly spread over the rest of the country. Spain also shows an extremely concentrated pattern with two key poles: Madrid and Barcelona. Great Britain shows a huge concentration of creative employment around London and neighbouring regions with other important 'hot

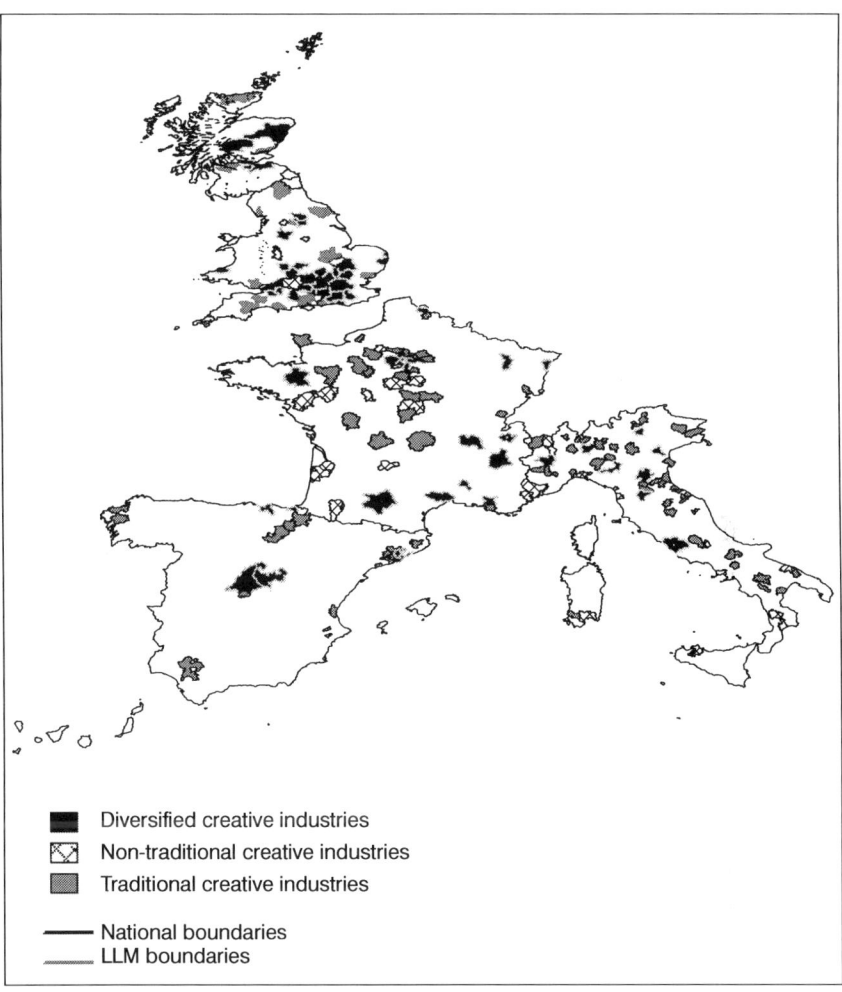

Figure 1.2 Local creative systems (LQ above 1 and minimum 250 employees in creative industries by LPS)

Sources: Our elaboration from ISTAT (Census 2001); INE (Census 2001); INSEE (Census 1999); ONS (Census 2007)
Note: LQs have been calculated for each country separately.

spots' around Manchester and Leeds, as well as around Glasgow and Edinburgh. A large amount of creative employment tends to be concentrated in London together with the South East and the South West, although it is, however, quite spread across their many LLMs, so that the spatial pattern in Britain could be argued to be simultaneously as 'concentrated' as it is 'distributed'. Finally, Italy shows another different pattern, one that is characterized by the existence of three big poles, Milan, Rome and to a lesser extent Turin. In addition, a more diffused and polycentric pattern is visible around the centre–north of the country, in Padua, Verona, Bologna and Florence.

Overall, Figures 1.1 and 1.2 show that employment in creative industries is concentrated in the four countries and clustered around the largest cities in each. However, the patterns of concentration and specialization show notable differences across countries. To better evaluate some of these characteristics we depart from an approach reliant on general indicators of concentration and utilize some common non-spatial indicators of concentration.

Spain shows the most concentrated pattern as 88.4 per cent of the employment in creative industries is concentrated in only 10 per cent of the LLMs, with a Gini index of 0.91 (maximum value 1). Italy seems to be the second country where the employment in creative industries is more concentrated, as 75.8 per cent is concentrated in 10 per cent of the LLMs (first decile) with a Gini index of 0.83. In France and Great Britain the employment in creative industries appears to be less concentrated in fewer LLMs: the share of creative employment in the first decile is 69 per cent for France and 70.9 per cent for Great Britain, with both having a Gini index of 0.76.

Quite similar results are obtained if the indexes are weighted by the share of total employment in the LLMs. The weighted Gini indicates that the patterns of concentration of employment in creative industries are significantly higher than the patterns of concentration of total employment.

Local creative systems and creative hubs

Most of the employment in creative industries is located in the LCSs, which confirms Pratt's thesis (1997, 2004) about the relevance of LCSs for the analysis and governance of the creative industries for countries other than the UK. This result is enhanced by other two findings. First, we find that the pattern of specialization by typology of LCS is also different across countries. Second, some of the largest LCSs are neighbours, forming large agglomerations or hubs of LCSs. These hubs contain a concentrated amount and huge national share of creative jobs, so they play a central role for the analysis and governance of the creative industries.

Whilst Figure 1.1 shows the absolute concentration of creative employment, LCSs are mapped in Figure 1.2. LCSs account for more than two thirds of the employment in creative industries in each country.

Their spatial distribution patterns again differ across countries. In France, there are fifty-eight LCSs (twenty diversified, twenty-three traditional and fifteen non-traditional), which have 694,000 employees in creative industries (70.6 per cent of the employment in creative industries). There are fifty-nine LCSs in Great Britain (thirty-five diversified, eighteen traditional and six non-traditional), which employ 1,054,000 people in creative industries (70.5 per cent of the employment in creative industries). In Italy there are sixty-one LCSs (eight diversified, forty-three traditional and ten non-traditional), which have 557,000 employees in creative industries (63.4 per cent of the employment in creative industries). Spain has only twenty-five LCSs (eight diversified and seventeen traditional), which have 437,000 employees in creative industries (65 per cent of the employment in creative industries).

We take into account that in some cases LCSs tend to be co-located forming large multi-sector agglomerations or hubs, such as in London and Paris. The largest hub is concentrated around London and is made up of twenty-seven LCSs, which have 541,000 employees in creative industries (52.5 per cent of the employment in creative industries in Great Britain). The second largest hub is located around Paris and comprises twenty-one neighbouring LCSs and employs 422,000 creative people (42.9 per cent of the employment in creative industries in France). The third hub is Madrid, with three LCSs and 208,000 employees in creative industries (31 per cent of the country). It is followed by Milan, with five LCSs and 171,000 employees in creative industries (19.5 per cent of the employment in creative industries in Italy), and Barcelona with nine LCSs and 129,000 employees in creative industries (19.2 per cent of the country). Rome is the sixth largest hub, although it is formed by only one LCS that has 117,000 employees in creative industries (13.4 per cent of the country).

A comparison of local creative systems across the largest cities

One key finding from our study is that the largest cities in the four countries – which tend to coincide with Europe's largest cities – appear to host the most important LCSs in each of the four countries and are the centre of the largest creative hubs in each country. In order to further our investigation, we compare the three largest LCSs in each of the four countries. This comparison includes capital cities such as Paris, London, Rome, Madrid; main industrial centres, such as Lyon, Manchester, Milan, Barcelona; and third-tier cities, such as Marseille, Glasgow, Turin, Valencia.

London has 28.7 per cent of the national employment in creative industries (405,000 jobs) and Madrid 27.8 per cent (205,000) (Table 1.3). In the same way, Paris pulls together about 17.6 per cent of the national creative industries' employment (173,000); Barcelona about 14.7 per cent (99,000), Milan about 13.3 per cent (146,000) and Rome about 11.4 per cent (117,500). The other cities account for a significant albeit much smaller portion of the national creative industries' employment with Turin employing 6.4 per cent, Valencia about 3.8 per cent, Lyon about 3.7 per cent, Manchester 3.5 per cent, Glasgow 2.3 per cent and Marseille 1.6 per cent.

Creative industries are particularly important for the economy in Paris (10.8 per cent of the local employment), Milan (9.5), London (9.0), Rome (9.0), Madrid (8.5), Turin (8.0) and Barcelona (7.4) (Table 1.4). Although lower, the shares are also significant for Manchester (5.8 per cent), Lyon (5.2), Glasgow (5.1), Marseille (4.4) and Valencia (4.2).

We also find that the overall relevance of traditional or non-traditional creative industries varies across such cities. Traditional creative industries account for more than 60 per cent of the total employment in creative industries in Valencia (70.3 per cent), Paris (69.5), Marseille (69.3), Barcelona (68.1), Glasgow (67.5), Lyon (62.1), London (61.4) and Madrid (61.1). On the other hand, non-traditional creative industries are particularly important in the economies of

Table 1.3 Employment in creative industries for the largest cities (LCS) in the country

	France			Great Britain			Italy			Spain		
	Paris	Lyon	Marseille	London	Manchester	Glasgow	Rome	Milan	Turin	Madrid	Barcelona	Valencia
Traditional creative industries	120,724	22,773	10,956	249,156	30,557	20,380	66,159	76,979	29,039	127,220	67,509	17,516
Printing and publishing	42,062	6,043	2,652	78,314	8,149	5,812	16,798	34,819	9,817	54,178	38,003	7,607
Architecture and engineering	23,297	11,389	4,585	73,138	15,352	9,875	18,793	27,187	14,852	34,980	15,872	5,662
Film, video and performing arts	55,365	5,341	3,719	97,704	7,056	4,693	30,568	14,973	4,370	38,062	13,634	4,247
Non-traditional creative industries	52,888	13,880	4,861	156,433	22,373	9,844	51,348	69,289	26,922	77,730	31,668	7,393
Software and computer services	14,056	5,034	751	104,558	16,250	6,281	44,525	49,929	19,779	53,901	20,873	4,564
Advertising	19,245	3,711	1,466	36,455	5,053	2,429	4,239	15,879	4,454	21,990	10,016	2,348
R&D	19,587	5,135	2,644	15,420	1,070	1,134	2,584	3,481	2,689	1,839	779	481
Total creative industries	173,612	36,653	15,817	405,589	52,930	30,224	117,507	146,268	55,961	204,950	99,177	24,909
Non-creative industries	1,427,203	672,979	345,894	4,095,580	858,871	562,128	1,182,975	1,394,903	639,390	2,196,308	1,238,319	563,165
Total	1,600,815	709,632	361,711	4,501,169	911,801	592,352	1,300,482	1,541,171	55,961	2,401,258	1,337,496	588,074

Sources: Our elaboration on data from ISTAT (Census 2001); INE (Census 2001); INSEE (Census 1999); ONS (Census 2007)

Table 1.4 Share of employment in creative industries on local employment for the largest cities (LCS) in the country

	France			Great Britain			Italy			Spain		
	Paris	Lyon	Marseille	London	Manchester	Glasgow	Rome	Milan	Turin	Madrid	Barcelona	Valencia
Traditional creative industries	7.5	3.2	3.0	5.5	3.3	3.4	5.1	5.0	4.2	5.3	5.0	3.0
Printing and publishing	2.6	0.9	0.7	1.7	0.9	1.0	1.3	2.3	1.4	2.3	2.8	1.3
Architecture and engineering	1.5	1.6	1.3	1.6	1.7	1.7	1.4	1.8	2.1	1.5	1.2	1.0
Film, video and performing arts	3.5	0.8	1.0	2.2	0.8	0.8	2.4	1.0	0.6	1.6	1.0	0.7
Non-traditional creative industries	3.3	2.0	1.3	3.5	2.4	1.7	3.9	4.5	3.9	3.2	2.4	1.3
Software and computer services	0.9	0.7	0.2	2.3	1.8	1.1	3.4	3.2	2.8	2.2	1.6	0.8
Advertising	1.2	0.5	0.4	0.8	0.5	0.4	0.3	1.0	0.6	0.9	0.7	0.4
R&D	1.2	0.7	0.7	0.3	0.1	0.2	0.2	0.2	0.4	0.1	0.1	0.1
Total creative industries	10.8	5.2	4.4	9.0	5.8	5.1	9.0	9.5	8.0	8.5	7.4	4.2
Non-creative industries	89.2	94.8	95.6	91.0	94.2	94.9	91.0	90.5	92.0	91.5	92.6	95.8
Total	100.0	100.0	100.0	100.0	100.0	100.0	100.0	100.0	8.0	100.0	100.0	100.0

Sources: Our elaboration on data from ISTAT (Census 2001); INE (Census 2001); INSEE (Census 1999); ONS (Census 2007)

Turin (48.1 per cent of the employment in creative industries), Milan (47.4), Rome (43.7) and Manchester (42.3). Two specific results are worth pointing out. On the one hand, despite the broader British discourse, traditional creative industries are fundamentally important for central London, and, on the other hand, despite the Italian focus on culturally driven industries, the three largest LCSs in Italy host large shares of non-traditional creative industries.

Conclusions

The research provides a comparative analysis of creative industries across France, Great Britain, Italy and Spain, a continuous neighbourhood of countries that includes four of the five largest producers of creative industries in the EU. The use of LLMs allows a rigorous study at the intra-regional level. Creative industries are divided into traditional and non-traditional in order to better understand the profile of these four very different countries.

Some of our findings are original whereas others confirm the results from previous national researches for an extended pool of countries (Lazzeretti *et al.* 2008; De Propris *et al.* 2009; Power and Nielsén 2010).

First, we find that the creative industries are important in the productive structure of these countries (4 to 6 per cent of the total employment) and that there are important differences in the national profiles regarding both the type of creative industries and their geographical distribution. This percentage is close to that found in other previous contributions.

Second, we find that creative industries are highly concentrated in the four countries, much more than other economic activity.

Third, most of the employment in creative industries is found to be localized in the LCSs. Furthermore, we found that in the four countries some of the largest LCSs are located close to one another, forming agglomerations or hubs. London and Paris are the largest of such hubs, followed by Madrid, Milan, Barcelona and Rome. These hubs have an enormous concentration and share of creative jobs. Despite the size of these creative hubs, other LCSs emerge around medium-sized cities, generating a map of creative industries that is diverse, heterogeneous and complex across the four countries. Furthermore, some places are found to specialize in a particular form of creativity, whereas other places show a more diversified creative pattern. These results suggest that the LCS is a relevant unit for the analysis and governance of the creative industries (as suggested by Pratt 2004) but that the largest metropolitan areas play a central role in the creative system and must also be considered key agents for the analysis, governance and the design of policy strategies for creative industries.

Thus, the spatial dimension of creativity has implications for the design and implementation of policy strategies. This is especially relevant in an EU context where the policy framework for creative and cultural industries tries to capture such diversity and reconcile it within a coherent approach. Our study shows that the geography of creativity across France, Great Britain, Italy and Spain mirrors the heterogeneity of places and their creative characteristics and endowments (including the size and sector distribution of the creative sector). This leads to a multiplicity of policy objectives and tools that have to be embedded in the European framework, somewhat paving the way for national-level awareness and initiatives.

Notes

1 LEG Eurostat 2000; OECD 2005; Gordon and Beilby-Orrin 2006; KEA European Affairs 2006; Towse 2007; UNCTAD 2008, 2010; DCMS 2009.
2 Twelve different lists of creative industries, coming primary and significant reports, have been taken into account. The final proposal is quite similar to the DCMS (2009) operative list with two differences: first, designer fashion has not been included in the 17.7, 18 and 19.3 NACE sectors as it is considered to be related more to 'manufacturing' than to 'creation' in Italy and Spain. A similar discussion for the UK can be found in the *London's Creative Sector* (GLA 2004), remarking that it is not possible to distinguish, on the basis of NACE codes alone, the manufacturing of clothing from the fashion industry. In addition, in line with Howkins (2007) and UNCTAD (2008), some parts of the R&D sector have been considered as creative industries.
3 The differences in the procedure as well as the morphology and density of each country produce differences across the LLMs. For example, the average surface by LLM is smaller in Italy (439 km^2) and Spain (626 km^2) than in the Great Britain (1,007 km^2), and they are particularly large in France (1,676 km^2).
4 The use of census data has some other restrictions regarding sector detail and the data not being recent, but it does assure homogeneity.
5 We refer the reader to Lazzeretti *et al.* (2008) for a detailed discussion on the advantages of using the LQ indicator of specialization and concentration, rather than other indicators such as the simple concentration coefficient, or Florida's (2002) mixed indicator.

References

Amadasi, G. and Salvemini, S. (2005) *La città creativa, una nuova geografia di Milano*, Milano: Egea.

Bassett, K., Griffiths, R. and Smith, I. (2002) 'Cultural industries, cultural clusters and the city: The example of natural history film-making in Bristol', *Geoforum*, 33: 165–77.

Baumont, C. and Boiteux-Orain, C. (2005) *Secteur culturel, metropolisation et centralités urbaines. Le cas de l'Île-de-France*, Dijon: Université de Bourgogne.

Bodo, C. and Spada, C. (2004) *Rapporto sull'economia della cultura in Italia, 1990–2000*, Bologna: Il Mulino.

Boix, R. and Galletto, V. (2006) 'Sistemas industriales de trabajo y distritos industriles marshallianos en España', *Economía Industrial*, 359: 165–84.

Boix, R. and Lazzeretti, L. (2012) 'Las industrias creativas en España: una primera panoramic', *Investigaciones Regionales*, 22: 181–206.

Bond, S. and Coombes, M. (2007) *2001-based Travel-to-Work Areas Methodology.* London: Office for National Statistics, Centre for Urban and Regional Development Studies.

Brinkhoff, S. (2006) 'Spatial concentration of creative industries in Los Angeles', Diplomarbeit, Berlin: Humboldt-Universität zu Berlin Geographisches Institut.

Capone, F. (2008) 'Mapping and analysing creative systems in Italy (1991–2001)', in P. Cooke and L. Lazzeretti (eds) *Creative Cities, Cultural Cluster and Local Economic Development*, Cheltenham: Edward Elgar, pp. 338–64.

Cooke, P. (2006) *Creative Industries in Wales: Potential and Pitfalls*, Cardiff: Cardiff Institute of Welsh Affairs.

Crewe, L. (1996) 'Material culture: Embedded firms, organizational networks and the local economic development of a fashion quarter', *Regional Studies*, 30 (3): 257–72.

DCA – Department of Communications and the Arts (1994) *Creative Nation: Commonwealth Cultural Policy*, Canberra: AGPS.

DCITA – Department of Communications, Information Technology and the Arts (2002) *Creative Industries Cluster Study*, Canberra: DCITA.

DCMS – Department for Culture, Media and Sport (1998) *The Creative Industries Mapping Document*, London: DCMS.

DCMS (2001) *Creative Industries Mapping Document 2001*, London: DCMS.

DCMS (2009) *Creative Industries Economic Estimates*, Statistical Bulletin, October, London: DCMS.

De Propris, L., Chapain, C., Cooke, P., MacNeil, S. and Mateos-Garcia, J. (2009) *The Geography of Creativity*, London: NESTA.

Florida, R. (2002) *The Rise of the Creative Class: And how it's Transforming Work, Leisure and Everyday Life*, New York: Basic Books.

Freeman, A. (2007) *London's Creative Sector: 2007 Update*, GLA Economics Working Paper no. 22, London: GLA.

García, M., Fernandez, Y. and Zobio, J. (2003) 'The economic dimension of the culture and leisure industry in Spain: National, sectoral and regional analysis', *Journal of Cultural Economics*, 27(1): 9–30.

GLA – Great London Authority (2004) *London's Creative Sector: 2004 Update*, London: GLA.

Gordon, J.C. and Beilby-Orrin, H. (2006) *International Measurement of the Economic and Social Importance of Culture*, Paris: Statistics Directorate, OECD.

Grabher, G. (2002) 'Production in projects: Economic geographies of temporary collaboration', *Regional Studies*, 36(3): 229–45.

Harabi, N. (2009) *Creative Industries: Case Studies from Arab Countries*, MPRA Paper no. 15628, Germany: University Library of Munich.

HM Treasury (2005) *The Cox Review of Creativity and Business: Building on the UK's strengths*, London: HM Treasury.

Howkins, J. (2007) *The Creative Economy: How People Make Money from Ideas*, 2nd edn, London, New York and Toronto: The Penguin Press.

INSEE – Institut National de la Statistique et des Études Économiques (1994) *Atlas des Zones d'Emploi*, Paris: DATAR, Ministère de l'Education Nationale and Ministère de l'Industrie et du Commerce Extérieur, Ministère du Travail, de l'Emploi et de la Formation professionnelle.

INSEE (1999) *Census Population Data*, Paris: INSEE.

ISTAT – Istituto Nazionale di Statistica (1997) *I sistemi locali del lavoro 1991*, edited by F. Sforzi, Roma: Istituto Poligrafico e Zecca dello Stato.

KEA European Affairs (2006) *The Economy of Culture in Europe*, Brussels: European Commission Directorate, General for Education and Culture.

Knell, J. and Oakley, K. (2007) *London's Creative Economy: An Accidental Success?* Provocation Series 3(3), London: The Work Foundation.

Lacour, C. and Puissant, S. (2008) *Medium-Sized Cities and the Dynamics of Creative Services*, Cahiers du GREThA, no. 2008–08, Pessac: France.

Lazzeretti, L. (2007) 'Culture, creativity and local economic development: Evidence from creative industries in Florence', in P. Cooke and D. Schwartz (eds) *Creative Regions:*

Technology, Culture and Knowledge Entrepreneurship, London and New York: Routledge, pp. 169–97.

Lazzeretti, L., Boix, R. and Capone, F. (2008) 'Do creative industries cluster? Mapping creative local production systems in Italy and Spain', *Industry and Innovation*, 15(5): 549–67.

LEG Eurostat – Leadership Group on Quality (2000) *Cultural Statistics in the EU*, Eurostat Working Paper, Population and Social Conditions Series, no. 3/2000/E/No1, Final report of the LEG, Luxembourg: Eurostat

Markusen, A., Wassall, G.H., De Natale, D. and Cohen, R. (2008) 'Defining the creative economy: Industry and occupational approaches', *Economic Development Quarterly*, 22(1): 24–45.

Ministère de la Culture (2005) *L'emploi culturel dans l'Union européenne en 2002: Données de cadrage et indicateurs. L'Observatoire de l'Emploi Culturel*, June, Paris: Département des Etudes, de la Prospective et des Statistiques.

Ministère de la Culture (2006a) *Aperçu statistique des industries culturelles*, May, Paris: L'Observatoire de l'Emploi Culturel, Département des Etudes, de la Prospective et des Statistiques.

Ministère de la Culture (2006b) *La mobilisation des actifs culturels de la France: De l'attractivité culturelle du territoire... à la nation culturellement créative*, May, Paris: L'Observatoire de l'Emploi Culturel, Département des Etudes, de la Prospective et des Statistiques.

Ministerio de Cultura (2008) *Anuario de Estadísticas Culturales*, Madrid: Secretaría General Técnica. Subdirección General de Publicaciones, Información y Documentación.

Nachum, L. and Keeble, D. (2003) 'Neo-Marshallian clusters and global networks: The linkages of media firms in central London, *Long Range Planning* 36(5): 459–80.

OECD – Organisation for Economic Co-operation and Development (2005) *Culture and Local Development*, Paris: OECD.

OECD (2007) *Competitive Cities. A New Entrepreneurial Paradigm in spatial Development*, Paris: OECD.

Power, D. and Nielsén, T. (2010) *Priority Sector Report: Creative and Cultural Industries*, Stockholm: Europe Innova. European Cluster Observatory.

Pratt, A.C. (1997) 'The cultural industries production system: A case study of employment change in Britain, 1984–91', *Environment and Planning-A*, 29(11): 1953–74.

Pratt, A.C. (2004) 'Creative clusters: Towards the governance of the creative industries production system?', *Media International Australia incorporating Culture and Policy*, 112: 50–66.

Pratt, A.C. (2006) 'Advertising and creativity, a governance approach: A case study of creative agencies in London', *Environment and Planning A*, 38(10): 1883–99.

Santagata, W. (ed.) (2009) *Libro bianco sulla creatività* [White paper on cultural industries], Milano: EGEA.

Scott, A.J. (1997) 'The cultural economy of cities', *International Journal of Urban and Regional Research*, 21(2): 323–39.

Scott, A.J. (2000) 'The cultural economy of Paris', *International Journal of Urban and Regional Research*, 24(3): 554–66.

Sedita, S.R. and Paiola, M. (2008) *Il Management della creatività: reti, comunità e territori*, Padova: CEDAM.

Sforzi, F. (2009) 'The empirical evidence of industrial districts in Italy', in G. Becattini, M. Bellandi and L. De Propris (eds) *A Handbook of Industrial Districts*, Cheltenham: Edward Elgar, pp. 327–42.

Sforzi, F. and Lasagni, A. (2008) 'Le determinanti dello sviluppo locale di attività ICT in Italia', *Economia e politica industriale*, 35(1): 155–67.

Sunley, P., Pinch, S., Reimer, S. and Macmillen, J. (2008) 'Innovation in a creative production system: The case of design', *Journal of Economic Geography*, 8(5): 675–98.

Tagliacarne Institute (2007) *Le attività economiche collegate alla valorizzazione del patrimonio culturale*, Report, Roma: Istituto G. Tagliacarne.

Tappi, D. (2005) 'Clusters, adaptation and extroversion: A cognitive and entrepreneurial analysis of the Marche music cluster', *European Urban and Regional Studies* 12(3): 289–307.

Towse, R. (2007) *Recent Development in Cultural Economics*, Cheltenham: Edward Elgar.

Turok, I. (2003) 'Cities, clusters and creative industries: The case of film and television in Scotland', *European Planning Studies*, 11(5): 549–65.

UNCTAD – United Nations Conference on Trade and Development (2004) *Creative Industries and Development*, Document TD(XI)/BP/13, Geneva: United Nations.

UNCTAD (2008) *Creative Economy. Report 2008*, Geneva and New York: UNDP and UNCTAD.

UNCTAD (2010) *Creative Economy. Report 2010*, Geneva and New York: UNDP and UNCTAD.

Yusuf, S. and Nabeshima, K. (2005) 'Creative industries in East Asia', *Cities*, 22(2): 109–22.

2 Why do creative industries cluster?

Luciana Lazzeretti, Rafael Boix and Francesco Capone

Introduction

Creative industries are not homogeneously distributed across the territory but they are concentrated in space (Scott 2005; Cooke and Lazzeretti 2008), forming geographical clusters (Lorenzen and Frederiksen 2008), creative cities (Florida 2002) and creative networks (Belussi and Staber 2010).

In the international debate, there is a growing interest in the study of the patterns of spatial location of creativity and its role in local and regional development (De Propris *et al.* 2009), although there are few studies on the concentration of 'creative industries' and on the reasons for their clustering.

This chapter explores the reasons for this phenomenon, focusing on four complementary approaches – culture and heritage, agglomeration economies, related variety and the creative class – and using an econometric model to develop a comparison between two countries aimed at making some generalizations. The two countries selected for the analysis – Italy and Spain – are not understood well enough from the point of view of the creative industries and are characterized by important endowments of cultural, artistic heritage and by different patterns of spatial clustering of creative industries.

The main results show the existence of some common determinants of creative industry clustering, of which the most important are the human capital, the creative class and the agglomeration economies. Urbanization economies are particularly important in Spain, where the creative industries cluster in the heart of the largest metropolitan areas. In Italy, where the creative industries are more distributed across the territory, forming networks of medium-sized cities, not only urban economies but also district-based localization economies are especially important, together with the presence of cultural and artistic heritage.

Theoretical framework

Creative industries

There exist several definitions of creative industries. One of the most popular comes from the Department for Culture, Media and Sport (DCMS 2001: 5), which defines creative industries as 'industries which have their origin in individual creativity, skill and talent and which have a potential for wealth and job creation through the generation and exploitation of intellectual property'. Based on the DCMS (2001) list of creative industries, Lazzeretti *et al.* (2008) propose an operationalization of this definition that facilitates inter-country comparison and includes: publishing; music, film, video and performing arts; architecture and engineering studios; research and development (R&D); software and computer services; and advertising (see Table 1.1 in the previous chapter).

Reasons for the clustering of creative industries

Culture, arts and heritage

One of the first explanations of the clustering of creative industries came from the field of 'cultural economics' (Towse 2003). Studies on cultural economics and those on clusters and cultural districts have intensified, creating a rich and interesting mass of literature. Among the many studies of cultural economy and arts management, in parallel with the interest in various cultural sectors (Throsby 2010), the debate has recently been extended to the implications of creativity and culture as a 'flywheel' of local economic development (Cooke and Lazzeretti 2008).

Cultural heritage includes historic places, buildings, monuments, paintings and artefacts, and is the reflection of intangible historical aspects of the local culture (traditions, customs, language, lifestyle, etc.). Heritage influences the creative industries from two points of views: first, art, culture, beauty and history affect the perceptions and attitudes towards creativity; second, it promotes cultural activities such as conservation, enhancement and economic management of these resources (Camagni *et al.* 2004). The 'cities of art' like Florence in Italy or Seville in Spain are good examples.

Sometimes, these elements are related to the historical role of the place as a regional, national or international capital. The territorial contexts are multifarious, and the fundamental role of forms of clustering is emphasized: from cultural districts (Frost-Kumpf 1998) to cultural clusters (Mommaas 2004), creative cities and, lastly, cultural quarters (Hall 2000).

Agglomeration economies

Notwithstanding the importance of the presence of cultural resources in the territories, the basic reasons for the clustering of creative industries are still recognized based on the traditional concept of 'agglomeration economies' (Trullén and Boix 2008; Campbell-Kelly *et al.* 2010). Agglomeration economies can be broadly defined as advantages in costs or quality due to the spatial concentration of productive resources and actors (population, firms, institutions and other collective agents). Agglomeration economies are classified as either internal or external to the firm, whereas external economies are usually divided into localization and urbanization economies. Creative industries are affected by agglomeration economies, which basically act as centripetal forces, fostering the incubation and attraction of creative industries in places with specific characteristics (localization economies) or in large cities and metropolises (urbanization economies) (Chapain and De Propris 2009).

Marshallian localization economies are associated with the concentration of many firms of similar characteristics in particular localities. From this point of view, creative industries concentrate to take advantage of the existence of a skilled labour market for these industries, of the existence of local suppliers specialized in other parts of the creative *filière*, and to benefit from local knowledge spillovers. Urbanization economies are related to the concentration of industry in general; to an increase in the total economic size of the city in terms of population, income, output or wealth; to urban labour market efficiency, flexibility and skills; to social and productive diversity; and to the density of agents (Glaeser *et al.* 1992; Florida 2002). Urbanization economies explain the concentration of creative industries since they benefit from the large size or capacity of the local consumption market, from the mixture of land uses, and from the variety of activities and people. These generate a dense and varied network of agents that fosters mutual economic and social support and knowledge transfer through cross-fertilization mechanisms, and promotes creativity and innovation.

Related variety

Analyzing the more recent determinants of clustering in evolutionary economics and new economic geography, a new evolving paradigm is the concept of 'related variety' (Frenken and Boschma 2003). A 'related variety' industry is defined in terms of industrial sectors that are related because of shared or complementary competences in a cognitive-based definition (Boschma and Iammarino 2009). In other words, a certain degree of cognitive proximity gives rise to effective communication and interactive learning among different industries that contribute to a higher capacity to absorb innovations from neighbouring sectors though cross-fertilization. In other words, 'related variety' means that there exists a relationship between industrial sectors and economic activities in terms of (effective and potential) competences, innovations and transfers of knowledge.

The concept of related variety has recently been applied to creative industries (Lazzeretti 2009) as particularly active in the process of cross-fertilization and cognitive relationships among different industries. In this context, related variety is supposed to promote creativity and innovation in local systems due to transversality and spillover processes of innovation in other sectors.

The role of human capital and the creative class

A fourth explanation of the concentration of creative industries is related to the seminal contribution of Florida (2002, 2005) through his concept of 'creative class'. Florida remarks that some places are poles of attraction for the creative class, and, accordingly, the driving force behind the development of a city turns out to be its ability to attract and retain creative individuals. Florida introduced the theory of the 3Ts (technology, talent and tolerance), which shifted the focus from the creative industries to the human factor and its creative habitat. The advantages derived from diversity are emphasized, together with the socio-demographic characteristics of the population (the bourgeois–bohemian or 'bobo' index) (Florida 2002). Creativity is a multifarious factor, a resource for innovation, but also a competitive advantage associated with culture and territory and a factor in attracting and developing creative industries.

The differential characteristic of creative industries is the 'creative content', related to the talent and the existence of a creative and educated class. The creative class includes a cohort of professional, artistic and scientific workers who share a common creative ethos and add economic value through creativity (UNCTAD 2008). Human capital (talent), in the form of a 'creative class', takes a prevalent role in the development of creative industries and creative jobs. This point was previously explained by Ciccone and Hall (1996), who assumed the existence of externalities related to human capital in cities. Lucas (1988) remarked that the externalities generated by the exchange of ideas not only depend on the concentration of people in an area, but also on the quality of human capital. Glaeser (2000) reports that access to human capital encourages firms to cluster. Florida (2002, 2005) associates human capital with talent and highlights that the economic geography of talent is highly concentrated. Thus, human capital externalities explain the concentration of activities, especially of creative activities, in concrete points of the space.[1]

Empirical model

The model

Despite the several theories explaining spatial concentration and clustering of creative activities, there are few contributions that explain spatial concentration of creative industries and not any specific theoretical model. This requires the development of an empirical model departing from the factors of concentration of creative industries previously exposed.

The concentration of creative industries and creative employment in medium and large cities suggest that the relationship between the clustering of creative employment and its determinants could follow power, log-normal, or Pareto distributions (Gibrat 1931; Zipf 1949). In fact, the initial exploration of the location quotients (LQ) of the jobs in creative industries by local production systems (LPSs) suggests that they follow an exponential distribution:

$$y = \alpha X^{\beta_1}$$

where y is the LQ of employment in creative industries (dependent variable), X is a set of variables, and a, b are the parameters to be estimated. This functional form can be linearized, taking logarithms by producing a log-linear equation where the estimated parameters can be interpreted as elasticities (relative variations).

Data and variables

The data used in this research come from the national census of population and activity in the two countries, provided by the respective national statistical offices.[2] Census data assure a complete coverage of the observations as well as inter-country comparability. We use the more recent homogeneous data available for each data set, which is 2001 for both Italy and Spain.

The territorial unit of reference in the research is the LPS. The territorial base for the LPS is the local labour market (LLM) – equivalent to the Travel-To-Work areas. The original data, provided by municipality (NUTS 5) are aggregated by LLM (equivalent to a NUTS 4 unit). The decision to refer to LLMs as a territorial unit of analysis is consistent with our main interest in the place, more than just the simple concentration of activity. LLMs go beyond the administrative definitions and better refer to the effective organization of the territory.[3] The LLM is used in the studies on Marshallian industrial districts in Italy and Spain as they define the boundaries of the local society (ISTAT 2005; Boix and Galletto 2006). Scott emphasizes their role as a

> locus of peculiar traditions, sensibilities, and norms [that have] great importance in the case of sectors that generate outputs with high levels of aesthetic or semiotic content, but it also carries weight in other types of sectors (including technology-intensive manufacturing) where informal know-how and tacit forms of knowledge play a major role in production.
>
> Scott (2006)

We use employment data and a LQ to measure sector specialization concentration.[4] The LQ of the jobs in creative industries by LPSs is proposed as a proxy for the concentration of creative industries and will be used as the dependent variable in the econometric estimates. The explanatory variables come from the theoretical determinants exposed in section 2 and use data of population, employment by sector, number of firms, educational levels, land coverage, patents and cultural assets.[5]

Three variables have been used as proxies for *historical and cultural heritage*. First, the extent of local artistic and cultural heritage designated as protected by the Ministry of Culture of Italy and Spain, and divided by the total population in the LPS in order to avoid over representing big cities;[6] second, the share of jobs in the LPS related to heritage and cultural sites (NACE 92.5 (Nomenclature générale des Activités économiques dans les Communautés Européennes [General Classification of Economic Activities in the European Community])); and third, a dummy to identify the capitals of the provinces, considered as a proxy for proximity to political power and funds.

Indicators for external economies have been divided in two families. *Localization economies* follow Marshall's (1920) concepts: structure and organization of industry, qualification of the local labour system, specialized suppliers, and knowledge and information spillovers. The range of information and

Table 2.1 Dependent and explanatory variables

Dependent variable $\quad LQ_{ij} = \dfrac{L_{ij}}{L_i} \bigg/ \dfrac{L_j}{L}$

Explanatory variables

History and cultural heritage

- Density of cultural heritage goods by population: $CH = M_{ij} / P_{ij}$
- Share of jobs in heritage and cultural sites: $L_{Mj} = L_{Mj} / L_j$
- Political power dummy: 0 = non-capital city; 1 = capital city

Localization economies

- Firm size in the LPS: $FS_j = L_j / F_j$
- Firm size in creative industries: $FS_{ij} = L_{ij} / F_{ij}$
- *Filière*: $\quad FIL_{ij} = 1 \bigg/ \left(\sum_i L_{ij} / L_{ij} \right)^2$
- Share of qualified jobs in creative industries: $Q_{ij} = QL_{ij} / L_{ij}$

Urbanization economies

- Size of the market: $\quad SM_{ij} = Pop_{ij}$
- Productive diversity: $\quad DIV_j = 1 \bigg/ \sum_j \left(L_{ij} / L_j \right)^2$
- Social capital: $\quad SK_{ij} = L_{ij} / Pop_{ij}$
- Density of employment: $\quad D_{ij} = L_{ij} / U_j$

Related variety

- Related variety: $\quad \displaystyle\sum_{g=1}^{G} P_{g,j} H_{g,j}$

Florida 3Ts: Technology

- LQ high-tech manufactures $\quad LQ_{HTMj} = \dfrac{L_{HTMj}}{L_{HTM}} \bigg/ \dfrac{L_j}{L}$
- Patents per employee: $\quad TP_j = PAT_j / L_j$

Florida 3Ts: Talent

- Creative class: $\quad CC_j = C_j / L_j$
- University graduates: $\quad HK_j = L_{ISCED(5,6)j} \bigg/ \sum L_{ISCED\,j}$

Florida 3Ts: Tolerance

- Foreign born: $\quad TO_j = FB_j / L_j$

Legend: i = municipality; j = sector or *filière*; L = employment; F = firms; M = cultural and heritage goods; QL = qualified employment; **Pop** = population; U = urbanized land (ha); PAT = patents; C = creatives; FB = foreign-born people.

indicators available for localization economies is, however, limited, particularly when the indicator usually used as a proxy for localization economies (the LQ) is, as in this case, the dependent variable. Thus, we have considered four families of indicators (Table 2.1).

The average firm size in the LPS (firm size) takes into account the preference for the organization of the industry in small or large firms (Glaeser *et al.* 1992; Combes 2000). A second indicator controls the effect of firm size in creative industries in the LPS (firm size in creative industries).

The specialization of the local labour system has been addressed using the share of qualified jobs in creative industries (ISCO (International Standard Classification of Occupations) categories 1 to 8) (Trullén and Boix 2008).

The inverse of a Herfindahl index inside the productive chain is proposed as a proxy for specialized suppliers (*filière*) (Capone and Boix 2008). It indicates the relative degree of homogeneity in the distribution of employment among sectors in creative industries by LPS, where more equilibrated compositions means more local suppliers.[7]

Urbanization economies relies on four indicators:

1   Ohlin–Hoover's potential size of the local system has been approached, using the *total population* in the LPS.
2   Jacobs' productive diversity has been computed using the inverse of a Hirschman–Herfindahl index of diversity of employment at two digits in the LPS (Henderson *et al.* 1995). Higher values indicate higher specialization (less diversity) of the economic structure (Combes 2000; Trullén and Boix 2008).
3   The effect of social diversity and social capital, measured by the density of jobs by population (Trullén and Boix 2008).
4   The potential effect of density of urban land approach on the density economies in the form of the number of employees by square metres of urbanized land (Ciccone and Hall 1996).

Related variety has been measured using the three-digit level entropy index proposed by Boschma and Iammarino (2009).[8]

Florida's creativity and the 3Ts are based on the measurement of technology, talent and tolerance (Florida 2002, 2005):

1   *Technology* includes two indicators: the LQ of high and medium-high technology manufacturing industries as defined by OECD (2003) and the density of local patent applications (Florida 2005).
2   *Talent* is also measured using two indicators: first, the proportion of creative jobs (creative class) of the total local jobs. Second, the share of local tertiary graduates (ISCED 5 and 6 (International Standard Classification on Education)) on total jobs as a proxy for Lucas' human capital.[9]
3   *Tolerance* has been interpreted as the share foreign workers have of the total local jobs.

Other control variables have been included. The linkages between creative industries and the knowledge economy have been contrasted by including the share of high and medium-high technology manufacturing industries and the share of knowledge-intensive services (except those classified as creative in our framework) as defined by OECD (2003), as well as the share of private per capita expenditures in R&D. Finally, a dummy has been included to control the relationship between creativity and Marshallian industrial districts (a widespread reality in both Italy and Spain), although no significant results were obtained.

Econometric estimation and results

The model has been estimated for each country separately. A two-step strategy was followed for estimations. First, in order to test separately the contribution of the different factors to the concentration of creative employment, partial regressions have been estimated for historical and cultural heritage, localization economies, urbanization and related variety, and the creative class (Appendix 2.1). Second, a full model, including all the economic and statistically significant variables in partial regressions, was estimated and reduced to a parsimonious specification (Appendix 2.2).

Partial regressions

Historical and cultural heritage

Historical and cultural endowments are associated with the differentials of concentration of employment in creative industries, although this only provides a small part of the explanation (between 14 and 20 per cent of the variance). The per capita number of ruins, listed buildings, museums, etc. is positively related to the concentration of jobs in creative industries in Italy, where an increase of 1 per cent in the per capita endowments is associated with an increase of 0.08 per cent in concentration. However, in Spain this relationship is negative, which is explained by the dispersion of the cultural heritage as well as by the fact that some medium and large Spanish cities are not rich in heritage.

We notice that the way the indicator is designed may not take into account the relevance or use of this heritage (e.g. visitors to museums). This should be captured more accurately by the indicator of share of jobs in heritage and cultural sites on the total local employment. This second indicator is positive. Although this is very small for Italy (0.01), it is much more important for Spain (0.13). The results of both indicators indicate the global correlation between heritage and concentration of jobs in creative industries, although with significant differences in the way it performs across the two countries.

On the other hand, the capitals of the provinces, used as a proxy for closeness to the political power or access to funds, are highly correlated with concentration, as the estimated coefficients are 0.62 for Italy and 0.72 for Spain. However, that could be also capturing the effect of urbanization economies, so that its real effect can only be evaluated in the full model.

Localization economies

Firm structure and localization economies explain about 39 per cent of the differentials of concentration in Italy and 52 per cent in Spain. Firm structure affects the concentration of creative industries in both countries. First of all, a larger average firm size in the LPS is negatively correlated with the concentration of jobs in creative industries (–0.13 for Italy and –0.52 in Spain). Second, a larger firm size in creative industries is positively associated with the concentration of creative industries, particularly in Italy, where an increase of 1 per cent in the average firm size of creative industries leads to an increase of 0.72 per cent in concentration.[10]

A more balanced distribution of the creative *filière* is also positively correlated with creative concentration (0.51 in Italy and 0.30 in Spain). The estimates for Spain (the information is not available for Italy) also include the percentage of qualified jobs in creative industries in the LPS, which is positively correlated with creative clustering (0.31).

Urbanization economies and related variety

Urbanization economies explain 25 per cent of the differentials in concentration in Italy whereas in Spain it explains up to 64 per cent. The population in the LPS (size of the local market) shows a small but significant impact on the concentration of creative industries, whereas an increase of 1 per cent only reports an increase of concentration of 0.07 per cent for Italy and 0.08 per cent for Spain (Appendix 2.1).

On the other hand, the diversity of the local productive structure proves to be much more important for concentration of creative jobs. It shows a high and positive correlation with the differentials in concentration of creative industries, reaching coefficients of 0.32 for Italy and 0.62 for Spain. The results of population and diversity indicators suggest options to foster creative industries in small and medium cities that show a highly diverse productive structure.

The rest of the variables regarding urbanization economies are not significant for Italy. In Spain the correlation of creative concentration with social capital (0.62) as well as with the related variety (0.46) are highly significant. In general, urbanization economies seem to be the principal cause in explaining the differences in the patterns of concentration of creative industries across both countries, due to their powerful impact in Spain.

Florida's creative class

Florida's 3Ts approach explains less than 1 per cent of the differentials of concentration of creative jobs in Italy and about 56 per cent in Spain. Despite this difference in the performance of the model, the estimated coefficients are quite similar in both countries.

The first T (technology) shows a small effect on concentration. The coefficients for the LQ of high-tech manufacturers are 0.05 in Italy and 0.09 in Spain. The estimated coefficients for the number of patents per employee are 0.01 in Italy and 0.04 in Spain.

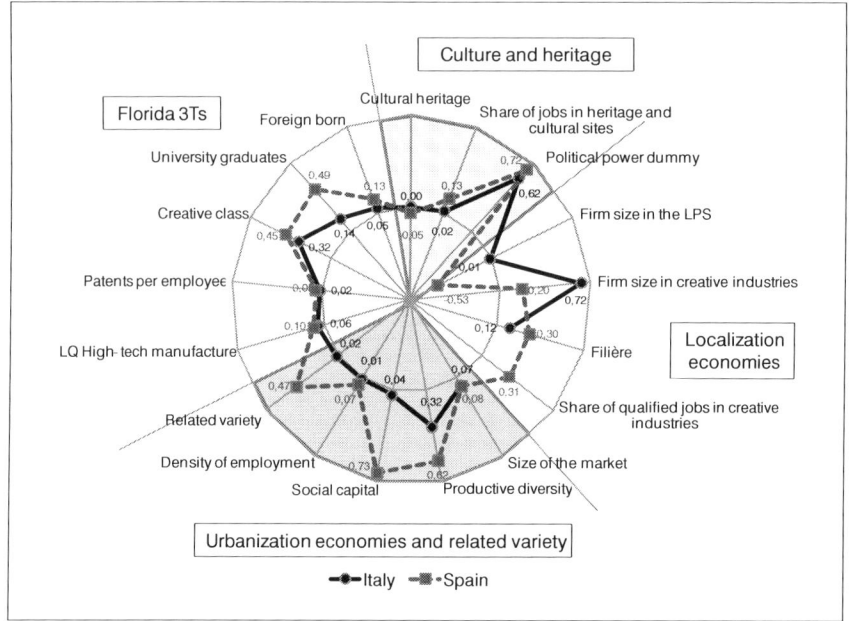

Figure 2.1 Results of the partial regressions, estimated coefficients

Source: Lazzeretti, Boix and Capone (2012: 11)
Notes: (a) dependent variable = Ln (LQ employees in creative industries); (b) all variables are natural logarithms; (c) partial regressions include history and cultural heritage (cultural heritage index; share of jobs in heritage and cultural sites; political power dummy); localization economies (firm size in the LPS; firm size in creative industries; internal creative filière; share of qualified jobs in creative industries), urbanization economies and related variety (size of the local market; productive diversity; social capital; density of employment; related variety), and Florida's creative class (LQ high-tech manufactures; patents per employee; creative class; university graduates; foreign born people); (d) robust Huber–White estimators. More details are presented in Appendix 2.1.

The second T (talent) proves to be much more important in explaining the differentials of concentration of jobs in creative industries. The share of creative class of the total employment shows an estimated coefficient of 0.32 in Italy, which rises to 0.44 in Spain. On the other hand, the share of resident employees with tertiary education levels shows coefficients of about 0.14 for Italy and 0.48 for Spain.[11]

The third T (tolerance) has been approached using the foreign-born index. Their effect on the differentials of concentration is positive and significant, although with a small effect: 0.04 in Italy and 0.12 in Spain.

Full model

The regressions combining the four sets of variables highlight the similarities and differences between both countries (Figure 2.1 and Appendix 2.2). First of all, the fit of the model is much better for Spain ($R^2 = 0.74$) and the causes of the differentials in concentration of creative jobs covers the global structure of the firms in the LPS (–0.19) and in creative industries (0.06), localization economies (share of qualified jobs in creative industries = 0.17), urbanization economies

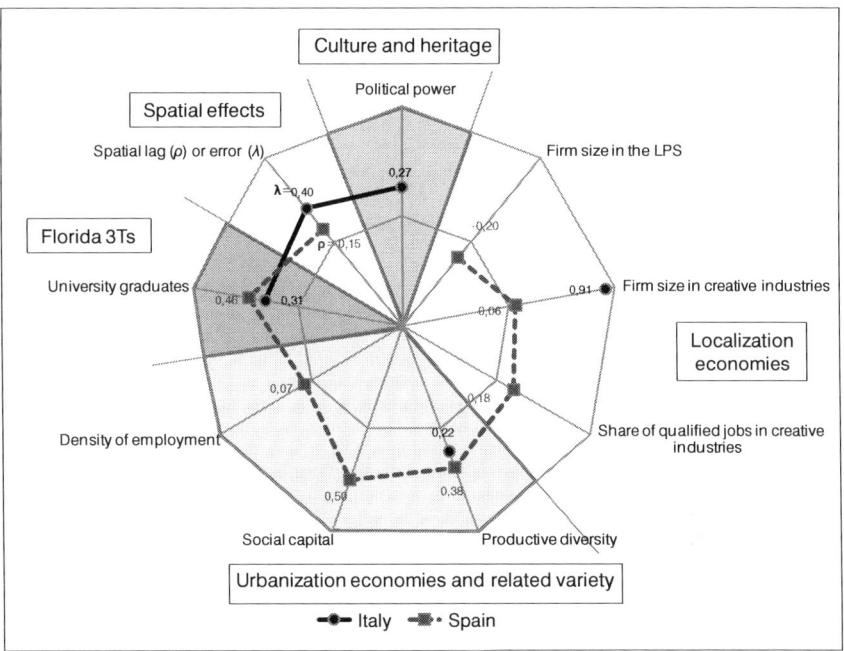

Figure 2.2 Results of the full model, estimated coefficients

Source: Lazzeretti, Boix and Capone (2012: 11)
Notes: (a) dependent variable = Ln(LQ employees in creative industries); (b) all variables are natural logarithms; (c) the full model estimated for Italy is an spatial error model (GM (generalized moments) iterated) including: history and cultural heritage (political power dummy), localization economies (firm size in creative industries), urbanization economies (productive diversity), Florida's creative class (university graduates), and a spatial error term (λ); (d) the full model estimated for Spain is an spatial lag model (IV (instrumental variable) robust) including: localization economies (firm size in the LPS; firm size in creative industries; share of qualified jobs in creative industries), urbanization economies (productive diversity; social capital; density of employment), Florida's creative class (university graduates), and a spatial lag term (ρ). More details are in Appendix 2.2.

(productive diversity = 0.37; social capital = 0.49; and density of employment = 0.07) and talent (share of university graduates = 0.46). This indicates that a large number of forces are correlated with the differentials of concentration of creative jobs in Spain, where urbanization economies and talent seem to be the main determinants. This is on the basis of the strong concentration of creative jobs in large cities and metropolitan areas.

In Italy, the fit (R^2) varies from 0.49 (non-spatial model) to 0.56 (spatial model). Although direct comparison between Spain and Italy cannot be performed using the R^2, the results suggests that, in Italy, a larger share of the reasons for the concentration of jobs in creative industries are still unmodeled. This is to say, other forces could have a relevant role in explaining concentration. Regarding the explained part, only the average firm size in creative industries (0.63), the dummy for political power/budget (0.37), the productive diversity (0.22) and the share of tertiary graduates (0.24) are economically and statistically significant (Figure 2.2 and Appendix 2.1).[12]

Common to both countries are the positive and significant coefficient for the productive diversity and the human capital (tertiary graduates) – even though the coefficient for Spain is double that of Italy – and the positive correlation with the average firm size of creative industries, although for Spain this latter coefficient is very small in the full estimates.

Spatial autocorrelation has been incorporated in the form of spatial lag and error effects based on a row standardized contiguity matrix. In Spain, the coefficient for the spatial lag ($\rho = 0.15$) is significant, and suggests the existence of spatial spillovers, where the concentration of jobs in creative industries is correlated with concentration in neighbourhood LPSs. In Italy, a process of spatial error dominates, with a large coefficient (0.39). This spatial error could be interpreted as the existence of spatial stochastic shocks between LPSs. However, in our opinion the coefficient could be affected by the existence of omitted variables in the specification of the model, and reinforces our previous belief about the existence of additional factors explaining the differentials of concentration.

Since it could be argued that differences between both countries could be due to a different composition of the creative industry in terms of more relevance of some activities, this fact has been also tested by dividing creative industries into traditional and non-traditional. The results suggest that traditional and non-traditional creative industries tend to co-agglomerate, and that their clustering determinants are not very different. A similar comment could be made about the changes in results if jobs were substituted by firms in the dependent variable. In this case, although there are variations in size of the coefficients, the reasons for the differentials of concentration points in the same direction.

Conclusions and discussion

The main purpose of this work was to contribute to the examination of the reasons of clustering of creative industries in Italy and Spain in order to identify the main differences between the two countries and any other factors useful in formulating some possible generalizations. For this purpose, we have adopted the classification of creative industries shared by most important European studies in order to facilitate future benchmarking.

As mentioned in the introduction, most of the works on creative industries are case studies or quantitative national surveys. There are few comparative studies and there is also a lack of analysis of the determinants of the phenomenon. To allow a comparison in this study, an exploratory econometric model was constructed, considering four theoretical approaches at the same time: *agglomeration economies*, divided into localization and urbanization economies; *cultural approach*, which considers the role of cultural heritage and the institutional and political cultural dimension; the theory of *creative class and Florida 3Ts*; and finally, the concept of *related variety*. Some of the most significant proxies were tested in both countries in order to make the model operative.

The results contribute to the investigation of the relationship between creativity and space, and show, first of all, the presence of two different spatial patterns. While in both cases the phenomenon of clustering is clear, in Italy its presence in creative industries is much more dispersed inside the territory. In Spain, it is actually concentrated around big metropolitan areas.

The details emerging from the local creative systems allow us to appreciate the variety in the different systems, both specialized and diversified into various typologies of creative industries.

A difference is also observable in the econometric model that highlights how the localization economies are more important in Italy and how urbanization economies are more diffused in Spain. In both countries, agglomeration economies are relevant, and this confirms the strong relationship existing between spatial concentration and creativity, as often recalled in the international literature on creative industries.

Regarding the related variety approach, we wondered whether the presence of this phenomenon has encouraged the clustering of creative industries thanks to cross-fertilization, and spatial and cognitive proximities. With regard to Spain, results are positive, while in Italy, estimations are not equally important. This issue supports the hypothesis that urbanization economies are a relevant factor nurturing related variety, especially in creative industries.

Regarding the cultural approach, the presence of an important artistic and cultural heritage is particularly relevant for Italy. In Italy, the 'heritage dependence' is probably significant as well as the correlation with institutional elements related to culture. The fact that much of the historical and artistic heritage in Italy is public influences the presence of *heritage dependent creative industries*.

In both countries, the role of capital cities is significant and emphasizes the importance of public and institutional actors for the development of creative industries. This role could even increase if, in addition to the considered economic activities, non-profit sectors, such as museums, were included in the analysis.

Finally, regarding the approach of creative class, its influence is the most common and generalizable aspect, together with the tendency to cluster in places. The strategic role of talents is present in both countries, but the indexes of tolerance and technology do not register the same relevance.

In conclusion, this study permits us to investigate the reasons for the clustering of creative industries, according to a multidisciplinary approach and from the perspective of an international comparison. Some common features were identified, but also many differences. Creativity and place are related, but the manner in which they are manifested are different from country to country. Consequently, it is important to continue these comparative analyses as they allow us to explore more fully the ways in which this phenomenon occurs, in order to develop more appropriate policies for creativity, considering all the differences between countries.

Appendix 2.1 Partial regressions

Dependent variable: LQ of the employment in creative industries

a) Historical and cultural heritage

	Italy	Spain
Constant	−0.4204***	−0.2619*
	(0.000)	(0.031)
Cultural heritage	0.0801***	−0.0516**
	(0.000)	(0.004)
Share of jobs in heritage and cultural sites	0.0182*	0.1348***
	(0.020)	(0.000)
Political power dummy	0.6222***	0.7204***
	(0.000)	(0.000)
R^2-adj	0.1393	0.1981
Mean VIF	1.08	1.02
Condition number	7.25	6.29
Observations	686	806

b) Structure of the industry and localization economies

	Italy (1)	Italy (2)	Spain
Constant	−0.9640***	−1.0693***	−1.8037***
	(0.000)	(0.000)	(0.000)
Firm size in the LPS	−0.1367*	–	−0.5262***
	(0.017)	–	(0.000)
Firm size in creative industries	–	0.7203***	0.2006***
	–	(0.000)	(0.000)
Filière	0.5158***	0.1185**	0.3014***
	(0.000)	(0.005)	(0.000)
Share of qualified jobs in creative industries	–	–	0.3113***
	–	–	(0.000)
R^2-adj	0.2261	0.3914	0.5293
Mean VIF	1.34	1.70	1.19
Condition number	8.77	7.01	28.71
Observations	686	686	806

c) Urbanization economies and related variety

	Log LQ employees in creative industries	
	Italy	*Spain*
Constant	−2.2035***	−2.6011***
	(0.000)	(0.000)
Size of the market	0.0743**	0.0831***
	(0.002)	(0.000)
Productive diversity	0.3242***	0.6248***
	(0.000)	(0.000)
Social capital	0.04420	0.7315***
	(0.269)	(0.000)
Density of employment	0.0113	0.0706***
	(0.571)	(0.000)
Related variety	0.0221	0.4661***
	(0.372)	(0.000)
R^2-adj	0.2532	0.6463
Mean VIF	2.06	1.91
Condition number	43.50	33.90
Observations	686	806

d) Human capital and creative class (Florida's 3Ts)

	Log LQ employees in creative industries	
	Italy	*Spain*
Constant	0.3840	1.0604***
	(0.283)	(0.000)
LQ High-tech manufacturers	0.0595***	0.0978***
	(0.000)	(0.000)
Patents per employee	0.0153	0.0489***
	(0.174)	(0.000)
Creative class	0.3205*	0.4464***
	(0.096)	(0.000)
University graduates	0.1447*	0.4859***
	(0. 040)	(0.000)
Foreign born	0.0483*	0.1294***
	(0.088)	(0.000)
R^2-adj	0.0709	0.5592
Mean VIF	2.33	2.31
Condition number	68.55	37.76
Probability Wu–Hausman	0.170	0.000
Observations	686	806

Notes: (a) dependent variable = Log (LQ employees in creative industries); (b) all variables are natural logarithms; (c) p-values are in parentheses and asterisks represent statistical significance (*** $p < 0.001$; ** $p < 0.01$; * $p < 0.1$); (d) robust Huber–White estimators. VIF: variance inflation factor.

Appendix 2.2 Full model

Parsimonious estimation. Dependent variable: LQ of the employment in creative industries

	Italy		Spain	
	OLS robust	Spatial error model	OLS robust	Spatial lag model
Constant	−1.1494***	−1.0645***	−0.7272***	−0.6307*
	(0.000)	(0.000)	(0.001)	(0.013)
Political power	0.2887***	0.2682***	–	–
	(0.000)	(0.000)	–	–
Firm size in the LPS	–	–	−0.2126***	−0.1968***
	–	–	(0.000)	(0.000)
Firm size in creative industries	0.8072***	0.9096***	0.0609***	0.0621***
	(0.000)	(0.000)	(0.000)	(0.000)
Share of qualified jobs in creative industries	–	–	0.1857***	0.1796***
	–	–	(0.000)	(0.000)
Productive diversity	0.2328***	0.2203***	0.4232***	0.3797***
	(0.000)	(0.000)	(0.000)	(0.000)
Social capital	–	–	0.6471***	0.4979***
	–	–	(0.000)	(0.000)
Density of employment	–	–	0.0748***	0.0721***
	–	–	(0.000)	(0.000)
University graduates	0.2489***	0.3106***	0.4615***	0.4642***
	(0.000)	(0.000)	(0.000)	(0.000)
Spatial lag (ρ) or error (λ)	–	0.3969***	–	0.1524***
	–	(0.000)	–	(0.000)
R^2-adj	0.4912	0.5665	0.7324	0.7448
Mean VIF	1.37	–	1.55	–
Condition number	23.17	–	55.26	–
Probability Wu–Hausman	0.3814	–	0.125	–
Robust LM-lag	25.16	–	16.54	–
Robust LM-error	87.36	–	7.55	–
Observations	686	686	806	806

Notes: (a) dependent variable = Log (LQ employees in creative industries); (b) all variables are natural logarithms; (c) p-values are in parentheses and asterisks represent statistical significance (*** $p < 0.001$; ** $p < 0.01$; * $p < 0.1$); (d) robust Huber–White estimators in non-spatial regressions; (e) spatial error model GM iterated; (f) spatial lag model IV-robust. OLS: ordinary least squares; LM: Lagrange multiplier.

Notes

1 Florida's theory has been criticized by some authors. Despite these criticisms, the contribution of the 'creative class' theory is recognized as redirecting the attention from the firm to the creative class, and so to the qualified human capital (Asheim 2009).

2 The exceptions are the number of cultural goods, which comes from the Ministry of Culture of each country, and the number of patents, which comes from each national Patent and Trademarks Office. In both cases the information encompasses geo-localized microdata by postal address, which is aggregated by local labour market.

3 They focus on the intensity of relations between residents and the workforce of a certain area, and they allow for the consideration of creative 'commuters' that work in the city, but reside outside the city limits. The existence of a homogeneous definition of LLM based on daily commuting flows in Italy and Spain allows the use of these units. By using the same methodology on 2001 census data, the Italian Institute of Statistics (ISTAT 2005) identifies 686 LLMs in Italy, whereas Boix and Galletto (2006) identify 806 LLMs in Spain. The picture that emerges for each country forms a pattern of local creative systems (LLMs where there is a high concentration of employment in specific creative industries).

4 The LQ has been used to measure the spatial concentration of creative industries in other chapters of this book. On the other hand, the census data we used comprises the universe of jobs in the territorial unit, and encompasses all the kinds of employment (wage earning, self-employment and special regimes of employment) in all the types of units (large firms, small firms, civil service, self-employment, etc.).

5 In spite of the limitations of some of these variables, they are well-known indicators used by reference works in quantitative frameworks.

6 We have also considered the number of museums localized in the LLSs registered by the Ministry of Culture in the two countries as a proxy for the cultural heritage and a dummy representing the United Nations Education, Scientific and Cultural Organization (UNESCO) World Heritage List, although results have been not significant. These indicators are used for 'historic and cultural heritage', as those assets protected by the state (e.g. historic/heritage designation) are used as a proxy for cultural facilities. Unfortunately, other desirable indicators as the local expenditures in culture are not available at an infra-regional level.

7 A second index has been calculated, departing from Dumais *et al.* (2002), and uses a mixed local and input–output approach to detect whether the presence of suppliers is above the local requirements, indicating the existence of a powerful chain of suppliers. However, this index has been removed from estimates as it has proved to be very collinear with other localization variables.

8 The value of the entropy indicator increases the more diversified the creative profile of a LPS is, where $P_{g,j} = \sum_{i \in S_g} p_{i,j}$ is the aggregation from three digit to two digit sectors of the share of each industry employment on the total employment $p_{i,LPS} = L_{i,j} \Big/ \sum_{i=1} L_{i,j}$, and $H_{g,j} = \sum_{i \in S_g} \dfrac{p_{i,j}}{P_{g,j}} \log_2\left(\dfrac{1}{p_{i,j}/P_{g,j}}\right)$.

9 *C* represents creative occupations or the creative class (ISCO-88 scientists, engineers, artists, cultural creatives, managers, professionals and technicians) to capture the effects of creativity.

10 In the estimations for Italy, the average firm size in the LPS and the average firm size in creative industries in the LPS are highly collinear, so that both have been estimated in separated regressions. Although the coefficient for the average firm size in the LPS in Italy is negative, as in Spain (although close to zero), this could be due to the collinearity of this variable with the variable *filière*. The larger impact for Italy

could be due to the smaller size of creative industries by LPS (the median is 1.5 in Italy against 5.5 in Spain), which contrasts with a similar median size for the complete industry in both countries (around three employees by firm by LPS).

11 The components of talent (human capital and creative class) are potentially endogenous. The results of a path analysis in partial regressions indeed suggest this possibility for Spain, although not for Italy. A Wu–Hausman test has been performed, testing the possible effects on the consistency of the estimations in both countries. The test confirms the results of the path analysis and suggests that the creative class can be treated as exogenous in both countries, whereas the percentage of tertiary graduates could be treated as endogenous in Spain in the partial regression (although not in the full regression). Two additional general methods of moments (GMM) regressions have been estimated for Spain, where the first includes as an instrument the percentage of secondary and tertiary graduates in 1991, and the second considers as instruments agglomeration economies and the percentage of knowledge-intensive services other than the creative ones. The effects of potential endogeneity do not hold in the full regression and the coefficient for the percentage of tertiary graduates is unusually high in IV estimations. Consequently, it is our opinion that the results of the Wu–Hausman test and the subsequent IV estimations are affected by the misspecification of the partial model, and the coefficient from OLS estimations is more correct.

12 It is noted that for both countries, in the full model, the significance of the creative class was absorbed by other variables with which it was highly correlated (firm size, diversity, etc.).

References

Asheim, B. (2009) 'Introduction to the creative class in European city regions', *Economic Geography*, 85(4): 355–62.

Belussi, F. and Staber, U. (2010) *Managing Networks of Creativity*, London: Routledge.

Boix, R. and Galletto, V. (2006) 'Sistemas industriales de trabajo y distritos industriles marshallianos en España', *Economía Industrial*, 359: 165–84.

Boschma, R. and Iammarino, S. (2009) 'Related variety, trade linkages and regional growth in Italy', *Economic Geography*, 85(3): 289–311.

Camagni, R., Maillat, D. and Matteaccioli, A. (eds) (2004) *Ressources naturelles et culturelles, milieux et développement local*, Neuchâtel: Institut de Recherches Économiques et Régionales, Éditions EDES.

Campbell-Kelly, M., Danilevsky, M., Garcia-Swartz, D.D. and Pederson, S. (2010) 'Clustering in the creative industries: Insights from the origins of computer software', *Industry and Innovation*, 17(3): 309–29.

Capone, F. and Boix, R. (2008) 'Sources of growth and competitiveness of local tourist production systems: An application to Italy (1991–2001)', *The Annals of Regional Science*, 42(1): 209–22.

Chapain, C., and De Propris, L. (2009), 'Drivers and processes of creative industries in cities and regions', *Creative Industries Journal*, 2(1): 9–18.

Ciccone, A. and Hall, R.E. (1996) 'Productivity and the density of economic activity', *The American Economic Review*, 86(1): 54–70.

Combes, P.P. (2000) 'Economic structure and local growth: France 1984–1993', *Journal of Urban Economics*, 47(3): 329–55.

Cooke, P. and Lazzeretti, L. (eds) (2008) *Creative Cities, Cultural Clusters and Local Economic Development*, Cheltenham: Edward Elgar.

DCMS – Department for Culture, Media and Sport (2001) *Creative Industries Mapping Document 2001*, London: DCMS.

De Propris, L., Chapain, C., Cooke, P., MacNeill, S. and Mateos-Garcia, J. (2009) *The Geography of Creativity*, London: NESTA.

Dumais, G., Ellison, G. and Glaeser, E.L. (2002) 'Geographic concentration as a dynamic process', *Review of Economics and Statistics*, 84(2): 193–204.

Florida, R. (2002) *The Rise of the Creative Class: And How it's Transforming Work, Leisure and Everyday Life*, New York: Basic Books.

Florida, R. (2005) *Cities and the Creative Class*, New York: Routledge.

Frenken, K. and Boschma, R. (2003) 'Evolutionary economics and industry location', *Review of Regional Research*, 23: 183–200.

Frost-Kumpf, H.A. (1998) *Cultural District: The Arts as a Strategy for Revitalizing our Cities*, Washington, DC: Institute for Community Development and the Arts, Americans for the Arts.

Gibrat, R. (1931) *Les inégalités économiques*, Paris: Librairie du Recueil Sirey.

Glaeser, E.L. (2000) 'The new economics of urban and regional growth', in G. Clark, M. Gertler and M. Feldman (eds) *The Oxford Handbook of Economic Geography*, Oxford: Oxford University Press, pp. 83–98.

Glaeser, E.L., Kallal, H., Sheinkman, J. and Schleifer, A. (1992) 'Growth in cities', *Journal of Political Economy*, 100(6): 1126–52.

Hall, P. (2000) 'Creative cities and economic development', *Urban Studies*, 37(4): 639–49.

Henderson, V., Kunkoro, A. and Turner, M. (1995) 'Industrial development in cities', *The Journal of Political Economy*, 103(5): 1067–109.

ISTAT – Istituto Nazionale di Statistica (2005) *I sistemi locali del lavoro. Censimento del 2001*, Roma: Direzione centrale censimento della Popolazione, territorio e ambiente.

Lazzeretti, L. (2009) 'The creative capacity of culture and the new creative milieu', in G. Becattini, M. Bellandi and L. De Propris (eds) *The Handbook of Industrial Districts*, Cheltenham: Edward Elgar, pp. 281–94.

Lazzeretti, L., Boix, R. and Capone, F. (2008) 'Do creative industries cluster? Mapping creative local production systems in Italy and Spain', *Industry and Innovation*, 15(5): 549–67.

Lazzeretti, L., Boix, R. and Capone, F. (2012) 'Reasons of clustering of creative industries in Italy and Spain', *European Planning Studies*, 20(8).

Lorenzen, M. and Frederiksen, L. (2008) 'Why do cultural industries cluster? Localization, urbanization, products and projects', in P. Cooke and L. Lazzeretti (eds) *Creative Cities, Cultural Clusters and Local Economic Development*, Cheltenham: Edward Elgar, pp. 155–79.

Lucas, R.E. (1988) 'On the mechanics of economic development', *Journal of Monetary Economics*, 22(1): 3–42.

Marshall, A. (1920) *The Principles of Economics*, London: McMillan.

Mommaas, H. (2004) 'Cultural clusters and post-industrial city: Towards the remapping of urban cultural policy', *Urban Studies*, 41(3): 507–32.

OECD – Organization for Economic Cooperation and Development (2003) *OECD Science, Technology and Industry Scoreboard*, Paris: OECD.

Scott, A.J. (2005) *On Hollywood. The Place, the Industry*, Princeton, NJ: Princeton University Press.

Scott, A.J. (2006) 'Creative cities: Conceptual issues and policy questions', *Journal of Urban Affairs*, 28(1): 1–17.

Throsby, D. (ed.) (2010) *The Economics of Cultural Policy*, Cambridge, UK: Cambridge University Press.

Towse, R. (ed.) (2003) *A Handbook of Cultural Economics*, Cheltenham: Edward Elgar.

Trullén, T. and Boix, R. (2008) 'Knowledge externalities and networks of cities in creative metropolis', in P. Cooke and L. Lazzeretti (eds) *Creative Cities, Cultural Clusters and Local Economic Development*, Cheltenham: Edward Elgar, pp. 211–37.

UNCTAD – United Nations Conference on Trade and Development (2008) *Creative Economy. Report 2008*, Geneva and New York: UNDP and UNCTAD.

Zipf, G.K. (1949) *Human Behavior and the Principle of Least-Effort: An Introduction to Human Ecology*, Cambridge, MA: Addison-Wesley.

3 Creative industries in Spain

The case of printing and publishing

Rafael Boix

Introduction

Creative industries are a highly relevant economic phenomenon. In 2005, they generated 6.1 per cent of the world gross domestic product (GDP) (US$2,706 billion) and 3.4 per cent of total world trade (Howkins 2007; UNCTAD 2010). They also provide wealth to the nations and regions that host them; an increase of 1 per cent in the share of creative industries among regional employment figures generates an average premium of €1,400 in the GDP per capita of the EU region (De Miguel *et al.* forthcoming).

Spain is the fifth-largest producer of creative industries in the EU and is a representative example of creativity in Mediterranean countries. Printing and publishing (P&P) are the most important creative industries in Spain, together constituting about 21 per cent of the country's creative GDP. Furthermore, P&P have two specificities in Spain: first, they operate on the basis of the Spanish language, spoken by about 400 million people worldwide. Second, they are hyper-concentrated in the metropolitan areas of Madrid and Barcelona, two of the main creative and P&P centres in the EU, with both showing characteristics of creative milieux. These specificities suggest that economies of scale could be operating in the industry from the angles of both demand and supply, one linked to sociocultural and historical patterns, and the other linked to the industry's spatial patterns of location.

This article proposes two contributions. It first provides an overview of the creative industries in Spain, focusing on the P&P industries. It then relates the relative importance of P&P in Spain to the economies of scale resulting from the size of the linguistic domain (demand approach) and agglomeration economies (supply approach).

Although most research focuses on only one of the two components of the industry (DCMS 2001), or in segments such as books (Hebbels and Boschma 2011) or newspapers (Driver and Gillespie 1993), this research focuses on both industries (printing and publishing) due to their strong interrelation in terms of input–output linkages and spatial co-location. The differences between both industries are taken into account by means of the differentiation between pure creative industries (publishing) and semi-creative industries (printing).

The overall effect of the linguistic domain is analyzed by comparing the size of both industries in Spain with other countries, and examining the patterns of exports by destination. The effects of agglomeration economies are revealed using the culture–agglomeration–creativity model in an intra-country econometric analysis (see Chapter 2 in this volume).

The results have shown that despite the advantages associated with the size of the linguistic domain, they are underused while powerful spatial economies of scale arise, generating very high levels of spatial concentration and the co-localization of both industries. The results have major implications for national and local specific strategies for P&P, and the places where these industries are located.

The text is divided into five sections. Following the introduction, the second section explores the characteristics of publishing as a creative industry and introduces the notion of a semi-creative industry in the case of printing. The third section offers an overview of the creative industries in Spain in comparison with the EU, while the fourth section focuses on the existence of economies of scale resulting from the size of the linguistic domain and agglomeration economies. The chapter ends with a set of concluding remarks.

Printing and publishing as creative and semi-creative industries

Printing and publishing

The origins of P&P date from the invention of the modern printing press by Gutenberg in roughly 1440 and its subsequent expansion throughout Europe (Eisenstein 2005). P&P as a whole is currently the largest creative industry in the world (representing 28 per cent of the market share of creative industries) and the third most exported creative industry (representing 8.15 per cent of the trade of creative goods and services) (Howkins 2007; UNCTAD 2010).

P&P is divided into two main industries. On the one hand, *publishing* is a knowledge-intensive service industry that focuses on the development, acquisition, copyediting, graphic design and production of literary contents (information products), as well as the dissemination and marketing of the contents in different formats (paper, electronic or other media).

On the other hand, *printing* focuses on the transference of contents to a certain medium, such as paper, metal, plastic, etc. It includes the printing of books, newspapers and magazines, commercial printing and other printed material, as well as other related activities such as binding or photoengraving. This part of the industry continues to be considered low-technology manufacturing, as it tends to require more mechanical and repetitive processes using machinery, and less qualified employees. Therefore, whereas publishing is a clear case of a creative industry, printing should be considered as a semi-creative industry.

Printing and publishing as creative and semi-creative industries

The *concept and definition* of creative industries differs according to the approaches, necessities and practices of different countries and organizations. Thus, to quote only some of the most significant sources, the Department for

Culture, Media and Sport defines creative industries as 'those industries which have their origin in individual creativity, skill and talent and which have a potential for wealth and job creation through the generation and exploitation of intellectual property' (DCMS 2001: 5). For the European Commission they are defined as 'those industries which use culture as an input and have a cultural dimension, although their outputs are mainly functional. They include architecture and design, which integrate creative elements into wider processes, as well as subsectors such as graphic design, fashion design or advertising (European Commission 2010).

Finally, for the United Nations Conference on Trade and Development they are defined as industries that

> (a) are cycles of creation, production and distribution of goods and services that use creativity and intellectual capital as primary inputs; (b) constitute a set of knowledge-based activities, focused on but not limited to arts, potentially generating revenues from trade and intellectual property rights; (c) comprise tangible products and intangible intellectual or artistic services with creative content, economic value and market objectives; (d) stand at the crossroads of the artisan, services and industrial sectors; and (e) constitute a new dynamic sector in world trade.
>
> (UNCTAD 2010: 8)

The publishing industry meets all of the characteristics and requirements outlined in these definitions. However, there is no consensus regarding the classification of printing as a creative industry. DCMS (2009) and Leadership Group on Quality Eurostat (LEG Eurostat 2000) do not include printing in their lists of creative industries, but instead consider it as a 'related industry' (Table 3.1). For World Intellectual Property Organization (WIPO 2003) printing is a 'core copyright industry', whereas in UNCTAD (2010) it is sometimes included to improve comparisons in which printing and publishing cannot be separated. This ambiguity is due to the fact that some creative products have a dual nature that divides their process into an intangible and a physical part, both with differentiated characteristics.

I propose the concept of semi-creative industries for this second category, which could include industries such as printing, clothing or housing goods (e.g. furniture or tiles). Thus, the *pure creative industries* could be characterized (Caves 2000; Handke 2004; Stoneman 2008; Throsby 2008; UNCTAD 2010) as: (a) the use of creative inputs to produce ideas, symbols and contents; (b) monopolistic or oligopolistic markets; (c) concentration in large corporations, often co-existing with small and medium enterprises (SMEs); (d) aesthetic qualities and product differentiation (experience goods); (e) concentration in the phases of creation and production of the value chain; (f) high and medium-high productivity; (g) innovation based on copyrights and trademarks (soft innovation) but also with expenditures in development; (h) spatial concentration to exploit local cultural assets, the creative class and urbanization economies; (i) co-localization with complementary semi-creative industries (Table 3.2).

Table 3.1 List of creative industries

Creative industries	UK DCMS (2009)	WIPO (2003) copyright industries	LEG Eurostat (2000)	KEA European Affairs (2006)	UNCTAD (2010)
Printing		×			×*
Publishing	×	×		×	×
Advertising and related services	×	×	×	×	×
Architecture	×	×	×	×	×
Arts and antique markets/trade	×	×	×		×
Crafts	×	×		×	×
Design/specialized design services	×	×	×	×	×
Designer fashion	×	×	×		×
Film/motion picture and video industries	×	×		×	×
Music/sound recording industries	×	×	×	×	×
Performing arts (theatre, dance, opera, circus, festivals, live entertainment)/Independent artists, writers and performers	×	×	×	×	×
Photography	×	×	×	×	×
Radio and television (broadcasting)	×	×	×	×	×
Software, computer games and electronic publishing	×	×	×	×	×
Heritage/cultural sites (libraries and archives, museums, historic and heritage sites, other heritage institutions)			×	×	×
Interactive media			×	×	
Other visual arts (painting, sculpture)			×		×
Copyright collecting societies				×	
Cultural tourism/recreational services				×	×
Creative R&D					×

* Only used for statistical reasons in comparisons.

Table 3.2 Characteristics of creative and semi-creative industries

	Creative industries	*Semi-creative industries*
Inputs	Creative	Humdrum
Outputs	Ideas, symbols, contents	Manufacturing
Production chain (main stage)	Creation and production	Production and reproduction
Markets	Oligopoly, monopolistic competition Large corporations and SMEs Aesthetic characteristics and product differentiation	Perfect competition SMEs and large corporations Price competition
Productivity	High and medium-high	Medium and medium-low
Innovation	Soft innovation: copyrights and trademarks; but also expenditures in development of product	Hard innovation: technological innovation (R&D, patents), but also soft innovation as designs and trademarks
Experience goods	Yes	Sometimes
Location factors	Culture and heritage Creative class Urbanization economies Co-location with complementary semi-creative industries	Scale economies Localization economies Co-location with complementary pure creative industries
Examples	Publishing, design, film and motion picture, music, performing arts, software, etc.	Printing, clothing, housing goods, toys

Semi-creative industries are characterized by: (a) 'humdrum' inputs to produce physical products embedding creative contents; (b) perfect competition markets; (c) SMEs with low average firm size; (d) competition in prices, even if products can be consumed as experience goods; (e) concentration in the phases of production and reproduction of the value chain; (f) medium and medium-low productivity; (g) technological innovation (R&D, patents) combined with non-technological innovation (designs and trademarks); (h) spatial concentration to take advantage of intra-firm economies of scale and localization economies; (i) co-localization with complementary pure creative industries (Table 3.2).

P&P meet the characteristics of complementary pure creative and semi-creative industries. First, creativity in P&P is expressed in the form of literary and aesthetic production translated into books; printed media translated into information in newspapers, journals and magazines; and printed graphic products (Stoneman 2008; UNCTAD 2010). Second, P&P is considered a 'downstream activity', as it is close to the market and derives its commercial value from low reproduction costs and easy transfer to other economic domains (UNCTAD 2010). Third, publishing is considered to be a mature sector demonstrating characteristics of monopolistic competition with a large number of sellers and buyers, low barriers of entry, differentiated products in the market and firms setting prices independently from competitors. As Canoy *et al.* (2005) explain, there is a trade-off between efficiency (economies of scale) and diversity. From the point of view of the structure of the market, there are some large companies co-existing with a plethora of small firms. The market is divided between local enterprises and some global corporations. In many cases, these large enterprises and corporations have significant market power (Schiffrin 2000; Canoy *et al.* 2005). On the other hand, the printing industry more closely resembles the behaviour of competitive markets: large number of firms, low barriers to entry, limited economies of scale, buyers with strong market power and difficulty in differentiating products.

Finally, even if P&P can be performed in the same enterprise unit, it is increasingly common to divide the two activities into separate units. However, in most cases, the complementariness of both processes requires an intimate spatial closeness (Driver and Gillespie 1993), such that the development of both parts of the industry has traditionally taken place in the same geographical space.

Creative industries, and printing and publishing in Spain: an overview

Empirical literature on creative industries, and printing and publishing in Spain

There is a lack of empirical research employing the creative industries approach in Spain. Most of the literature relies on the idea of a 'cultural sector', or on purely sector-specific studies. Only a few researchers have focused on the creative industries approach: Centro Europeo de Empresas e Innovación de Navarra (CEIN 2005) has provided an introduction to the capacity of creative industries to generate entrepreneurial projects in some creative firms in Spain; Casani (2010) coordinated research based on twenty different creative firms in Spain; and Lazzeretti *et al.* (2008) have provided initial measurements of creative industries in Spain and their patterns of spatial concentration (see also Chapter 1).

Institutional and academic studies have relied on different issues. Institutional studies include the satellite account on the cultural industry in Spain (Ministerio de Cultura 2010), book reading and buying habits in Spain (Ministerio de Cultura 2009), the figures and trends of the internal trade of books in Spain (FELC 2009), the distribution of books and periodical publications (FANDE 2010), the profile of the Spanish firms in the publishing industry (MKM 2007) and the facts and trends of the digital book in Spain (Neturity 2011).

Past academic research on P&P in Spain has focused on analysis of the country's book industry (Martínez 2001; Palma *et al.* 2009), the structure and distribution of multimedia groups and their concentration in the market and territory (Gámir 2005), the attitude of the Spanish book industry with respect to e-books (López and Larrañaga 2010) and the factors concerning competitiveness of the printing industry in Spain (Redondo 1999). In general, this research characterizes P&P in Spain as a mature and highly competitive industry, with a large number of agents and effective task distribution (Ávila and Porto 2004).

Basic magnitudes and comparison with the EU

As yet, no general research providing an overview of the creative industries in Spain exists. To provide the basic magnitudes of the creative sector in Spain, I followed UNCTAD's (2010) definition of creative industries and used the culture satellite account (Ministerio de Cultura 2010) and the national accounts (Spanish National Institute of Statistics – INE) (see Table 3.1). By using the satellite accounts, a special elaboration of the national accounts, one can take advantage of the fact that the cultural sector is included in the classification of creative industries by UNCTAD, and can thus obtain certain specific data not identified in the national accounts. The rest of non-cultural sectors are complemented using the national accounts.[1]

The data reveal five stylized facts about the creative industries as a whole and two regarding P&P in particular:

1   Creative industries are relevant in the Spanish economy. They amount to 5.6 per cent of the Spanish gross value added (GVA) (€56,129 million) and 6.3 per cent of employment (1.26 million jobs) in 2008 (Table 3.3).
2   Spain is the fifth-largest producer of creative industries in the EU, although it does not specialize in them. Spain supplies 9 per cent of total production in the EU but only 6.9 per cent of production in creative industries. Furthermore, the contribution of creative industries to the Spanish GDP is lower than the EU average (6.6 per cent) and well behind the most specialized countries (Denmark 8.7 per cent, Sweden 8.5 per cent, and Finland 7.7 per cent) (Figure 3.1).
3   The most important creative industries in Spain are P&P (20.4 per cent of the creative GVA) and architectural and engineering activities (21.3 per cent of the creative GVA).[2] These figures are closer to the EU average.
4   The share of creative industries in total Spanish production has decreased from 6.1 per cent in 2000 to 5.6 per cent in 2008. This loss of influence is not unique to Spain, as Power and Nielsén (2010) reported the same trend among other European economies including France, the UK and Belgium. In the Spanish case, this has been due to the accelerated growth of construction and low-tech services in the country's economy during that period.
5   During the period from 2000 to 2008, all the creative industries in Spain grew in nominal terms, with the exception of fashion. The higher increases were in research and development (R&D), culture and heritage (in both cases due to the effort of the public sector), and architecture and engineering (due to the expansion of the construction sector). The other creative industries showed more moderate behaviour and grew less than the average of the Spanish economy. For this reason, some creative industries saw a reduction in their share of the total economy, particularly advertising, and P&P (Table 3.3).
6   P&P as a whole represents 1.15 per cent of total production (GVA), similar to the EU and the Organisation of Economic Co-operation and Development (OECD) average. Spain contributed 6.5 per cent of the EU production in publishing industries and 9.7 per cent to printing industries in 2008. This involved about 8,000 firms, €11.400 million of GVA and 249,000 jobs (Figure 3.2).

Table 3.3 Gross value added in creative industries in Spain, 2000–08

	Million euro		Percentage of creative industries		Percentage of Spanish economy	
	2000	2008	2000	2008	2000	2008
Architecture and engineering	5,109	11,931	14.7	21.3	0.90	1.20
Printing and publishing	8,369	11,426	24.0	20.4	1.47	1.15
Software and videogames	4,465	7,180	12.8	12.8	0.78	0.72
Radio and television	3,096	4,856	8.9	8.7	0.54	0.49
Advertising	3,163	4,146	9.1	7.4	0.55	0.42
Film and video	2,236	3,218	6.4	5.7	0.39	0.32
Painting and sculpture	1,869	2,912	5.4	5.2	0.33	0.29
Fashion (including production)	2,803	2,384	8.0	4.2	0.49	0.24
Performing arts	770	1,671	2.2	3.0	0.13	0.17
Heritage	446	1,206	1.3	2.1	0.08	0.12
R&D	214	702	0.6	1.3	0.04	0.07
Libraries and archives	312	614	0.9	1.1	0.05	0.06
Recorded music	394	597	1.1	1.1	0.07	0.06
Interdisciplinary	1,590	3,286	4.6	5.9	0.28	0.33
Total creative industries	34,836	56,129	100.0	100.0	6.09	5.64

Sources: Culture satellite account (Ministerio de Cultura 2010) and national accounts (INE)

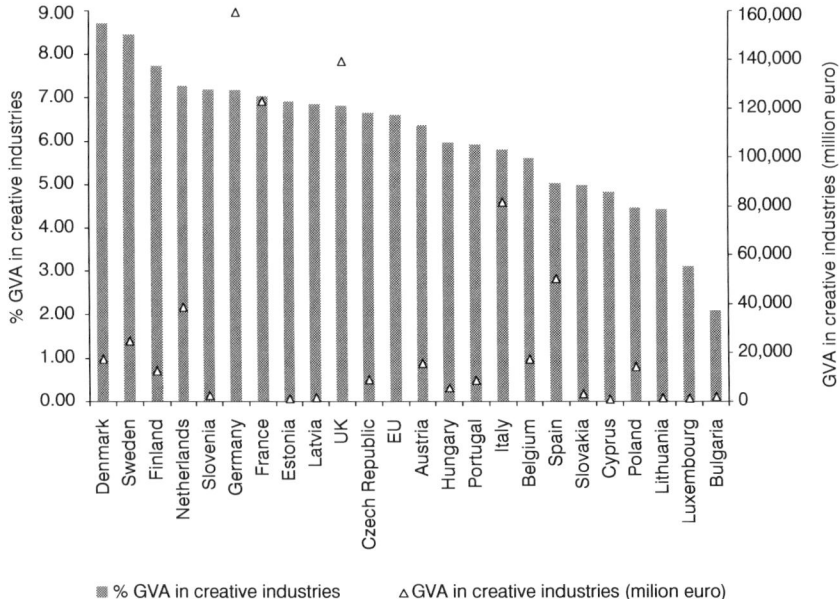

Figure 3.1 Gross value added in creative industries in the EU countries, 2008

Source: Eurostat, Structural Business Survey and National Economic Accounts
Note: Greece, Ireland, Malta and Romania are excluded because of data unavailability in Eurostat.

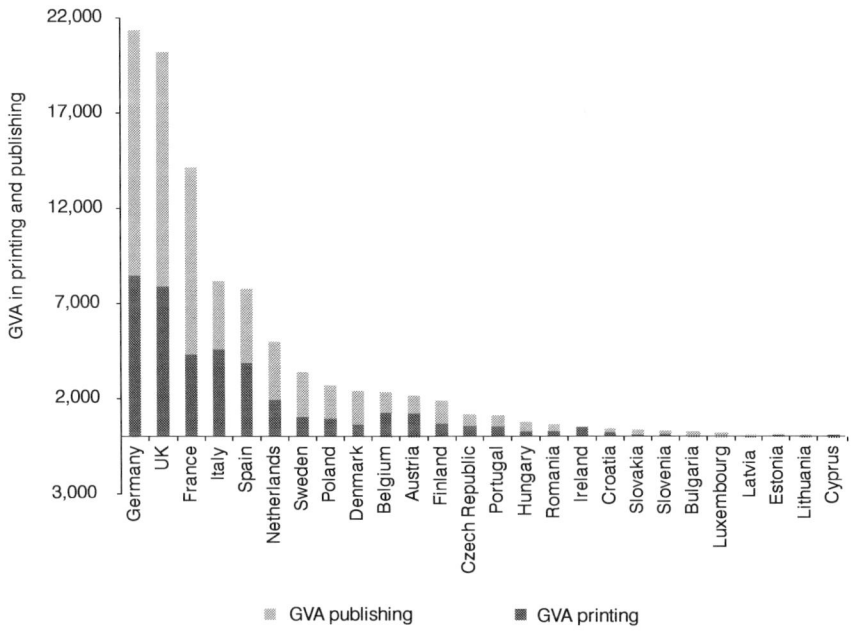

Figure 3.2 Gross value added in printing and publishing industries in the EU countries,
2007

Source: Our elaboration from Eurostat, Structural Business Statistics

7   However, the contribution of P&P industries to creative production is higher in Spain (20.4 per cent) than in the EU (12 per cent) due to the relatively smaller size of the rest of the creative industries in Spain, and to the fact that the contribution of the printing industry in Spain is higher than the EU average. Thus, whereas in Spain P&P is divided about 50 per cent for each industry, the EU average is 40 per cent for printing and 60 per cent for publishing. A similar pattern appears in other countries such as Portugal (51 per cent printing), Italy (57 per cent), Belgium (55 per cent) and Austria (57.5 per cent).

Economies of scale in printing and publishing industries in Spain: linguistic factor and urban creative milieux

Linguistic factor

Language is the basis for key aspects of creative industries, and is particularly relevant for the publishing industry (ICEX 2007). It is the main avenue for the introduction of cultural products and in turn becomes a strategic input. The importance of language in this context is derived from four factors: first, the number of speakers and their distribution generates network economies; second, it offers the capacity to absorb a linguistic market in terms of purchasing power; third, the characteristics that are inherent in a language, such as alphabet, openness to other languages or ease of interaction with information and communication technologies (ICTs); and finally, in countries where knowledge of foreign languages is low, the language also acts as a barrier for the introduction or diffusion of contents generated in other countries, as the consumption is carried out in the local language. These characteristics determine the economies of scale of a language and its contribution to production in a country (Martín 2003; Gámir 2005; García Delgado *et al.* 2008).

In the case of Spain, Spanish is spoken as a mother tongue by more than 80 per cent of the population and co-exists with other official languages, namely Catalan, Gallego and Euskera. However, the majority of Spanish speakers are found in the Americas, from the US to Argentina. This places Spanish somewhere between the second and fourth most spoken language in the world, depending on the source of data. For example, Lewis (2009) estimates that Spanish is the second most spoken language (329 million speakers in forty-four countries) together with English (328 million speakers in 112 countries) (Table 3.4). For Moreno and Otero (2006), using the United Nations Educational, Scientific and Cultural Organization's (UNESCO) data, Spanish is the fourth most spoken language globally with 392 million speakers, 6.1 per cent of the world population and 6.2 per cent of the world economy in terms of production.

The question is: Does language confer significant advantages to P&P in Spain? This leads to the following hypothesis:

*H*1: Spanish P&P is obtaining significant economies of scale associated with the Spanish language.

Table 3.4 Twenty most spoken languages in the world

Rank	Language	Total countries	Speakers (millions)
1	Chinese (12 varieties)	31	1,213
2	Spanish	44	329
3	English	112	328
4	Arabic (16 varieties)	57	221
5	Hindi	20	182
6	Bengali	10	180
7	Portuguese	37	178
8	Russian	33	144
9	Japanese	25	122
10	German (standard)	43	90
11	Javanese	5	85
12	Lahnda (two varieties)	8	78
13	Telugu (tel)	10	70
14	Vietnamese	23	69
15	Marathi	5	68
16	French	60	68
17	Korean	33	66
18	Tamil	17	66
19	Italian	34	62
20	Urdu	23	61

Source: Our elaboration of Lewis (2009)

However, three facts support contrary evidence to the H1 hypothesis, beginning with the internal composition of P&P. The effect of language is mainly exerted within the content sector of the industry. However, the relative contribution of publishing to the Spanish economy and to the European publishing industry is lower than the EU average, thus indicating that the country's publishing industry is not taking full advantage of the size of its linguistic market.

Furthermore, other less-spoken European languages such as German (90.3 million speakers in forty-three countries) or Italian (61.7 million in thirty-four countries) are associated with higher absolute and relative sizes of both the printing and the publishing industries in their countries, suggesting that the advantages of scale associated with the Spanish language are underused.

The final factor is the behaviour of exports. Publishing accounts for approximately 82 per cent of P&P exports (63 per cent books, 15 per cent newspapers and journals, and 4 per cent others). Its value and contribution towards total exports decreased from a maximum of 0.9 per cent of exports in 2003 to 0.37 per cent in 2010, while its positive contribution to the trade balance also decreased from 780 to 190 million euros in the same period.

Table 3.5 Printing and publishing industry exports by region of destination (percentage), 2000 and 2009

	EU	America	Other	Total
2000	45	51	5	100
Printing	79	18	3	100
Publishing	34	61	5	100
2009	57	40	4	100
Printing	94	2	4	100
Publishing	29	68	3	100

Source: Our elaboration of FECL (2009)

Changes in the typology of exported goods and the destination markets have also been important (FECL 2009). The strength of the euro has affected the competitiveness of Spanish P&P such that printing exports have increased their concentration in the EU as destination markets (from 79 per cent in the year 2000 to 94 per cent in 2009),[3] while publishing has increased its share of exports to America (from 61 to 68 per cent) and reduced its share within Europe (Table 3.5). Mexico is the main destination for publishing, followed by Argentina, Portugal, France, Brazil and the US.[4] This provides evidence that cultural and linguistic patterns are important for the success of publishing but not for printing. In any case, despite their positive effect, the potential economies of scale associated with the Spanish language have been insufficient to boost the production of the Spanish publishing industry.

The role of agglomeration economies: geographical clusters and the emergence of urban creative milieux

Lazzeretti *et al.* (2008) have shown that one of the most distinctive features of creative industries is their high spatial concentration, particularly in Spain (see also Chapter 1). For example, the concentration index of Gini reached the extreme value of 0.91 for the creative industries (very high concentration), far more concentrated than the rest of the economy.[5] Although Spain is not specialized in creative industries, it holds two of the major creative agglomerations of Europe: the metropolitan areas of Madrid and Barcelona.

Boix *et al.* (2012) have also shown that with large metropolitan areas such as Madrid and Barcelona, the creative industries have a preference towards the most central areas of the city. Lazzeretti *et al.* (see Chapter 2) have linked this pattern to the intensity of the urbanization economies in Spain, particularly those related to productive diversity and social networking. This pattern is further reinforced by localization economies and the concentration of the creative class in the largest cities.

P&P tend towards high levels of spatial concentration. For example, an indicator of concentration such as the Gini index calculated for the EU regions shows values of 0.73 for printing and 0.80 for publishing. Here, the regions of Madrid and Catalonia (Barcelona) host the highest EU levels of employment in printing, jointly with Lombardia and Île-de-France. The highest levels of employment in publishing are found in Île-de-France (75,000 employees) and Inner London (47,000), followed in third place by Madrid (22,000), with Catalonia (16,000) ranking in seventh place.

A location quotient can offer initial confirmation of the processes of P&P clustering (Figure 3.3, regions with a location quotient above 1). Most of the clusters are found in Germany, The Netherlands and the UK. However, only two clusters are found at a regional level in Spain: Madrid and Barcelona (Figure 3.3). This demonstrates that P&P could also be highly concentrated in Spain.

This observation is confirmed by the Gini index. Using local labour markets as territorial units and applying 2010 data, the index was 0.9 for P&P as a whole, 0.89 for printing and 0.93 for publishing.[6] Even when weighting by the distribution of total employment, the index was still above 0.70. The metropolitan areas of Madrid and Barcelona shared 49 per cent of Spanish jobs in printing and 60 per cent in publishing.

In addition, in these metropolitan areas, the publishing industry was extremely concentrated in the city centres, which in both cases accounted for more than 70 per cent of firms and roughly 80 per cent of jobs. The printing industry followed a slightly different intra-metropolitan pattern of location, as the city of Madrid had a concentration of 40 per cent of the metropolitan jobs and Barcelona 27 per cent. However, other significant percentages were concentrated in medium-sized cities in close proximity to the central city. This was due to two reasons: first, printing produces less added value by unit of land, so printing companies thus prefer less central locations. Second, it requires spatial proximity to publishing activities and other clients, since a relevant share of its market is located within city centre (Figure 3.4).

This leads to a specific pattern where publishing activities generally seem not to be affected by the traditional process of incubation in the central city and subsequent spread to the rest of the metropolitan area (Hoover and Vernon 1959). On the other hand, printing activities seem to resolve the trade-off between centrality (i.e. their proximity to publishing) and a preference for lower land rents by establishing themselves in places that are close to the city centre (Figure 3.4). In fact, in Madrid and Barcelona, most of the firms are still located in the most central parts of the city and most of the births and deaths happen in this same space (Figure 3.5).

This raises a second question: What are the reasons for the hyper-concentration of P&P in the metropolitan areas of Madrid and Barcelona? This in turn leads to the following hypotheses:

*H*21: The co-location of both parts of the industry (P&P) reinforces the patterns of concentration.

*H*22: However, the reasons for the concentration of a creative industry (publishing) and a semi-creative industry (printing) must be different.

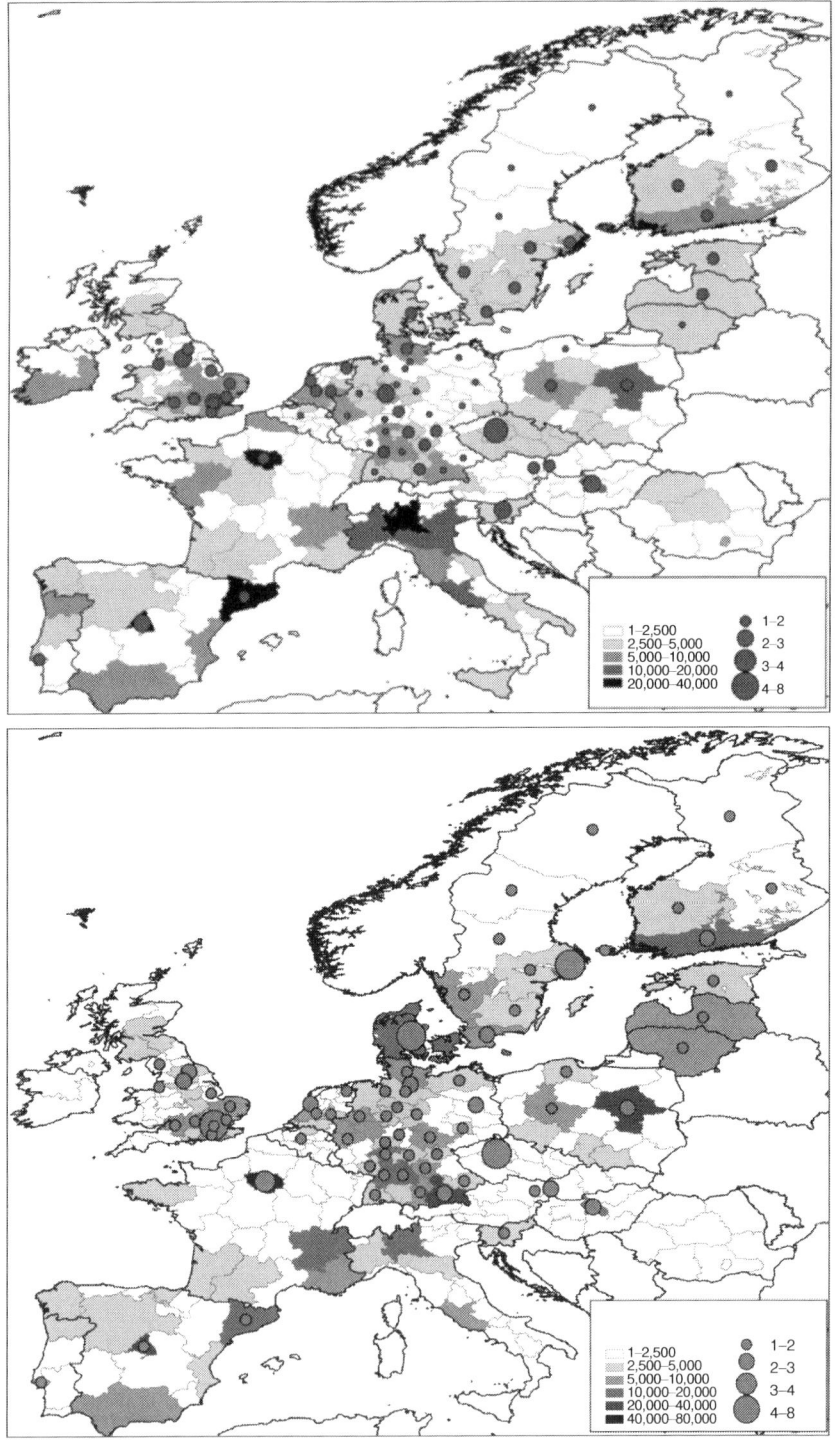

Figure 3.3 Printing and publishing employment and clusters in EU regions (NUTS 2):
a) Printing; b) Publishing

Source: Our elaboration from Eurostat

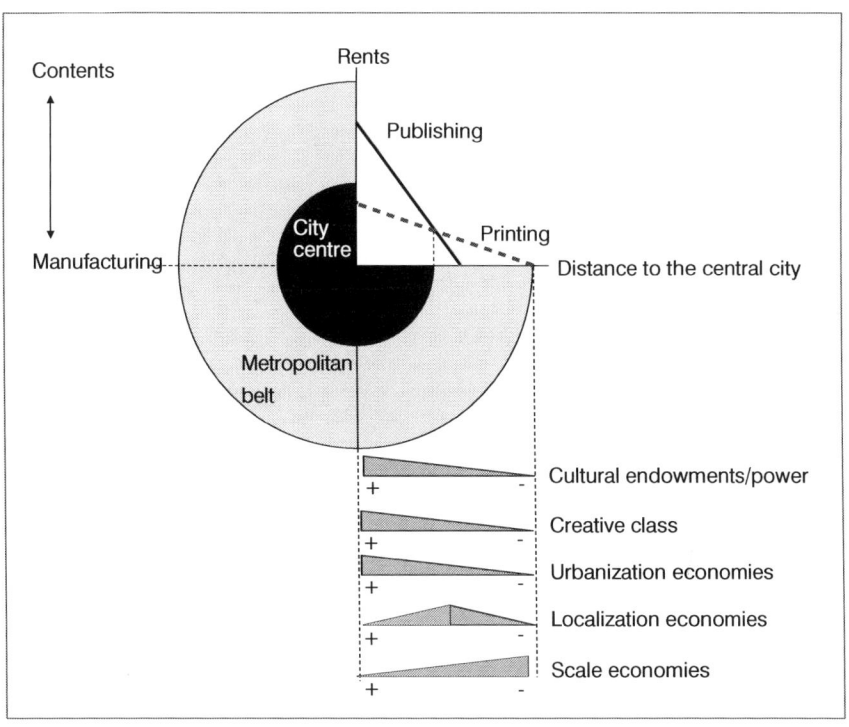

Figure 3.4 Land rents and forces affecting the rents of creative industries in a von Thünen–Alonso framework

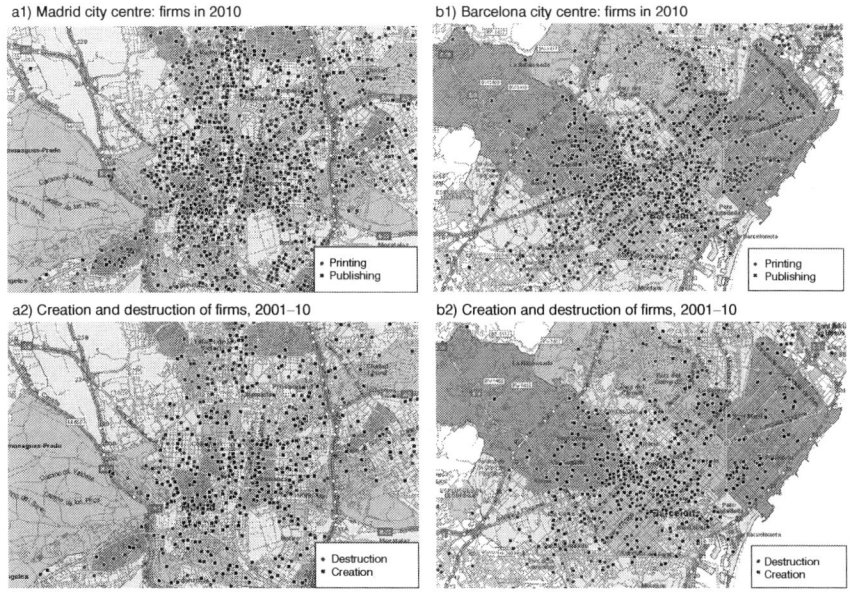

Figure 3.5 Localization of printing and publishing firms in the central part of the cities of Madrid and Barcelona

Source: Our elaboration from SABI (Sistema de Analisis de Balances Iberico (Bureau van Dijk))

*H*221: A creative industry based on contents and copyrights (in this case publishing) is differentially affected by specific creative forces (such as culture or the creative class), and general forces related to the generation of higher rents, such as urbanization economies.

*H*222: A semi-creative industry (in this case printing) is differentially affected by the traditional forces of agglomeration of industries, particularly economies of scale and localization economies.

To explore these hypotheses, we depart from the culture and heritage, agglomeration and creative class (CAC) model introduced by Lazzeretti *et al.* (see Chapter 2). This is an empirical model in which the concentration of creative industries is explained in an econometric regression by three main groups of factors: cultural endowments and proximity to the political power, agglomeration economies (including internal economies of scale, localization economies and urbanization economies), and the location of the creative class.[7] As the H2 hypotheses consider that each sector is co-located, such that the localization of printing affects publishing and vice versa, this version of the CAC model results in a system of two equations, where the location of each sector endogenously determines the location of the other:

Printing = f (culture and heritage, agglomeration economies, creative class, publishing)

Publishing = f (culture and heritage, agglomeration economies, creative class, printing)

The results of the estimates (Table 3.6) showed that for both industries, it was important to co-locate. This was particularly the case for publishing, since printing firms can take advantage of locating in neighbouring cities.

The concentration of the printing industry within a given space was correlated with the existence of intra-firm economies of scale, specialization in the industry and the diversity of the place, even if these industries preferred less populated areas in order to avoid higher land rents. On the other hand, publishing concentration was related to heritage and political power, specialization, urbanization economies associated with the size of the place and the intensity of personal networks, and the creative class.

These results give evidence favourable to all the H2 hypotheses: the relevance of co-location for both industries (H21), the different nature of the forces affecting each industry (H22), and the direction (sign) and relative intensity with which each force is operating in each industry (H221 and H222).

In the particular case of Madrid and Barcelona, these two areas are the only places in Spain that enjoy a complete model of knowledge (high levels of analytic, synthetic and symbolic knowledge) and work as an innovative milieu, generating localization and urbanization economies, facilitating investment and concentrating the creative class, which is fundamental for the content industries.

Table 3.6 Estimates of the CAC model for the printing and publishing industry, final regressions (including coefficients only statistically significant at 10 per cent)

	Printing	*Publishing*
Constant	1.3722***	–1.2464**
Culture and political power		
Heritage	–0.0699***	0.1010
Political power	–	0.8245***
Agglomeration economies (general)		
Scale economies: firm size in the industry	1.1283***	–0.6115***
Localization economies: firm size in the place	–0.2719***	–
Localization economies: diversity of the creative chain	–0.2261***	–0.1504*
Urbanization economies: population	–0.2571***	0.2472***
Urbanization economies: diversity of the place	0.2806***	–
Urbanization economies: variety of the place	–0.3289***	–
Urbanization economies: social diversity	–	0.8286***
Agglomeration economies (co-localization)		
Specialization in publishing (LQ)	0.2380***	–
Specialization in printing (LQ)	–	0.5084***
Creative class		
Creative class	–	0.5069***
Foreign born	–	0.0696***
R^2-adj	0.7424	0.3208

Notes: (a) Dependent variables: location quotients of the P&P industries. All variables are in logarithms (except political power dummies). The data for the dependent variable are for the year 2010 and the rest are lagged to 2001 to reinforce causality. Chapter 2 provides details about the elaboration of the rest of variables; (b) Robust Huber–White estimators; (c) P&P are tested to be endogenous when introduced as explanatory in the IV equation and endogeneity is rejected so that we provide the results of the OLS model (more efficient) and not the IV model; (d) Statistical significance: *** 1 per cent; *** 5 per cent, ***10 per cent. OLS: ordinary least squares.

Conclusions

This chapter provides an overview of the creative economy and creative industries in Spain, and an in-depth analysis of the P&P industry. P&P are not only the most important creative industries in Spain but also present two particularities related to the size of the linguistic domain of the Spanish language, and to their hyper-concentration in the metropolitan areas of Madrid and Barcelona, two of the largest creative and P&P agglomerations in the EU.

From the analysis, it can be concluded that Spain is the fifth-largest producer of creative industries in the EU but is not specialized in the production of creative industries. P&P are the most important creative industries in Spain, although both have different characteristics, as publishing is a pure creative industry whereas printing behaves like a semi-creative industry.

I attempted to relate the size of the linguistic domain to the existence of economies of scale for the P&P industries in Spain. However, the preliminary evidence demonstrates that even if some advantages are detected for the publishing industry, the potential economies of scale of the language are underused. Regarding general policy strategies, this finding suggests the need for a more active policy of interaction with the American markets, the main potential buyers. In fact, the expansion of exports to American markets, and particularly the US, constitutes one of the new priorities of the Ministry of Culture.

On the other hand, the printing industry seems to be scarcely affected by the size of the linguistic domain and seems to be more closely related to price competition and outsourcing processes. It may thus be most affected by the shift toward digital books and the digital press. In this case, policies should be adjusted in order to reinforce the most creative part of the semi-creative industry: qualification of the workforce and specialization in the quality-based market segments.

This chapter also explores the reasons for the hyper-concentration of creative industries in the metropolitan areas of Madrid and Barcelona, as they indicate the existence of powerful agglomeration economies. In this case, the conclusion of the confirmatory analysis was that both the printing and the publishing industries agglomerate and co-agglomerate in order to take advantage of the spatial economies of scale. The differences between the super-agglomerations (Madrid and Barcelona) and the rest of Spain were extreme due to the huge competitive advantages that the P&P industry finds in these locations.

Furthermore, the factors affecting the spatial concentration of a creative (publishing) and semi-creative industry (printing) proved to be different. Concentration in the content industry is positively affected by specific creative forces such as cultural heritage, proximity to political power, the concentration of the creative class and general forces such as urbanization economies. Concentration in the semi-creative industry is determined by general forces such as intra-firm economies of scale, localization economies and urbanization economies, even if part of the urbanization economies (those associated with higher land rents) acts as centrifugal force.

Thus, the spatial specificities of P&P in Spain, possibly the most neglected point in policy formulation for these industries, prove to be quite basic. From the point of view of Madrid and Barcelona, policy at the local level is crucial to facing the changes within the industry and favouring their competitive bases. We suggest at least two relevant directions for these policies: first, addressing the complementary role of cluster-specific policies, urban general policies and the strategies of large conglomerates with headquarters in the city; second, reinforcing the expansion to other linguistic markets via specific market segments, and the products in which each of these metropolitan areas is specialized.

Acknowledgements

The author would like to thank the Ministry of Science and Innovation for financially supporting this research (ECO2010–17318 MICINN Project). The research also benefited from the cooperative project between the University of Valencia and the Institut d'Estudis Regionals i Metropolitans de Barcelona.

Notes

1 Unfortunately, as UNCTAD (2010) remarks, not all countries elaborate culture accounts yet. As a result, for the comparison with other EU countries it is necessary to use Eurostat structural business statistics and national accounts databases. These data are not usually available in the necessary level of detail, thus producing differences in the size and share of the creative sector (and sometimes industry by industry) between national and European data.
2 The figures of architecture and engineering are inflated due to the boom in construction in Spain.
3 France (40 per cent of the exports) and the UK (37 per cent) are the main destinations for this subsector.
4 To complete the picture, it is necessary to remark that the patterns of imports are also extremely concentrated. For example, 42 per cent of the imports of books come from China and another 28 per cent from the UK (FECL 2009). The printing sector is also observing big increases in imports from China and other Asian countries for all the EU countries. Almost 100 per cent of the imports from these countries are printing orders, where the products are printed in China due to the lower costs of labour and low shipping fees. This affects particularly those segments of the market that are labour-intensive, as children's books with mobile parts (FECL 2009).
5 I calculated the Gini index for Spain using local labour markets as territorial units and employment data, as in Lazzeretti *et al.* (2008) and Chapter 1. The results using provinces (NUTS 3) as territorial units are quite similar. Moreover, even when the Gini index is weighted by the rest of the economy, it still reaches a value of 0.75. Gini index is defined between 0 (the industry is perfectly and equally distributed) and 1 (all the industry is concentrated in one spatial unit).
6 In this case, 2010 data come from the social security register and includes all types of firms and employment.
7 The detail of this model can be found in Chapter 2. I reproduced the estimates using the same variables as Lazzeretti *et al.* (2008), although in order to provide more updated results, I used the social security registers from 2010 as the dependent variable data regarding employment, rather than the census of 2001. Both sources of data cover the entire population.

References

Ávila, A.M. and Porto, S. (2004) 'El sector editorial en España', *Boletín Económico del ICE*, 2796: 39–50.
Boix, R., Trullén, J. and Galletto, V. (2012) *Barcelona ciutat creativa*, Barcelona: IERMB i Ajuntament de Barcelona.
Canoy, M.F.M, van Ours, J. and van de Ploeg, F. (2005) *The Economics of Books*, Munich: CESIFO Working Paper no. 1414.
Casani, F. (ed.) (2010) *Industrias de la creatividad 20+20*, Madrid: EOI.

Caves, R.E. (2000) *Creative Industries: Contracts between Art and Commerce*, Cambridge, MA and London: Harvard University Press.

CEIN – Centro Europeo de Empresas e Innovación de Navarra (2005) *XXI ideas de sectores para el siglo XXI. Informe industrias creativas*, Pamplona: CEIN.

DCMS – Department for Culture, Media and Sport (2001) *Creative Industries Mapping Document 2001*, London: DCMS.

DCMS – (2009) *Creative Industries Economic Estimates Statistical Bulletin January 2009*, London: DCMS.

De Miguel, B., Hervás, J.L., Boix, R. and De Miguel, M. (forthcoming) 'The importance of creative industry agglomerations in explaining the wealth of the European regions', *European Planning Studies*.

Driver, S. and Gillespie, A. (1993) 'Information and communication technologies and the geography of magazine print publishing', *Regional Studies*, 27(1): 53–64.

Eisenstein, E.L. (2005) *The Printing Revolution in Early Modern Europe*, Cambridge, UK: Cambridge University Press.

European Commission (2010) *Green Paper: Unlocking the Potential of Cultural and Creative Industries*, Brussels: EU Commission, COM(2010) 183, DG Education and Culture.

FANDE – Federación de Asociaciones Nacionales de Distribuidores de Ediciones (2010) *XV Estudio de perfil del sector de la distribución de libros y publicaciones periódicas*, Madrid: FANDE.

FECL – Federación Española de Cámaras del Libro (2009) *Comercio exterior del libro 2009*, Madrid: FECL.

Gámir, A. (2005) 'La industria cultural y los grupos multimedia en España, estructura y pautas de distribución territorial', *Anales de Geografía*, 25: 179–202.

García Delgado, J.L., Alonso, J.A. and Jiménez, J.C. (2008) *Economía del español: una introducción*, Barcelona: Ariel.

Handke, C.W. (2004) 'Defining creative industries by comparing the creation of novelty', paper presented at Workshop Creative Industries, *A Measure for Urban Development?*, WIWIPOL and FOKUS, Vienna, Austria, 20 March.

Hebbels, B. and Boschma, R. (2011) 'Performing in Dutch book publishing 1880–2008: The importance of entrepreneurial experience and the Amsterdam cluster', *Journal of Economic Geography*, 11(6): 1007–29.

Hoover, E.M. and Vernon, R. (1959) *Anatomy of a Metropolis: The Changing Distribution of People and Jobs within the New York Metropolitan Region*, Cambridge, MA: Harvard University Press.

Howkins, J. (2007) *The Creative Economy: How People Make Money from Ideas*, 2nd edn, London: The Penguin Press.

ICEX – Instituto Español de Comercio Exterior (2007) *La internacionalización de las industrias culturales españolas*, Madrid: ICEX.

KEA European Affairs (2006) *The Economy of Culture in Europe*, Brussels: European Commission Directorate, General for Education and Culture.

Lazzeretti, L., Boix, R., and Capone, F. (2008) 'Do creative industries cluster? Mapping creative local production systems in Italy and Spain', *Industry and Innovation*, 15(5): 549–67.

LEG Eurostat – Leadership Group on Quality (2000) *Cultural Statistics in the EU*, Eurostat Working Paper, Population and Social Conditions Series, no. 3/2000/E/No1, Final report of the LEG, Luxembourg: Eurostat.

Lewis, M.P. (ed.) (2009) *Ethnologue: Languages of the World*, 16th edn, Dallas, TX: SIL International.

López, M. and Larrañaga, J. (2010) 'El e-book y la industria editorial española', *Revista Interamericana de Bibliotecología*, 33(1): 85–103.

Martín, A. (2003) *El valor económico de la lengua española*, Madrid: Fundación Santander Central Hispano.

Martínez, R. (2001) 'El sector editorial español', *Información Comercial Española*, 792: 109–23.

Ministerio de Cultura (2009) *Hábitos de lectura y compra de libros en España 2008*, Madrid: Ministerio de Cultura.

Ministerio de Cultura (2010) *Cuenta Satélite de la Cultura en España*, Madrid: Ministerio de Cultura.

MKM (2007) *Informe sobre las industrias culturales de España. Volumen II. Sector Editorial*, Madrid: ICEX.

Moreno, F. and Otero, J. (2006) *Demografía de la lengua española*, Madrid: Instituto Complutense de Estudios Internacionales.

Neturity (2011) *2a Encuesta sobre el libro digital en España*, Madrid: Neturity.

Palma, L., Martín, J.L. and Jaén, M. (2009) 'El mercado del libro en España, 1989–2006. Un análisis económico', *Estudios de Economía Aplicada*, 27(1): 223–50.

Power, D. and Nielsén, T. (2010) *Priority Sector Report: Creative and Cultural Industries*, Stockholm: Europe Innova, European Cluster Observatory.

Redondo, A. (1999) 'Factores de competitividad en el sector de artes gráficas en España', *Dirección y organización: Revista de dirección, organización y administración de empresas*, 21: 116–25.

Schiffrin, A. (2000) *The Business of Books: How the International Conglomerates Took over Publishing and Changed the Way we Read*, London: Verso.

Stoneman, P. (2008) *Soft Innovation in Creative and Non-creative Industries*, The National Endowment for Science, Technology and the Arts Working Paper, London: NESTA.

Throsby, D. (2008) 'Modelling the cultural industries', *International Journal of Cultural Policy*, 14(3): 217–32.

UNCTAD – United Nations Conference on Trade and Development (2010) *Creative Economy Report 2010*, Geneva and New York: UNDP and UNCTAD.

WIPO – World Intellectual Property Organization (2003) *Guide on Surveying the Economic Contribution of the Copyright Industries*, Geneva: WIPO.

4 Creative and cultural industries in Austria

Michaela Trippl, Franz Tödtling and René Schuldner

Introduction

Creative and cultural industries are portrayed as key sectors in the emerging knowledge-driven economy and they are ascribed to play an increasingly important role in regional development and prosperity (Power and Nielsén 2010; UNCTAD 2010). Creative industries comprise very different subsectors such as new media, design, publishing, visual arts, cultural sites, performing arts, etc. They invent, produce and distribute goods and services that rely heavily on creativity and intellectual capital as primary inputs (UNCTAD 2010). Drawing on a symbolic knowledge base (Asheim and Gertler 2005), these industries exhibit strong innovation potentials and a high level of entrepreneurship (see, for instance, OECD 2005, 2007). They usually employ highly qualified and skilled labour, and often attract further talent to the respective locations (Florida 2005; Costa 2008). As a consequence, creative and cultural sectors are on the top of the policy agenda in many countries and regions (Power and Scott 2011).

A considerable body of work has demonstrated that creative activities are unevenly spatially distributed across space. Location patterns and tendencies of spatial clustering of creative and cultural industries have been analyzed for countries such as the US, Italy and Spain, the UK and the Nordic countries (Scott 1997; Cinti 2008).[1] These studies suggest that creative and cultural industries locate and cluster in large urban areas. At the same time, however, there is evidence showing that creative and cultural activities are also present in other types of regions and places positioned at lower levels of the urban hierarchy (De Propris *et al.* 2009).

As in many other countries, creative and cultural industries have been a 'fashion' of policy in several Austrian regions in the past decade. Recent studies have provided insights into the evolution and innovation performance of these sectors in Austria. The location pattern and clustering processes of creative and cultural industries, however, have not been investigated so far and are thus not well understood. Vienna, as a major internationally renowned 'city of culture' seems to be a key location for these sectors, but we have little systematic evidence of the more detailed spatial pattern. The aim of this chapter is to shed light on the geographical dimension of creative and cultural industries in Austria. Based on relevant theories, existing studies and data on the spatial distribution of employees, we seek (a) to investigate the location pattern of creative and cultural industries in Austria; and (b) to examine to which extent these industries are subject to clustering processes in the large urban areas and their cores.

The remainder of this chapter is divided into three sections. The second section provides a short review of the different strands of literature dealing with the location pattern and clustering tendencies of creative and cultural sectors. Then the third section contains the empirical part of the chapter. After some notes on the data and methods used and a brief characterization of the sectors under investigation in terms of size and structure, we will present and discuss the main results of our empirical analysis of the geographical dimension of creative and cultural industries in Austria. In conclusion, the key findings are summarized and some key questions are identified for further research.

Spatial clustering of creative and cultural industries: the view from the literature

Cities have always been the core centres of cultural activities (see e.g. Mumford 1961). The creative and cultural sectors, however, are quite heterogeneous, leading to specific spatial clustering processes and challenging the usefulness of too simple explanations for their geographical concentration tendencies (Power and Nielsén 2010). Relevant activities include 'traditional' cultural activities such as publishing, architecture and engineering studios as well as 'non-traditional creative industries' such as research and development (R&D), music, film, video and performing arts (see, for instance, Lazzeretti *et al.* 2008). The location patterns and the theoretical explanations offered for spatial concentration processes seem to differ between particular subsectors of creative and cultural industries.

Relevant concepts and arguments for enhancing one's understanding of the geographical distribution of creative and cultural activities can be based on market and customer access (central place theory), production interdependencies (agglomeration economies and cluster concept), innovation and knowledge interactions (concept of symbolic knowledge base), and the embeddedness of activities, in particular socio-economic milieux of creativity (literature on the creative class and on cultural districts).

Some cultural activities (such as large theatres, orchestras and music halls) can be considered as being highly specialized service activities where considerations of Christaller's central place theory can be applied (Maier and Tödtling 2006). There are usually only a few excellent opera houses, theatres and museums in a country, and they need a certain threshold of demand and good accessibility. Arguably, such activities attract not only regional and national customers but, increasingly, international clients and tourists. As a consequence, they are often found in the highest ranking cities as well as the touristic centres of a country. In Austria, the most important cities, including Vienna, Graz, Linz and Salzburg, are key centres in this regard. Other subsectors of traditional cultural activities (such as architecture and engineering studios, cinemas, smaller theatres and publishing), in contrast, are certainly less specialized and have lower thresholds. They might also be found at lower levels of the urban hierarchy and can be expected to show a more dispersed pattern. Some intra-industrial heterogeneity, however, is likely to exist. Leading firms in sectors such as architecture are often located in large metropolitan regions, whereas smaller firms from that industry are more evenly distributed across space.

Close to such cultural activities, in particular to the 'high cultural' ones, we might observe the presence of related activities in the fields of music, theatre, fine arts and media (such as arts studios, painting, tapestry and restoration, manufacture of instruments, recording, etc.) as well as schools and touristic activities, partly supporting the high cultural ones. Cinti (2008) in a literature review on this topic refers to such areas of concentration as 'cultural clusters or districts'. Relying on Frost-Kumpf (1998) and Hitters and Richards (2002), he defines them as a 'well-defined and labelled city area where a high concentration of culture stimulates the presence of concurrent services and activities' (p. 71). To some extent we find here Marshallian arguments of localization economies as well as Porter's (1998) cluster arguments of production advantages that result from the presence of highly specialized suppliers, qualified labour, sophisticated demand and rivalry. Lazzeretti (2008) focuses on the dynamic side of such clustering phenomena and identifies a process she terms cultural 'districtualization'. Lazzeretti (2008) provides empirical evidence for cultural sub-clusters (museums, music) for Florence (Italy) and Seville (Spain).

Lorenzen and Frederiksen (2008) – based on Maskell and Lorenzen (2004) and Scott (2005) – highlight the role of localization and urbanization economies for innovation in cultural industries. They argue that localization economies (i.e. clustering of cultural industries in specialized locations) support efficiency, product flexibility and incremental innovation in such sectors, pointing to the impact of specialized labour markets, institutions and knowledge spillovers. Urbanization economies (i.e. location of cultural industries in large cities), in contrast, offer externalities from diversity and support, in particular product novelty and radical innovation. The key point made by these authors, thus, is that cultural industries located in clusters and large cities benefit from different kinds of advantages of innovation (De Propris *et al.* 2009).

Other scholars such as Martin and Moodysson (2011) and Garmann-Johnsen (2011) have been stressing the importance of knowledge interactions and innovation linkages in clusters of creative industries. The key argument raised in this strand of literature is that these industries are largely based on 'symbolic' knowledge (Ashcim and Gertler 2005) that needs a certain degree of spatial proximity of actors for its successful transfer and exchange. Creative industries that are concentrated in particular locations and regions, thus, have an innovation advantage in comparison to firms located outside those places.

Finally, Florida (2002, 2005) also provided strong arguments for the spatial concentration of creative industries in particular cities. Florida focused on the location preferences of highly qualified and creative people (the so-called 'creative class'), highlighting that they are attracted to specific places that offer a favourable living environment, diversity and tolerance. This stimulates the concentration of creative people and related industries in particular socio-economic milieux of larger cities. Boschma and Fritsch (2009) have analyzed the location pattern of the creative class in seven European countries (The Netherlands, England, Norway, Finland, Germany, Sweden and Denmark) and found members of the creative class to be strongly concentrated in the main cities of the investigated countries.

A recent study done by Power and Nielsén (2010) provides some support for the arguments raised above, showing that different sectors of the creative and cultural industries exhibit different cluster and location tendencies. The most concentrated industries are those active in the fields of the reproduction of computer media, sound recording and video recording as well as the manufacture of media, musical instruments and the publishing of software. Amongst the least concentrated industries were activities such as advertising and printing.

To summarize, there is a consensus in the literature reviewed above that creative and cultural industries tend to be concentrated not just in the largest cities of a country but also in other types of regions and places positioned at lower levels of the urban hierarchy. In the following section we will investigate the location pattern of creative and cultural industries in Austria to find out to what extent these sectors are an urban phenomenon in that country and where these activities are concentrated.

Spatial clustering of creative and cultural industries in Austria

Data and methods

There exists no commonly agreed definition or delineation of creative and cultural industries (UNCTAD 2008). On the contrary, a range of different definitions and approaches to capture those sectors could be found in the literature (for an overview, see UNCTAD 2010). A useful definition of these sectors has been suggested by Lazzeretti *et al.* (2008). They draw a distinction between two main groups, namely traditional cultural industries (comprising publishing, architecture and engineering studios, and music, film, video and performing arts) and non-traditional creative industries (including R&D, software and computer services, and advertising).

In this chapter we adopt the definition of creative and cultural industries as it has been proposed by Lazzeretti *et al.* (2008). In contrast to the work done by Lazzeretti and her colleagues who used the NACE (Nomenclature générale des Activités économiques dans les Communautés Européennes [General Classification of Economic Activities in the European Community]) Rev. 1 (2003) classification of economic activities our analyses are based on the NACE Rev. 2 (2008) classification structure. Furthermore, whilst Lazzeretti *et al.* (2008) examined creative and cultural industries at the three-digit level, we will look at these sectors at the four-digit level.

We use the most recent employment data (year 2009) provided by the Public Employment Service Austria (AMS). The AMS employment data have the advantage that they are not based upon 'place of residence' but upon 'place of work' (where people are employed, regardless of where they live). Thus, potential commuting effects can be disregarded in the interpretation of the results presented below.

We focus on labour market districts as territorial units of analysis to investigate the location pattern in creative and cultural industries in Austria. Labour market districts are geographical entities made up of several municipalities but they are smaller than NUTS 3 regions. The delineation of labour market districts is rather similar to that of public administration (political) districts (OECD 2002). Our analysis of the spatial dimension of these sectors rests on different steps. We look at the spatial distribution of absolute numbers of employees in both sectors and calculate location quotients (LQs) of employment to identify the key places of creativity and cultural activities in Austria. Furthermore, by looking at the sectoral composition of creative and cultural industries, we investigate whether or not districts with high LQs of employment show different specialization patterns. Finally, to further characterize the location pattern and to find out whether or not neighbourhood effects exist, we conduct a spatial autocorrelation analysis (Moran's I). The results of these research steps will be presented in 'Location patterns of creative and cultural industries in Austria' below. Before discussing our findings on the location pattern, we will provide a brief overview of the size, structuring and dynamics of the Austrian creative and cultural sectors.

Characterization of creative and cultural industries in Austria

In Austria creative and cultural industries have developed dynamically in the recent past. In the period 2001–2006 Austria showed the highest average annual employment growth in these sectors amongst all European countries, starting, however, from a rather low level (Power and Nielsén 2010). Recent studies (Rammer *et al.* 2008; Voithofer *et al.* 2010) point to a high rate of new firm formation, a high level of qualification of employees and a dominance of small companies. Two thirds of all Austrian firms within creative and cultural industries are single-person enterprises (Voithofer *et al.* 2010). Importantly, recent work suggests that the Austrian creative and cultural sectors are highly innovative. In the period between 2005 and 2007, not less than 59 per cent of the Austrian firms active in creative and cultural industries have introduced new products or services to the market, 31 per cent carried out R&D activities and 46 per cent reported supporting firms from other industries in their innovation activities, thus contributing to the growth of the whole economy (Rammer *et al.* 2008).

Our own analysis based on recent employment data provides clear support for the importance of these sectors in Austria. In the year 2009 the creative and cultural industries employed not fewer than 138,263 workers (Table 4.1), representing 4.3 per cent of total employment. The share of creative and cultural sectors in total employment in Austria is similar to that found for other countries (see e.g. Pratt, 1997; Hall, 2000; Lazzeretti *et al.* 2008; and also Chapter 1). Table 4.1 provides some interesting insights into the structuring of these industries and the relevance of different subsectors in Austria. It is shown that 43.8 per cent (60,495 employees) can be found in non-traditional creative industries, while 56.2 per cent (77,768

Table 4.1 Employment in creative and cultural industries in Austria, 2009

	Employees	
	no.	*%*
Non-traditional creative industries		
Software and computer services[a]	37,213	61.5
Scientific research and development[b]	7,269	12.0
Advertising and market research[c]	16,013	26.5
Total non-traditional creative industries	60,495	100.0
Traditional cultural industries		
Printing and reproduction of recorded media[d]	20,384	26.2
Motion picture, video and television programme production, sound recording and music publishing activities[e]	4,854	6.2
Architectural and engineering activities[f]	34,623	44.5
Creative, arts and entertainment activities, museums and other cultural activities, recreation activities[g]	17,907	23.0
Total traditional cultural activities	77,768	100.0

Notes:
[a] NACE codes: 5821, 5829, 6201, 6202, 6203, 6209, 6311, 6399.
[b] NACE codes: 7211, 7219, 7220.
[c] NACE codes: 7311, 7312, 7320.
[d] NACE codes: 1811, 1812, 1813, 1814, 5811, 5813, 5814, 5819.
[e] NACE codes: 5911, 5912, 5913, 5914, 5920, 1820.
[f] NACE codes: 7111, 7112.
[g] NACE codes: 8552, 9001, 9002, 9003, 9004, 9102, 9103, 9321, 9329.

employees) are working in traditional cultural industries. The non-traditional creative segment is thus somewhat smaller in size than the traditional cultural one. The most important subsectors (measured by number of employees) of non-traditional creative industries comprise computer programming activities (around 15,000 employees), advertising agencies (13,700 employees), data processing, hosting and related activities (12,000 employees) as well as computer consultancy activities (6,000 employees). Other subsectors play a minor role in comparison. The largest subsectors within traditional cultural industries are engineering activities and related technical consultancy (26,000 employees), 'other printing' (10,000 employees) and architectural activities (8,500 employees). Other traditional cultural activities are clearly lagging behind in terms of number of workers and are therefore less significant. In Austria, both the creative and cultural industries are thus characterized by the dominance of a few subsectors.

Location patterns of creative and cultural industries in Austria

Whilst there are various studies on creative and cultural industries in Austria dealing with the size, structure and dynamics of these sectors, little is still known about their spatial distribution. The location pattern of creative and cultural

Table 4.2 Key places of creative and cultural industries in Austria, 2009

Rank*	Name of district (province)	Traditional and non-traditional		Traditional cultural		Non-traditional creative	
		No.	LQ	No.	LQ	No.	LQ
1	Vienna (Vienna)	46,985	1.43	23,342	1.27	23,643	1.65
2	Linz (Upper Austria)	9,718	1.14	5,168	1.08	4,550	1.22
3	Graz (Styria)	9,554	1.42	5,748	1.52	3,807	1.29
4	Salzburg (Salzburg)	6,568	1.38	4,318	1.62	2,250	1.08
5	Innsbruck (Tyrol)	5,095	1.16	2,939	1.19	2,156	1.12
6	Tulln (Lower Austria)	3,081	3.29	1,665	3.16	1,416	3.45
7	Mödling (Lower Austria)	2,817	1.36	1,335	1.15	1,482	1.64
8	Klagenfurt (Carinthia)	2,420	1.06	1,483	1.16	937	0.94
9	Baden (Lower Austria)	2,360	2.10	1,273	2.02	1,087	2.22
10	St. Pölten (Lower Austria)	2,040	0.68	1,319	0.78	721	0.55
11	Wr. Neustadt (Lower Austria)	1,693	1.41	937	1.39	756	1.44
12	Wels (Upper Austria)	1,648	0.77	834	0.69	814	0.87
13	Korneuburg (Lower Austria)	1,642	2.72	836	2.46	806	3.05
14	Vöcklabruck (Upper Austria)	1,484	0.98	1,059	1.25	425	0.64
15	Gänserndorf (Lower Austria)	1,471	2.88	742	2.59	729	3.26
16	Bregenz (Vorarlberg)	1,454	0.74	1,003	0.91	451	0.53
17	Mistelbach (Lower Austria)	1,257	2.13	715	2.16	541	2.10
18	Steyr (Upper Austria)	1,252	1.06	589	0.88	662	1.28
19	Villach (Carinthia)	1,245	1.14	717	1.17	528	1.10
20	Dornbirn (Vorarlberg)	1,153	1.15	716	1.27	437	0.99
21	Amstetten (Lower Austria)	1,121	1.19	648	1.22	472	1.15
22	Krems (Lower Austria)	1,074	1.66	692	1.90	382	1.35
23	Hallein (Salzburg)	1,019	1.79	705	2.20	314	1.26
24	Eisenstadt (Burgenland)	967	1.24	588	1.34	378	1.11
25	Freistadt (Upper Austria)	925	2.39	500	2.30	425	2.51

* The ranking is based on the sum of absolute numbers of employees in creative industries and employees in cultural industries.

industries in Austria has not been examined so far. In the following we will analyze the spatial dimension of non-traditional creative industries and traditional cultural industries in Austria based on the definitions of the sectors and the data specified in the previous section.

Where are the main centres of creative and cultural activities in Austria? To identify the key places, as a first step we look at the location of absolute numbers of employees at the district level. As shown in Table 4.2, cultural and creative industries are unevenly distributed across space. Our analysis shows that the nation's capital city, Vienna, clearly has the lead, providing employment opportunities for not fewer than 47,000 workers. The share of creative and cultural industries in total employment in Vienna, however, seems to be rather low (6.1 per cent). Comparing it with the percentages found in Chapter 1 for Paris (10.8 per cent), London (9.0 per cent), Rome (9.0 per cent) and Madrid (8.5 per cent) clearly suggests that Vienna lags behind these big European capitals as regards the relative importance of the creative economy. Other Austrian cities and regions are of minor importance when compared internationally.

In the following, we will analyze the geographical concentration of creative and cultural industries separately. Mapping and analyzing the location of non-traditional creative industries (see Table 4.2) shows a high concentration of employment in the nation's capital city Vienna (23,643 workers). Other important centres of creativity in Austria are the regional capitals (i.e. the capital cities of provinces, 'Landeshauptstädte'), particularly Graz (capital city of the province of Styria, 3,807 workers), Linz (Upper Austria, 4,550 workers), Salzburg (Salzburg, 2,250 workers) and Innsbruck (Tyrol, 2,156 workers). Together, the top-five centres of creative activities (made up of Vienna and the regional capitals mentioned above) employ not fewer than 36,403 workers. This corresponds to more than 60 per cent of the total employment in creative industries in Austria, pointing to a strong concentration of creative activities and jobs in larger cities. This finding is not surprising and in line with what one might reasonably expect (see 'Spatial clustering of creative and cultural industries: the view from the literature' above). Interestingly, however, we also find rather high absolute numbers of employees in smaller cities and districts such as Tulln, Mödling and Baden, which are located close to Vienna. There is, thus, also some indication of suburbanization processes in creative industries that will be further analyzed and discussed below.

The analysis of the spatial distribution of employees in traditional cultural industries (Table 4.2) provides a similar picture. In this sector, Vienna again performs as the key hot spot (23,342 employees), followed by the provincial centres Graz (5,748 workers), Linz (5,168 workers), Salzburg (4,318 workers) and Innsbruck (2,939 workers). Together, the top-five places account for 53 per cent of the total employment in cultural sectors in Austria. Again, some smaller districts in the vicinity of Vienna (specifically Tulln, Mödling, Baden, St Pölten) also exhibit rather large number of workers in traditional cultural industries (Table 4.2).

The results presented above suggest that employment in creative and cultural sectors is not exclusively an urban affair, as there is some evidence of suburbanization processes. Another result worth mentioning is that (apart from some exceptions) those districts that perform as centres of non-traditional creative industries also tend to be the core places of traditional cultural industries. While it is not surprising to find this result for the larger cities, it could not be immediately expected for smaller districts, which, however, show a similar pattern. Creative and cultural activities thus tend to coincide in specific places of Austria.

To identify geographical concentration tendencies of creative and cultural industries independently of the size of the districts, we calculated LQs of

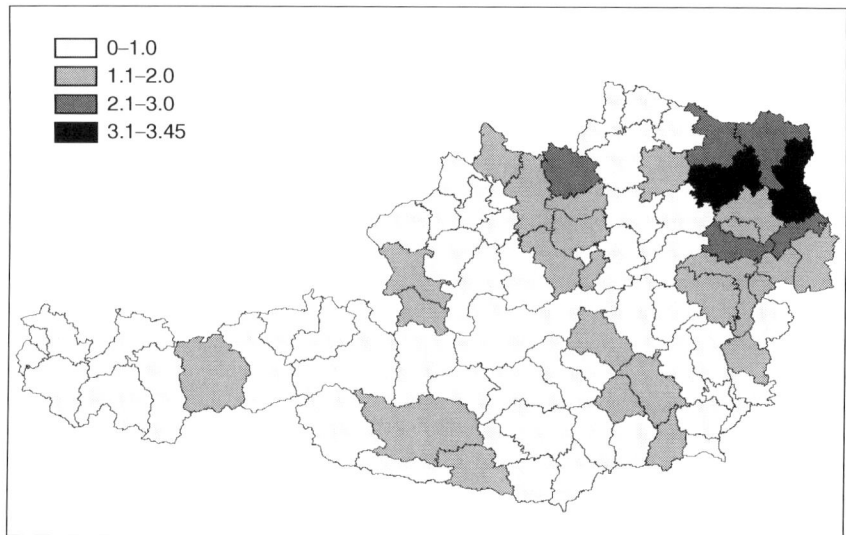

Figure 4.1 Location quotients of employment (minimum 200 employees) in non-traditional creative industries, 2009

employment. Looking at the LQs of employment in the creative and cultural sectors confirms the findings from the analysis of the spatial concentration of absolute numbers of workers presented above. In non-traditional creative industries not fewer than thirty-one districts have a LQ higher than 1. In traditional cultural industries we could identify forty-four districts exhibiting a LQ above 1. Districts that specialize in creative industries also tend to be centres of cultural activities. This holds true for not fewer than twenty-eight districts and confirms the finding from the analysis of absolute numbers of employees reported above. In Austria, creative and cultural activities thus show a tendency to cluster together in specific places. However, there are also some notable exceptions to this pattern. We could identify three districts that specialize in the creative sectors only and sixteen districts specialize exclusively in cultural industries. It is interesting to see that non-traditional creative industries are more concentrated compared to traditional cultural industries.

In the following, we will look at creative and cultural activities separately. Focusing on the creative sectors, we find a strong clustering of this segment in the larger cities (Vienna, Linz, Graz, Salzburg, Innsbruck and Klagenfurt) *and* in the districts surrounding these major urban centres (Figure 4.1). The larger urban centres and their hinterlands thus constitute distinctive spatial agglomerations of creative activities. The only exception in this context is Innsbruck, which seems to perform as 'island of creativity' in the western part of Austria. Apart from that, all other major urban centres are surrounded by districts exhibiting high shares of employment in creative industries. In some cases these districts have even higher LQs than the urban centres they are surrounding. This holds particularly true for Vienna (LQ 1.65), which is surrounded by three districts with a LQ higher than 3 (Tulln, Korneuburg, and Gänserndorf) and two districts with a LQ higher than 2 (Baden and Mistelbach).

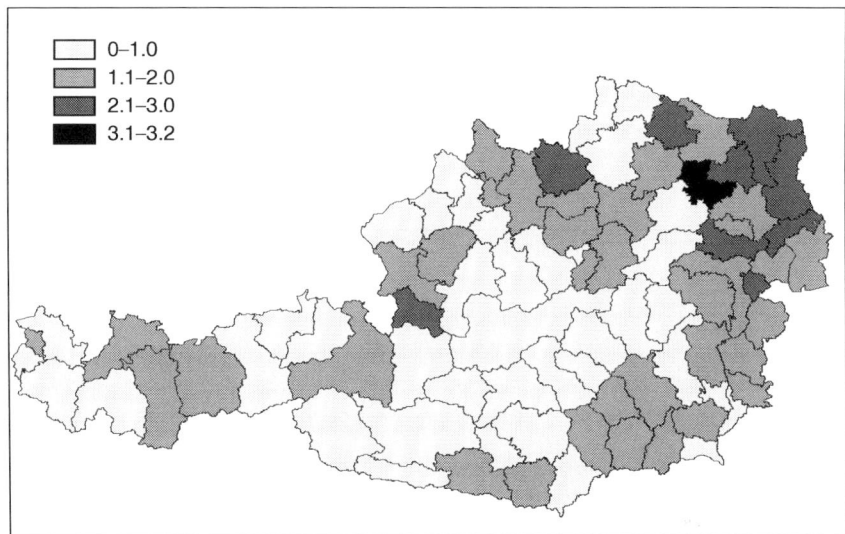

Figure 4.2 Location quotients of employment (minimum 200 employees) in traditional
cultural industries, 2009

Looking at LQs of employment in traditional cultural industries, we find a more
dispersed pattern (Figure 4.2). Not fewer than forty-four Austrian districts exhibit
a LQ above 1. Nevertheless, the spatial organization of traditional cultural sectors
resembles similarities with that observed for non-traditional creative industries:
districts located in close geographical proximity to large cities such as Tulln (LQ
3.16), Korneuburg (LQ 2.46), Gänserndorf (LQ 2.59) and Baden (LQ 2.02) in the
neighbourhood of Vienna (LQ 1.27), Freistadt (LQ 2.3) in the neighbourhood of
Linz (LQ 1.08) or Hallein (LQ 2.2), which is close to Salzburg (LQ 1.62), tend to
outperform the major urban centres they are surrounding.

To summarize, there is a marked concentration of employment in creative and
cultural industries in terms of absolute numbers in major cities. Vienna clearly
has the lead followed by main provincial centres such as Linz, Graz, Salzburg
and Innsbruck. This result corresponds to our hypotheses and is in line with the
view from the literature (see above). The analyses of employment share (LQs),
however, have led to somewhat surprising and unexpected findings. It was shown
that it is not the major cities but smaller districts surrounding the urban centres in
Austria that exhibit the highest LQs of employment. This finding holds true for
both non-traditional creative industries and traditional cultural ones.

The high concentration of creative and cultural industries outside the main
cities and urban centres in Austria needs further analyses and explanations. As
noted above, both the non-traditional creative sectors and the traditional cultural
ones are extremely heterogeneous in nature, covering very different subsectors.
One might expect that the sectoral composition of creative and cultural industries
in the large cities clearly differs from that in the surrounding areas. The urban
centres can be expected to specialize in higher-order activities such as R&D,
computer programming and consultancy, architectural and engineering activities

as well as performing arts and museums, whilst the surrounding areas specialize more in rather standardized activities such as, for instance, diverse printing activities (see also 'Spatial clustering of creative and cultural industries: the view from the literature' above). One might hypothesize that the strong clustering of creative activities in districts surrounding the larger cities is related to a specific spatial division of labour between the centres and their hinterland. This implies a concentration of more creative activities in the city centres and a dispersal of routine activities to surrounding areas.

In order to test this assumption, we analyze and compare the sectoral composition of creative and cultural industries in the major urban centres and their surrounding districts. In the case of the latter, we focus only on those districts that exhibit a LQ higher than 2.

Our analysis provides little support for the hypothesis that the urban cores and their surrounding districts exhibit diverging patterns of specialization. As revealed in Table 4.3, there are only few sectoral differences between large cities (Vienna and Linz) and their neighbouring districts as regards the specialization pattern in creative industries. Looking at Vienna and its surrounding areas (eastern agglomeration) we find that computer programming activities (around 20 per cent), data processing, hosting and related activities (between 21 and 40 per cent), advertising agencies (around 20 per cent) and computer consultancy activities (around 12 per cent) are important. Vienna thus has similarities with its neighbouring districts concerning the specialization pattern in non-traditional creative industries. There are only two notable exceptions in this regard. Vienna clearly outperforms its neighbouring districts with respect to scientific R&D. At the same time, it has a comparatively lower share in data processing, hosting and related activities than most of its surrounding districts.

In the case of the northern agglomeration (Upper Austria's capital Linz and the neighbouring district Freistadt) we can also observe similarities in the specialization pattern between the core centre (Linz) and the neighbouring area (Freistadt). Computer programming activities and advertising activities clearly dominate. In contrast to the eastern agglomeration, in the northern agglomeration scientific R&D is not only concentrated in the core centre. On the contrary, the share of R&D is even higher in the surrounding area of Freistadt than it is in Linz. This specific pattern is due to the fact that Freistadt is home of the Software Park Hagenberg, a science park that hosts several university institutes, R&D labs, competence centres and a University of Applied Sciences.

Whilst there are only few differences in the specialization pattern within larger agglomerations (i.e. the centres do not differ greatly from their surrounding areas), remarkable differences exist between the larger agglomerations. As revealed in Table 4.3, the northern agglomeration is by far more specialized in computer programming activities than the eastern one, whilst it clearly lags behind its eastern counterpart as regards computer consultancy activities, and data processing, hosting and related activities.

Looking at traditional cultural industries we find a more complex pattern of specialization (Table 4.4). First, similar to non-traditional creative industries,

Table 4.3 Sectoral composition of non-traditional creative industries in selected Austrian districts (percentages), 2009

Subsector	Eastern agglomeration								Northern agglomeration		Austrian average
	Vienna	Gänserndorf	Korneuburg	Mistelbach	Hollabrunn	Tulln	Baden	Bruck/Leitha	Linz	Freistadt	
Software publishing (58.2*)	3.70	4.50	5.88	4.03	5.38	4.75	2.78	2.45	2.91	2.16	3.37
Computer programming activities (62.01*)	19.29	18.86	22.97	21.51	18.01	21.07	24.37	18.50	39.64	54.11	24.873
Computer consultancy activities (62.02*)	10.09	12.24	13.86	12.51	12.63	12.39	15.01	11.78	4.98	3.12	10.103
Other computer programming, consultancy and related activities (62.0*)	4.30	6.10	5.04	5.99	4.53	4.52	4.21	6.78	1.38	0.98	3.20
Data processing, hosting and related activities (63.11*)	20.72	36.61	34.03	34.46	39.73	26.64	24.97	32.33	13.12	11.51	19.777
Other information service activities not elsewhere classified (63.99*)	0.12	0.27	0.12	0.02	0.37	0.08	0.00	0.00	0.00	0.00	0.191
Advertising agencies (73.11*)	21.55	17.72	15.02	17.14	13.14	19.83	17.66	23.11	19.69	10.82	22.584
Other advertising and market research (73.1, 73.2*)	4.80	3.71	3.08	4.34	6.20	3.37	3.26	5.06	7.21	4.63	3.89
Scientific research and development (72*)	15.42	0.00	0.00	0.00	0.00	7.34	7.75	0.00	11.07	12.68	12.02
Total	100.00	100.00	100.00	100.00	100.00	100.00	100.00	100.00	100.00	100.00	100.00

*NACE classification(s)

Table 4.4 Sectoral composition of traditional cultural industries in selected Austrian districts (percentages). 2009

Subsector	Eastern agglomeration									Western agglomeration		Northern agglomeration		Austrian average
	Vienna	Gänserndorf	Korneuburg	Horn	Mistelbach	Bruck/Leitha	Baden	Tulln	Mattersburg	Salzburg	Hallein	Linz	Freistadt	
Other printing (18.12*)	7.75	14.44	19.76	61.82	17.86	9.96	23.70	25.95	29.48	15.08	6.61	9.03	13.83	12.94
Reproduction of recorded media (18.20*)	0.06	0.27	0.00	0.00	0.00	0.00	0.00	0.06	0.00	16.61	32.54	0.20	0.07	1.81
Rest printing (18.11. 18.13, 18.14*)	2.50	3.14	4.98	0.00	1.39	1.31	4.71	7.18	3.97	2.18	1.06	3.21	2.30	2.82
Publishing activities (58*; without software publishing)	14.81	11.77	14.48	6.15	7.42	7.82	9.80	10.71	4.68	10.56	7.63	8.58	6.73	10.46
Motion picture, video, television. etc. (59*)	7.67	1.80	3.68	1.42	2.30	2.09	3.69	5.34	1.54	2.68	2.02	2.25	2.12	4.43
Architectural activities (71.11*)	11.45	6.22	9.00	8.14	6.78	7.64	10.53	8.99	11.96	5.74	7.90	7.99	6.80	10.88
Engineer activities and related technical consultancy (71.12*)	19.78	30.26	24.65	10.19	26.68	30.60	28.63	23.17	30.27	24.52	19.43	50.75	56.47	33.64
Performing arts (90.01*)	7.86	5.70	7.85	1.60	9.75	5.64	2.38	4.95	1.11	12.62	5.49	8.39	5.27	5.96
Supporting activities to performing arts (90.02*)	7.14	7.25	4.64	0.88	11.80	4.37	1.72	3.57	3.25	0.63	0.17	0.30	0.60	2.94
Other creative arts and entertainment activities (90.03. 90.04*)	6.46	2.71	2.71	0.88	3.22	5.02	6.98	2.35	1.45	0.50	0.44	3.88	1.27	3.55
Museums and historical sites (91.02, 91.03*)	7.79	11.63	3.22	3.75	5.43	20.82	2.32	4.01	5.38	1.83	4.12	2.37	1.83	4.56
Other (85.52.93.21.93.29*)	6.72	4.81	5.02	5.15	7.38	4.72	5.54	3.71	6.90	7.06	12.58	3.06	2.72	6.03

* NACE classification(s)

we can observe some differences *between* larger agglomerations regarding the specialization in specific subsectors of cultural industries. The western agglomeration (Salzburg and Hallein) has by far the highest share in the subsector 'Reproduction of recorded media' than its eastern and northern counterparts. The northern agglomeration specializes more in engineering activities and related technical consulting than the eastern and western ones. This reflects the general economic specialization of the wider region in the steel, engineering and automotive industries. The eastern agglomeration has higher shares of employment in 'Supporting activities to performing arts' and 'Museums and historical sites'. Second, we also find some marked differences *within* larger agglomerations between the centres and their surrounding areas. In the eastern agglomeration this holds particularly true for the subsector 'Other printing', where Vienna's share is clearly lower than that of its surrounding areas. The peripheral district of Horn represents an extreme case in this regard. Not less than 60 per cent of all traditional cultural activities located in that district are in this subsector. Moreover, compared to its surrounding areas, Vienna also has a low share in engineering activities and related technical consulting, but a higher share in publishing activities, as well as in motion picture, video, television. In addition, Vienna as an internationally recognized 'city of culture' outperforms many (but not all) of its neighbouring districts in the fields of performing arts, supporting activities to performing arts and other creative arts and entertainment activities.

Finally, we conducted a spatial autocorrelation analysis to find out to what extent high concentrations of creative and cultural districts in neighbouring districts are related to each other, i.e. whether or not such a relation and mutual influence among Austrian districts exists. The spatial autocorrelation analysis suggests that there is indeed a positive correlation of employment in non-traditional creative industries (Moran's I 0.4260) and in traditional cultural industries (Moran's I 0.3001) between neighbouring districts. Randomization tests show that these results are significant (at the 99 per cent level). The spatial pattern, thus, is far from being random. On the contrary, the spatial autocorrelation analysis suggests that certain interdependencies or complementarities between neighbouring districts prevail. These could be a joint output market, a joint labour market, industry-specific knowledge spillovers, and so on. To examine the precise nature of these interdependencies is a key issue for future research (see also 'Conclusions' below).

Conclusions

As in many other countries, creative and cultural industries have been growing dynamically in the past few years in Austria. Recent studies have provided valuable insights into the size, development pattern and innovation capacity of the Austrian creative and cultural sectors. However, no attempts have been made so far to analyze the location pattern of these industries for Austria and consequently little is known about their spatial organization. In this chapter we sought to deal with this research gap by investigating to what extent creative and cultural industries are geographically concentrated in Austria and by identifying and mapping the main centres of creative and cultural activities. Drawing on different strands of literature we expected a strong clustering of creative and cultural industries in space, particularly in the nation's largest urban centres.

Our empirical analyses, however, have shown that this is only partly the case. Although we found a strong concentration of employment in creative and cultural industries in the major cities in absolute terms, we could not provide support for the hypothesis that creative and cultural industries are exclusively an urban phenomenon. Looking at LQs of employment we observed surprisingly high values for districts surrounding the large cities, in particular Vienna, Linz and Salzburg. This finding was supported by a spatial autocorrelation analysis. The spatial pattern was found to be far from random. Moran's I values pointed to a strong and positive correlation of high concentrations of employment in creative and to a lesser extent in cultural industries between neighbouring districts.

A more detailed analysis of the sectoral composition of non-traditional creative industries in the major urban centres and their surrounding districts has shown that there are only a few differences in the specialization pattern between the core cities and their neighbouring districts. Pronounced differences, however, were found to prevail between larger agglomerations. There was thus some indication for a spatial division of labour, but not within the agglomerations between the core city and the surrounding areas, but between these agglomerations. For traditional cultural industries a more complex pattern could be identified. We found differences in the specialization pattern both within and between larger agglomerations.

Further analyses are required to enhance one's understanding of the spatial dimension of creative and cultural industries in Austria. One of the key issues of future research should be to examine the reasons for the high concentration of these sectors in some districts located outside but in close proximity to the main urban centres. Does this pattern of suburbanization result from a relocation of firms and employment and, if yes, to what extent is it driven by lower costs and the availability of land and office space in the hinterland of larger cities? To what extent does it reflect a spatial division of labour within multi-locational firms between centres and their hinterland, or, alternatively, residential preferences of freelancers? Furthermore, due attention should be devoted to the question of whether and in which ways creative and cultural industries located in the urban centres differ from those further out. For the creative sector our analysis of the sectoral composition has suggested that there are only a few differences in the specialization pattern between large cities and their surrounding areas. However, this does not necessarily mean that they are similar. In spite of specializing in the same subsectors, there might be strong differences between the core centres and other places as regards the character of activities (creative content, support, distribution), and related factors such as the qualification level of the workforce, revenues, innovation capacity, etc. Finally, the existence of positive neighbourhood effects needs close scrutiny. The spatial autocorrelation analysis suggested strong interdependencies between neighbouring districts showing a specialization in creative and cultural sectors. As outlined above, access to common input and output markets, joint labour markets providing highly qualified workers with specific skills, production interdependencies and knowledge spillovers might play a key role in generating this pattern. To empirically investigate the precise nature of interdependencies is a worthy subject for future research.

Note

1 See also Chapters 1 and 2 for an international comparison between European countries and regions.

References

Asheim, B. and Gertler, M. (2005) 'The geography of innovation', in J. Fagerberg, D. Mowery and R. Nelson (eds) *The Oxford Handbook of Innovation*, Oxford: Oxford University Press, pp. 291–317.

Boschma, R. and Fritsch, M. (2009) 'Creative class and regional growth: Empirical evidence from seven European countries', *Economic Geography*, 85(4): 391–423.

Cinti, T. (2008) 'Cultural clusters and cultural district: The stare of art', in P. Cooke and L. Lazzeretti (eds) *Creative Cities, Cultural Clusters and Local Economic Development*, Cheltenham: Edward Elgar, pp. 73–92.

Costa, P. (2008) 'Creativity, innovation and territorial agglomeration', in P. Cooke and L. Lazzeretti (eds) *Creative Cities, Cultural Clusters and Local Economic Development*, Cheltenham: Edward Elgar, pp. 183–211.

De Propris, L., Chapain, C., Cooke, P., MacNeill, S. and Mateos-Garcia, J. (2009) *The Geography of Creativity*, Interim report, London: NESTA.

Florida, R. (2002) *The Rise of the Creative Class: And how it's Transforming Work, Leisure and Everyday Life*, New York: Basic Books.

Florida, R. (2005) *The Flight of the Creative Class*, New York: Harper Collins.

Frost-Kumpf, H.A. (1998) *Cultural District Handbook: The Arts as a Strategy for Revitalizing our Cities*, Annapolis Junction, MD: American for the Arts.

Garmann-Johnsen, I. (2011) 'The geography of innovation dynamics: Analysis of the fashion design industry in Oslo, Norway', unpublished paper (submitted to *European Urban and Regional Studies*), Norway: University of Agder.

Hall, P. (2000) 'Creative cities and economic development', *Urban Studies*, 37(4): 639–49.

Hitters, E. and Richards, G. (2002) 'The creation and management of cultural clusters', *Creativity and Innovation Management*, 11(4): 234–47.

Lazzeretti, L. (2008) 'The cultural districtualization model', in P. Cooke and L. Lazzeretti (eds) *Creative Cities, Cultural Clusters and Local Economic Development*, Cheltenham: Edward Elgar, pp. 93–121.

Lazzeretti, L., Boix, R. and Capone, F. (2008) 'Do creative industries cluster? Mapping creative local production systems in Italy and Spain', *Industry and Innovation*, 15(5): 549–67.

Lorenzen, M. and Frederiksen, L. (2008) 'Why do cultural industries cluster? Localization, urbanization, products and projects', in P. Cooke and L. Lazzeretti (eds) *Creative Cities, Cultural Clusters and Local Economic Development*, Cheltenham: Edward Elgar, pp. 155–79.

Maier, G. and Tödtling, F. (2006) *Regional- und Stadtökonomik, 1: Standorttheorie and Raumstruktur*, 4th edn, Vienna and New York: Springer.

Martin, R. and Moodysson, J. (2011) 'Innovation in symbolic industries: The geography and organization of knowledge sourcing', *European Planning Studies*, 19(7): 1183–1230.

Maskell, P. and Lorenzen, M. (2004) 'The cluster as market organization', *Urban Studies*, 41(5–6): 991–1009.

Mumford, L. (1961) *The City in History: Its Origins, its Transformations, and its Prospects*, New York: Harcourt, Brace & World.

OECD – Organisation for Economic Co-operation and Development (2002) *Redefining Territories. The Functional Regions*, Paris: OECD.

OECD (2005) *Culture and Local Development*, Paris: OECD.

OECD (2007) *International Measurement of the Economic and Social Importance of Culture*, Paris: OECD.

Porter, M. (1998) *On Competition*, Boston, MA: Harvard Business School Press.

Power, D. and Nielsén, T. (2010) *Priority Sector Report: Creative and Cultural Industries*, Stockholm: Europe Innova, European Cluster Observatory.

Power, D. and Scott, A. (2011) 'Culture, creativity, and urban development', in A. Pike, A. Rodríguez Pose and J. Tomaney (eds) *Handbook of Local and Regional Development*, London and New York: Routledge, pp. 162–71.

Pratt, A. (1997) 'The cultural industries production system: A case study of employment change in Britain, 1984–91', *Environment and Planning A*, 29(11): 1953–74.

Rammer, C., Müller, K., Kimpeler, S. and Georgieff, P. (2008) Dritter Österreichischer Kreativwirtschaftsbericht, Vienna: ARGE Creativ Wirtschaft Austria in der Wirtschaftskammer Österreich.

Scott, A.J. (1997) 'The cultural economy of cities', *International Journal of Urban and Regional Research*, 21(2): 323–39.

Scott, A.J. (2005) *On Hollywood. The Place, the Industry*, Princeton, NJ: Princeton University Press.

UNCTAD – United Nations Conference on Trade and Development (2008) *Creative Economy Report 2008*, Geneva and New York: UNDP and UNCTAD.

UNCTAD (2010) *Creative Economy Report 2010*, Geneva and New York: UNDP and UNCTAD.

Voithofer, P., Eidenberger, J., Gavac, K., Leheyda, N., Meyer, J., Müller, B., Rammer, C., Vanberg, M., Holzinger, F. and Schmidmayer, J. (2010) *Vierter Österreichischer Kreativwirtschaftsbericht*, Vienna: Creativ Wirtschaft Austria, Wirtschaftskammer Österreich.

5 Creative industries in the United Kingdom

Lisa De Propris

Introduction

The debate on creativity and the creative economy has occupied scholars and policy makers in the UK, Europe, the United States, and as far east as China, Singapore and Australia. These concepts have entered our vocabulary as our economies are undergoing another fundamental change.

The demise of Fordism coincided with the end of mass production and Taylorist factories in the UK and Europe, but not the end of mass consumption. To reconcile the two, economies of scale have been pursued by manufacturing complexes in East Asia where labour has been abundant and cost-effective. During this transition, advanced economies have shifted to post-Fordist organizations of production that have enabled flexibility, modularity and above all variety through innovation. Post-Fordism sustained the conversion of the manufacturing sector from being based on mass and volume production and price competition to being able to offer customized and bespoke goods in imperfectly competitive markets. It is likely that the current transformation of the manufacturing sector started when identical functional objects had to project different impressions to demanding and discerning consumers. The tertiarization of advanced economies enabled manufacturing to change its nature as it created services and tasks that extracted information from consumers or enabled consumers to be better catered for. Post-Fordism led the way to the knowledge economy: this epitomized the centrality of the know-how and the peripherality of the making. The knowledge economy mirrored a techno-scientific paradigm that revolved around the dynamic processes of inventing and innovating that have been the driving force behind the creation and satisfaction of consumers' needs. These engaged smaller sized firms but also universities and the state as key stakeholders. With knowledge becoming the hinge of the new competition, human capital became the fundamental economic input – at the expense of capital and surely land. What came first is probably not so relevant, but as advanced economies were occupied with creating value to compete on knowledge-intensive goods, the actual making of such goods was moving east. It is unclear how advanced economies are contemplating maintaining control over the 'thinking', the 'knowledge creation' end of production, when the 'making' has detached itself from it already.

The step from knowledge workers to creative class has been in reality a long leap. Our economies are again at a crossroads. One of the key aspects of the knowledge economy has been the recognition that the fluidity between tacit and codified knowledge enables knowledge exchanges and spillovers, both drivers of the learning dynamics recorded in detail in the academic literature. In other words, workers can become *knowledgeable* as they absorb, learn and apply new knowledge. We are witnessing the beginning of a sustained flow of knowledge-intensive activities also moving east, both to co-locate with the 'making' and due to the increasing absorptive capacity of eastern countries' labour force. The creative class is different.

The literature on the creative class has emphasized the solid link that creative talent has with the *place* and in particular with cities. On closer examination, a main theme has run through the scholarly and policy-making debate on the creative class, creative industries and creative cities: in a very slippery space, creative industries have been found to be anchored in creative cities and creative places.

In the UK, it can be argued that the interest that the government has demonstrated in creative industries over the last decade has been motivated by the need to identify a niche of economic activities that is commercially viable, creates innovation and value to the economy, but also that can be pegged down.

This work brings together some of the recent contributions on British creative industries so as to better understand what has been done so far, and what is worth applying ourselves to in the future.

From technology to creativity

The concept of a creative economy surfaced as a by-product of an academic debate that started by looking at the creative class.

The work by Florida (2002, 2008) on the creative class showed something new to the world. He identified professions that were recognized for the first time as producing economic value thanks to their ability to generate soft innovations or creative goods or services. The debate on the creative economy started therefore within the sociological realm, stressing the link between talent, creative content, professions and ultimately their economic contributions. Florida's work brought to the fore a varied group of highly skilled people whose contribution to the economy had until then been ignored; these ranged from artists to computer scientists. His study showed that creative talents were able to *produce* creative value in services and goods, although such value could not be captured by standard innovation measures.

The most radical difference between Florida's work and the dominant knowledge economy paradigm is the emphasis placed on the overlap between people's working and living spaces, suggesting that there is a 'Starbucks' generation' that tends to use public spaces to reconcile work and life to maximize their quality of life, and in so doing is able to create and innovate. Indeed, the gay and bohemian indexes introduced by Florida are nothing else but proxies that capture a *creative atmosphere* that is nurtured by creative people and attracts creative people. The underlying quality of such a creative atmosphere is its ability to deny pre-existing schema and to grant a true opportunity for novelty. Talking about the emergence of the post-industrial *new economy*, Webber (1993: 28) had already recognized a new way of understanding 'work': 'in the new economy, conversations are the most important form of work. Conversations are the way knowledge workers discover what they know, share it with their colleagues, and in the process create new knowledge for the organization.' It is indeed through conversations that tend to occur outside orthodox workplaces that knowledge is created, exchanged, multiplied, adapted and absorbed. Such knowledge provides in part the foundation for the creative buzz of the creative class, a creative class that would surely include Harvard dropout Mark Zuckerberg, inventor of Facebook, whose ability to imagine a completely new way of social interaction (virtual social networking) borne out of his computing skills but also a personal, everyday hobby. The fact that the company is still loss making is irrelevant with respect to the radical innovation that it represents, and the relatively basic technology it relies on.

It should not be a surprise if creativity and creative activities were somehow unearthed outside mainstream business or economics disciplines, since the latter have been until recently entrenched in the debate on the knowledge economy that dominated the 1990s and the early 2000s. The central tenet of the knowledge economy was indeed technology and hard innovation; and the focus was on industries that were heavily reliant on standard innovation inputs such as R&D expenditure and human capital, and were producing innovations that could be codified in patents. Examples of this are the biotech industries and more recently green tech.

Creativity can be defined as 'the ability to come up with ideas and artefacts that are new, surprising and valuable' (Boden 2003: 1). According to Florida (2002: 31), 'creative work is often downright subversive, since it disrupts existing patterns of thought and life'. Creativity is often associated with art expressions, such as music, literature, poetry or design; as such these tend to be cultural expressions of a community or a society at a certain point in time. Despite its romanticized connotation, the adoption of the concept in the economic and business discourse has altered such a vision in so far as creativity could be now considered 'the most highly prized commodity in our economy' (Florida 2002: 4).

Creative dynamism has been associated with urban spaces as only creative cities are able to attract and retain sufficient talent to reproduce virtually their creative processes (Florida 2002). The emergence of the creative class marked a renewed interest in the city as a unique place for fast economic growth. In this context, the work of Jane Jacobs (1961, 1984) was rediscovered as it brought to the fore the determinants of cities' development in terms of the socio-economic advantages derived from the co-location of a multiplicity of very different activities: the serendipitous cross-fertilization between such activities. The results were potentials for innovations and creativity as well as a multifaceted place where work and life absorb each other and feed into each other (Scott 2006).

The creative economy: definitions

The concept of creative economy has evolved in the UK academic and policy debate drawing on the contribution of Florida on the creative class and on the frame-setting role of the Department for Culture, Media and Sport (DCMS) in providing clear pegging points for the broader academic and policy debate that focused, in particular, on creative industries.

The first understanding of the creative economy was introduced as a result of work sponsored by the DCMS. These include the mapping documents (1998, 2001) and the annual *Creative Industries Economic Estimates Statistical Bulletin*. It can be argued that the DCMS' measurement efforts have paved the way for broader research, especially thanks to the definitional clarity it introduced.

The DCMS' *Creative Industries Mapping Document* defined creative industries as those industries that

> are based on individual creativity, skill and talent. They also have the potential to create wealth and jobs through developing and exploiting intellectual property. The creative industries include: Advertising, Architecture, Arts and antique markets, Computer and video games, Crafts, Design, Designer Fashion, Film and video, Music, Performing arts, Publishing, Software, Television and Radio.
>
> (DCMS 1998)

Despite the soft nature of Florida's characterization of the creative class, when this was translated into economic activities by the DCMS in the UK, the classification of creative industries was framed within a hard innovation approach. This is in part what the DCMS classification has been so widely criticized about, since it dismissed activities that had a creative content but were not technology intensive. This has meant that creative industries became separated from cultural industries, with the latter disappearing from the DCMS policy debate.

Indeed, it can be argued that in providing a clear classification of creative industries, the DCMS has steered the academic and policy debate cherry-picking some sectors, whilst overlooking other arguably equally important sectors such as cultural and experience-based activities, including heritage, archives, museums, libraries, tourism and sport. Pratt (2008: 14) provides an interesting explanation for the choice of creative over cultural industries: he argues that the term 'creative' was 'politically agile' since it matched the neoliberal agenda of the newly elected New Labour. Indeed, Pratt (2008) argues that creative industries had crucial 'economic, commercial and individualistic dimensions' that made them fundamentally different from the 'publicly funded and non-commercial orientated arts sector'. In other words, creative industries were meant to capture an innovative portion of the economy that was predominantly dominated by the private sector – small or medium-sized firms. Recently, Cooke and De Propris (2011) suggest that the policy agenda endorsed by the government saw a preference for those creative industries that were more intense in hard innovation and high tech. This approach developed within a techno-scientific paradigm that privileged the emergence of worldwide acclaimed university-centred clusters in sectors such as biotech, nano-tech, medical devices or aerospace, and technology-intensive sectors in which innovation processes tend to rely on the triple helix. Creative industries were therefore meant to capture those activities that had developed in the crevices of an increasingly tertiarized and knowledge-intensive economy. The only caveat to this critique is the inclusion in the listing of three probably softer sectors: 'Performing arts, Arts and antique markets' and 'Crafts'. It can be argued that 'Arts and antique markets' and 'Crafts' ought to be considered as cultural industries and a recent classification by the UK Art and Humanity Research Council suggests just that. However, the inclusion of 'Performing arts' served the purpose of privileging London, which is undoubtedly the core of such activities in the UK.

More recently, the DCMS commissioned Frontier Economics (2007, 2009) to consider a more detailed classification scheme of creative industries without, however, undermining the original classification. Frontier Economics proposed an operational classification that was much more disaggregated in terms of Standard Industrial Classification (SIC) codes as it utilized five-digit SIC codes. This enabled a much more fine-grained representation of each creative sector. However, this was not the most relevant novelty; instead, what was proposed was to differentiate within each creative industry various 'layers' corresponding to stages in the creative value chain of that particular sector (KEA European Affairs 2006; Andari *et al.* 2007; O'Connor 2008; UNCTAD 2008). Within each creative industry activities were grouped in up to five layers where layer 1 corresponded to activities with the highest creative content – the so-called creative core; layer 2 included those activities that are directly related to the original creative content; activities in layers 3 and 4 had a more significant manufacturing content and coincided with the actual execution or production of the original creative content, together with the selling of them wholesale; finally, layer 5 included the least creative activities, such distribution and retail of creative goods and services (Figure 5.1).

Despite the intrinsic differences, both classifications remain strongly attached to the techno-scientific paradigm described above. The lack of a real conversation about the validity and robustness of either classification system has meant nevertheless that in the UK scholars and policy makers have been looking at and focusing on the same thing, channelling *intelligence* and funding in the same direction. Whether the industries in questions were capturing part or all of the creative 'capital' of the country was beside the point and deemed irrelevant. In this context, sectors that had a very different nature such as cultural and experience-based activities were set aside. This approach has distanced the UK debate from the EU one, for instance, which has been crucially centred on the role of culture as an engine of local socio-economic development.

Very recently, the UK Arts and Humanity Research Council (AHRC) has proposed an alternative way of classifying the creative economy (Table 5.1). It will be very interesting to see whether some of its philosophy will be absorbed by government departments. The classification distinguished activities that

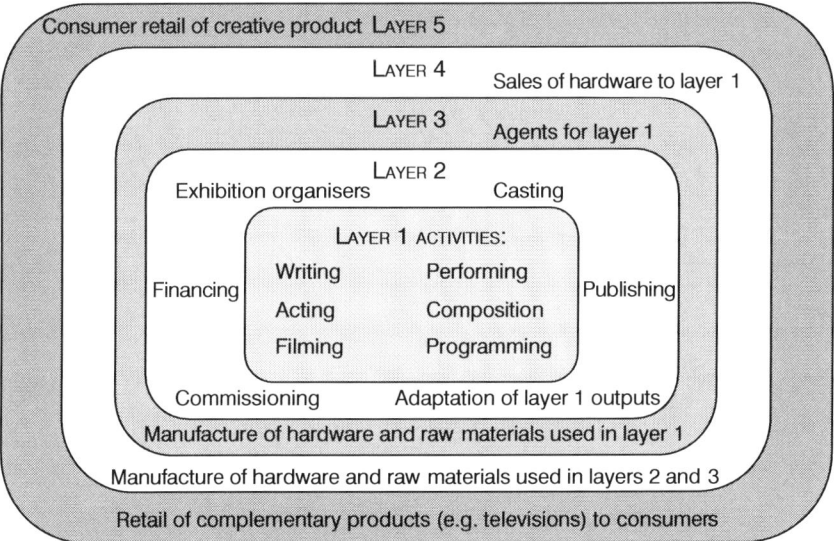

Figure 5.1 Frontier Economics' sector classification

Source: DCMS (2007), in De Propris *et al.* (2009)

Table 5.1 The Arts and Humanity Research Council's creative economy

Cultural promotion and preservation	Creative activities	Creative communications	Creative interfaces
• Museums, galleries, libraries and archives • Heritage services • Arts and antiques markets • Archaeological work • Exhibitions and festivals	• Music • Performing arts • Visual, literary and graphic art • Video and computer games • Architecture • Craft • Design and fashion	• Advertising, branding and 'experience economy' • Publishing and printed media • Film, television, radio, 'new media' and other broadcasting • Internet, social networking and other new media	• Creative interactions with business • Creative R&D with science and technology • Cultural production alongside new technologies • Ethical interactions with technological advances • Regulations • Intellectual property

Source: AHRC 2011, in www.ahrc.ac.uk (accessed 18 July 2011)

are associated with 'Cultural promotion and preservation' from those that are strictly 'Creative activities' and 'Creative communications'; at the same time, it acknowledges the importance of 'Creative interfaces'. The latter category is of particular interest since it captures agents, service providers and intermediaries whose role is to connect creative and cultural producers with users and consumers, the latter including people and businesses in other creative and non-creative sectors. It also includes firms that liaise with the regulatory world for intellectual property or ethical issues. This conceptualization of the creative economy is probably the most adequate representation of its complexity, including the fact that it comprises not only creative and cultural producers but crucial creative and cultural intermediaries. Further research on this is necessary not least to ascertain whether it is able to present a better representation of the UK creative economy. The challenge of this latter taxonomy is also that it needs to be empirically tested, starting from the identification of the relevant sector classification according to the British Office for National Statistics' SIC coding and then to the application of mapping and measuring techniques.

The creative economy: an understanding

Conceptually, the academic debate started with the mapping of the UK creative class to ascertain how it stood when compared with the US. Cooke and Clifton (2007: 5) find that in England and Wales, the creative class tends to concentrate in urban areas that are 'diverse, bohemian, socially cohesive and which offer higher levels of cultural opportunity' in the same ways as Florida finds for North American cities. In particular, the creative class accounts for about 40 per cent of the workforce in England and Wales and it tends to concentrate in a corridor around London that goes from Cambridge down to Oxfordshire, Wokingham, Reading and to Brighton. Other regional hot spots are Newcastle in the north-east, Manchester in the north-west and Cardiff in Wales (Cooke and Clifton 2007: 5). A study by the Greater London Authority (GLA 2004) also found that in 2004 creative industries in London employed a proportionally higher number of people in 'creative occupations' than any other region in the UK (see also Knell and Oakley 2007).

From employment to firms and sector activities, a wealth of studies started looking at creative industries drawing on the DCMS classification. Contributions flourished along two parallel avenues: quantitative aggregate studies and qualitative case study analyses.

Quantitative aggregate studies have scrutinized the extent of the phenomenon with a view of reaching a better understanding of its weight and role in the UK economy. The first of these studies was probably by Pratt (2004), where he finds that by 2003 a third of England's creative industries were in London and one quarter overall in the south-east. This distribution is showing a strong path dependency tendency as London has remained UK's creative capital. De Propris *et al.* (2009) present *The Geography of Creativity* in Britain by mapping the spatial distribution of creative industries by means of firm level data at the regional and Travel-To-Work levels. The study utilized both the DCMS classification of creative industries and the one suggested by Frontier Economics. This meant its findings are the most comprehensive in terms of sector definitions and geographical scale. The mapping relied on location quotients to capture the relevance of an industry within the broader economy of a particular place irrespective of the absolute number of firms actually present. This enabled meaningful agglomeration of firms in specific sectors to be flagged up, reflecting the tendencies of firms to cluster. The regional analysis showed that London is a cluster of clusters, as it presents an agglomeration of firms in all creative industries except 'Art and antiques' and 'Craft'. In particular, 'Video, film and photography' and 'Radio and TV' show levels of agglomeration almost three times the national average. London's neighbouring regions benefit from a significant spillover effect: the east, south-east and south-west regions show high location quotients, in particular in 'Architecture', 'Advertising', 'Publishing', 'Software and computer games' (De Propris *et al.* 2009) (see Figure 5.2 and Table 5.2). The report also found that overall the main cities across Britain were home to a number of creative activities.

The spatial distribution of creative industries unveiled in the report shows that they tend to cluster and therefore to benefit from the well-known agglomeration economies; but in addition to that they locate near other creative industries especially in urban areas. De Propris *et al.* (2009) provided evidence of industries' co-location by means of a correlation analysis: 'Advertising', 'Designer fashion' and 'Software, computer games and electronic publishing' were found to co-cluster. At the same time, 'Music and the Performing Arts', 'Publishing', 'Video, film and photography' and 'Radio and TV' were found to co-locate in urban areas.

The explanation for the overlap of many creative industries in cities is twofold. On the one hand, it can be suggested that they benefit from cross-sector synergies – so-called urbanization economies. Co-clustering provides value chain knowledge spillovers as well as serendipitous knowledge seeding across unrelated sectors. In addition creative industries seem to be attracted by other industries with which they have crucial technological similarities. Depending on their nature, centripetal forces attract creative industries around two dominant technological platforms: digital and design (Chapain *et al.* 2010; Cooke and De Propris 2011). This is a very new and interesting phenomenon that requires further investigation, since it can provide evidence of what sectors could be potentially targeted by policy making to support the growth of creative industries and their impact on the wider economy.

In parallel to these studies, the academic debate has been enriched by many case study analyses of creative clusters, creative quarters or creative places. The scholarly debate has been very careful to reconcile quantitative with more qualitative studies on the basis that they are complementary and shed light on different and equally important aspects of this complex, multifaceted and multi-layered phenomena.

The creative economy is complex, to the extent that it includes activities that have very different economic, social and artistic values. For instance, it is becoming increasingly accepted that to measure innovation, each creative industry might have to rely on appropriate output indicators as patents are clearly inadequate to carry out this task. For instance the work by Stoneman (2009: 2) shows that creative activities produce soft innovation that embodies 'both innovation in aesthetic products and aesthetic innovation in non-aesthetic products'. Considering the publishing industry, he argues that each industry ought to construct indicators that are unique to it but that best reflect the innovation and

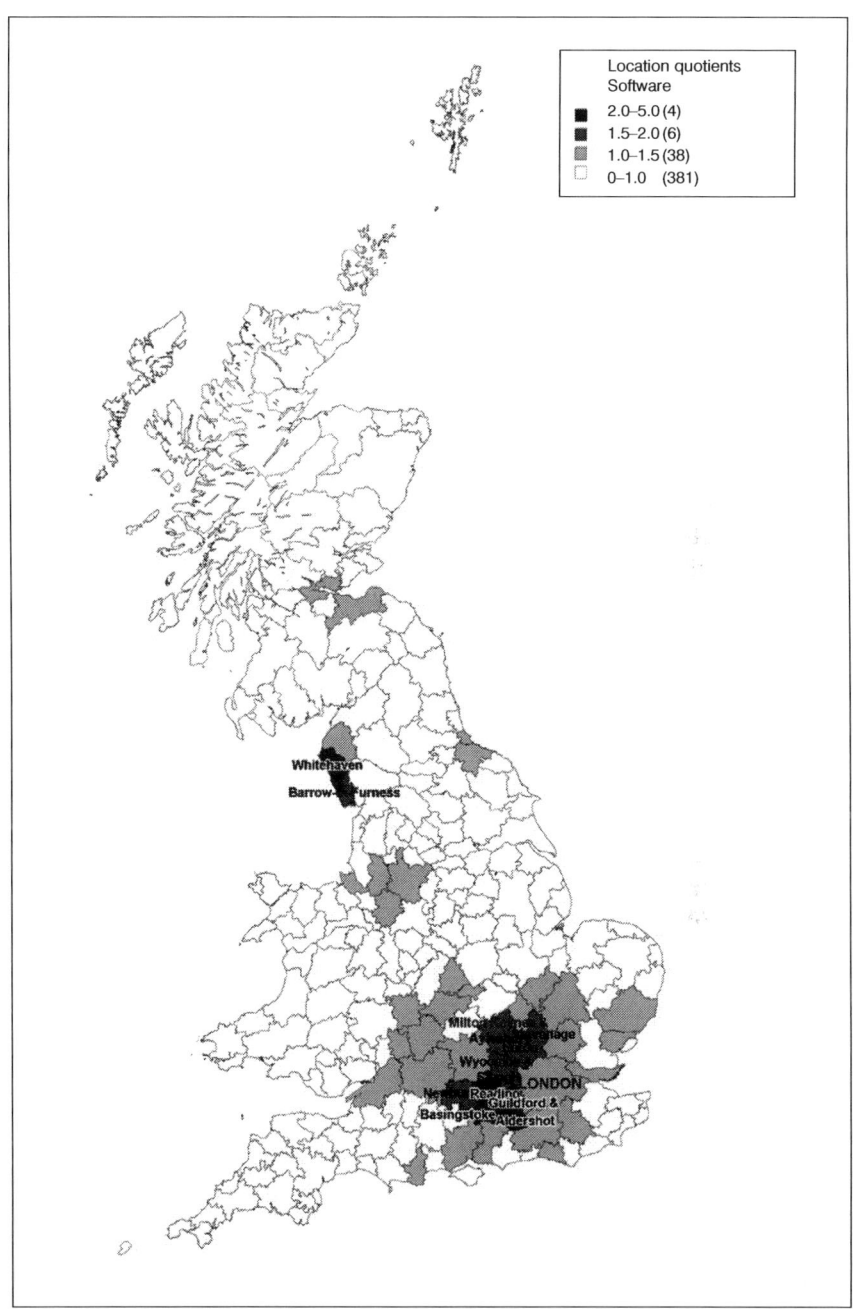

Location quotients
Software

- 2.0–5.0 (4)
- 1.5–2.0 (6)
- 1.0–1.5 (38)
- 0–1.0 (381)

Whitehaven

Barrow-in-Furness

Milton...
Aylesbury...enage
Wyo...
New... Reading LONDON
Basingstoke Guildford &
Aldershot

Figure 5.2 Map of software, computer games and electronic publishing, location quotients by travel-to-work area (TTWA) (DCMS definition), 2007

Source: De Propris *et al.* (2009)

Table 5.2 Creative clusters in the UK

Industry	Travel-to-work area level (LQ)
Advertising	South of London (from St Albans to Tunbridge Wells and Guildford), a south belt around Manchester and Birmingham and its south counties (Warwickshire and Worcestershire). Percentage higher than average agglomeration in Harrogate and Ripon and Blackpool
Architecture	Concentrated in hot construction spots such as Aberdeen, Newcastle and Southampton/Portsmouth
Arts and antiques	Very evenly distributed across the UK
Designer fashion	Midlands, North London and around Manchester
Video, film and photography	Very highly concentrated in London and its surrounding area (towards Oxford and Guildford, as well as Slough and Wycombe), and Brighton, Bristol and Bath
Music and the visual and performing arts	London, Brighton, Bath and the South West of England (Isles of Scilly, Penzance, Bridport and Lyme Regis)
Publishing	Oxford, Bath and Minehead. Significant specialisation in London, Cambridge, Peterborough, Ludlow and the North of Scotland
Software, computer games and electronic publishing	Clustering around the West of London, around the triangle Oxford–Cambridge–Reading; between Blackpool and Manchester
Radio and TV	Very strong level of concentration with high agglomeration in London and its surrounding areas (Wycombe and Slough), Brighton, Bristol, Cardiff and the North of Wales and Scotland

Source: De Propris *et al.* (2009)

creative output of that sector. More general indicators might incorrectly estimate the phenomena.

At the same time, the creative economy is multifaceted as it includes firms producing goods, services and experiences, as well as intermediaries, mediators and agencies that bridge consumers and producers. Finally, the increasing interconnectedness of linkages means that creative activities are necessarily organized across different levels: individual, community, local, regional, national and international.

An in-depth understanding of such complexity can only be reached with more qualitative case studies that are able to unpick the different layers and tendencies inside a particular creative phenomenon.

Studies on creative places have included in-depth studies of 'cultural quarters' in the UK (Roodhouse 2010); an exploration of London' cultural places (Evans *et al.* 2006), Scottish film cluster (Turok 2003), the fashion services firms clustering in the Lace Market in Nottingham (Crewe 1996), the London media cluster (Nachum and Keeble 2003), the advertising sector (Grabher 2002; Pratt 2006), the Birmingham Jewellery Quarter (De Propris and Wei 2009) and the fashion designer cluster (Sunley *et al.* 2008; Sunley *et al.* 2011).

What about the cultural economy?

Cultural or experience sectors have recently gained credibility thanks to the contributions of northern and Continental European scholars (Lazzeretti *et al.* 2008; Lazzeretti and Capone 2009; Lorentzen and Hansen 2009) who have focused on embedded and place-based resources to generate economic activities that are associated with the value of having the first-hand, authentic experience of certain phenomenon. The European Commission debate has also been mostly centred on themes that include culture (multiculturality), cultural assets (historical and heritage) and leisure activities.

It is beyond the remit of this chapter to disentangle the definitional tension between creative and cultural industries, although we have presented arguments that attempt to explain the UK pragmatic approach to this matter. There is no doubt, however, that the bohemian atmosphere depicted by Florida as ideal to attract creative talent alludes more to a context imbued with art and cultural content, than labs populated by scientist in white coats. Hesmondhalgh and Pratt (2005) also used creative and cultural industries interchangeably, whilst Cunningham (2002) noted how cultural industries had been rebadged and recently enveloped in the catch-all term 'creative industries'.

The starting point to understanding of the link between culture and its economic valorization needs to be traced back to the work of Adorno and Horkheimer (1973) on the emergence of mass culture and the commodification of art and its accessibility to the masses. Despite the inevitable controversial debate, cultural industries emerge as an expression of cultural productions no longer available to the few, but available to the many. This also meant the beginning of cultural policy (Hesmondhalgh and Pratt 2005) as the government started to be called into question so that such culture could be made affordable for the masses.

In this context, culture tends to coincide with the expression of communities' traditions and costumes at a particular point in time. It is not unusual, therefore, to see culture and cultural activities being described as expressions of the identity of specific communities or as the expression of common grounds across a multiplicity of identities. Cultural industries can be argued therefore to be different from creative industries in so far as they reflect the uniqueness of a place, of a time or of a society.

More recently, culture seems to have awaken the interest in some quarters of the UK government, since the DCMS website seems to suggest that its remit also includes a broad range of socio-economic activities comprising the arts, broadcasting, creative industries, the historic environment, Internet and international information and communication technologies (ICT), licensing and gambling, libraries, museums and galleries, sport, telecommunications and broadband, and tourism. Again, the DCMS also pledges to be committed to 'cultural and sporting activities' as well as 'tourism, creative and leisure industries'.

It is not clear whether this reflects a substantial change of focus or is just a cosmetic exercise. However, a couple of recent publications have unearthed the economic value of more traditional cultural sectors in the UK economy. Deloitte (2008) looked at the contribution of the *visitor economy* and finds that in 2007 the 'Visitor' sector directly accounted for 3.7 per cent of gross domestic product (GDP) and supported 1.36 million jobs, but the total – direct and indirect effect – was up to 8.2 per cent of UK GDP. At the same time, the 'Creative industries report' published by UK Trade and Investment (UKTI 2010: 30) portrays the UK's experience industries as attractive industries for foreign investment. The report acknowledges that 'the UK is one of the world's leaders in the aptly named "experience economy" – the creation and operation of visitor attractions such as museums, art galleries, heritage sites, gardens, zoos and leisure parks'.

Overall the cultural and experience-related activities coincide with an ample sector of the economy that has expanded over the last decades as the UK has become more affluent and society more eager to consume leisure goods and services.

Drawing on the Deloitte UKTI reports, and expanding on them, Boix and De Propris (2012) have attempted for the first time to define and map experience industries in the UK. They have isolated those industries that capture cultural activities related to nature, heritage or art with other that are more associated with the experiential value of an activity in a place. These industries include:

- other entertainment activities (including artistic and literary creation and interpretation, operation of arts facilities, fair and amusement park activities);
- libraries, archives and museums;
- sporting activities;
- other recreational activities (including gambling; motion picture, television and other theatrical casting; recreational activities at parks and beaches).

At the same time, as these industries are typically attendance-based (Lorentzen and Hansen 2009), it is important to also consider the ancillary industries that enable visitors to access the experience assets. This means considering industries such as:

- hotels, camping sites and other accommodation;
- restaurants, bars;
- travel agencies, tour operators and tourist assistance activities;
- membership organizations for the pursuit of cultural and recreational activities.

Lazzeretti and Capone (2009: 1669) have already argued the importance of tracing the 'integrated *filière* of tourism' to understand and assess the economic contribution of the tourism sector in Italy and in particular their agglomeration in local tourist systems. An understanding of how economic activities dis-integrate but link up to one another along the value chain is in line with a post-Fordist organization of production (whether of goods or services).

Even in this realm of scholarly activities a number of definitions are emerging: visitor economy, tourism, cultural industries, leisure industries and experience-related industries. It is beyond the scope of this discussion to look into them, but it is worth noting that they all capture an increasingly important part of the economy, probably the only part of the economy that, in this time of increasing globalization, cannot be that easily relocated abroad. Furthermore, these economic activities are developing in places that are peripheral or coincide with second-tier cities, and are trying to capitalize and maintain an authentic economic identity for their sustainable socio-economic well-being.

The classification suggested by Boix and De Propris (2012) is not free from controversial issues. In fact, the mapping exercise has shown that such industries behave quite similarly to 'Arts and antiques': they spread quite thinly across space and tend to weight more heavily in rural and more peripheral areas. So, this probably confirms the fact that the 'Arts and antiques' industry ought to be more appropriately considered as a cultural industry rather than as a creative one. De Propris *et al.* (2009) found for instance that the only negative correlation coefficient was the one between all other creative industries and 'Arts and antiques', suggesting that the latter is fundamentally different from the other creative industries..

Another concern is the difficulty in accurately capturing two key cultural and experience-related industries: food and craft (including garments, glass, furniture, jewellery and ceramic tableware). Both are plagued with operational problems as it is difficult to single out the 'cultural and experience' component in these sectors. In both cases, mass production and handcrafted products are statistically undistinguishable. For these sectors, therefore, case study analyses tend to dominate the debate, but more rigorous and aggregate investigations have been so far absent.

Concluding remarks

The steer of the UK government to focus on creative industries and the certainty of their definitions and classifications has pushed the scholarly and policy debate much further than in other countries; however, it has also silenced any opportunity to open up a conversation on the link between creativity and culture and their combined impact on the economy. As important as creative industries can be in promoting radical innovations and technological leaps – think for instance of digital technology – we would argue that they do not exhaust the economy's innovation capacity, which it can be argued also includes culture and leisure activities. There is an increasing understanding that the latter are not only able to generate soft and incremental innovations, and that they are key users of technologies like design and digital, which in turns can spawn further innovations.

In a different way, as creative industries tend to concentrate in urban areas (De Propris *et al.* 2009), cultural and leisure industries tend to spread across urban and rural economies, promoting a more balanced and diffused economic development.

In the current political climate, it is not clear how the government will take the creative economy agenda forward. Budget cuts to theatres, museums and all sorts of heritage sites seem to suggest that whether it is creative or cultural, what matters is that it is commercially viable and profit making. The public sector is withdrawing from the economy even in sectors or circumstance where cases of textbook market failures would suggest some role for the government. This view reflects the belief that the driving force in the economy to create growth and jobs must lie with the private sector, namely businesses. Also the good old *triple helix model* – key to the knowledge economy paradigm – has been somewhat kicked into the long grass. It is too soon to have a feel for what will be the outcome of this approach. It might be time for all of us to pick up and read another book by Florida (2010) and hope that the current harshness will yield the 'great reset'.

References

Adorno, T. and Horkheimer, M. (1973) *Dialectic of Enlightenment*, 1st edn 1947, London: Allen Lane.

Andari, R., Bakhshi, H., Hutton, W., O'Keeffe, A. and Schneider, P. (2007) *Staying ahead: The Economic Performance of the UK's Creative Industries*, London: The Work Foundation.

Boden, M.A. (2003) *The Creative Mind: Myths and Mechanisms*, London: Routledge.

Boix, R. and De Propris, L. (2012) *The Experience Economy in the UK*, mimeo.

Chapain, C., Cooke, P., De Propris, L., MacNeill, S. and Mateos-Garcia, J. (2010) *Creative Clusters and Innovation: Putting Creativity on the Map*, London: NESTA.

Cooke, P. and Clifton, N. (2007) 'The "Creative class" in the UK: research briefing', *Regions*, 266, special issue on *The Role of Culture in the Economic Development of Old Industrial Regions*.

Cooke, P. and De Propris, L. (2011) 'A policy agenda for EU smart growth: The role of creative and cultural industries', *Policy Studies*, 32(4): 365–75.

Crewe, L. (1996) 'Material culture: Embedded firms, organizational networks and the local economic development of a fashion quarter', *Regional Studies*, 30(3): 257–72.

Cunningham, S.D. (2002) 'From cultural to creative industries: Theory, industry and policy implications', mimeo, Brisbane: Queensland University of Technology.

DCMS – Department for Culture, Media and Sport (1998) *Creative Industries Mapping Document*, London: DCMS.

DCMS (2001) *Creative Industries Mapping Document*, London: DCMS.

De Propris, L. and Wei, P. (2009) 'Creativity and space: The opportunity of an urban creative jewellery cluster', *Creative Industries Journal*, 2(1): 37–56.

De Propris, L., Chapain, C., Cooke, P., MacNeill, S. and Mateos-Garcia, J. (2009) *The Geography of Creativity*, London: NESTA.

Deloitte (2008) *The Economic Case for the Visitor Economy*, final report, September, London: Deloitte.

Evans, G., Foord, J., Gertler, M., Tesolin, L. and Weinstock, S. (2006) *Strategies for Creative Spaces: Lessons Learned*, London: LDA.

Florida, R. (2002) *The Rise of the Creative Class: And how it's Transforming Work, Leisure, Community and Everyday Life*, New York: Basic Books.

Florida, R. (2008) *Who's Your City? How the Creative Economy is Making Where You Live the Most Important Decision of Your Life*, New York: Basic Books.

Florida, R. (2010) *The Great Reset*, New York: Harper Collins.

Frontier Economics (2007) *Creative Industry Spillovers: Understanding Their Impact on the Wider Economy*, A report prepared for DCMS, London: Frontier Economics.

Frontier Economics (2009) *Creative Industry Performance. A Statistical Analysis for the DCMS*, London: DCMS.

GLA – Greater London Authority (2004) *London's Creative Sector: 2004 Update*, London: GLA.

Grabher, G. (2002) 'Production in projects: Economic geographies of temporary collaboration', *Regional Studies*, 36(3): 229–45.

Hesmondhalgh, D. and Pratt, A.C. (2005) 'Cultural industries and cultural policy', *International Journal of Cultural Policy*, 11(1): 1–13.

Jacobs, J. (1961) *The Death and Life of Great American Cities*, New York: Random House.

Jacobs, J. (1984) *Cities and the Wealth of Nations*, New York: Random House.

KEA European Affairs (2006) *The Economy of Culture in Europe*, Belgium: European Commission.

Knell, J. and Oakley, K. (2007) 'London's creative economy: An accidental success?', *Provocation Series* (London: The Work Foundation) 3(3).

Lazzeretti, L. and Capone, F. (2009) 'Spatial spillovers and employment dynamics in local tourist systems in Italy (1991–2001)', *European Planning Studies*, 17(11): 1665–83.

Lazzeretti, L., Boix, R. and Capone, F. (2008) 'Do creative industries cluster? Mapping creative local production systems in Italy and Spain', *Industry and Innovation*, 15(5): 549–67.

Lorentzen, A. and Hansen, C.J. (2009) 'The role and transformation of the city in the experience economy: Identifying and exploring research challenges', *European Planning Studies*, 17(6): 817–27.

Nachum, L. and Keeble, D. (2003) 'Neo-Marshallian clusters and global networks: The linkages of media firms in central London', *Long Range Planning*, 36(5): 459–480.

O'Connor, J. (2008) *The Cultural and Creative Industries: A Review of the Literature*, A report for Creative Partnerships, London: Arts Council of England.

Pratt, A.C. (2004) 'Mapping the cultural industries: Regionalization. The example of South-East England', in A.J. Scott and D. Power (eds) *The Cultural Industries and the Production of Culture*, London: Routledge.

Pratt, A.C. (2006) 'Advertising and creativity, a governance approach: A case study of creative agencies in London', *Environment and Planning A*, 38(10): 1883–99.

Pratt, A.C. (2008) 'Creative cities: The cultural industries and the creative class', *Geografiska Annaler: Series B-Human Geography*, 90(2): 107–17.

Roodhouse, S. (2010) *Cultural Quarters*, Bristol: Intellect.

Scott, A.J. (2006) 'Creative cities: Conceptual issues and policy questions', *Journal of Urban Affairs*, 28(1): 1–17.

Stoneman, P. (2009) *Soft Innovation*, London: NESTA.

Sunley, P., Pinch, S., Reimer, S. and Macmillen, J. (2008) 'Innovation in a creative production system: The case of design', *Journal of Economic Geography*, 8(5): 675–98.

Sunley, P., Pinch, S. and Reimer, S. (2011) 'Design capital: Practice and situated learning in London design agencies', *Transactions of the Institute of British Geographers*, 36(3): 377–92.

Turok, I. (2003) 'Cities, clusters and creative industries: The case of film and television in Scotland', *European Planning Studies*, 11(5): 549–65.

UKTI – UK Trade and Investment (2010) *UK Creative Industries*, London: UKTI.

UNCTAD – United Nations Conference on Trade and Development (2008) *Creative Economy. Report 2008*, Geneva and New York: UNDP, UNCTAD.

Webber, A.M. (1993) 'What's so new about the new economy?', *Harvard Business Review*, 71(1): 24–42.

6 Leisure, culture and experience economy as a creative strategy in the periphery

Does North Denmark benefit from the experience economy?

Anne Lorentzen

Introduction

Experiences have been connected with economy due to a growing leisure demand in the Western world. Today many people give a high priority to their leisure time, and as a consequence they are assumed to require the existence of amenities close to their place of residence. Quality of place is a factor that is thought of as playing a considerable role in the decisions people make on where to settle, and this is the reason why quality of place is seen strategically as a lever of demographic and economic development of local economies. Quality of place includes among other things attractive natural environments as well as urban qualities, a supply of culture and facilities for leisure activities. From a production perspective it has been argued that cultural factors represent sources for local entrepreneurship, regional differentiation and competitive advantage through creative industrial cluster building (Cooke and Lazzeretti 2008). Earlier works on experience economy and place developed the hypothesis that experience economy may function as a lever of growth for peripheral regions, due to an assumed decentralized pattern of location and consumption (Lorentzen 2009). A parallel can be seen in creative industry research. Collis *et al.* (2010) summarize research that shows how creative industrial activity increasingly takes place in outer suburbia and peri-urban regions.

In Denmark politicians and planners have shown a growing interest in the notion of experience economy as a lever of local and regional growth in less favoured areas (Lorentzen 2011). Experience economy is thus seen as a tool of industrial policy, both directly as creator of employment in industrial sectors providing experiences and indirectly as a factor of attraction for potentially new citizens in general and of a highly educated labour in particular. In North Denmark, the regional development strategy formulates the experience economy as a strategic focal point (Region Nordjylland Vækstforum 2007). The Danish municipalities have also started to work with the experience economy, most often motivated by incentives from higher levels of territorial administration such as the region and the Danish government. The experience economy focus of urban and local development policies seems to be a Scandinavian specialty, whereas other European countries talk about cultural industries and Britain in particular of creative industries (Flew and Cunningham 2010: 114). The different policies share the intention of identifying and enabling economic growth in post-industrial economies and to some extent they overlap in terms of sector focus (Flew and Cunningham 2010: 118).

The question that this chapter discusses is the extent to which peripheral regions are actually able to develop, based on a development of local experience offerings. The question can be divided in two, namely to what extent the periphery is able to develop experience economy offerings, and what is the role of culture and creativity in the local experience economy. Second, what implications do these offerings have for demographic and broader economic growth and differentiation? The chapter discusses this question based on empirical statistical evidence of the industrial and demographic development of North Denmark, a peripheral region of Denmark. Not only is this region located at a considerable distance from the Danish core, it is also characterized by internal centre–periphery relations in the regional capital of Aalborg. This enables a regional as well as a sub-regional analysis of the weight, composition and dynamic of the experience economy of the periphery, and the role it plays for demographic and industrial development.

The chapter proceeds in the following way. First the theoretical foundation of the chapter is developed. This section discusses how notions of the experience economy and society and the creative industry can be connected with local development of post-industrial non-core localities. A methodology section leads to the empirical part, which presents the findings of a study of the experience economy of North Denmark, where this economy is particularly well developed. The chapter ends with a conclusion of the empirical analysis and perspectives for future policy and research. It is suggested that differentiated local policies are developed, and new types of industrial lock-in are avoided.

Theoretical framework of the study

The experience economy

While there are arguments that consider the role of amenities, culture and entertainment as connected to the spatial and social development of the knowledge economy, as Florida (2002) does, it seems fruitful to also consider the increased focus on experiences, culture and entertainment as a phenomenon and even a 'paradigm' (Lorentzen 2009) in itself. It can thus be argued that the focus on urban qualities, leisure and culture is just one aspect of the increased focus on luxury (non-basic) consumption, which has been foreseen by Tofler in 1970 (Tofler 1970) and later described in more detail by Schulze in the 1990s (Schulze 2005). Tofler envisaged the emergence of a 'provision system of psychic gratification' as a response to the growing affluence of the Western societies, while Schulze discussed the changes in the value system of the modern society towards hedonism, leading to an 'experience society'. Florida's description of the preferences of the creative class as an affluent class in search of entertainment can also be seen in this perspective. However, it can be argued that the mega-trend towards luxury and hedonistic consumption in Western societies is probably more generalized among different social groups, than Florida's work on the specific 'creative class' lets on, in particular in countries with relatively equal income distribution as, for example, in Scandinavian countries.

Pine and Gilmore's work on the experience economy takes Tofler's visions of an emerging system of experience provision to the shop floor of private businesses (Pine and Gilmore 1999). According to these authors every business may add psychic gratification as part of their product with the aim of enhancing its competitive edge in the market. They apply the notion of 'experiences' to make their point. The development of experience offerings is not only connected to specialized experience makers. On the contrary experiences are developed deliberately by many kinds of businesses to leave positive, memorable impressions with the customers. When describing how experiences may enhance the value of the products the authors apply the metaphor of the theatre to explain how experiences can be seen as the play, the business management as the stager, and the basic products as props for the experience. The aim of this type of innovation is to arouse the interest and loyalty of the customers. The experience economy can be seen as a mega-trend in strategic management in which the customer relationship has the highest priority. The ability to innovate by developing experience offerings provides businesses with a competitive advantage.

In comparison the creative industries are not defined by their customer relationship but by the artistic or creative input into their innovation process. Howkins (2002: 116) lists fifteen sectors as belonging to the core creative industries, namely advertising, architecture, art, crafts, design, fashion, film, music, performing art, publishing, research and development (R&D), software, toys and games, TV and radio, and video games. This list is grossly agreed upon by the EU (Flew and Cunningham 2010: 114–15). It can be argued that most of the listed creative industries produce experience offerings, and that their location contributes to the vibrancy of the city. However, some experience economy fields are usually not included in the listings of creative industries, but are nevertheless an integrated part of today's hedonistic consumption. Such fields are heritage tourism, sport, festivals and leisure activities (Flew and Cunningham 2010: 114–15).

Experience economy and place

If we focus on products in which the experience offering is the *core* (a game, a movie), compared to products in which the experience is an add-on (rural ecological narratives, or lotteries offered together with dairy products), a distinction can be made between *footloose* or *place bound* experience offerings (Lorentzen 2009). Manufactured experience products are footloose (books, games, video films, toys) because production and consumption is usually not collocated, and because both processes can in principle take place everywhere, where the general conditions allow it. Experience services (sports event, theme restaurant meals, art exhibitions) require the collocation and simultaneity of consumption and production. The consumer needs to 'be present' sometimes even as co-producer of the experience.

Considering this relationship between experience and place a distinction can be made between (a) place in products; (b) products in place; and (c) place as products, as developed in Smidt-Jensen and Lorentzen (2011). First, experience offerings may draw value from places. Places can be seen as constructed by social practices and narratives about them, and businesses may draw on such narratives when developing their products and presenting them to the market. Examples are regional foods (Arthur 2011) and Swiss watches (Crevoisier and Jeannerat 2009). The use of local narratives makes local purchase of otherwise footloose products appear particularly interesting. Second, places may draw value from hosting experience offerings. This is the Florida perspective, according to which the quality of place is enhanced by the number of, for example, festivals, galleries, cafes and areas for recreational use. It can be added that the quality of place would also win by the clustering of some creative industries. Third, places may provide experiences due to the beauty of their natural or constructed environment, its history or the localized competences. The place can be consumed by watching it, staying or living in it or by performing different activities in it. The economic value of such places can be direct by the payment of entry fees or more indirectly by comparatively high prices of housing, hotel rooms or other local offerings.

Based on these three perspectives in relation to experience economy and place it can be argued that place bound experience offerings are of particular importance to local development because of (a) the potential alliance between producers and places; (b) the collocation of production and consumption of experiences; and (c) the role of place as factor of attraction to businesses, citizens and tourists. In all three perspectives an impact on employment, industrial transformation and demography can be seen as a potential outcome.

This argument has raised the interest of small transforming cities in participating in the rush for culture, creativity and wealth (Miles 2006; Allingham 2009; Lassen *et al.* 2009; Lorentzen and Krogh 2009; Waitt and Gibson 2009; Lorentzen 2011). Even rural areas have embarked on experience-based development strategies (Scott 2010; Arthur 2011).

The experience economy and local development in the periphery

Obviously places are not equally equipped to develop experience economy, and compared to big cities, or core areas, peripheral localities have different potential quantitatively as well as qualitatively. Core areas represent both economies of scale, which allow them to develop big, expensive productions, and economies of scope, which allow them to differentiate the offer and to develop specialized productions. Both size and variety are connected to the experience offerings of big cities. Creative and cultural industries are known to cluster in big cities (Pratt 2004; Scott 2006; Cooke and Lazzeretti 2008). Big cities often also host important historic monuments that serve them as flagships in the global competition. The demand for experiences in big cities is also both big and differentiated. Peripheries, on the other hand, are characterized by small cities, natural environment and tranquillity. Traditional industries prevail. The distance to the core calls for local solutions, and a social and cognitive proximity among local actors can be seen as a potential resource in local development. Conditions seldom allow economies of scale and scope as in big cities. However, due to globalization, specialization based on niche strategies may develop within some fields of inherited or newly developed competences. Different types of international festivals offer themselves as examples (historic, gastronomic, artistic) (Bradley and Hall 2006).

Creative industries are known to cluster in big cities, but have been shown to disperse into suburbs and peri-urban regions due to affordability and locality preferences (Collis *et al.* 2010: 107). More labour-intensive and artisanal creative small and medium enterprises (SMEs) (Flew and Cunningham 2010: 114) are likely to locate in the periphery, compared to the highly capitalized and industrialized industries, locating in the big cities. In particular arts and crafts as well as performing arts are creative industries that may develop in connection with rural tourism (Scott 2010).

Peripheries differ, and according Arzeni *et al.* (2002) four main types of periphery can be found in Europe today. They differ in relation to their distance to the core; their nature, culture and leisure values; their economic structure; and their demography. The potential for experience economy in relation to the four types can be characterized in the following way.

Type 1 regions are found near an urban centre. They may benefit from the facilities and amenities of the centre, and serve as residential areas for people working in the centre. They may develop experience offerings directed to the citizens of the core as well as for tourists. Type 2 regions are more distanced from the centre and have natural, cultural and leisure values, which attract visitors, and based on which a heritage industry may develop. Creative SMEs are most likely to locate in type 1 and type 2 peripheries, where they find affordability as well as a certain market.

Type 3 regions are distanced from the centre, and agriculture prevails. We find holidays on farms and theme parks in such areas. Type 4 regions are remote areas in demographic decline. Due to low accessibility the potential to economize on experiences are limited. However, even remoteness can be turned into an asset. Adventure tourism or wellness and recreation are options for the rural periphery.

In sum, the distinction between different types of peripheries indicates the different potential of experience-based development and creative industries, depending on accessibility, natural and cultural values, economic structure and demography. It also implies a need to differentiate experience-based local development strategies. The questions are therefore to what extent are the different types of peripheries able to develop experience economy offerings and creative industries? And what implications do the development of these industries have for demographic and broader economic growth and differentiation?

Empirical method and research questions

The research is based on data from Statistics Denmark regarding the composition of employment, unemployment figures and population changes at municipal, regional and national level.

The analysis of the experience economy in the North Denmark Region is based on employment data of twenty-seven subcategories from Statistics Denmark. Place-based experience economy has been operationalized as 'hotels and restaurants' and 'associations, culture and renovation'. In relation to these subcategories the development of employment in hotels and restaurants is closely linked to tourism, while the categories of 'associations, culture and renovation' can be seen as related to the consumption of culture and leisure by the local population, and seasonally by tourists. This group includes creative industries such as performing arts, and arts and crafts. The analysis assesses the relative size in employment of both statistical subgroups at the regional and the municipal level. The year 2008 was the most recent available at the time of research, which implies that the impact of the financial crisis is not reflected.

The relative size of the experience economy employment is discussed in relation to the differentiated potential of the municipalities, understood as their geographic experience resources, which is a combination of their experience values and their accessibility.

The role of place-based experience economy to job creation is analyzed by correlating the relative size of the experience economy to the levels and dynamics of unemployment at municipal level. The role of the experience economy as attraction for settlement is analyzed by relating the relative size of the experience economy employment in the municipalities to population changes. Finally the relationship between experience economy development and the emergence of new knowledge-based sectors is assessed. The subsectors financing and insurance are used as a proxy for knowledge-based sectors.

The full empirical study reported here was published in Lorentzen and Krogh (2009) in a report funded by the Centre for Regional Development at Aalborg University.

The place bound experience economy of North Denmark and its eleven municipalities

What is the overall role of place bound experience economy (PBEE) in the region of North Denmark? The following analysis compares the weight of the PBEE in North Denmark, Denmark as a whole, Denmark outside Copenhagen, and in the city of Copenhagen.

In Denmark employment in PBEE amounted to 8.33 per cent as a national average. The city of Copenhagen weighed heavily in this mean with 13.45 per cent of its employment in these sectors. This is due to the position of Copenhagen as a metropolitan city with its vast supply of culture, and its large share of Danish tourism. To assess the situation of North Denmark, therefore, it seems

Table 6.1 Place bound experience economy (PBEE) in the eleven municipalities of North Denmark as a share of employment (percentage), 2008

	PBEE total	Culture	Hotels and restaurants
North Denmark	7.90	4.29	3.61
Læsø	11.64	5.29	6.35
Frederikshavn	9.20	4.37	4.83
Aalborg	9.00	6.73	2.27
Hjørring	8.37	4.59	3.78
Jammerbugt	7.80	4.22	3.58
Morsø	7.42	4.39	3.03
Rebild	6.45	2.72	3.73
Thisted	6.45	3.81	2.64
Mariagerfjord	6.25	3.87	2.38
Brønderslev	6.16	3.77	2.39
Vesthimmerland	6.07	3.48	2.59

Source: Our elaboration on data from Statistics Denmark

more reasonable to compare this region with Denmark outside Copenhagen city (DK - C). In this comparison employment in the PBEE has a greater share in North Denmark (7.9 per cent) than it has in DK - C (7.49 per cent). As a traditional tourist region it is no surprise that in North Denmark a greater share of employment is found in hotels and restaurants (3.61 per cent) compared to DK - C (3.43 per cent), but also employment related to culture (associations, culture and renovation) has a greater share in North Denmark (4.29 per cent) than in DK - C (4.06 per cent) (based on Denmark Statistics).

Even though it is present everywhere in North Denmark, the analysis of PBEE employment shows that its weight is quite different among the eleven municipalities. Table 6.1 thus illustrates how five of the eleven municipalities are characterized by a PBEE employment at or above the regional mean, while six municipalities show an employment in the PBEE sectors below this mean.

The municipalities of Læsø, Frederikshavn, Aalborg and Hjørring show an employment of PBEE above the mean, while Jammerbugt is only slightly below the mean. Morsø, Rebild, Thisted, Mariagerfjord, Brønderslev and Vesthimmerland have clearly less than the regional average employment in PBEE. Also Læsø, Hjørring and Frederikshavn municipalities have a higher employment in hotels and restaurants than the regional average. Figure 6.1 shows the location of the eleven municipalities of North Denmark.

Differentiated geographic experience resources

The background for the development of PBEE in North Denmark in general is no doubt the quality of the natural environment, and in particular the sandy

Figure 6.1 The municipalities of North Denmark

Source: Region of North Denmark

beaches along the North Sea coast, which have been the object of tourism for decades, and in particular since the 1960s, with the boom in the number of holiday cottages as second homes. In addition the many forests and plantations, moors and lakes offer opportunities for leisure activities. Sparsely populated as it is, one major attraction is that the region does not appear to be crowded, even in midsummer.

The eleven municipalities differ from each other according to some important parameters of relevance for the development of PBEE. The parameters can be summarized as follows: accessibility, urban qualities, quality of the natural environment, history/authenticity, and visibility. Together these parameters are suggested as the key geographic resources from which the PBEE can develop.

Accessibility to markets, labour and supplies are key to economic development and in the experience economy accessibility to localized experience offerings is equally important. In terms of accessibility the municipalities differ. Aalborg municipality and in particular the city of Aalborg represent an infrastructural node with regional, national and international accessibility with airport, intercity railway and European motorway. A number of municipalities are connected with the European motorway and railway, namely Brønderslev, Rebild, Frederikshavn, Hjørring and Mariagerfjord (the latter has no railway). Very poor accessibility characterizes Morsø, Thisted and in particular Læsø municipalities, while Jammerbugt and Vesthimmerland have got reasonable regional accessibility. These differences in accessibility imply that Aalborg has a regionally central position, which enables neighbouring municipalities to attend PBEE in Aalborg. Nationally and internationally Aalborg is not a node, but rather an accessible periphery. Morsø, Thisted and in particular Læsø are characterized by a peripheral situation with low accessibility, meaning that they lack a key factor for growth and innovation, also in relation to PBEE. In total, the municipalities exist in an infrastructural hierarchy with Aalborg at the top and Læsø at the bottom.

A common characteristic of the municipalities is that they provide a high quality natural environment. Beautiful coastlines and beaches, forests and plantations, moors and lakes characterize the municipalities. Particularly attractive landscapes are, however, found in Hjørring and Jammerbugt with the beautiful broad sandy beaches. The two seas, the desert and dramatic plantations of Skagen in Frederikshavn municipality are also unique, and with the newly created national park in Thisted represent flagships with high experience economy potential. One rural municipality has a huge and well-known adventure park in easy reach of the main city of Aalborg.

This pretty rurality also implies, however, that urban resources are scarce in the region with one main city, Aalborg, and two second tier cities, Hjørring and Frederikshavn. This means that three of the eleven municipalities have important experience resources that the other municipalities do not have. They have theatres, concert halls, shopping malls and streets, and a built environment of historic buildings among other things. Aalborg also hosts dynamic creative clusters and incubators. The other municipalities are rural with only one town bigger than 5,000 inhabitants (Thisted).

History and authenticity or heritage is a potential resource in all municipalities. Cloisters, manor houses, traditional fishing villages, and remnants from the Danish Bronze Age abound, and these resources are also being developed in different ways. Historic buildings (Skagen), historic trades (Læsø) and historic narratives (Frederikshavn) are developed as experience offerings.

The analysis of the geographic experience resources shows that there is a considerable concentration of localized experience resources in Aalborg and the traditional tourist destinations on the North Sea. At the same time accessibility mainly supports Aalborg and the neighbouring municipalities, while other municipalities are in less favourable infrastructural positions, rendering their attractions less accessible.

The different geographic experience resources are reflected in the employment figures in Table 6.1, showing that the most urbanized municipalities have the largest share of employment in PBEE. Some of these at the same time also have the most famous beaches. The least accessible municipalities have the lowest employment in PBEE. The suburban municipalities have equally low employment in PBEE, which may reflect their reliance on the experience supply of the capital city. The high share of employment in PBEE of Læsø merely reflects the lack of alternative employment.

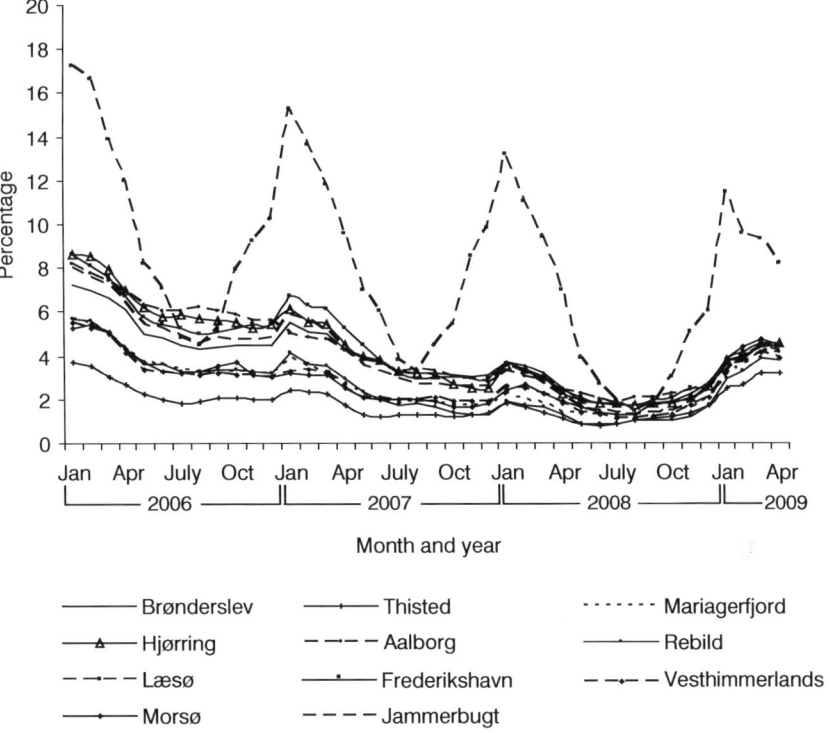

Figure 6.2 Full-time unemployment (in per cent of work force) in the municipalities of North Denmark, 2006–09

Source: Lorentzen and Krogh (2009), based on data from Statistics Denmark

The experience economy as a lever of employment?

High unemployment is the main characteristic of North Denmark. However, the region has benefited considerably from the economic upturn that has characterized Denmark more than its neighbouring countries since about 2004. Figure 6.2 shows the unemployment rate between March 2006 and January 2009 in the eleven municipalities. The figure shows how the unemployment rates differ slightly between the municipalities in terms of level as well as in relation to seasonal variations. Six municipalities have relatively low levels of unemployment, namely Thisted, Mariagerfjord, Vesthimmerland, Morsø, Rebild and Brønderslev while high rates of unemployment can be found in Læsø, Aalborg, Frederikshavn, Hjørring and Jammerbugt. These municipalities also have the highest seasonal variations in employment.

As a lever of development the experience economy should contribute positively to employment. A simple correlation between the level and seasonal variation of employment with the share of experience economy of the municipality has been made.

PBEE share of employment ⟍ Unemployment rate	High share	Low share
High	Læsø Frederikshavn Aalborg Hjørring Jammerbugt	
Low		Thisted Rebild Vesthimmerland Mariagerfjord Morsø Brønderslev

Figure 6.3 Share of experience economy employment and unemployment rate of 11 municipalities of North Denmark, 2008

Figure 6.3 combines the results from Table 6.1 and Figure 6.2 in a simple two-by-two matrix. From this matrix it can be seen that the municipalities with the highest share of employment in PBEE also are those with the highest unemployment rates. These are also characterized by considerable seasonal variations in employment.

This implies two things. First, the experience economy employment is not big enough to solve the employment problem, which on the other hand would have been more serious without this employment. Second, experience-based employment goes along with seasonal variations of employment. This is because such employment is widely connected to the tourist services. In Denmark these service sectors are busy during summer but much less so outside the main season. A case in point is the small island of Læsø with unemployment rates during winter of 12–17 per cent of the registered labour force while in summer it is only around 2–4 per cent.

Further, the quality of the employment generated in PBEE can be described by the level of education of the people employed. Smidt-Jensen *et al.* (2009: 857) find that the education level in these sectors is considerably lower than the Danish mean, and that it is also lower in small rural municipalities than in large urban municipalities. It is also much lower in 'hotels and restaurants' than in 'culture', implying that the tourism-related jobs are of a particularly low quality. These differences also apply to North Denmark, where the education level in the PBEE trades of the regional capital of Aalborg is considerably higher than in more rural municipalities, and the difference in education level of the two PBEE subgroups is significant (Statistics Denmark, RAS (register-based labour force statistics) (registerU22).

Share of PBEE in total employment / Demographic growth	High share	Low share
Positive growth	Aalborg Jammerbugt	Vesthimmerland Rebild Mariagerfjord Brønderslev
Negative growth	Læsø Hjørring Frederikshavn	Thisted Morsø

Figure 6.4 Share of place bound experience economy employment and demographic growth in 11 municipalities of North Denmark, 2008

The experience economy as a lever of demographic growth?

North Denmark is the smallest region of Denmark measured by population (590,515 inhabitants in 2009), and it has stagnated demographically while the Danish population as a whole grew 1.85 per cent between 2005 and 2009. The future looks equally bleak, especially because young people tend to leave the region.

An analysis shows that in North Denmark six of the municipalities have positive demographic growth, while five of them show negative growth. Positive demographic growth can thus be found in the Aalborg, Rebild, Vesthimmerland, Brønderslev, Jammerbugt and Mariagerfjord municipalities. Of these only three municipalities have a natural demographic growth, meaning that there is an excess of births over deaths, which again means that the relative number of young families in Aalborg, Rebild and Brønderslev is higher than in the rest of the region. Negative demographic growth on the other hand characterizes Hjørring, Thisted, Morsø, Frederikshavn and the island of Læsø. The question of whether experience economy is related with positive demographic growth can now be analyzed in relation to the eleven municipalities (Lorentzen and Krogh 2009).

Figure 6.4 shows that a large share of PBEE employment can be related to positive as well as negative demographic growth. However, if we exclude Aalborg as the big urban municipality with specific characteristics (and which represents both high PBEE employment and positive demographic growth) we can see the contours of a *reverse* relationship between PBEE share of employment and demographic growth. Four municipalities present low PBEE employment and positive demographic growth, while three municipalities have a comparatively high share of PBEE employment and negative demographic growth. This means that a high share of PBEE is not enough to make citizens stay in the municipality and that municipalities attract citizens for reasons other than their offers of place bound experience. Which other factors could explain positive demographic growth? A look on the map of the region in Figure 6.1 shows that the municipalities with positive demographic growth all are neighbouring the capital of Aalborg. In other words they have become part of the commuting area around Aalborg due to good accessibility and moderate housing prices.

The experience economy as a lever of new industries?

Industrial diversification is of great importance to peripheral regions. Localized experience offering are seen as a lever for other industries, as they represent a reason for knowledge-intensive branches of industry to establish themselves in search of qualified labour. The question can therefore be posed: can a positive relationship be detected between PBEE employment on the one hand and employment in knowledge-intensive sectors on the other hand in the region and its eleven municipalities? In the present study the 'knowledge economy' has been operationalized as the statistical categories 'business services' and 'financing and insurance' as they are called in Statistics Denmark.

The employment share of North Denmark in knowledge services in 2008 was 10.4 per cent of total employment, of which 8.2 per cent were employed in business services. This figure is quite low in a Danish perspective. This is true both in comparison to Denmark as a whole, and in comparison to Denmark outside Copenhagen. Denmark outside Copenhagen employs 12.9 per cent of the labour force in knowledge services (North Jutland: 10.4 per cent) and 10.2 per cent in business services (North Jutland: 8.2 per cent). North Denmark is lagging behind the rest of the country in terms of knowledge economy. This means that in the region of North Denmark the relatively high employment in PBEE does *not* correspond to a high share of employment in knowledge services at the regional level.

In relation to knowledge economy development the municipalities also differ. Their share of employment in knowledge services can be seen in Table 6.2.

The table shows that only one of the eleven municipalities is above the Danish mean in relation to employment in knowledge services, and this is Aalborg, the regional capital. With 13.9 per cent of its total employment in knowledge services, and 11.53 per cent in business services, the city distances itself from all other municipalities, and also raises the mean for the region. The other municipalities have far lower shares of employment in knowledge services, but also differ considerably. No clear categorization offers itself, but for the purpose of analysis the municipalities have been divided in two groups. One group has around 9 to 10 per cent of employment in knowledge services (Rebild, Brønderslev, Jammerbugt, Frederikshavn, Hjørring), and the other has below 8.6 per cent (Mariagerfjord, Vesthimmerland, Thisted, Morsø, Læsø).

Based on this grouping is it now possible to illustrate, at the municipal level, if there exists any positive relationship between the share of employment in PBEE

Table 6.2 Knowledge services in the eleven municipalities of North Denmark as share of employment (percentage), 2008

	Knowledge service	Of which business services
Aalborg	13.87	11.53
Rebild	9.73	7.84
Brønderslev	9.14	9.19
Jammerbugt	9.14	6.91
Frederikshavn	8.84	6.83
Hjørring	8.80	6.72
Mariagerfjord	8.56	6.46
Vesthimmerland	8.08	5.73
Thisted	7.47	5.34
Morsø	6.65	4.32
Læsø	4.87	2.96

Source: Lorentzen and Krogh (2009), based on data from Statistics Denmark

on the one hand and the share of knowledge services on the other hand? Is PBEE followed by industrial diversification? For this purpose Figure 6.5 compares the share of employment in PBEE with the share of employment in knowledge services in a simple two-by-two matrix. Figure 6.5 shows that four municipalities are characterized by low shares of both types of employment, PBEE and knowledge services. Four municipalities show high shares of employment in both types of economy. One municipality, Læsø, has a high level of employment in PBEE and the lowest level of knowledge services employment, while two municipalities have high shares of knowledge services employment and low levels of PBEE employment. This means that two thirds of the municipalities show a positive correlation between the two types of economy! The municipalities that have high shares of both types of employment are the urbanized, and relatively big, municipalities (Aalborg, Frederikshavn, Hjørring) plus one small municipality (Jammerbugt). Low shares of both types of economy are found in relation to the small, rural municipalities (Thisted, Mariager, Vesthimmerland, Morsø). Two municipalities have a different combination, namely relatively high levels of employment in the knowledge services, in combination with low shares of employment in the PBEE (Brønderslev, Rebild). And finally, one small rural municipality, the island of Læsø, has a very high share of employment in PBEE and almost no employment in knowledge services. The question is now: What sense can be made of this pattern?

First it seems that cities attract PBEE as well as knowledge services (Aalborg, Hjørring Frederikshavn). Second, small rural municipalities have difficulty in relation to both economies (Thisted, Mariager, Vesthimmerland, Morsø). Third, suburban position in relation to Aalborg has positive implications for knowledge services employment, which tends to be higher than in municipalities at a greater distance from Aalborg (Brønderslev, Rebild, Jammerbugt). Cheap rent and good

PBEE / Knowledge services	High share	Low share
High share	Aalborg Frederikshavn Hjørring Jammerbugt	Brønderslev Rebild
Low share	Læsø	Thisted Mariager Vesthimmerland Morsø

Figure 6.5 Experience economy and knowledge economy in 11 municipalities of North Denmark, share of employment (high vs low), 2008

connections to Aalborg is available in these municipalities. Also the easy access to Aalborg discourages a local development of PBEE because of the easy access to the many attractions of the neighbouring city (Brønderselv, Rebild). Finally, a remote location may represent an opportunity for PBEE due to the qualities of the natural environment, but not for knowledge services (Læsø).

This means that PBEE and knowledge services both share a preference for urban environments. PBEE further exploits natural environments, in particular sandy beaches (Jammerbugt and Læsø), while knowledge services benefit from suburban locations, which are cheaper, but reasonably close to industrial customers in the big city. Based on this analysis PBEE cannot be seen as the way to industrial diversification in rural areas. Positive synergies between experience and knowledge economy are more likely to develop in urbanized municipalities and regions.

Conclusion of empirical analysis

The chapter set out to establish whether the experience economy and creative industries represent a road to development in peripheral regions. First, does the experience economy develop at all in peripheral regions? And if this is the case, what implications does the experience economy have for broader development in terms of demography and industrial diversification? The study of North Denmark has produced some nuanced answers to these questions.

First, PBEE has developed in North Denmark, where it is significant even in a national comparison. A sub-regional analysis shows that PBEE develops in relation to urban areas and traditional tourist areas characterized by unique natural attractions. Creative industries, local culture producers, contribute to their vibrancy. On the other hand suburban municipalities and remote rural municipalities only have small PBEE employment.

Second, a high share of PBEE employment is connected with high and seasonal unemployment. This can be explained by the significant role of tourist services in the region, which are most in demand in the summer time. Municipalities with no significant PBEE have better and less seasonal employment. With this background a development of PBEE can be seen more as a supplementary employment opportunity than as a solution to employment problems.

Third, North Denmark is stagnating demographically in spite of a significant PBEE sector. Aalborg, the capital, of course shows a positive relationship between PBEE and demography. But at the sub-regional level it is possible to detect a *reverse* relationship between PBEE share of employment and demographic development. It is thus not the search for experiences that generate a positive demography, but rather cheap housing in the suburbs and good accessibility to the capital.

Fourth, North Denmark is lagging behind in terms of knowledge services development in spite of a significant PBEE sector. In the urbanized municipalities, a significant PBEE sector is accompanied by a relatively big knowledge services sector, mostly so in Aalborg, the capital. Two suburban municipalities, representing cheap rents and good accessibility, have also developed employment in the knowledge economy, however, without high PBEE employment. Rural, more or less remote, peripheries have no significant development in either of the sectors, knowledge services or PBEE.

In sum PBEE development is spatially unequal, as it is connected to cities and traditional tourist areas, but is not present in remote rural areas. The wider developmental impact of PBEE in terms of demography and industrial diversification in new sectors can be seen only in relation to more urbanized municipalities, and in particular the capital, Aalborg. In most places the PBEE seems to represent a new type of service-based industrial 'lock in' with little prospect of upgrading and diversification in the local economy (Martin and Sunley 2006).

Perspectives and further research

The results of the study shall now be discussed in relation to the theoretical framework above. First the results will be related to the different types of peripheries. North Denmark evidently consists of several sub-regions. The municipalities, which function as suburbs, represent a version of type 1 periphery. They serve among other things as residential areas for the labour force of the centre, but do not, as expected, develop a significant PBEE supply of their own. Instead they access the abundant supply in the centre. The more distant municipalities with famous beaches represent type 2 regions. They have developed significant tourist services and some creative cultural industries. Remote areas in demographic decline with low accessibility, or type 4 areas, include three municipalities. Small

PBEE and knowledge services sectors should be a characteristic of them all, but one of them, a very small beautiful island, has a very large PBEE sector, because there are no other employment alternatives. Type 3 regions, or agricultural regions, is not a separate group among the municipalities in North Denmark, as all the municipalities in question are characterized by big rural areas. One of them hosts a famous theme park, in accordance with the theory.

While the framework may thus help to systematize the rural peripheries, it has one major flaw. It fails to grasp the role of small cities, which in this study has proven to represent the most important geographical framework for PBEE development. It is in the cities that demographic growth and industrial diversification can be found, and in which it can be argued that virtuous circles of development can be identified in connection with PBEE.

The implication of this is that regional and local development strategies need to recognize the crucial role of cities in the new economy. This further suggests that small municipalities rather than competing against each other should find their role in relation to the regional dynamos of development. More research on the role of post-industrial small cities is needed to inform such strategies.

References

Allingham, P. (2009) 'Experiential strategies for the survival of small cities in Europe', *European Planning Studies*, 17(6): 905–23.

Arthur, I.K. (2011) 'En undersøgelse af perspektiverne for oplevelsesøkonomi i fødevaresektoren: En pilotundersøgelse i Thisted Kommune', in A. Lorentzen and S. Smidt-Jensen (eds) *Planlægning i oplevelsessamfundet*, Aarhus: Aarhus Universitetsforlag.

Arzeni, A., Eposti, R. and Sotte, F. (2002) *European Policy Experiences with Rural Development*, Kiel: European Association of Agricultural Economics.

Bradley, A. and Hall, T. (2006) 'The festival phenomenon: Festivals, events and the promotion of small urban areas', in D. Bell and M. Jayne (eds) *Small Cities. Urban Experience Beyond the Metropolis*, Oxon: Routledge, pp. 77–89.

Collis, C., Felton, E. and Graham, P. (2010) 'Beyond the inner city: Real and imagined places in creative place policy and practice', *The Information Society*, 26(2): 104–12.

Cooke, P. and Lazzeretti, L. (2008) 'Creative cities: An introduction', in P. Cooke and L. Lazzeretti (eds) *Creative Cities, Cultural Clusters and Local Economic Development*, Cheltenham: Edward Elgar, pp. 1–22.

Crevoisier, O. and Jeannerat, H. (2009) 'Territorial knowledge dynamics: From the proximity paradigm to the multilocation paradigm', *European Planning Studies*, 17(8): 1223–41.

Flew, T. and Cunningham, S. (2010) 'Creative industries after the first decade of debate', *The Information Society*, 26(2): 113–23.

Florida, R. (2002) *The Creative Class*, New York: Basic Books.

Howkins, J. (2002) *The Creative Economy. How People Make Money from Ideas*, London: Penguin Books.

Lassen, C., Smink, C. and Smidt-Jensen, S. (2009) 'Experience spaces, aeromobilities and environmental impacts', *European Planning Studies*, 17(6): 887–903.

Lorentzen, A. (2009) 'Cities in the experience economy', *European Planning Studies*, 17(2): 829–45.

Lorentzen, A. (2011) 'Sustaining small cities through leisure, culture and experience economy', in A. Lorentzen and B. van Heur (eds) *Cultural Political Economy of Small Cities*, Oxfordshire: Routledge.

Lorentzen, A. and Krogh, R. (2009) *Oplevelsesøkonomi, udvikling og planlægning i nordjyske kommuner*, Aalborg: Institut for Samfundsudvikling og Planlægning, Aalborg Universitet.

Martin, R. and Sunley, P. (2006) 'Path dependence and regional economic evolution', *Journal of Economic Geography*, 6(4): 395–437.

Miles, S. (2006) 'Small city, big ideas: Culture-led regeneration and the consumption of places', in D. Bell and M. Jayne (eds) *Small Cities. Urban Experiences beyond the Metropolis*, Abingdon, Oxon: Routledge, pp. 233–43.

Pine, J.B. II and Gilmore, J.H. (1999) *The Experience Economy. Work is Theatre and Every Business is a Stage*, Boston, MA: Harvard Business School Press.

Pratt, A.C. (2004) 'Mapping the cultural industries', in D. Power and A.J. Scott (eds) *Cultural Industries and the Production of Culture*, Abingdon: Routledge, pp. 19–36.

Region Nordjylland Vækstforum (2007) *Vækst og Balance. Erhvervsudviklingsstrategi for Nordjylland 2007–10*, Aalborg: Region Nordjylland Vækstforum.

Schulze, G. (2005) *Die Erlebnisgesellschaft*, Frankfurt/Main: Campus Verlag.

Scott, A.J. (2006) 'Creative cities: Conceptual issues and policy question', *Journal of Urban Affairs*, 28(1): 1–17.

Scott, A.J. (2010) 'The cultural economy of landscape and prospects for peripheral development in the twenty-first century: The case of the English Lake District', *European Planning Studies*, 18(10): 1567–89.

Smidt-Jensen, S. and Lorentzen, A. (2011) 'Planlægning i oplevelsessamfundet. Indledning', in A. Lorentzen and S. Smidt-Jensen (eds) *Planlægning i oplevelsessamfundet*, Aarhus: Aarhus Universitetsforlag.

Smidt-Jensen, S., Skytt, C.B. and Winther, L. (2009) 'The geography of the experience economy in Denmark: Employment change and location dynamics in attendance-based experience industries', *European Planning Studies*, 17(6): 847–62.

Tofler, A. (1970) *Future Shock*, New York: Bantam Book.

Waitt, G. and Gibson, C. (2009) 'Creative small cities: Rethinking the creative economy in place', *Urban Studies*, 46(5–6): 1223–46.

7 Creative industries and creative city policy in Japan

Masayuki Sasaki

Preface: the era of creative cities

Neoliberal globalization, which has advanced rapidly since the 1980s, mainly in the areas of finance and economics, has plunged the world into a money game, putting global cities in competition with one another and causing an expansion of regional and social disparities in the midst of a dog-eat-dog rivalry for survival. However, it seems that being sunk into the worst worldwide depression in eighty years has presented people with an opportunity for reflection, and they have begun to recognize the need to diverge from market fundamentalism and escape from financially centred globalization (Sasaki 2010a, 2010b).

In the midst of this environment, global society is transitioning away from the existing socio-economic system, and a need has arisen to question and rethink existing theories in the humanities and social sciences domains as well. In the field of urban studies, reconsidering the global, creative and sustainable cities that began to appear around the beginning of the twenty-first century has become an urgent task (Sassen 2010).

The 'creative city' has emerged in the spotlight of twenty-first-century urban theory, taking the place of global cities. In the midst of the transition to knowledge- and information-based economies, and against the historical backdrop of the decline of Fordist cities based on manufacturing, the theory of creative cities has conceptualized 'urban regeneration through culture and creativity' based on a number of successful examples. The concept is rapidly becoming popular around the world, extending into realms related to creative industries, creative economies and the creative class, with many variations. In the US especially, it has given impetus to competition between cities to attract the creative class (Florida 2002).

However, simply attracting the creative class does not create a creative city. To develop creative industries, which are the economic engine of creative cities, as Andy Pratt (2010) indicates, the intrinsic values of the city's cultural capital and resources must be mobilized. Moreover, without the formation of networks and clusters based on the creativity and spontaneity of creators and artists, one cannot hope for sustainable development of the city's economy (Pratt 2010). In addition, urban policy concerns that are solely focused on attracting the creative class can lead to heightened social tensions.

In the beginning, the urban concept of the creative city was born out of the experience of European Cities of Culture and European Capitals of Culture promoted by the EU. It was an experiment in not only urban economic revival but social and cultural revival as well, using culture and creativity to create new industries and jobs and to solve problems of homelessness, the environment, etc. (Landry and Bianchini 1995; Landry 2000).

In light of the many livelihoods threatened by the current worldwide depression, creative city theory is impacting creative solutions to social inclusion issues, such as seeing that homeless people are not socially ostracized, conquering the disparities that have arisen in the knowledge and information economy, and solving the problem of refugees that has been brought about by rapid globalization.

The paradigm shift from global cities to creative cities has become a fact, and the building of a creative city network proposed by the United Nations Educational, Scientific and Cultural Organization (UNESCO), which has been emphasizing preservation of cultural diversity since 2004, has encouraged a move away from competition between cities and toward a network of cities.

Japanese cities have struggled to emerge from a long period of economic stagnation since the economic bubble burst in the 1990s, and this is one reason for the growing interest in creative cities and urban regeneration through arts and culture. Two Japanese cities that have moved in this direction are Kanazawa, where indigenous business leaders and citizens have created the Kanazawa Creative City Council and begun promoting a grass roots movement for a creative city, and Yokohama, where the former mayor adopted 'the artistic creative city strategy' and established a bureau for promoting 'Creative City Yokohama'.

Features of Japanese creative industries

At the turn of the century, the British government under Tony Blair and the former mayor of London announced a policy promoting 'creative industries' – that is, those industries that have their origin in individual creativity, skill and talent and have a potential for wealth and job creation through the generation and exploitation of intellectual property. They include thirteen sectors: advertising, architecture, crafts, design, designer fashion, film, fine arts and antiques, game software, music, performing arts, publishing, software, and television and radio. In 2000, these industries produced more than £120 billion and employed roughly 1,320,000 people in the UK. They ranked second in terms of the percentage of gross domestic product (GDP) and third in employment among industries in London (DCMS 1998, 2001).

Because of a shortage of official statistics about the creative industries in Japan, the author collected data from interviews and documents provided by each industry group, in addition to various government figures. Estimates about the size of Japanese creative industries were made from these data and then compared to the UK data. Table 7.1 shows that the market for the thirteen industries amounts to 38,834 billion yen (US$353 billion), and the industries employ 1,408,780 people. Comparing Japan and the UK based on this data, Japan is higher in absolute terms

Table 7.1 Market size and employment in creative industries, UK versus Japan (exchange rate £1 = ¥185), 2000

	Market size			Employment	
	UK £ billion	*UK billion*	*Japan billion*	*UK*	*Japan*
Publishing	18.5	3,422.5	4,815.0	140,800	169,395
TV and radio	12.1	2,238.5	3,738.6	102,000	135,000
Film	3.6	666.0	1,806.6	44,500	75,288
Music	4.6	851.0	2,142.6	122,000	119,002
Advertising	16.0	2,960.0	10,189.9	92,800	154,382
Game software	1.0	185.0	1,210.0	21,500	29,000
Software	36.4	6,734.0	10,722.8	555,000	555,253
Design	26.7	4,939.5	665.2	76,000	46,861
Designer fashion	0.6	111.0	25.0	11,500	4,500
Fine arts	3.5	647.5	84.5	37,000	23,500
Crafts	0.4	74.0	384.6	23,700	25,900
Performing arts	0.5	92.5	48.8	74,300	58,200
Architecture	1.7	314.5	3,000.0	20,900	12,500
Total	125.6	23,236.0	38,833.6	1,322,000	1,408,780

Source: Dentsu Research Institute (2001–10)

in both employment and market size. However, when differences in the scale of GDP and total employment between the two countries are taken into account, employment in the UK cultural industries is roughly twice than that of Japan, and the market is roughly three times larger. This could be seen as an indication of future growth potential for creative industries in Japan. The only industries in which Japan has a superior market size are the game software and crafts industries. The UK is superior to Japan in the design, performing arts, music, and film industries.

Next, we will examine the economic and industrial features of Japanese creative industries – manga (comics), animation, and game software – that form the basis of 'Japan's cool'.

In 2000, the global market for manga, animation, and game software was 34 trillion yen (US$300 billion), which is nearly as much as the 39 trillion yen (US$355 billion) spent globally on advertising and represents roughly one third of the 100 trillion yen (US$900 billion) global new-media content market. Within Japan in 2005, the markets for manga, animation, and game software were 502 billion yen, 227 billion yen and 314 billion yen respectively, amounting to a total of 1.043 trillion yen (US$9.5 billion), or about 10 per cent of the entire new-media content market of roughly 13.7 trillion yen (US$124 billion). However, when character products (products derived from manga characters) and entertainment facilities are included, the scale of the combined market is between 3 and 5 trillion yen (US$27–45 billion). The manga market, in particular, is showing world-leading growth. In

2005, 135 million copies of manga magazines, such as *Shonen Jump* and *Shonen Magazine*, were printed. There are 183 manga magazines, which, along with manga books, represent 37.4 per cent of all publications sold and 22.9 per cent of total publishing sales. With shops that specialize in original and second-hand copies of manga publications, such as the *Mandarake* shops examined by Douglas McGray in 'Japan's gross national cool' (2002), appearing in places like Los Angeles and Bologna, manga is becoming an internationally competitive industry that represents Japan's cool. The number of manga artists in Japan has grown by 1,000 in the past 10 years, totalling 4,080 artists. However, the number of copies of *Shonen Jump* printed today is half of the 6.5 million copies printed at its peak in 1994, and some commentators have noted that while its popularity abroad is increasing, it seems to be at a crossroads in Japan (Dentsu Research Institute 2001–10).

In the animation sector, the market in Japan has continued to grow from 159 billion yen (US$1.45 billion) in 2000 to 259 billion yen (US$2.35 billion) in 2006. The success of director Hayao Miyazaki's *Spirited Away*, which won the Golden Bear at the 2002 Berlin International Film Festival and an Oscar at the 2003 Academy Awards, has brought international acclaim to animation as art. Today, 60 per cent of all of the animated programmes shown worldwide are produced in Japan; in Europe, this figure is 80 per cent or more. In terms of market scale, 259 billion yen is a record high. Even as Japanese films have generally declined under pressure from Hollywood productions, animated films such as Miyazaki's are succeeding in their use of a mixed-media promotional strategy that includes publishers, broadcasters and advertising agencies, which has contributed greatly to box office receipts. In addition, the spread of digital technology has given rise to a boom in DVD remakes of classic animated films.

In the game software industry, 487 billion games were shipped from Japanese companies in 2005; 48 per cent were sold in Japan and the rest were sold abroad. Exports of Japanese games amounted to 232.7 billion yen (US$2.1 billion), while imports were just 3 billion yen, creating an enormous industry export surplus. With the appearance of hit games such as 'Super Mario', 'Pocket Monsters', 'Dragon Quest' and 'Final Fantasy' and the development and spread of specialized game consoles such as the PlayStation2 and Nintendo DS, Japanese game hardware and software have joined forces to conquer the world market.

In the Japanese music industry, known around the world as J-Pop, music album production, mostly in the form of CDs, amounted to 367.2 billion yen (US$3.33 billion) in 2005. The figure shows a declining trend that has continued since the peaks of 607.5 billion yen (US$4.7 billion) in 1998 and 588.1 billion yen (US$4.5 billion) in 1997. However, more than anything, this is a reflection of the music industry as a whole. In Japan, the total music market amounted to approximately 1.6 trillion yen (US$14.5 billion), which includes approximately 347.7 billion yen (US$3.16 billion) for music videos and DVDs, 113.5 billion yen (US$1.03 billion) for use of copyrights, 12.2 billion yen (US$110 million) for Internet and mobile downloads, and 746.6 billion yen (US$6.79 billion) for karaoke machines. At the same time, imports of music software amounted to 21 billion yen (US$190 million), while exports were only 2.2 billion yen (US$20 million).

A notable feature of J-Pop industries is that, until recently, they have not sought government assistance under industrial or cultural assistance programmes but have developed through their own efforts in the private market. Until recently, the aim of cultural programmes has been largely to protect cultural assets and support traditional arts and high culture. In industrial programmes, even support for information and communications technology (ICT) industries has tended to favour the hardware sectors, and there has been almost no support for cultivating creators of ICT content.

With this lack of support for creative industries, many talented creators have gathered in the manga industry because the cost of training is relatively low, making it easy to enter the field. For example, Masuzo Furukawa, the president of Mandarake, which publishes a magazine that has been a point of entry for aspiring young manga artists, explained the conventional wisdom in the field in an interview with the author: 'All you need to become a manga artist is a pencil and paper, so any young person with talent could easily enter the field.'

The general structure of J-Pop industries is characterized by the combination of groups or venture companies consisting of highly creative creators of original content and their support staff, together with producers that procure funding and edit the original material. Producers are generally part of the large-scale information culture or mass media industries and direct circulation, distribution, advertising and promotion. For example, in the animation industry, the creator, who is the animation director, and the director, who is his or her manager, generally work on joint projects with producers from television or film companies. Of the 437 animation production companies in Japan, less than 50 act as general contractors for the entire production process. The others are all small subcontractors.

Therefore, when an animated television programme is made, the 50 million yen paid by the sponsor is reduced to about 12 million yen by payments to the advertising agents and broadcasting companies before it reaches the general contractor. Then, because it is common practice to subcontract some work, such as the artwork, photography and audio production, and demand is high to produce low-cost, high-ratings content, creators other than famous animation directors face intense competition. This has created an environment that fails to encourage improvement in quality across the industry as a whole. In addition, in recent years, this subcontracting structure has spread to South Korea, hollowing out the Japanese content creation industry.

This situation has caused and encouraged the concentration of the animation industry in Tokyo. Talented young people are drawn to Tokyo to obtain work from the skilled producers at the large publishing and mass media companies concentrated in the capital. Moreover, talented producers from other large cities, such as Osaka, are moving to Tokyo of their own accord. Consequently, 72 per cent of all animation employees are concentrated in cities in the Tokyo metropolitan area, such as Mitaka and Kokubunji, which are located in the western suburbs of Tokyo (Tokyo Metropolitan Government 2010).

The common foundation for the significant popularity of J-Pop culture in places such as South Korea, Taiwan, Hong Kong and Singapore is the spread of an

American lifestyle as a result of globalization and economic development in these countries. This has led to the creation of equivalent urban spaces in cities such as Tokyo, Seoul, Singapore and Taipei. The phenomenon in which the characters and backgrounds in manga and other animation are indicative of no particular nation and in which images from outside Japan are used with success has been attributed to cultural neutrality or blankness. However, it has been none other than today's Tokyo that has given rise to J-Pop culture, which expresses a different sort of cool from the old Japanese images of Mt. Fuji and geishas.

As Douglas McGray (2002) has noted, J-Pop culture has already formed a large market centred in East Asia. Recently, South Korean pop culture has also spread to countries such as Japan and Taiwan, where it is being very well received. Hit television dramas such as *Winter Sonata* and films and television dramas in the 'Korean wave' are now more popular than Japanese offerings, and Korean online games now make up 30.4 per cent of the world market.

This phenomenon of mutual penetration of East Asian cultures is not only the result of the creative industries in one country selling their output to the Asian market. For example, J-Pop stars such as Tetsuya Komuro have become popular in the Asian market due to the sales efforts of Hong Kong's *Star TV*. Likewise, the Japanese television drama *Oshin* achieved broad popularity due to the work of an Australian production company. Thus, the mutual-penetration phenomenon has arisen in the context of global media strategies; for this reason, the 'neutrality' of J-Pop offerings as cultural products has been convenient.

The rapid growth in South Korea's culture industries and the new cultural exchanges between Japan and South Korea were primarily due to (a) policies implemented by the former South Korean President Kim Dae Jung to promote South Korean culture industries and open South Korea to the popular culture of Japan; and (b) the success of the joint hosting of the soccer world cup. The development of creative industries in Asia depends on each country's government and people having a mutual respect for the cultures of other countries, as well as the continuation of friendly relations.

However, the concentration of culture in the capitals and large cities is a problem that needs to be corrected throughout Asia. If the growth of creative industries promotes and solidifies their concentration in cities such as Tokyo, Seoul and Shanghai, it could lead to uniformity and reduced diversity in cultural output and reduced competitiveness in the creative industries in the long term. Therefore, there is a need for 'cultural decentralization' policies that expand the cultural programmes in provincial areas and promote creative industries in small and medium-size provincial cities. Based on such policies, it is also important to encourage the growth of diverse creative cities in each region and develop networks between them.

Creative city challenges in Japan: culture-based production system

Based on discussions with Landry and Florida, in this chapter 'creative cities' are defined as cities that cultivate new trends in arts and culture and promote innovative

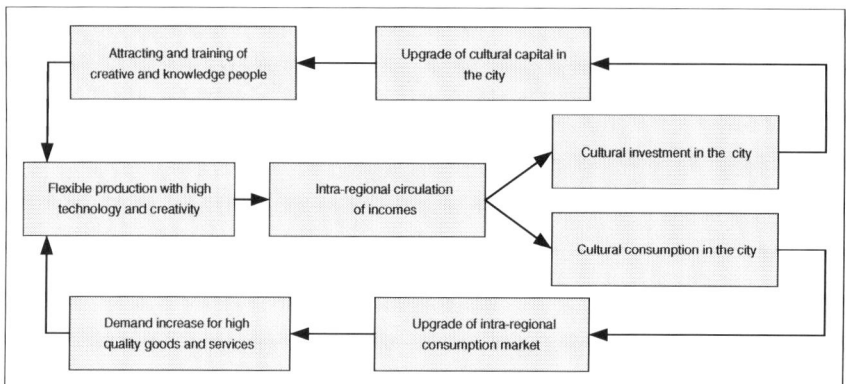

Figure 7.1 Cultural mode of production model

Source: Our elaboration

and creative industries through the energetic creative activities of artists, creators and ordinary citizens; contain many diverse creative and innovative milieux; and have a regional, grass roots ability to find solutions to global environmental problems such as global warming (Sasaki 2001).

Based on empirical analyses of some cities, the author defined a 'cultural mode of production model' (see Figure 7.1) as a well-balanced system of cultural production and consumption that takes advantage of accumulated cultural capital to produce products and services that are high in economic and cultural value in a system where consumption stimulates production (Sasaki 2003, 2007).

This definition encompasses the elements of the creative city detailed below. First, not only should artists, scientists, workers and craftsmen involve themselves with creative work, but all citizens should evolve (or expand) their free creative activity. The result is increased satisfaction with their lives. To make this a reality, it is necessary to encourage the production of useful and culturally valuable goods and services and to improve the work environment in factories and offices. Second, the ordinary lives of citizens should be artistic. Thus, it is necessary to ensure that citizens have sufficient income and free time to be well off. In addition, high-quality consumer goods must be available at reasonable prices, and people should be able to appreciate arts and culture, such as the performing arts, at a low price. Third, universities, technical schools, research institutes, theatres, libraries and cultural institutions that support the creative activity of science and the arts in a city have to function as the creative support infrastructure. Fourth, environmental policy is crucial because it preserves a city's historical heritage and environment and improves amenities. Consequently, citizens are able to enhance their creativity and sensitivity. Fifth, a city has to have a well-balanced economic base that supports a sustainable and creative region. Finally, in terms of public administration, a creative city is composed of a creative, integrated urban policy; a cultural policy that is unified with its industrial policy; and an environmental policy that is managed democratically using public finances.

Table 7.2 Characteristics of Kanazawa and Yokohama

	Kanazawa (UNESCO Creative City)	Yokohama
Population	450,000 (Human-scale city)	3,600,000 (Modern, large city)
Economic aspects	Small and medium-sized companies, Traditional arts and crafts	Large companies, Port, car and high-tech industries
Cultural aspects	Traditional and contemporary art	Contemporary art, art NPOs
Cultural budget	4,000 yen/capita	2,500 yen/capita
Creative city initiatives	Business circle, citizen group, mayor's office	Mayor's office, art NPOs

Source: Our elaboration
Note: NPO – non-profit organization

In the next sections, the chapter provides specific advice for developing urban policies for the cities of Kanazawa and Yokohama (see Table 7.2).

Kanazawa as a UNESCO Creative City

In terms of population, surroundings and defining characteristics, the city of Kanazawa has much in common with Bologna, Italy, a creative and sustainable city. Kanazawa is a human-scale city of 450,000 people. It is surrounded by mountains, which are the source of two rivers that run through the city. Kanazawa has also preserved its traditional cityscape and arts and crafts. As a mid-size city, Kanazawa has maintained an independent economic base while also maintaining a healthy balance in terms of development and cultural and environmental preservation. Kanazawa established the Kanazawa Arts and Crafts University soon after World War II. In addition to nurturing traditional arts and crafts, the city has also produced leaders in industrial design, and local talents have become innovators in the traditional crafts. Kanazawa has also become a national leader in historic preservation, as evidenced by the meticulous preservation of the Tokugawa-era castle town district.

In addition to preserving its historical landscape and traditional arts and crafts, Kanazawa has also produced leading orchestra conductors and chamber music ensembles. Other civic achievements in the area of cultural creativity include the nurturing of local artists through the establishment of the citizens' art village and the twenty-first century contemporary art museum.

As the trend toward globalization quickly intensified in the latter half of the 1980s, the textile industry that had sustained Kanazawa's high growth rates over the years began to decline. In September 1996, the Kanazawa Citizens' Art Village opened in a vacated spinning factory and adjacent warehouses. The mayor of Kanazawa opened the 24-hour facility in response to citizen requests for a public arts facility that they could use in the evening after they had finished their daytime responsibilities. The facility comprises drama, music, 'eco-life'

Figure 7.2 Kanazawa Twenty-First Century Art Museum (outside view)

and art studios that occupy four separate blocks of the old spinning compound. Two directors that are elected by the citizens oversee the management of each studio. The active use and independent management of the facility is a remarkable example of a participatory citizens' cultural institution in contemporary Japan. Thus, through the active participation of the citizenry, abandoned industrial facilities were used to construct a new cultural infrastructure, a new place for cultural creativity.

Another example of re-imagining existing facilities and utilizing them in creative ways in Kanazawa is the Twenty-First Century Art Museum (Figures 7.2 and 7.3), which opened in October 2004. The art museum is in an area of the central city that many feared would lose its vitality when the prefectural offices that used to be there moved to the suburbs. In addition to collecting and exhibiting contemporary art from around the world, the new museum also solicits and features locally produced traditional arts and crafts. Along with this fusion of the global and the local with the modern and the traditional, the new museum pursued a policy of stimulating local interest and talent in the arts. To this end, the first museum director, Mino Yutaka, solicited local schools and the general citizenry to participate in educational tours he dubbed 'museum cruises'. In the first year, the museum attracted around 1.5 million visitors – three times the population of the city. Furthermore, the revenue generated from the tours exceeded 10 billion yen. Since 2008, the museum has also sponsored open-air exhibits, which livened up a

Figure 7.3 Kanazawa Twenty-First Century Art Museum (inside view)

relatively quiet part of town and allowed people to view the work of local artists and studios that produce both contemporary and traditional works. Such policies are a shining example of creatively fusing the traditional and modern through culture as part of urban regeneration.

With the museum at the centre of industrial promotion efforts in the areas of fashion and digital design, the city of Kanazawa has been promoting development in the creative industries. Thus, one can see how the promotion of arts and culture has led to the development of new local industries in contemporary Japan. As Figure 7.4 shows, the city of Kanazawa is an excellent example of how the accumulated creativity in a city with a high level of cultural capital can be used to promote economic development. With a history as a centre of craft production in the Edo era, Kanazawa clearly illustrates the historical stages of economic development from craft production to Fordism (mass production) and, finally, to a new era of culture-based production in the contemporary creative cultural industries.

The creative city strategies of Kanazawa also demonstrate the importance of citizen and government collaboration in forums such as the Creative Cities Council of Kanazawa, which brought together experts from various fields and people from inside and outside the government to deliberate on and decide matters of public policy. Such a forum and mode of deliberation and decision making is clearly congruous with the ideal of urban creativity. The experiences of Kanazawa

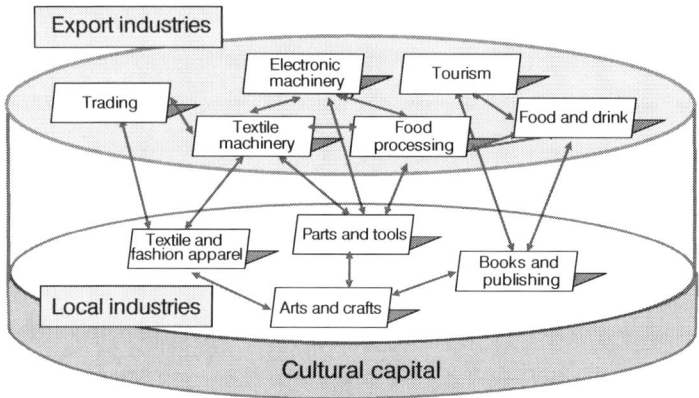

Figure 7.4 Culture and economy of Kanazawa City

described above are befitting of an UNESCO Creative City in the Crafts and Folk Art category. In October 2008, the city applied to UNESCO for recognition and was registered in June 2009.

In 2009, facing the challenges posed by the current global financial crisis, the city of Kanazawa implemented the Monozukuri (craftsmanship or art of manufacturing) Ordinance for the protection and promotion of traditional arts and crafts and other new industries. The former mayor of Kanazawa described the aims of the ordinance as follows:

> I think that the present society has lost sight of the meaningfulness of work and the basic way of life. In such an age, we should re-evaluate and cherish the spirit of Monozukuri, which leads to the creation of values. Without such efforts, we might lose our solid foundation of societies. Fortunately, the city of Kanazawa has a broad base of the milieu of craftsmanship handed down from the Edo period. The arts of Kanazawa's traditional craftworks include, among other things, ceramic ware, Yuzen dyeing, inlaying and gold leafing. We aim to protect and nurture the traditional local industries while working to introduce new technologies and innovative ideas. We also applied to UNESCO's Creative Cities Network in the Crafts and Folk Art category. The ordinance is intended to recognize anew the importance of Monozukuri and the pride in Monozukuri so that the region as a whole can support Monozukuri industries in order to realize the lively city, Kanazawa. The ordinance applies to the fields of agriculture and forestry as well. Therefore, we are planning to develop an authorization system for Kanazawa-brand agricultural products and to open the Kanazawa Forestry Academy. We are also aspiring to build cooperation between businesses and universities through the opening of institutes for research and promotion of Kaga-yuzen silk dyeing and Kanazawa gold leaf craftwork. I assume that diversified Monozukuri will pave the way for diversified urban development.
>
> (Interview with the former mayor of Kanazawa, October 2010)

As this section describes, in Kanazawa, ongoing mayor-led administrative and private efforts – the 'two wheels of one cart' – are working together to turn Kanazawa into a creative city.

The 'Creative City Yokohama' experiment

Yokohama, a 150-year old port city that has become one of Japan's largest urban centres, stands in stark contrast to the image of Kanazawa as an Edo-era castle town with a long and rich history. At the height of the economic bubble, the city of Yokohama pursued a large-scale waterfront development project to create a new central business district with the aim of shedding its image as a city of heavy industry. However, with the collapse of the economic bubble and the subsequent construction boom in central Tokyo, Yokohama suffered a double blow. Since the beginning of 2004, however, Yokohama has embraced a new urban vision and embarked on a project to reinvent itself as a creative city of art and culture.

The contents of this new urban vision are fourfold: (a) to construct a creative environment where artistic and creative individuals would want to live; (b) to build a creative industrial cluster to spark economic activity; (c) to utilize the city's natural assets to these ends; and (d) to utilize citizen initiatives to achieve the vision. By 2008, the city aimed to attract close to 2,000 artists and nearly 15,000 workers to its creative industrial cluster.

In April 2004, former mayor Nakada opened a special 'Creative City Yokohama' office. At the centre of the new office's activities has been the establishment of several 'creative core districts' in the general vicinity of the port. These creative districts utilize numerous historic buildings, such as old bank buildings, warehouses and vacant offices, to house new creative spaces for citizen artists and other creative individuals. The Bank ART 1929 project (Figure 7.5) was the start of this ambitious undertaking. The project was under the guidance of two non-profit organizations (NPOs), which were selected via a competitive process and are in charge of organizing an array of exhibits, performances, workshops, symposiums and various other events that have attracted participants from Tokyo and Yokohama.

Since their inception, the creative corridors have expanded to incorporate numerous vacant buildings and warehouses in the vicinity. As of March 2007, the economic ripple effect of the creative corridors on the local economy was estimated to be around 12 billion yen (US$100 million). In July 2007, an arts commission in Yokohama comprising public and private individuals and institutions was established to support and attract artists and other creative individuals to the region.

The experimental Kogane Cho Bazaar is a good example of the numerous activities that are underway in Yokohama. The event was held in an area that had become filled with gangs and prostitutes after the chaotic period that immediately followed the war. Though the area developed into a shopping district with over 250 shops, in recent years, many of the shops had closed down, and the area was in decline. Many young students and artists collaborated with local businesses

Figure 7.5 The Bank ART 1929 project in Yokohama

to carry out the bazaar's projects. The diversity on display during the planning sessions for the event was a clear illustration of how cultural projects can lead to social inclusion. Indeed, the planning events featured the participation of local residents, university students, artists and all manner of specialists to create an art event to enliven an area blighted by a plethora of vacant shops.

Finally, to mark the 150th anniversary of the opening of the port of Yokohama, an international creative cities conference aimed at building a creative cities network in Asia took place in 2009.

The case of Yokohama is remarkable in the sense that the policy aim of utilizing the creativity inherent in art and culture for the purpose of urban regeneration also led to a restructuring of the politics related to cultural policy, industrial policy and community development. In other words, the new organizations that emerged to revitalize Yokohama as a city of art and culture transcended the bureaucratic sectionalism that typically plagues policy formation and administration in creative fields while also constructively engaging NPOs and citizens in the formation and administration of policy. Throughout Japan, urban policies and projects based on art and culture have given rise to socially inclusive politics.

The most significant thing about the case of Yokohama is the reorganization of previously separate administrative units in charge of cultural, industrial and urban policies to create two new core organizations, the Artistic and Cultural City Creation Division and the Creative City Promotion Section, to promote the use of artistic and cultural creativity in urban revitalization. If this idea is effectively applied, Yokohama will take the lead in the movement to develop creative cities in Japan. Naturally, some conflict is to be expected between previously vertically organized administrative units, but the best way to restore creativity in the city is to make the organization more creative, which in turn will bring out more creativity in individuals. Creative reform of the 'culture of bureaucratic organization' will bring Yokohama closer to its goal of becoming a creative city.

In Kanazawa, the business sector and individual citizens took the lead in starting the Kanazawa Creative City Council, making proposals that stimulated the city government to take steps toward making Kanazawa a creative city. Meanwhile in Yokohama, setbacks in the waterfront urban development project, 'Minato Mirai', led the former mayor to criticize the failure of the project and propose a new strategy for the city. Thus, efforts to develop creative cities vary based on the historical background of the city.

Briefly, theoretically Yokohama is a case in which a city voluntarily chose the 'cognitive–cultural' system of production (Scott 2008) after the collapse of the Fordist and neoliberal paradigms. On the other hand, Kanazawa has experienced a more continuous and smooth – although not unplanned – evolution of historical local traditions.

Conclusion: developing creative cities through networking

The trend of decentralization in creative industries began with the creative city policies in Kanazawa and Yokohama. Following these successful examples, other cities, including Sapporo, Sendai, Nagoya, Kobe and Fukuoka, have begun a push to become creative cities. The discussion that follows outlines the steps the author considers necessary to achieve this goal.

First, it is necessary to conduct an intensive analysis of the embedded culture of the city, increase the shared awareness of fusing contemporary arts with traditional culture, clarify the need to become a creative city, and elaborate a creative city concept for the future with an understanding of the historical context of the city.

Second, in developing concepts, artistic and cultural creativity must be recognized as factors that impact many other areas, including industry, employment, social systems, education, medical care and the environment. In order to link cultural policy to industrial policy, urban planning and environmental policy, vertical administrative structures must be made horizontal, ordinary bureaucratic thinking must be eliminated and organizational culture must change.

Third, art and culture must be recognized as central social infrastructures in the knowledge and information society, and systematic planning must be used to bring out the creativity of the city's people. Specifically, diverse creative milieu and space for industrial and cultural creation must be established in the city, and creative producers must be fostered to take charge of this task.

Fourth, creative policy cannot be effectively promoted if it is limited to the city government. It is essential to obtain the cooperation of a broad selection of citizens, including business leaders and NPOs, perhaps in the form of a creative city promotion council. The most important thing for the promotion of creative cities is the establishment of research and educational programmes for developing the necessary human resources.

In order to realize and develop creative cities, not only do we need the global-level inter-city partnerships promoted by UNESCO, but we also need to learn from partnerships seen at the Asian and national levels. Collaboration among the public, private and civic sectors within the cities is also essential. The author appeals for the formation of a multi-layered and multifaceted partnership and encourages each city to provide diversified platforms toward this end.

References

DCMS – Department for Culture, Media and Sport (1998) *Creative Industries Mapping Document*, London: DCMS.

DCMS (2001) *Creative Industries Mapping Document*, London: DCMS.

Dentsu Research Institute (2001–10) *White Paper of Information Media Business*, Tokyo: Dentsu Research Institute.

Florida, R. (2002) *The Rise of the Creative Class*, New York: Basic Books.

Landry, C. (2000) *The Creative City: A Toolkit for Urban Innovators*, London: Comedia.

Landry, C. and Bianchini, F. (1995) *The Creative City*, London: Comedia.

McGray, D. (2002) 'Japan's gross national cool', *Foreign Policy*, 130 (June–July): 44–54.

Pratt, A.C. (2010) 'Creative cities: Tensions within and between social, cultural and economic development: A critical reading of the UK experience', *City, Culture and Society*, 1(1): 13–20.

Sasaki, M. (2001) *The Challenges for Creative Cities*, in Japanese; translated into Korean 2004, Tokyo: Keiso Shobo.

Sasaki, M. (2003) 'Kanazawa: A creative and sustainable city', *Policy Science* (Ritsumeikan University), 10(2).

Sasaki, M. (2007) 'Towards an urban cultural mode of production: A case study of Kanazawa, Japan', in M. Nadarajah and A.T. Yamamoto (eds) *Urban Crisis: Culture and the Sustainability of Cities*, Tokyo: United Nations University Press, pp. 156–74.

Sasaki, M. (2010a) 'City, culture and society (CCS): Opening up new horizon of urban studies', *City, Culture and Society*, 1(1): 1–2.

Sasaki, M. (2010b) 'Urban regeneration through cultural creativity and social inclusion', *Cities*, 27(1001): S3–S9.

Sassen, S. (2010) 'The city: Its return as a lens for social theory', *City, Culture and Society*, 1(1): 3–11.

Scott, A.J. (2008) *Social Economy of the Metropolis*, Oxford: Oxford University Press.

Tokyo Metropolitan Government (2010) *Report on the Situation and Problem of Creative Industries*, Tokyo.

Part II

Innovation, creative space and symbolic value

8   Complexity geography and the rise of the green creative city

Philip Cooke

Introduction

Today, promotion of creative industries as catalysts of economic growth has been common but not equally successful everywhere. For years London's Millennium Dome seemed a great white elephant until rescued by Las Vegas entertainment investment. Sheffield's Rock Music Museum (National Centre for Popular Music) is just one of the many casualties of misplaced optimism towards the power of symbolic infrastructure. Ironically, independent movie mogul Harvey Weinstein saved the former aspiration when he opened the 'British Music Experience' in the former facility, now renamed as the O2Arena in 2009 (Mugan 2009). Indeed, it seems the creative industry contribution to economic development is hard to plan successfully. Nevertheless, the UK as one of the countries pioneering the 'creative city' (Landry and Bianchini 1995) unquestionably takes the concept of creative industries contributing to economic welfare completely seriously, establishing a Ministry of State (Department for Culture, Media and Sport – DCMS) to oversee the broad field and give definition to the platform. In this case the notion of 'platform' captures the diversity and sometimes 'related variety' (Frenken *et al.* 2007) of the many activities that make up the category of 'creative industries'. These are more than a vertical sector or cluster; rather they comprise networks of firms and organizations that cross-pollinate the distinctive creative elements that coalesce therein. As such and in their organically shifting forms they are difficult to pin down and predict behaviourally or locationally.

The conceptual dimension of this chapter considers the creative industries to be amenable to regional innovation systems (RISs) analysis (Cooke and Schwartz 2008) especially in terms of their 'related variety' spillovers across the wider economy. Because its empirical focus is TV, film and digital media it is more framed within the RIS paradigm, but where relevant reference is also made to the related variety literature (Hoekman, Frenken and van Oort 2009). However, the key future challenge for creative industry thinking is something that has scarcely entered the radar of its leading exponents and practitioners. This concerns the fusing or welding of a somewhat exclusive not to say *effete*, mainly urban, post-modern aesthetic concern with a more robust and socially inclusive climate change concern that would presage 'green creativity' and green creative industry in both urban and rural settings. Indeed, the economic impact of future creative industries can only be fully realized if they move away from a present, possibly debilitating specialization formed in the 'experience economy' cul-de-sac of the recently ended long boom and embrace the greater variety implied in the imperatives of creative and eco-diversity in the future economy. In thinking how this might be achieved, attention will be devoted to certain important multi-level governance failures, notably by the EU in its 'Europe 2020' economic recovery strategy. Contrarily, this spotlights eco-innovation but ignores creative industry for reasons discussed elsewhere as an abiding *technophilia* among the higher functionary levels of the EU (Cooke and De Propris 2012, forthcoming).

So, no guidance from the large and slow level of complexity as the 'resilience' perspective on dynamic systems would put it (Folke 2006). What about the middle level of multi-level system dynamics? National governments generally set more or less adequate regulatory frameworks albeit typically according to their vertical governance 'silos'. This extends to regional governments in highly devolved settings for the same reasons. Moreover, if there are, as in a devolved setting like Wales in the UK, sensitivities to sustainability pervading all policy areas, it is the control dimension of planning (i.e. withholding inappropriate building permissions) that connects rather than the aesthetic. Nevertheless, more and more, green construction must in fact engage with building aesthetics, if not develop an engaging green aesthetics of its own. Hence, micro-control but also positive micro-management of new green aesthetics is most obviously the province of the smallest, fastest most innovative scale of the multi-level governance system, the city and its constituent firms and citizens. What such a green aesthetics would look like is envisaged from some real-time practices already implemented in some Nordic cities. Accordingly, the chapter proceeds as follows. The conceptual framework will be summarized and the current literature on innovation in creative industries and eco-innovation more broadly will be reviewed. This will be followed by the setting of the succeeding discussion in the RIS and related variety frameworks. Initial findings on the evolution of policy and practice exemplar, which is Creative City Cardiff's (CCC) TV, film and digital media platform, will be presented. Then the evidence from elsewhere (notably Nordics) on urban eco-innovation as currently practised will be discussed. In conclusion, the implications arising for creating *imagined* policy methodologies for the sustainable city will be explored.

Systems of innovation: the complexity perspective

Innovation systems thinking at the national level is too blunt an instrument to integrate creative and eco-innovation thinking. If it remains too wedded to a 'productivist' narrative the problem may arise at the regional level. But the latter remains the correct level for imagining how these two distant 'partners' are to be integrated. A clarification comes from complexity science, where innovation thinking is unencumbered by neo-Schumpeterian baggage although it nevertheless remains compatible with this perspective. In the complexity sciences

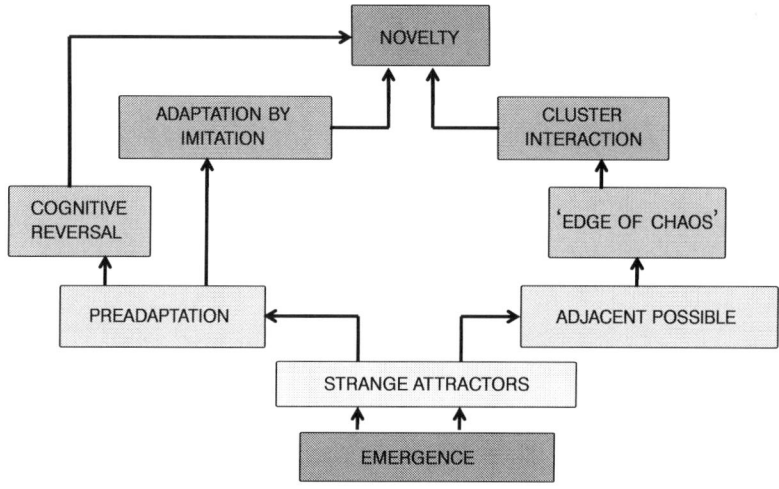

Figure 8.1 The nature of emergence of innovation: a complexity perspective

such 'controllers' as system planners or designers are excluded in favour of complex adaptive system effects. One of these of particular interest for students of regional development is the phenomenon of 'strange attractors'. Innovation occurs mainly horizontally as regional path dependence leads to novelty, possibly because of an external destabilization (resilience effect) or simply because of an endogenous system topology. The latter allows for path interdependence of the kind discussed by Martin and Sunley (2010) in what is termed 'revealed related variety', when that which could never have been predicted occurs and results in innovation or novelty of some kind. It is crucial to underline this non-physics-like process that is non-reductionist and non-predictable because human systems are concerned with life and evolutionary biology teaches that life, its mutations and speciations cannot be predicted *ex ante*, only understood *ex post*. Such processes are in Kauffman's (2008) terms, essentially 'lawless'. In Figure 8.1 a scheme is elaborated of the complex 'emergence' into innovation through 'preadaptation' and the 'adjacent possible' in relation to 'attractors' and especially 'strange attractors' from Kauffman (2008).

What occurs in Figure 8.1 is that Martin and Sunley's path interdependence evolves on the plane of a complex adaptive system. In analogue form, this is a regional economy that is invested with a topology. The topological routeways (path dependencies) favour certain deviations and disfavour others. At a given point they meet, as we shall see the meeting of socio-technical systems (STS) from another co-evolutionary multi-level perspective (MLP; Geels 2007), because they are not only natural attractors but also, particularly, when they are 'strange attractors'. Strange attractors display 'revealed relatedness' rather than obvious relatedness. While both can facilitate innovation, that caused by 'strange attractors' has the possibility of being the most radical kind. This is because an adjacent possible that is utterly unknown is being explored. Contrariwise in

Figure 8.1 the 'preadaptation' route is either moderately surprising because it involves a 'cognitive reversal' of an existing innovation – Kauffman's favourite metaphor of the tractor chassis, that always broke due to the weight of the engine, being replaced by the engine itself being bolted to the back axle and drive-train. Alternatively 'preadaptation' is incremental innovation and quite close to 'imitation' because it takes an innovation from one field and applies it to another. Innovation agencies sometimes facilitate this by mounting innovation 'fashion shows' where, for instance, a 'smart textile' in automotive seats can be a solution to the quest for stay-clean medical uniforms in hospitals. The harder, more rewarding innovation route comes where strange attractors merge at what complexity theorists call 'the edge of chaos' which is both stable and unstable with much interaction, communication and 'buzz' going on between, for example, clusters or more precisely innovation-spotting members of two or more clusters.

Given that coherent patterns of order emerge from the self-organization of interacting agents according to local rules (e.g. a cluster) without a global controller or designer, path dependence itself constitutes an *attractor* of path-dependent interaction. This means that strong path dependence on a particular industry attracts agents to it and repels or ignores agents that have no cause for interaction with it. Such attractors take a number of 'dynamical' (or dynamic) forms dependent upon such parameters as their energy-flow, their connection density or 'connectivity' in the resilience sense of governance links, and the diversity or variety of agents (innovative potential, in resilience terms). Some attractors are orderly, being set at a stable or equilibrium point. This means they are in a high degree of isolation from one another, as might be the case in a regional economy with a high degree of low related variety clusters (including industry forms, such as oligopolies, that are not clusters in the economic geographical sense), thus they have no impulse to interact. When parameters 'go critical', as with a surge or collapse of energy ('shock'), a tension arises between stability and instability. These are attractors that are stable and unstable at the same time or, in complexity terms, 'on the edge of chaos', meaning capable of change in some significant way. Chaos theory talks of 'strange' or fractal attractors in this context. This is the point where agents interact and adapt in ways that may result in mutation or 'speciation' in the presence of diversity or variety from which novel attractors can occur. This cannot be predicted in a physics-like way. Thus attractors are forms of path dependencies and strange attractors are path interdependencies far from equilibrium agents or clusters that cannot be predicted. New attractors thus emerge from this self-organizing process themselves as emergence where stability and instability intersect. Thus 'smartphones' emerge from convergence of mobile telephony and Internet computing with characteristics like 'apps' and 'crowdsourcing' that cannot be predicted. Disruptions generate variety and the spontaneous emergence of novelty depends on variety (Allen 1998).

In Kauffman (1995) his super-computer simulations provide an analogy for regional development and innovation. First he reiterates that the number of connections between agents in a complex system determines the dynamics of the system. When these numbers are small, the system displays stability and high path dependence. This is because with a small number of connections constraints or divergences between paths are few. However, when connectivity is very high, system dynamics are highly unstable because the conflicting constraints imposed on each other by agents are numerous. Moreover, at a state with neither too few nor too many connections the dynamic of at the 'edge of chaos' arises. This is neither stable enough to obstruct potential for innovation and change nor so unstable as to destroy path dependence. The dynamic of 'living systems' is to be 'changeable' according to Kauffman.

System evolution is influenced by 'clusters' with high internal but low external links to other clusters. Weak ties clustering across the system stabilizes it. However, clustering towards the 'edge of chaos' with strengthening cluster interactions produces innovation, change and novelty. System self-organization thus gives emergence first to new clusters and, second, their interconnection in 'platforms'. This occurs first, possibly in 'shadow themes' between clusters or informal interactions that, if successful, may become formal interconnections. This produces regional organization in terms of webs and networks that are superior to hierarchies for finding innovation (see also Arthur 2009). Closely linked clusters establish power differences (platforms) within and between clusters, constraining others, but in a less destabilizing way than if there were very close interactions between all clusters. Only interaction between diverse entities gives rise to potential transitions associated with path interdependence.

The 'adjacent possible' refers in effect to the fulcrum of evolution, connecting the restless character of economic or ecological life to progress beyond the current *status quo ante*. It is a cumulative capacity in which the more variety the system displays, 'the easier is the creation of still further novelty' (Kauffman 2008: 151). However, because the further out from the present human capability for prediction dramatically decays, such novel moves are generally fairly short-range but adjacent. Adjacency means 'close at hand' but it implies no particular directionality. Thus it can be straightforward, or an angle forwards, sideways or, interestingly, backwards. This captures the Schumpeterian notion of innovation being intimately bound up with new combinations of knowledge, including recombinations of old knowledge as well as of combinations of new and old and even, conceivably, new and new knowledge.

In a recent study, Sunley *et al.* (2008) focusing upon 'soft' innovation dynamics specifically in the design industry in the UK, found that design innovation requires the combination of a wide range or platform of knowledge. Design emerges from the interaction between different network nodes that synthesize and recombine knowledge to produce emergent effects and new designs. They further found that relations with clients, as well as firms' routines and competences, are highly important to design innovation compared to inter-firm cooperation or the local cultural environment. These system effects in 'soft innovation' make it amenable to normal systems of innovation analysis. In this, key roles are played, first, by the 'platform' of potentially, but not always realized, interlocking 'related variety' nodes of commercial, market-facing business activity, and the intertwining institutional knowledge-flows that may be sourced in many ways by firms. Training of skilled staff, consulting of design archives or pattern libraries, 'sampling' retro tunes, consulting film libraries and photographic archives all lead to soft innovation that saturates contemporary culture.

Eco-innovation shares much of this retro-design thinking with the creative industries. We can easily see this in three typical elements in the 'package' of eco-innovations that have characterized sustainable city strategies. The first is the policy rejection of 'productivist' agriculture and industrialized food production and procurement for cuisine under public management. Copenhagen's 'Dogma' programme achieved complete replacement of 'conventional' by organic food from local farms in all public canteens by 2009. This echoes the move, begun in modern times in culinary transition regions like Northern California (Alice Waters and 'Chez Panisse'), Wales (home of the first organic gastro-pub 'The Walnut Tree' in 1969) and Southern Sweden (Värmland and Region Skåne). Such restaurants led to the privileging of local, fresh, seasonal, preferably organically farmed cuisine over that habitually provided by an industrial agriculture that saturated its produce in chemical fertilizers, pesticides, herbicides and fungicides, and supermarkets that procured globally products that lost freshness, taste and nutritional value in the process. Farmers and franchisees who chose the 'productivist' route became debt-slaves to an unholy alliance of the chemical, capital equipment and credit industries. The recent global fiscal and economic crisis was induced in large measure by consumption excesses associated with this pernicious and prevalent 'productivist' regime extended into the sub-fields of debt-fuelled housing and mobility. Until then, even hitherto reluctant eco-consumers were turning away from the disease-inducing (obesity, diabetes, cardiovascular) content of 'conventional' food making the organic food segment the fastest-growing in Western markets (Cooke and Rehfeld forthcoming).

The second 'productivist' problem system faced by eco-innovation concerns the supply of energy. Throughout the equivalent period during which carbon-fuelled 'productivist' agriculture and food distribution were enveloping vast populations of consumers with their hegemonic regime, electricity generation and supply was doing the same. Massive carbon-fuelled power stations were constructed and linked in scale-driven supply systems known as the 'grid'. Such were the technical but, more importantly, regulatory 'lock-ins' associated with grid-thinking that in all but a few developed regions there was no alternative to buying energy from what were often state monopoly providers. This further meant no choice regarding the mix of energy consumers were forced to buy: if they had concerns about the nature of the supply and subsidy regime that furthered the interests of the nuclear energy industry the only way to escape was to go 'off-grid'. As with organic food, counter-cultural centres pursuing this 'politics of the personal', like the Alternative Technology Centre in Wales (1973), its affiliate, the Urban Centre for Alternative Technology, set up in 1980 at Bristol and other notable institutions including the New Alchemy Institute in Hatchville, Cape Cod, Massachusetts, US, Small Earth in Boxtel, The Netherlands, and the Nordic Centre for Renewable Energy at Thisted in North Jutland, Denmark all made major, often unheralded, energy eco-innovation contributions to living 'off-grid'. 'Feed-in tariffs' are one such eco-innovation available in more enlightened countries since the turn of the millennium. 'Smart grids' are another: in passing, one little-known 'dissipative structure' that rocked the grid regime in Denmark was set in motion by the last-named Nordic Centre for Renewable Energy. Complexity theorist Ilya Prigogine developed the concept of 'dissipative structures' to describe the coherent space–time structures that form in open systems in which an exchange of matter and energy occurs between a system and its environment (Nicolis and Prigogine 1989). As part of their voluntary work, the Nordic Centre collected all the designs of each enterprise engaged in wind turbine design and manufacturing in Jutland, the main centre. In line with their counter-cultural proto-freedom of information principles, they then proceeded freely to distribute every firm's design to every other thus ensuring all had state-of-the-art product design knowledge. This greatly aided the whole Jutland industry, whose dominant design eventually triumphed globally, although the hippy-run centre gained only notoriety for that act from the industry.

After food and energy, probably the third retro-design concept shared by eco-innovators and creatives specifically concerns construction methods. These are the most obvious connection with green aesthetics potential since they embody materials and ways of thinking about design and architecture that can be and are being deployed in contemporary leading-edge architecture. Key elements here are use of traditional building materials, waste recycling and sustainability in building production. The goal of green building is to increase the efficiency of resource use (including energy, water and materials) and to reduce any building's negative impacts on the environment during its life cycle. 'Zero energy' buildings achieve the key green building goal of reducing energy use and greenhouse gas emissions. Given the complex environmental, energy, economic and financial system crises faced by governments everywhere, it may be considered intellectually absurd that greater attention and policy support has yet to be given to raising standards for promoting eco-innovation and achievement of such energy efficiency on the EU-wide scale.

Even at national level there is laggardness. Thus the UK government has made its commitment to be the 'first in the world' to require zero carbon homes by law from 2016. The requisite energy efficiency standard will be required of all new homes. Beneath the large, slow governance system, smaller, swifter systems nevertheless function. At the meso-governance system level of Wales, the plan of zero carbon building as the standard for all new homes is to be met by 2011, earlier than the UK at 2016. This suggests better alignment in the potentially asymmetrical relationship between system *potential* (related variety) and *connectedness* (networks) that can prevail away from the upper, slower regulatory heights of the supranational or even the national governance levels. This can be seen in the sustainable parliament building that houses the Welsh government. This was designed by Richard Rogers and completed in 2006. It has won a substantial number of awards for sustainable construction that recognize the green principles within its design (e.g. British building standards agency, BREEAM; Steel Design; and Chicago Athenaeum). It has low environmental impact through the use of renewable (timber) and low energy solutions to construct heat and maintain the building. For example, the roof plane around the top building turns down to form a funnel into the debating chamber, allowing ventilation and natural light. Natural ventilation is used in nearly all areas of the building.

Offices do not have air conditioning as outlets in the floor push cool air into the rooms. The earth heat exchange system uses the ground as both a heat source and a heat sink. A biomass boiler fuelled by local wood chips helps to reduce carbon-dioxide emission. Rainwater is collected at roof level and circulated through roof-supporting columns for use in building services and window washing.

Other instances of green aesthetics include Malmö, Sweden's first stage waterfront housing at the Western Harbour developed in 2001. The houses were designed as sustainable buildings with well-insulated and high-efficiency electrical equipment to minimize heat and electricity consumption, using a 100 per cent renewable energy supply. The waste management system was designed to use waste and sewage as an energy source. Each unit was designed to use no more than $105kW/m^2/year$, including household electricity. Finally, in China, where eco-cities are de rigueur, an example of a zero-energy office building is the seventy-one-story Pearl River Tower, designed by US signature architects Skidmore, Owings and Merrill (Cooke and Zhang 2012). It was designated one of the most energy-efficient skyscrapers in the world when completed in 2010. It uses both energy efficiency measures and a mains distributed renewable energy generation system based on solar and wind power. The 2.3 million square (sq ft) foot tower innovates in sustainable design by incorporating the newest sustainable technology and engineering elements, including remotely controlled integrated wind turbines and photovoltaic energy systems, double-skin curtain walls, a chilled ceiling system, under-floor ventilation, air and daylight harvesting systems. The tower has received economic support from government subsidies that support the application of renewable energy technologies.

Regional indicators of innovation in creative industries

An important recent finding is that the creative economy contributes more innovation to the economy than manufacturing (Chapain *et al.* 2010). UK Office of National Statistics (ONS) data analyzed as part of a *National Endowment for Science, Technology and the Arts* (NESTA) funded project on the subject reveal that overall some 26 per cent of UK firms are innovators, meaning they have introduced product or process innovations over a specified period. However, the equivalent creative industry statistic for the same period is 34 per cent. On a combined innovation analysis the project's creativity index scores UK industry overall at 41 per cent but creative industry at 57 per cent between 2004 and 2006 (see Table 8.1). Innovation performance varies among creative industries. The most innovative is software, with a creativity index of 81 per cent from 2004 to 2006. Firms in sectors such as advertising, publishing, architecture and designer fashion are also innovative, but firms in film, video and photo, and arts and antiques are below average for total creative industries. Returning to manufacturing innovation for momentary comparison though, it is clear that 'soft

Table 8.1 Firms in creative industries by type of innovation outputs (percentage of all firms), 2004–06

	Goods innovation	Service innovation	Process innovation	Product or process innovation	Index of creativity
Advertising	n.a.	26	n.a.	26	65
Architecture	11	28	17	32	61
Arts and antiques	11	20	10	23	33
Designer fashion	31	n.a.	n.a.	32	57
Film, video and photo	10	18	9	20	45
Publishing	30	19	14	35	62
Software	38	55	26	59	81
Total creative industries	17	30	16	34	57
Engineering-based manufacturing	32	14	21	39	63
Other manufacturing	32	14	23	40	59
Retail and distribution	13	18	8	21	34
Knowledge-intensive business services	9	26	18	31	53
Other services	6	16	6	18	27
All industries	14	18	12	26	41

Source: Our elaboration on data from ONS

innovation' in general is marginally below that for manufacturing in general and engineering-based manufacturing in particular, especially for standard product and process innovations.

Given the different innovation patterns across creative industries, one would expect that these would impact differently on the regional innovation performance depending on the level of concentration and the weight of these industries within the regional economy. Overall, creative industry firms represent between 9.6 per cent (in Wales) and 17.7 per cent (in London) of all firms across the eleven British regions. The highest proportions of creative firms can be found in London, the South East, the East, the South West and the North West. Some creative industries weight more on regional economies than others, and this is the case for software, arts and antiques, and architecture. While software and architecture display high innovation performance at the national levels, this is not the case for arts and antiques, as shown in Table 8.1. Nevertheless, most of the British regions seem to present a concentration of activities in one or more creative industries.

Moving to indicators of eco-innovation patenting, it is difficult to separate out the eco-innovations from the more general manufacturing and services innovations listed in Table 8.1. Some may even be hidden in creative industry categories like architecture, film, (green) software and designer fashion (organic cotton, silk, linen and hemp). *Tencel* is an organic cotton substitute made from

Table 8.2 Global patent shares in renewable energy and automotive abatement

Country	Renewable energy	Country	Automotive emissions
EU25	45	EU25	50
Germany	19	Germany	33
Japan	18	Japan	29
US	17	US	15
UK	6	France	6
Denmark	5	UK	5
Australia	4	Sweden	3
France	3	Italy	2
Canada	2	Austria	1
Netherlands	2	Canada	1
Sweden	2	Australia	1
Rest of the world	22	Rest of the world	4

Source: OECD, Compendium of Patent Statistics 2007, in Smith (2008)

the cellulose released in wood pulp processing. It has been patented by Austrian firm Lenzing Fibres as has its ecological fabric softening agent Modal. In Smith (2008) are listed by country patent shares for two of the main eco-innovation areas: renewable energy and automotive emissions. The main results are given in Table 8.2. They show that the EU25 countries together register easily the best performance in these patent fields at 2007. They further show that Germany, Japan and the US were neck and neck in 2007 in renewable energy patenting while the same three led in automotive abatement although the US trailed the first two somewhat. In both fields the UK lagged well behind the leaders but was ahead of most competitors. Patenting by the UK in these two fields accounted for approximately 5 per cent of global patents. In the absence of other evidence, except that the UK share of its exports in ecological products and services is 6 per cent, we can reasonably presume that patenting (equivalence) in UK is considerably lower in eco-innovation than in the creative industries. This is not surprising, nor is it so compared with industry in general because sustainable technologies often do not involve patented knowledge because they are 'medium-tech'.

UK sector analysis

Television

According to the 2009 Annual Business Inquiry by the ONS the UK television industry provides approximately 80,000 jobs through broadcast television, cable and satellite and the independent production sector (Chapain *et al.* 2010). This employment contribution amounts to just over a tenth of the entire workforce in the creative media sector in the UK and is up from approximately 56,000 jobs in 2006 (Chapain *et al.* 2010). In addition, according to Skillset (the Sector Skills Council for the Creative Industries), when taking into account the related sectors as mentioned above, the employee population expands to 188,150 of which 24 per cent are freelancers. While the number of those employed in the UK TV production sector is high, it is reported that the sector is only comprised of 1,450 businesses, divided into:

- ten (terrestrial) broadcast television companies (e.g. BBC, ITV, Channel 4, Five, S4C, SMG, etc.);
- around 250 cable and satellite broadcasters (e.g. BSkyB, UKTV, Virgin Media, etc.);
- around 1,100 independent production companies (Chapain *et al.* 2010).

Based on these figures, the sector has a small number of large businesses and a large number of small and medium enterprises (SMEs). Due to the recession, there are an increasing number of firm mergers and acquisitions within this industry (Chapain *et al.* 2010).

The British TV production industry continues to benefit the UK as a whole; however, the concentration of these firms has traditionally been in close proximity to the major broadcasters. For England, this would be predominantly London and the South East due to the BBC, ITV, Channel 4 and Five sites nearby. Two thirds of the actual industry is located in London; however, smaller clusters are present throughout the UK. An example is Manchester, which is growing in prominence due to the BBC's Media City in Salford Quays, which currently has several working SMEs onsite and is expected to be fully opened in 2011 (Chapain *et al.* 2010). For Wales, this concentration of TV production firms is in Cardiff, largely due to the presence of the three major broadcasters: BBC Wales, ITV Wales and the Welsh-language channel S4C. Similar to Manchester's Media City, Cardiff is finalizing plans to be the home of the BBC Drama Village, which would further connect the TV production cluster in the area, increase employment in the TV production industry, and have a positive economic impact on Cardiff and the nation as a whole. With the construction of the media village, Cardiff's TV sector employment will increase with 1,500 jobs (above the national salary average) and bring in an estimated £300m (net) to the Welsh economy over a five-year period (Chapain *et al.* 2010). Furthermore, all of these locations are also home to several prominent independent production firms.

Eco-innovation

Regarding renewable energy, Wales now has fifteen biomass power stations, including two in the pipeline and three co-firing arrangements with large coal burning power stations. Amongst these is Europe's first commercial scale biomass power station in Port Talbot, which became fully operational in June 2008. Producing 13.8 MW of renewable energy the station generates 104 GWh per year, sufficient to meet the needs of around 31,000 homes. The Cardiff-based renewable energy company Eco2 designed and managed construction of the power station, for a project originally proposed by the Western Log group, using boilers sourced from Aalborg Energie Technik in North Jutland, Denmark. The plant is fuelled with 160,000 tonnes per year of clean wood that has come from sustainable, managed forests and sawmills. With trees drawing carbon dioxide from the atmosphere as they grow, the carbon dioxide produced in combustion results in no net increase of the gas. By generating electricity in this way, some 47,000 tonnes of equivalent fossil fuel carbon dioxide emissions are avoided. In 2010, Wales also opened the largest biomass power station in Europe. It is eight times the size of the UK's next-biggest biomass-fuelled power station. The plant created 150 full-time jobs and delivers 70 per cent of the Welsh renewable energy target for 2010 displacing 3.5 million tonnes of carbon dioxide emissions from older power stations. Wood chips from sustainable forests in the US, Canada, Eastern Europe and South America will be shipped in to fuel the station.

The aforementioned Eco2, one of the UK's leading renewable energy research and development (R&D) firms, was not involved in this huge investment and it is nowadays repositioning itself as a global leader in tidal energy systems. Most of Cardiff-based Eco2's contracts are with UK and, increasingly, European clients. Eco2 has a business model said to be common in eco-business, whereby the firm calls on a group of ten or so investors to fund projects and take a return subject only to capital gains rather than corporation tax. This is realized when the project is sold or a project client makes the final payment. This enables Eco2 to be a tax-efficient, knowledge-based research, development and innovation vehicle. Amongst its clients is the Sleaford Renewable Energy Plant for whom a straw-fired power station opened in late 2008. Eco2's first such plant, generating 38 MW, was built at Ely, Cambridgeshire for Energy Power Resources Ltd. The new one is the UK's largest straw-fired biomass burner and first in Eco2's new £1bn programme to develop up to ten biomass facilities across Europe. It will create eighty jobs, bringing £6m a year to local farmers in fuel supply contracts and £20m for local construction firms. It will power the equivalent of 65,000 homes, one quarter of all houses in Lincolnshire. Having begun in the wind farm business, in which the firm owns a number of farms with two awaiting planning permission, wind energy has now scaled up beyond Eco2's capacity, hence the move into biomass. The company's most recent development is in tidal energy as it partners fellow Cardiff firm Tidal Energy Limited to develop 'DeltaStream' – an innovative technology designed to generate electrical power from tidal stream resources. A 1 MW tidal energy turbine has been successfully trialled in Milford Haven, Pembrokeshire in partnership with Carbon Connections Ltd along with Cardiff and Cranfield Universities. Accordingly an important research-led eco-innovation supply chain exists in Wales, focused on Cardiff, from where other initiatives like the Low Carbon Research Institute at Cardiff University manage renewable energy networks of firms and intermediary organizations across the economy and around the UK's main energy port at Milford Haven in West Wales.

Description of the cluster nodes and networks

From the creative industry perspective, Wales has a creative economy that is mainly supported through the TV/film/new media production industry. In 2002, it was reported that Wales employed 4 per cent of the UK total in the audiovisual industry, which equated to 600 businesses and £350m (Chapain *et al.* 2010). Of these firms, the majority are related to TV and film or with a focus in one of those particular sectors based on the similar supply chain. This leaves only a small portion of the firms related to radio. Furthermore, to narrow down the location, within Wales, there are several areas that have concentrations of TV production firms, largely based on satellite BBC Wales production studios in the area; however, Cardiff is where they are the most prevalent. Cardiff, as a local authority, has the highest saturation of creative industry employment in Wales at 4.6 per cent with Gwynedd, in Northwest Wales, having the second highest level at 4.1 per cent (Chapain *et al.* 2010). Cardiff's hinterland, the South Wales Valleys, has been improving in terms of the creative industries; however, this may be addressed with the BBC Drama Village as a number of BBC employees reside in this area and one of the long-term goals of the Drama Village is peripheral regeneration.

The TV industry employs 3,800 people in Cardiff, of which BBC Wales directly employs 1,226 (full and part-time) (Chapain *et al.* 2010). Outside the large networks, Cardiff has a growing independent TV sector with some 200 firms, led by Boomerang, Green Bay Productions and Calon TV. The independent TV sector alone makes up almost 7 per cent of the creative businesses in Cardiff, while 28 per cent of those employed in the creative industries are employed in TV production. The relationship between employment and firms is characteristic of the larger British TV industry. A recent study concluded that 24 per cent of creative firms in Cardiff had only one full-time member of staff (Chapain *et al.* 2010). This is supported by the survey findings for this study that had 64 per cent of firms surveyed with five or less employees and 22 per cent with one employee.

The number of firms in the same sector may be impressive given the relatively small size of Cardiff as a capital city (330,000 serving a metro-region of one million and Wales as a whole at three million); however, that does not necessarily mean there is an actual TV production cluster. In defining a cluster, the Cardiff TV production sector meets three of the four criteria: there is a geographic agglomeration of firms in the same sector, the firms are competitive and the firms have links with other actors. However, the level of cooperation within the cluster is not present largely due to intellectual property rights (IPR) protection. This has been alluded to by both firms and policy makers who consider Cardiff to have a creative cluster that meets the aforementioned criteria, but not a TV production cluster. This is based not only on the proximity of the firms but also on the data collected, the overlap between the industries (see the innovation process section) and the level of cooperation.

From the eco-innovation viewpoint, in Wales, there has long been a close relationship with Hydrogen Fuel Cells (HFC) technology since the technology, the predominant motive force in rocket engineering, was invented by Swansea scientist William Grove in 1857. Coincidentally, Wales is identified as one of

Europe's top sixteen HFC regions in research by Nygaard (2008). Among achievements warranting that status are the prototype 'Tribrid Bus' developed at the University Glamorgan, the 'H2Wales' network based at Baglan Energy Park, Port Talbot and the car-design work of Connaught Engineering and the Naro car company. But HFC is not the most prominent technology design in the Welsh renewable energy equipment spectrum. That accolade probably belongs currently with the production of energy from biomass. Here is a sphere in which Welsh research is at the global forefront, mainly through its grassland research institute, the Institute of Biological, Environmental and Rural Sciences (IBERS, formerly the Institute of Grassland and Environmental Research – IGER), since 2008 part of the University of Wales, Aberystwyth. In 2004 IGER opened a biofuels research and commercialization division due to its evolving expertise in understanding and improving the calorific content of feedstock plants by experimenting with ryegrass, short rotation willow and *miscanthus* (Asian elephant grass). This connects to our earlier point regarding 'revealed related variety' because this research institute manages to combine innovation at interfaces among organic food, biofuels and tourism, promoting indigenous entrepreneurship in three industries on which Wales has been path dependent for centuries.

IBERS conducts much industrial contract research and advisory activity. This interweaves with the three noted sectors in the following ways. First, IBERS advised the tourist theme park business 'Oakwood Leisure' in Pembrokeshire on a green tourism plan for a new leisure complex named 'Bluestone' for the uniquely coloured stone quarried nearby of which many Neolithic monuments like Stonehenge are composed. The €130 million leisure park consists of 340 sustainably sourced wooden chalets and a Celtic village of eighty adjoining buildings part-located in the Pembrokeshire Coast National Park. Additional facilities include a snowdome, waterworld park, indoor tropical garden and sports centre. It houses 2000 residents and receives 5000 day visitors. Bluestone directly employs 600 catering and hospitality staff and indirectly supports 100 jobs with its suppliers. By offering a 'green tourism' solution Oakwood finally achieved planning permission to go ahead with such a development, which included building on two fields that were inside the National Park boundary. The project was grant aided by the National Park Authority through its Sustainable Development Fund and by the UK government's (DEFRA) carbon-neutral crops scheme. University of Wales, Bangor's Centre for Alternative Land Use (CALU) was also consulted. IBERS advised Bluestone on its renewable energy strategy, which consists of 3 MW of biomass burning combined heat and power (CHP) units. Initially IBERS favoured *miscanthus* but opted finally for short-rotation willow wood chips as the main fuel source. These are grown by fifty farmers in a localized supply chain managed by an energy company called Pembrokeshire Bioenergy. Completing the green symbolism of this tourism project is the Bluestone culinary strategy, which is to supply tourist food from a localized food network of mainly but not exclusively organic farms. Among its suppliers are successful food 'aggregator' firms such as Castell Howell Foods based at nearby Cross Hands Food Park, a major West Wales centre for food processing and packaging.

Towards the green creative industry solution

The foregoing discussion identifies a medium-sized city-region, Cardiff, and its hinterland(s) of South and West Wales combining pronounced evidence of a mature creative industries agglomeration in 'convergent media'. This is perceived as sufficiently capable to warrant decentralization of BBC (UK) drama away from London and into the sustainably designed 'Drama Village' on the waterfront at Cardiff Bay where it shares space with another iconic green building, the Welsh 'Senedd' building. More recently this has also been joined by further green buildings of some architectural merit in the form of Number 3 'Senedd' Square. Located next to the National Assembly's 'Senedd', the 66,215 sq ft building joins other environmentally friendly commercial developments such as Caspian Point and Scott Harbour as part of the regeneration of Cardiff's waterside business district. Architects Scott Brownrigg and sustainability consultants Arup designed the building with environmental sustainability to the fore, incorporating state-of-the-art green technologies and systems, including a biomass boiler, chilled beams and rainwater harvesting. These eco-features, which have seen the building achieve the prestigious BREEAM 'excellent' status, will also reduce energy, water, maintenance and replacement running costs by up to 50 per cent against a comparable building.

The offices also boast an innovative design, with timber louvres, feature exterior glazing and a full-height atrium with staircase and lifts, designed to provide panoramic views over the city. The atrium features an eye-catching sculpture by internationally renowned artist Claire Morgan called Pressure Makes Diamonds, which uses coal and iron to represent the industrial history of Cardiff Harbour.

These creative and eco-friendly elements point the way to a broader perspective of *green creativity*, which also begins to embody artistic solutions that reference place history (Cardiff was once the world's largest coal exporting port) in the local geology whereby the earth's crust pressure was responsible for the formation of compressed carbon, here, in the form of high calorific steam coal, elsewhere in the form of diamonds. Other 'critical regionalist' architecture in this waterside business district includes the Millennium Centre, Cardiff's Opera House, which is constructed upon a slate base and sidewall elements. Slate was the main resource industry of North Wales, performing a community-bonding role comparable to the coal-mining and export industries of South Wales. In the Millennium Centre it is presented in all its numerous hues from light grey through green and dark blue to light and dark purple.

The Environment Building conference centre is also situated in Cardiff Bay on the edge of its barrage, and accessible via the new Cardiff Bay Barrage Coast Path. Offering coffee-making facilities, services and an interactive white board screen linked to a computer, the building can be hired for small conferences. The main meeting room offers panoramic views across the water. In order to promote sustainability the building is powered by a biomass boiler using wood chips from debris collected from Cardiff Bay. Although these designs are guided in a light-touch manner by the 'One Wales, One Planet' sustainable economy strategy of the Welsh government, which from 2007–11 was a coalition between Labour and Plaid Cymru (the Party of Wales), it is likely that had the smaller Plaid Cymru partner not been present the green regime would have been considerably less. Until recently Plaid Cymru and the Greens fought elections as a coalition in Wales. Hence, it is from below that the impetus for green creativity has come and from parts of Wales that are principally rural, agricultural and renewable energy producing as well as being largely inhabited by native speakers of the Welsh language (see Cooke and Rehfeld forthcoming). To what extent is this kind of arrival at green creativity an experience shared elsewhere and to what extent is it unique? Green creativity in the built form has unquestionably been reached from different starting points in Europe, Asia and elsewhere but the precise path dependence to it in Wales is probably unique, or only vaguely comparable with the experience of other peripheral minority language or cultural regions in the world.

Scandinavian exemplars

At this point it is appropriate to turn the focus towards two Nordic experiences of moving towards the 'sustainable city' as both a creative and an eco-innovation hub. The first of these is Copenhagen and the second Stockholm. Both cities have acted as role models of a kind for Chinese 'eco-city' planning though inevitably at a larger scale and also influenced in a leading case by the practice in eco-building of Singapore. Towards the end of the final section, attention will be devoted to two further cases of 'sustainable city' planning currently underway in Sweden to demonstrate certain complexity science principles that are now deployed to connect diverse eco-innovation elements involving the creative industries of 'convergent media' and 'smart textiles', the eco-innovations of 'green logistics' and the 'food academy', and the 'sustainable business hub' (SBHUB) and 'recycling' capabilities in the planning of sustainable cities.

As noted, for its first and best communicated initiative, Copenhagen tackled the important climate change issue of agro-food emissions. This they did by transforming food procurement from conventional to organic, which in Copenhagen and four other 'Dogma' towns included schools, hospitals, day care and long-term care homes. Together, these city strategies on organic canteen food alone contributed to a 2.25 per cent reduction in carbon dioxide (CO_2) emissions from their institutional food chains. In the further important emissions sphere of mobility, renewable energy vehicles were promoted and bought for bus, car and light truck or van fleets. Comparably, passenger transport CO_2 emissions were reduced by 10–15 per cent in Copenhagen (1996–2006) following the establishment of urban environmental zones and clean technology measures. Next, in regard to waste management, another significant climate change contributory factor, in Copenhagen up to 80 per cent of city household waste is used in Energy from Waste (EfW) power plants while over 70 per cent of all waste is recycled. Finally, regarding energy, a further major contributor, more than 25 per cent of electricity generation in Copenhagen is from renewables, notably wind (4 per cent) and solar power (3 per cent) in addition to waste (26 per cent). Other towns approved building of biogas from waste biofuels power plant. Copenhagen had, from 1990 to 2005 reduced overall CO_2 emissions by 23 per cent with the further reduction aim of 35 per cent during 1990–2010. These achievements led to Copenhagen, home to the EU's Environmental Protection Agency, being elected Environmental Capital of Europe and International Solar City. In the Copenhagen 'Carbon Neutral Plan' for 2025 the city committed to further reduce carbon emissions by 20 per cent by 2015 through fifty specific initiatives, many involving more efficiency in the energy (wind, geothermal, solar replacing coal) and transportation grids.

In Stockholm's Hammarby suburb, a sustainable community has been constructed. Hammarby Sjöstad is a lakeside area south of Stockholm city centre. Originally planned for development as part of Stockholm's bid for the 2004 Olympic Games, this formerly disused, polluted brownfield site is now one of Europe's leading eco-towns. The bid failed; however, work was already underway to clean and redevelop the area for the Olympic Village and it was decided to retain this momentum to create positive change. Formerly derelict and polluted, the site was transformed with an emphasis on ecology and environmental sustainability. The construction of Hammarby Sjöstad is still under way. It is envisaged that the area will eventually house some 35,000 people on completion in 2015. In addition there is a new school, church, shops, offices and a park all located on a 7.6 hectare brownfield site within easy reach of Stockholm's inner city. Hammarby Sjöstad is a good example of the Swedish 'green welfare state' shared value approach to eco-cities and shows how it can promote sustainable development, new jobs, growth and welfare into the future. As well as being ecologically innovative, it is also socially ambitious in line with the Swedish government mandate that all citizens should be provided with a decent, safe, affordable home that will be sustainable in the long term.

Imagining the sustainable city as a green creativity model

To translate the foregoing and somewhat 'structural' analysis of the intersections or cross-pollinations among the related varieties of creative and eco-innovation, it is helpful to reintroduce 'design thinking' of the kind discussed by the likes of Lester and Piore (2004) and Martin (2009). Here, the 'global controller' is not excluded though she may still not be highly individualistic in methodology. In Sweden, two regions recently adopted the EU idea of 'Grand Challenges' to drive their innovation strategies. Both Region Skåne (main city Malmö) and Västra Götaland (main city Gothenburg) did this. In the early parts of this chapter, we outlined an approach to regional economic change analysis that paid attention to the following key elements: multi-level relationships in governance and corporate structures and relations; and resilience as an expression of a region's capabilities in absorbing 'shocks to the system' and returning to the position before destabilization, or, more likely, engaging in some form of search behaviour for the adjacent possibilities of innovating after the creative destruction process had calmed down. The other, more common form of displaying resilience with the support of regional innovation agencies was to identify 'preadaptive' innovations that could be transferred from one industry or cluster to a different one. In some European regions like Bavaria and Lower Austria this is normal whereas in Värmland, in Sweden, there is more of a search across a relatively narrow span of related regional industries for user and design-driven innovation in the 'adjacent possible'. In the key comparative case of Skåne region, also in Sweden, this quest for the 'adjacent possible' is even more to the forefront across a broader front where grand challenges have imposed shocks on the RIS. These range from climate change imposing harsher winters on shared infrastructures in the Öresund region, de-industrialization with the major closure of Kockums shipyard in Malmö and its rapid transformation into a 'cognitive–cultural' quarter housing the media, information and communication technology (ICT) and many other clusters as well as the Regional Development Agency in close proximity. Downsizing of established large ICT corporations faced with massive global competition emanating from Asia, and China in particular, has been another shock, resiliently responded to by 'open innovation'. Finally the demographics of ageing have also imposed strains on the system, with recognition that services are deteriorating and efforts being made to respond with innovations that optimize on infrastructure, ICT, food and health care expertise and capabilities in the region, as well as serving Sweden and the wider world. Exploiting the region's proximity and relatedness advantages has been key to the response made thus far. Indeed, each cluster is connected into a set of interlocking circles that represent two strategic grand challenges the overall Region Skåne strategy is meant to address, as shown in Figure 8.2 (Cooke and Eriksson 2012).

In the remaining space, the main 'transversalities' are summarized for each of the clusters in the Region Skåne innovation system discussed above. This shows recognition that regional industries have suffered significant shocks from climate change, energy scarcity, corporate 'global shift' and downsizing, and health care issues such as ageing of the population. In different ways, as with 'food academy' and 'mobile heights' ('smartphones'), the response to destabilization is to engage in some form of 'platform-building' among clusters to produce innovative solutions with regional industry neighbours (Howe 2009; Shirkey 2010). Linkage is particularly pronounced towards the 'gaming' technologies of 'media evolution', and to the 'food academy'. The technology projects they are working on include: sustainable technologies; new kinds of 'crowd' or user-driven innovation; and the use of gaming and simulation to stimulate learning and change management in meeting the shocks imposed by grand challenges such as climate change.

'Iconic projects' is the characteristic approach taken in Västra Götaland region centred upon Gothenburg. The strategic decision was taken to concentrate initially on meeting the grand challenges of climate change and health care, the first not least because the region had been one of the first in the world, in 2003, to

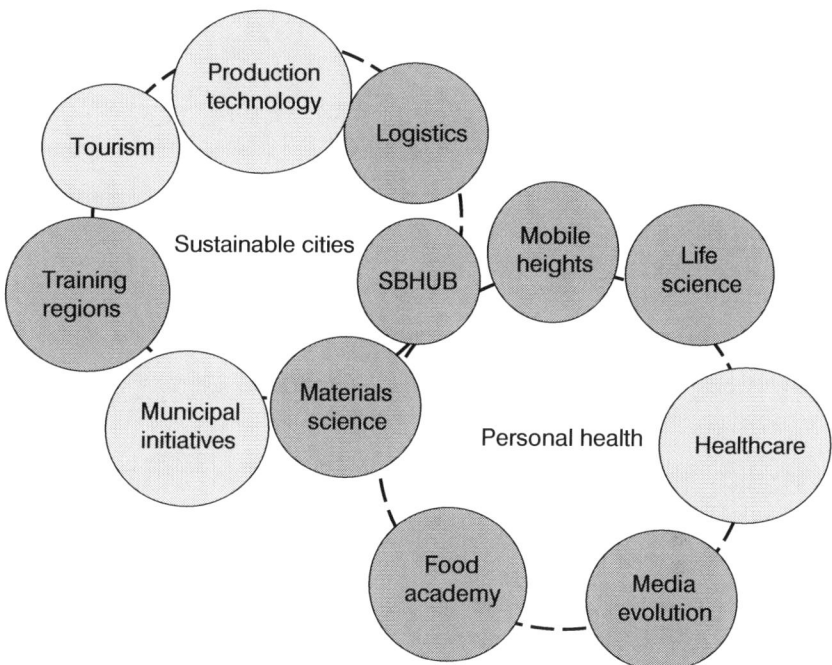

Figure 8.2 Region Skåne's two strategic 'Grand Challenges' innovation platforms

Source: Centre for Advanced Studies, Cardiff University

publish a climate change response strategy report, *Gothenburg 2005*, involving policies for 'smart energy' that have more recently evolved into the strategic 'climate change' target of Västra Götaland being totally 'fossil fuel free' by 2030. This became known as the 'Gothenburg model' of the Lisbon Strategy. However, having got the regional position on that grand challenge worked out well in advance gave scope for the new environmental strategy to be down to earth and practical. This means focusing on 'iconic projects' that are committed to as innovation, learning and collaborative platform management 'laboratories' (Figure 8.3). Thus the particularization of the 'climate change' grand challenge involves translating it into a 'sustainable cities' initiative triggered by an actual infrastructure commitment to a new tunnel. This brings together numerous regional clusters involved in renewable automotive fuels, forest plastics and petroleum and health. At a more detailed level this assembles pilot projects mixing expertise in cluster firm logistics, public transport, visioning (computer graphics and imaging) and green accounting. It links to a RIS relationship with Chalmers University and firms like Asta AB. A comparable 'Iconic project' approach is being taken in health care where the project in question involves a new Health Imaging Facility at the University Medical School. This connects transversally to digital signals processing (data compression) and medical diagnostics engineering expertise at Chalmers University and one of its spin-out firms, Medfield Diagnostics.

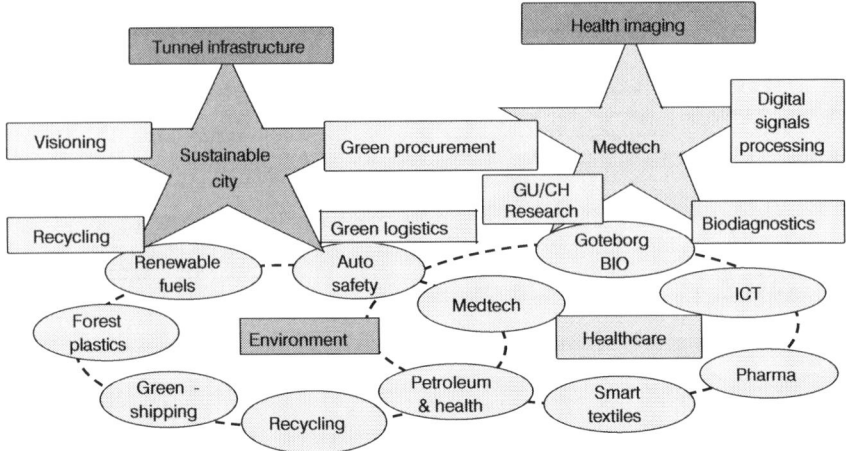

Figure 8.3 Västra Götaland's 'Iconic projects' approach

Source: Centre for Advanced Studies, Cardiff University
Note: GU: Gothenburg University, CH: Chalmers University

Conclusions

Three key conclusions can be drawn from the foregoing account. First, active thinking about the emergence and evolution of a new 'green aesthetic' is in its infancy. Both creative industries analysis, on the one hand, and 'eco-innovation' on the other have largely operated in sealed containers or intellectual 'silos'. However, in this first, evolutionary way of thinking about their pre-figurative and, in the form of 'sustainable cities', actual *emergence* through convergence to distinctive policy models, some pointers for the future have become firmer. First, nearly all sustainable cities are water-based, which may be a sign that in future we will all be living near water even if we are currently not. But work is needed to think out the non-water-based sustainable city of the future. Moreover, most such thinking is still urban rather than rural.

Second, the analytical difficulties in bridging the 'silos' between creativity and sustainability are not that great if the thinker or planner is informed by theory, particularly evolutionary geographic theory and its complementary perspective from complexity sciences. These posit 'relatedness', namely that potential cross-pollinating clusters or industries will find ways, to survive not least, by identifying a significant other where knowledge spillovers and semi-tacit knowledge may be exchanged and innovation discovered. This is assisted enormously where judicious innovation agencies perform this 'brokering' function (transversality) through RISs encompassing creative and sustainability perspectives. Furthermore, complexity science envisages ways this happens. First existing innovations may be adapted in a new context (preadaptation) or the nearby unknown may be jointly explored. Such innovations as 'green gaming' or 'sustainable simulations' may join 'green procurement' and 'smart textiles' where such complex adaptive system clusters can be taken to 'the edge of chaos' (Nicolis and Prigogine 1989).

Finally, methods are being worked out in practice, through transversality measures and instruments to achieve precisely this. It is a communicative and collaborative process that derives its evolutionary fuel from narratives, discourses and in some instances from the insights of 'organizational' or 'research-based' theatre (Schreyögg and Höpfl 2004). In such circumstances, based on the idea of 'living labs', revealed related variety may be explored, simulated and even 'gamified' to facilitate design planning. This is the inevitable mid-process between complex adaptive innovation system evolution that can, on occasion, appear 'lawless' in its hybridization of 'strange attractors' and the still not necessarily rationally designed 'work of genius' necessitated to bring forth the realized sustainable habitat. More design research is clearly needed to further improve the aesthetic content of 'green architecture' so that it more prominently represents its function in its form.

References

Allen, P. (1998) 'Complexity, organization and knowledge: The law of excess variety', in E. Mitleton-Kelly (ed.) *Proceedings of the 'Organizations as Complex Evolving Systems' Conference*, Warwick, UK: University of Warwick and London, London School of Economics and Political Science, pp. 7–29.

Arthur, B. (2009) *The Nature of Technology*, London: Penguin.

Chapain, C., Cooke, P., De Propris, L., MacNeill, S. and Mateos-Garcia, J. (2010) *Creative Clusters and Innovation: Putting Creativity on the Map*, London: NESTA.

Cooke, P. and De Propris, L. (2012) 'For a resilient, sustainable and creative European economy, in what ways is the EU important?', in P. Cooke and D. Parrilli (eds) *Innovation, Global Change and Territorial Resilience*, Cheltenham: Edward Elgar.

Cooke, P. and De Propris, L. (forthcoming) 'A policy agenda for smart growth: The role of creative and cultural industries', *Policy Studies*.

Cooke, P. and Eriksson, A. (2012) 'Resilience, innovative "White Spaces" and cluster-platforms as a response to globalization shocks', in P. Cooke and D. Parrilli (eds) *Innovation, Global Change and Territorial Resilience*, Cheltenham: Edward Elgar.

Cooke, P. and Rehfeld, D. (forthcoming) 'Path dependence and new paths in regional evolution: In search of the role of culture', *European Planning Studies*, 19.

Cooke, P. and Schwartz, D. (2008) 'Regional knowledge economies: An UK–EU and Israel perspective', *Tijdschrift Voor Economische Geografie*, 99(2): 178–92.

Cooke, P. and Zhang, F. (2012) 'China: beyond the global production line', in P. Cooke and D. Parrilli (eds) *Innovation, Global Change and Territorial Resilience*, Cheltenham: Edward Elgar.

Folke, C. (2006) 'Resilience: The emergence of a perspective for social-ecological systems analysis', *Global Environmental Change*, 16(3): 253–67.

Frenken, K., van Oort, F. and Verburg, T. (2007) 'Related variety, unrelated variety and regional economic growth', *Regional Studies*, 41(5): 685–97.

Geels, F. (2007) 'Analysing the breakthrough of rock 'n' roll (1930–70). Multi-regime interaction and reconfiguration in the multi-level perspective', *Technological Forecasting and Social Change*, 74(8): 1141–1431.

Hoekman, J., Frenken, K. and van Oort, F. (2009) 'The geography of collaborative knowledge production in Europe', *The Annals of Regional Science*, 43(3): 721–38.

Howe, J. (2009) *Crowdsourcing*, New York: Three Rivers Press.

Kauffman, S. (1995) *At Home in the Universe. The Search for the Laws of Self-organization and Complexity*, Oxford: Oxford University Press.

Kauffman, S. (2008) *Reinventing the Sacred*, New York: Basic Books.

Landry, C. and Bianchini, F. (1995) *The Creative City*, London: Demos.

Lester, R. and Piore, M. (2004) *Innovation: The Missing Dimension*, Cambridge, MA: Harvard University Press.

Martin, R.L. (2009) *The Design of Business,* Boston, MA: Harvard Business Books.

Martin, R.L. and Sunley, P. (2010) 'The place of path dependence in an evolutionary perspective on the economic landscape', in R. Boschma and R.L. Martin (eds) *Handbook of Evolutionary Economic Geography*, Cheltenham: Edward Elgar, pp. 62–92.

Mugan, C. (2009) 'The story of pop music', *The Independent*, 10 March.

Nicolis, G. and Prigogine, I. (1989) *Exploring Complexity*, New York: W.H. Freeman.

Nygaard, A. (2008) 'Regional innovation systems and emerging Hydrogen Fuel Cells clusters', paper presented at the Workshop *Climate Change and Eco-innovation: Regional Perspectives*, Aalborg University, 12 November.

Schreyögg, G. and Höpfl, H. (2004) 'Theatre and organization: Editorial introduction', *Organization Studies*, 25(5): 691–704.

Shirkey, C. (2010) *Here Comes Everybody*, London: Penguin.

Smith, K. (2008) *The Challenge of Environmental Technology: Promoting Radical Innovation in Conditions of Lock-in*, final report to the Garnaut Climate Change Review, Hobart, Australia: Australian Innovation Research Centre.

Sunley, P., Pinch, S., Reimer, S. and Macmillan, J. (2008) 'Innovation in a creative production system: The case of design', *Journal of Economic Geography*, 8(5): 675–98.

9 From cultural cluster to creative cluster

The case of art restoration in Florence

Luciana Lazzeretti and Tommaso Cinti

Introduction

An important debate on the role of creativity and culture as factors of local economic development has been enriched by new suggestions (Storper and Scott 2009), which mainly concern the issues of innovation and creativity (Pratt and Jeffcutt 2009). Formerly, culture was basically considered as a good to preserve, and only afterwards as a possible gain, if properly advanced in itself and from an economic point of view (Towse 2003). At present, the focal point of the debate is on culture's capacity to produce knowledge and so the attention has shifted to innovative processes, human capital and creative cities and industries (Belussi and Staber 2011). A new phase in the development of the relationship between culture and economy has thus opened, which overcomes that of economic enhancement of culture, putting innovation and creativity at the centre.

Creativity takes place beyond organizational boundaries (Staber 2004), often concentrated in cultural clusters (Scott 2004) and it is also characterized by a collective process (Jeffcutt and Pratt 2002). It is important to manage 'situated creativity' and the role of place in creativity and novelty becomes crucial for creative networks (Potts *et al.* 2008).

With our contribution we focus upon the current debate in order to understand whether, within a cultural cluster, culture – aside from representing a flywheel of economic development through the exploitation and enhancement of cultural resources – is also capable of generating innovation.

Normally in traditional industrial literature, technology is the primary driving force of innovation and with this study we will potentially bridge innovation studies with culture and creative economics literature.

Our specific goal is to identify what elements can contribute to transforming a cultural cluster into a creative cluster and to understand whether cities of arts can be considered as examples of *creative milieu*. This chapter is intended to better shape a research objective to which not enough importance was attached, notwithstanding the current euphoria, over the economic developmental potential of cultural industries and 'culture-led' policies to revitalize declining or stagnant regions/cities.

To this purpose, we focus on the case of laser technologies for restoration in Florence, which constitutes an interesting example of innovation led by a creative capacity, engendered by creative environments in art cities. Specifically, the field of laser innovation applied to the restoration and cleaning of cultural assets (e.g. ablative laser technological systems) is one of the most thriving and successful technologies newly available in Europe (Schreiner and Strlic 2006).

In addition, the present case study is meant to start investigating the cultural cluster of restoration as a creative cluster, and to reconstruct, on the one hand, the genesis of the innovation under study and, on the other hand, the role of the strategic actors involved in the innovation process.

The development process of the innovation entailed a 'cross-fertilization' among apparently distant sectors (i.e. medical diagnostics and cultural goods). It also profited from the location in an art city like Florence, a creative milieu where high technology blends perfectly with significant cultural heritage.

The study is arranged as follows. After this introduction, the main characteristics of the creative capacity of culture and the city of art as a creative milieu are revisited. The research scheme and the methodology of investigation are then described, followed by the history of the laser technologies for restoration, examined from its genesis to its international diffusion, focusing on the Italian and Florentine experiences. Then we reconstruct the rise of the Florentine creative cluster throughout a series of research projects financed by the Tuscany Region. Finally some conclusions complete the study.

Theoretical framework

The paths for the creative capacity of culture

Nowadays, in the era of the creative economy (Florida 2002),[1] the production of culture has also turned into an increasingly important resource for innovation, as it is able to activate new industrial *filières* and to regenerate not only products but also places and industries (Andersson, Andersson and Mellander 2011).

In this contest the city of art may became a creative city if it is characterized by a large endowment of creative resources, which identify it as a creative place (i.e. creative industries, creative class, creative atmosphere), and by the presence of a network of economic, non-economic and institutional actors, who are able to generate ideas and innovation (creative cluster).

By creative capacity of culture (CCC), we intend culture's ability to rejuvenate places, sectors, *filières* or professions, and to generate ideas and innovations through processes of cross-fertilization and serendipity (Cunha, Clegg and Mendonca 2010). It involves searching out new and different relationships, and preferably the 'unusual' relatedness that is the basis of the innovation process.[2] It is the ability to create ties (*relatedness*) and recognize unusual relations able to generate incremental and radical innovations. The example of 'Coca Cola' is emblematic. In fact it was originally thought up as a medicament and later it became the most popular cold drink thanks to the new use developed by the consumers.

Creativity also promotes searching and lateral thinking (De Bono 1971)[3] and it is advanced by lateral proximity, which is basically measurable in terms of the

Creative habitat	Creative spillovers
A place likely to attract a creative class that elects it as its life and working place. Its attractive quality may be due not only to its human capital, but also to its creative firms	Knowledge spillovers generated by lateral thinking, which is typical of artists as well as of creative industries and other creative actors. Ideas are 'in the air', shaping the atmosphere of creative habitats
Lateral proximity	
A cognitive proximity favoured by informal environmerts. Its effectiveness depend on 'cogritive distance' (relatedness). Cognitive distance is measurable in terms of related/unrelated knowledge and on the various typologies of linkages and nexuses which creative actors are liable to find	
Creative absorptive capacity	Creative economies
The ability to transform generic creativity (exploration) into goal-oriented creativity (exploitation), so as to generate and even transfer ideas and innovations	External agglomeration economies achieved in creative milieux, that are cross-fertilization economies which can compose the advantages of specialisation with those of diversification

Figure 9.1 The new creative milieu: key points

Source: Our elaboration on Lazzeretti (2009)

cognitive distance among creative actors (see Figure 9.1). The CCC is founded on a multifaceted idea of proximity, diversified not only on a geographical basis but also cognitively (Boschma 2005).[4] The main objective becomes the search for 'relatedness', which constitutes the *incipit* (opening) of the development paths for CCC.

According to this perspective, recently recalled in recent studies of new evolutionary geography (Boschma and Martin 2010) that analyze transversality and lateral innovation phenomena in Jacobian clusters developed by the related variety approach (Cooke *et al.* 2011), we identify four main paths of development of the CCC that can give rise to different typologies of innovation – incremental (renewing) or radical (novelty) – and may relate to places or other economic contexts (see Table 9.1). Some exemplifications are proposed here regarding the case of restoration, the object of this study.

An example of *economic renewal* is represented by the rejuvenation of the traditional profession of restorer. 'New' restorers are not only artistic, but also an example of sophisticated technological craftsmen that combine handiwork skills with scientific and technical knowledge in highly specialized subjects. Furthermore, because of their localization in the historical centre of the city of Florence, restorers are, in addition, considered a creative class, a creative firm and an important source of urban regeneration (*urban renewal*) (Lazzeretti 2003).

Table 9.1 The innovation paths for the creative capacity of culture

Renewing	Novelty
Urban renewal pertains to the idea that culture can rejuvenate places using strategies like: • city branding; • physical renovation and flagship developments; • culture-led and driven strategies.	*Cross-fertilization* is the ability to search and build new relationships (relatedness): • inside a cultural cluster/district; • among 'related' cultural clusters/ sectors; • among 'unrelated' clusters/sectors; • across time (the rebirth of a cultural district).
Economic renewal pertains to the idea that culture can rejuvenate mature or declining: • sectors; • products; • *filières;* • professions.	*Serendipity* is the capacity to discover pleasant or valuable things by chance and recognizes unusual correlations that become the basis for an innovative idea: • new uses for a product; • multiplicity of interest (diversification); • technological correlations.

Source: Our elaboration on Lazzeretti (2009)

However, the most relevant aspect of our findings is probably the analysis of restoration as an example of *cross-fertilization* and *serendipity* that we have further delved into in this study.

The central points to consider are the 'relatedness' and the ability to look for and build new relationships. In previous studies (Lazzeretti 2003), processes of cross-fertilization inside a cultural cluster were identified (i.e. the restoration cluster), which can arise with regard to different professional abilities (specializations) within the same productive *filière* or the same cluster/district; relatedness is based essentially on social and physical proximity.

The institutional proximity can also be found among 'related' cultural clusters. In fact, Florentine institutional actors belonging to different clusters work as 'connection nodes'. This certainly occurs in the clusters of restoration, and museums where the restoration activities are exhibited.[5] Furthermore, it is possible to encounter cluster-to-cluster relationships outside the city, relating the same kind of actors from different places, and even from different countries, such as in the case of the relationships between Florentine and Chinese restorers (*virtual proximity*).

However, the most important and innovative situation is certainly that of cross-fertilization *among 'unrelated' clusters/sectors* through which we introduce the new concept of *lateral proximity*. An example is given by the case under study, i.e. the *cross-fertilization* between the biomedical and medical diagnostics sector and that of the preservation of cultural goods. The presence in the same territory of institutes of applied physics and institutions for preservation purposes together with a considerable artistic heritage was probably at the origin of the implementation of laser technologies of optometry for cleaning stone materials (Salimbeni *et al.* 2002). The laser-cleaning technologies in art conservation were discovered by chance while using a laser to make a holographic archive of statues and monuments (Asmus *et al.* 1974). This represents an emblematic example of serendipity by *inter-sectoral technological correlations* that has taken place in a world-renowned city of art, Venice.

The new creative milieu

Thus, do cities of art represent environments potentially favourable to innovation? Can these art cities, wherein the preservation and economic enhancement of culture take place, be also considered as an important type of creative environment? In order to reply to these questions, we have developed a preliminary concept of new creative milieu (NCM) and applied it to the city of art.

In previous studies, the NCM has been defined as 'an informal, collective open space, physical, virtual or just ideal, able to release the CCC within cultural clusters/districts or other environments, and characterized by processes of lateral thinking and problem finding' (Lazzeretti 2009: 289). Summarizing, there are four key factors that contribute to its definition: creative habitat, lateral proximity, creative spillovers and creative economies, described in Figure 9.1.[6]

We cannot investigate them more extensively in this work. It should be enough to recall how the case of laser technologies in conservation represents a valid example of serendipity and cross-fertilization among unrelated sectors taking shape in a city of art. Thus, Florence demonstrated a favourable creative habitat where a network of economic, non-economic and institutional actors endowed with creativity and belonging to a cultural cluster managed to change an innovative idea into a successful innovation. The general context and the information setting contributed to this achievement, probably by shortening the cognitive distance between actors belonging to working sectors and situations that were only apparently distant (lateral proximity across sectors). Further in-depth research is certainly required to complete the analysis of the forces at work in this field, but the examination of the innovation's genesis and development, led through the identification of the main networks involved in the projects that made it possible, can give us a first remarkable result.

Research scheme and methodology

The object of the analysis is the restoration cluster in Florence, which is a significant field for investigating the relationship between culture and economy. The purpose is to answer the following research questions: Is the cultural cluster of restoration also a creative cluster? Is the city of art of Florence a favourable creative milieu for the developing of innovations? Who are the players capable of triggering and leading the innovation process?

While culture, according to the cultural district approach, was considered as a flywheel of economic development, here we shift from culture to creativity and try to analyze restoration as a creative cluster by focusing on creative actors and considering the city as a creative milieu. From this point of view, restoration is a creative industry, wherein the phenomena of cross-fertilization and serendipity emerge thanks to the case of the laser cleaning technologies.

Interest in the analysis emerged at the time of the restoration of the Gates of Paradise by Ghiberti,[7] which was carried out using the laser technology by some strategic actors from the Florentine and Tuscan setting. This fact led us to reconstruct the history of the laser innovation, specifically referring to what was going on, and also analyze the relational dynamics among that group of actors by examining the main funded projects.

The on-field analysis was achieved by using two different methodologies for collecting information. In the first stage, we conducted some in-depth interviews with privileged interlocutors, in terms of their role in the development of laser technologies for restoration. The interviews were made following the 'snowballing' method (Goodman 1961), which implies that the first person questioned is asked to supply the names of other subjects who also played a key role in the process, then the following person is asked the same question, and so on. This procedure was accomplished with the interviews of the main actors recommended in this way.[8]

This first stage proved that the laser technology had been the result of a collaboration among different actors, motivated by a common planning activity. Consequently, in the second stage, an analysis of the projects was carried out. An ad hoc database was collected with the information provided by IFAC–CNR,[9] an institution that had participated in almost all the projects and coordinated half of them. Throughout this course of action, twelve projects were selected, covering a time frame of nearly fifteen years (1995–2009). In order to draw up the governance structure and the relational dynamics in the creative cluster, as well as to highlight the role of different actors, the database was arranged in a workable form for the application of social network analysis (Wasserman and Faust 1994), with the purpose of finding the inter-subject relationships deriving from common participation in the projects.

The city of art as a new creative milieu

The genesis of innovation of laser technologies in conservation

The application of laser for the restoration of cultural goods started in the 1970s, with the works of John Asmus (Asmus *et al.* 1974), who first tested the potentialities of laser in cleaning a column in the Church of St Gregory in Venice. Asmus realized that the ruby laser technique, usually applied to holographic processes, could also be effective for cleaning the dome's columns. This 'accidental' discovery led Asmus to develop a series of tests on several materials, which he undertook between 1972 and 1974.

The importance and great potential of this technology was soon understood all over Europe, and in the subsequent years the countries with the greatest cultural endowments started to plan and implement activities aimed at developing the use of laser (Salimbeni *et al.* 2002). However, it was not until 1994, with the approval of two European projects,[10] that it was possible to implement and start the serial production of the first neodymium laser, which used optic fibre to transport radiation to the light-emitting hand-piece (Vergès-Belmin *et al.* 2003).

In 1995, the first conference on Lasers in Conservation of Artworks (LACONA) was held in Crete. Since then the international community, made up of physicists specializing in the restoration of cultural heritage, restorers (the real end-users) and developer enterprises, regularly meet every two years.

In Europe, many initiatives to develop laser-technology testing were undertaken, with several of them benefiting from the funding received through European projects.[11]

However, although there had been wide experimentation to determine the impact of using lasers in the preservation of cultural heritage, a well-developed laser system for restoration fully accredited by restorers and conservators by the late 1990s was still non-existent in Europe.

In this situation, Tuscany has emerged as the place where the greatest persistence was shown to test the use of laser for preserving and restoring cultural and art goods.

This undertaking was made by a public body, the Workshop for Hard Stone (Opificio delle Pietre Dure – OPD), a centre of excellence in restoration with headquarters in Florence, through a local firm who made a first attempt in 1979. The result of the application of a carbon dioxide (CO_2) laser was not encouraging, because the laser was too powerful and the marble absorbed too much heat. However, in spite of the failure, this first test gave the opportunity to make OPD more aware of the use of laser.

About ten years later, in 1992, OPD collaborated with IFAC to address the cleaning of paintings, and later the cleaning of stone material. This experience encouraged OPD to deem feasible the design of a more appropriate device, and IFAC, having specific competencies in laser technology, suggested that the ideal implementer of such a programme could be El.En., a firm also located in Florence.

To do this, the project, called SMART CLEAN, got off the ground (Margheri *et al.* 2000) and developed a new laser system, the Nd:YAG, which obviously required a preliminary analysis of effects on different materials. The partnership of the El.En. Group in the project certainly represented a significant factor in the effort: in fact, the Florentine firm, with internationally recognized know-how in medical ablation techniques using lasers, offered the opportunity to plan a low-cost implementation of the product, which could very well be included in its batch production of biomedical lasers.

Accordingly, in 1996, the physicians started an extensive stage of analysis, for the most part on stone materials, which allowed El.En. to create a new laser product, modified with regard to both its impulse and duration. The last puzzle piece in the innovation development was filled by local institutions, which supported the testing and application of laser to restore pieces of the art present in the territory.

The phases of the innovation process: a walk through the project activities

The twelve projects selected, who were by some means associated with the use of laser in restoration, allow us to reconstruct the various stages of the innovation process.

The research and development (R&D) activity was concentrated in the 1990s, particularly with regard to stones and metals. The early 2000s were mainly characterized by the *in loco* testing and experimentation of laser technology, and the field of application was extended to include other materials, such as masonry, frescos and paintings. At present, the innovation process is going through a period of exploration, searching new paths in the conservation and archeometric application of laser to cultural assets, with particular reference to metals.

The very first projects were led by IFAC, in the framework of a series of initiatives taken by CNR, and were characterized by intense research, aimed at verifying the applicability of the technologies of photoablative laser to preservative restoration. At this initial stage, the institute took in other actors with complementary competencies, such as restorers, physicists, chemists, laser specialists and experts in laser systems engineering, revealing its interdisciplinary approach.

In 1997–2000, the programme of the Tuscany Region on Regional High-Technology Network marked a key moment in the development of laser technology, for three particular reasons. First, the central unit of the partnership (IFAC, OPD, El.En.) was formalized and will be thus maintained for the following twenty years, during which time it will invest time and resources trying to find new applications of this technology to the sector of restoration. Second, the implementation of a prototype was made, the so-called SMART CLEAN, which will be produced and commercialized by El.En., and lay the groundwork for its further improvements and adjustments. Third, En.El. was able, thanks to the funding of this project, to invest in the production line of lasers for restoration.

In the course of the project, a comparison among different typologies of laser was made in order to choose the most appropriate for each kind of material to be restored, with the resulting identification of the various optimum methodologies, and their translation into parameters of laser emission for the use in restoration. But the really substantial step forward in the innovative process was the implementation of a prototype neodymium, the YAG laser (the aforementioned SMART CLEAN). This had several innovative factors: it was transportable, and radiation was transmitted by an optic fibre cable, allowing a convenient use in restoration yards. In fact, the operator was able to direct the laser radiation precisely to the affected area by moving only the optic hand-piece, and leaving the rest of the machine still. A few tests were made at the Rucellai Palace in Florence and the Chapel of the Square in Siena, with the Superintendence of both towns very satisfied with the results.

At that point (2000), research addressed a laser system capable of varying not only the strength and the repetition frequency of the impulse, but also its length, which is a useful characteristic for restoring stone and other materials. The result was a prototype neodymium YAG laser called VARIO, which was characterized by a variable length of impulse, and consequently could be used on different materials. R&D having progressed to such a good point and the tool having been tested, the network resolved to undertake technological transfer and started to involve a substantial number of firms, from both the restoration sector, and others, like diagnostics and information and communications technology (ICT) sectors.

Another project financed by Tuscany Region (Optocantieri) was aimed at enlarging the network and starting to actually use laser technology, with the cleaning of some artworks from three sites: the Miracle Square (Pisa); the Old Palace and the Cathedral Santa Maria del Fiore (Florence); and the 'Fonte Gaia' (Siena). A key factor, in the latter case, was that end-users were directly involved, as they were given the opportunity to try the laser and validate its technology.

In parallel with the projects more typically addressed by R&D and technological transfer, the European funds allowed the undertaking of extensive networking and dissemination activities worldwide. The aim was to create an international, multidisciplinary community that would promote the recognized, validated use of laser for cultural assets restoration. The project, 'COST Action G7', together with the two Culture 2000 Programmes, represented an important opportunity to spread into Europe, as they brought into the international debate the opportunities/ threats deriving from the laser option, even trying to advance a sort of 'Italian line' for the solution to the problem.

Finally, the latest developments in this field concern the exploration of innovative paths arising from the real demands of operators. Specifically, two projects are now underway whose purpose is to diversify the application of laser in the area of cultural assets ('Authentico' for anti-falsification guarantee and 'Start' for a new laser systems applied to restoration diagnostics and works).

The art restoration cluster in Florence: from cultural cluster to creative cluster

Figure 9.2 shows the structure of the cultural cluster of restoration as it was identified in the analysis of Florence (Lazzeretti 2003). The study focused on the detection of a critical mass of actors that, through the economic enhancement of cultural and artistic resources, triggered relational dynamics capable of contributing to the economic development of the territory.

Currently, our interest lies in understanding whether, and eventually which, of these actors have played a key role in the innovation process leading to the utilization of laser technologies for the restoration of artworks.

The role of the key actors in the initiation of the innovative process, and the (human, technical, scientific, financial and relational) resources involved in it are now examined in detail.

The twelve projects selected covered a time frame of fifteen years (1995–2010) and include a total of eighty-one actors. As regards localization, it is interesting to note that half of the subjects who took part in these activities are localized in Tuscany.[12]

The analysis of the typology of actors confirms that the greatest role in the innovation was played, on one part, by research centres and, on the other, by firms and institutional actors. On the whole, these three sets covered about 88 per cent of all actors involved and, in particular, there was a marked prevalence of the world of research (50 per cent of the total), followed by the industrial world

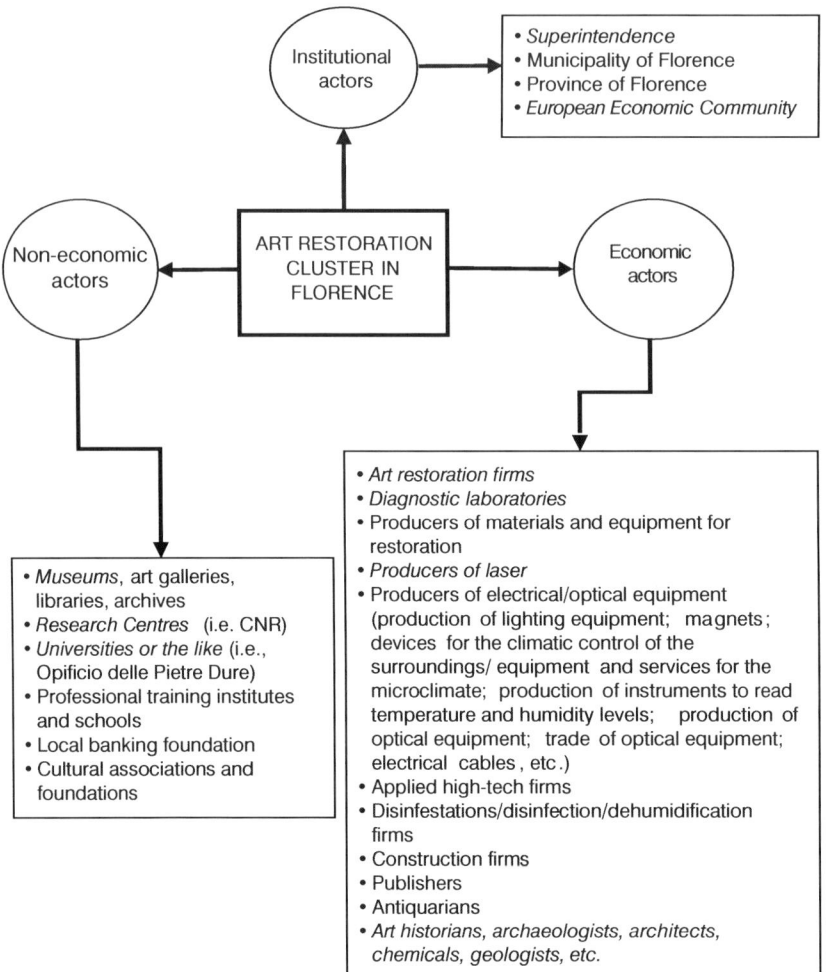

Figure 9.2 The cultural cluster of restoration in Florence

Source: Our elaboration
Note: In italics are the creative actors participating to the development of the technological innovation of laser in the filed of artistic restoration.

(21 per cent), and the institutions (18 per cent). It is worth noticing that the only large firm is El.En., and this is because regional project funds are only granted to small and medium firms.

The survey of the competencies of the participating actors shows that these projects required a broad multidisciplinarity. One third of the sample comprises subjects directly connected with the field of preservation and promotion of cultural assets (20 per cent), and restoration (15 per cent). A significant presence is obviously that of optoelectronics (15 per cent), the economic sector owning the technical competencies for laser development. To complete the picture of the technical capabilities required, chemistry and physics registered at 11 per cent.

Another relevant point concerns the financial resources to which the actors involved were able to access: more than five million euros overall were invested into the twelve projects. The actors who received the most public money were research centres (61 per cent) and universities (19 per cent), while firms, despite their fairly substantial involvement, received a little less than 6 per cent of the total resources.

Finally, some interesting results can be seen from the point of view of the competencies involved: apart from optoelectronics, which, as it might be expected, had the highest share of financing (25 per cent), the other actors to receive the most funding were diagnostics (20 per cent) and ICT (19 per cent), while smaller percentages were allocated chemistry and physics (7 per cent), and restoration (5 per cent).

After describing the main characteristics of the actors involved in the twelve projects, we analyzed the structure of the relationships within the network in order to understand in more detail who had actually played the most active role and governed the innovation process. It is in fact possible, with the assistance of social network analysis, to draw up the network, the place occupied by each subject and the main ways of relationship governance.

The participation rates of actors again show the prevalence of IFAC, who entered into partnership in eleven of the projects. As already mentioned, this data is partly affected by the methodology used to build the sample; nevertheless, it certainly indicates the significant activity of the CNR Institute in the planning stage. The figures for other organizations, such as OPD, the Department of Environmental Sciences of Siena University and the El.En. Group, are also quite significant.

As sixty-six actors out of eighty-one (i.e. 81.5 per cent of the total) participated in only one project, we can infer a small cohesion, which indicates that the central unit that carried out the innovation activities comprises an extremely small number of actors.

The density indexes show that the average number of projects to which each couple of actors co-participated was 0.3219, and that 30.5 per cent of the total number of couples were co-members in one or more projects. These figures alone convey the image of a loosely cohesive network, especially if related to its small size, but it is also necessary to combine this information with the indexes presented below, which help to better define the network.

The first index is the degree of centrality, which corresponds to the number of direct connections a single actor has built. Under this profile, the network appears strongly centralized around IFAC, who co-participated in the projects with a total number of seventy-eight organizations, that is, 97.5 per cent of all the actors. Other subjects who show a certain degree of centrality are all foreign actors, and their central position in the network mainly derives from their participation in the 'COST Action G7' alone. An exception worth noting is offered by the cases of the Romanian National Institute of Research and Development for Optoelectronics (INOE–Romania), the Spanish Instituto de Química-Física 'Rocasolano' (IQFR), and the Greek Institute of Electronic Structure and Laser (FORTH–IESL), whose visibility in the network is the result of more well-structured relations.

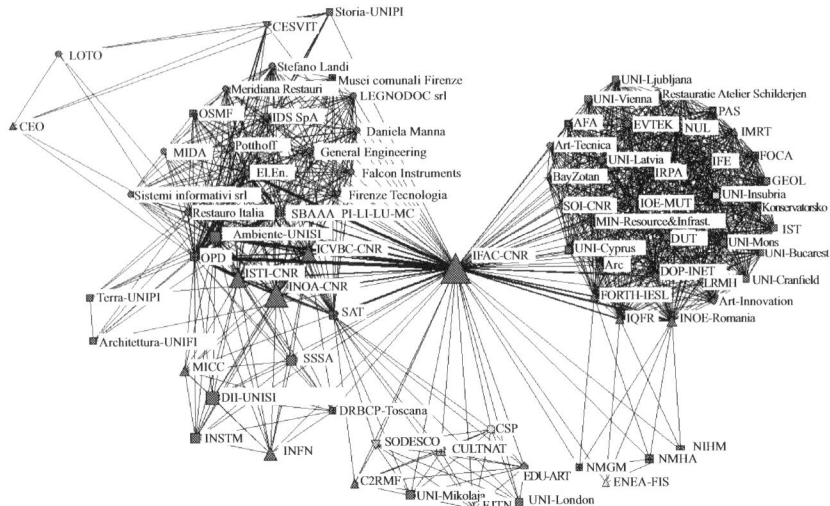

Figure 9.3 The network of laser for restoration (c ≥ 1)*

Source: Lazzeretti, Capone and Cinti (2011: 165)
Legend: The different shades of gray of the nodes indicate the site (black for Tuscany, light grey for the rest of Italy, dark grey for Europe, white for non-European countries); the different shapes of the nodes show the typology (a triangle for research centres, a square for universities, a circle for firms, a plus sign inside a square for the agencies, a coloured circle inside a square for academies, a plus sign for associations); the dimension of each node is a proportional representation of the financial resources received. * The value expressed by 'c' stands for the minimum number of projects shared by each couple of actors.

The second index is the betweenness centrality, which denotes the importance attached to a certain actor in a relationship network, in terms of its role as a go-between contact with other subjects. In this respect, IFAC also maintains its central position, and is established as the coordinator – because of its part as well as its action – of the relationships developed through the planning activities. However, another visible feature is the significant presence of other local actors who work as intermediate centres and connectors: OPD and Siena's Department of Environmental Science are privileged interlocutors as regards laser development, as well as the Archaeological Superintendence of Tuscany (Soprintendenza Archeologica Toscana – SAT) and then there are Pisa's Department of Historical Science of the Ancient World, other CNR institutes and El.En.

The examination of the centrality indexes can be combined with the analysis of the relational topology as it is revealed in a graphic representation of the network of actors (Burt and Minor 1983) who participated in the twelve projects. By looking at Figure 9.3, it is possible to make some interesting remarks.

First of all, the Institute of Physics clearly represents the most central node around which the others catalyse: therefore, it is the actor who holds the most (relational) power within the network and has a connector role.

Second, two macro-blocks take shape: the Tuscan one on the left and the European one on the right. In this regard, IFAC works as a 'bridge' between the

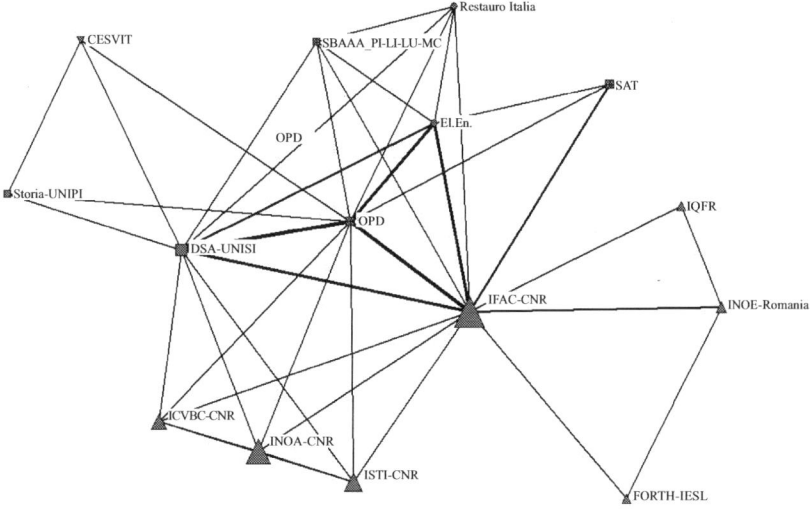

Figure 9.4 The network of laser for restoration (c ≥ 2)

Source: Our elaboration

local and the international levels. It can also be considered a so-called 'cut-point', which means that once it is removed, the constituents of the network increase: in our case, for that event, they would become two – one with a marked local profile and the other European; specifically, the actors who take on a first-rate role as connectors are SAT on the one hand, and INOE–Romania, FORTH–IESL and IQFR on the other.

Third, we can observe that the subjects who received the largest shares of funds for the projects (the biggest nodes) are not necessarily the most central: if we look at the list of actors having a high betweenness and centrality, we can see that as many as nine of them do not appear among the first fifteen for financial resources received.

Considering higher levels of co-participation, i.e. including in the analysis only the couples of actors who took part in at least two projects (Figure 9.4), we observe:

- a sharp reduction of the size of the network, which decreases from eighty-one to fifteen nodes;
- international openness almost completely disappearing;
- the preservation of a central block of subjects mostly belonging to the research system, but also to institutions and industry.

Only six actors participate in at least three projects, and only four take part in four projects. The pattern of the network presents a nucleus corresponding to the group of actors who offered an essential contribution in the development of the technology, thus confirming the previous analyses: they are OPD, IFAC,

El.En. and Siena's Department of Environmental Sciences. In this respect, it is important to recognize the role of a 'triple-helical' lever of innovation (Etzkowitz and Leydesdorff 1998). In fact, the highest degree of participation (i.e. in five projects) is registered only by three actors.

Going back to the initial scheme of the cultural cluster of restoration (Figure 9.2), we can now state that some of those players have actively participated in the development of the innovation. The organizational structure that has followed this process is characterized by a circular architecture of relationships, which shows knowledge sharing among research centres (including universities), firms and institutions. Unlike the classical linear model 'research, development, production and marketing', in the analyzed case we note that the development phase provided constant feedback to the process, re-orienting the research towards new combinations of existing know-how.[13] This has allowed not only the fine-tuning of the laser technology with more adequate parameters, but also the opening up of new potential applications for this technology.

Political institutions, in particular, play a twofold role: on the one hand they represent the main interlocutor of the R&D players (in this case, actors such as the Superintendence of Cultural Heritage and the institutes of restoration), while on the other hand they have economically fuelled the process by financing the projects (Tuscany Region).

Moreover, two types of relationships emerge: those strictly to do with R&D activities, where the end-users participation as interlocutors of institutions, and those spreading to developing firms and research centres in the phase of technological transfer. Figure 9.5 highlights the modelling of relations both in general and specifically as regards R&D and technology transfer.

Conclusions

To summarize, this chapter enters into the recent debate involving culture, creativity and innovation by presenting a successful case of innovation that has taken place in a city of art, and which can be interpreted through the lens of the CCC perspectives.

What we previously studied as an example of economic enhancement of culture in cities of art is now proposed as a case of innovation developed by a creative cluster. In other words, restoration firms are no longer just cultural industries capable of economically enhancing cultural heritage, but they have become creative resources and actors within the creative city.

As regards the questions that we attempted to investigate with the present work, we can provide roughly positive answers.

The cultural cluster can be considered as a creative cluster, since it was capable of developing such an important innovation as that of laser technologies for artworks, even though not all the identified actors played the same role. The innovative idea initially emerged in Venice and has found Florence a suitable environment for developing thanks to the financial support of the Tuscany Region and some European projects. In this context, Florence has proven to be a creative

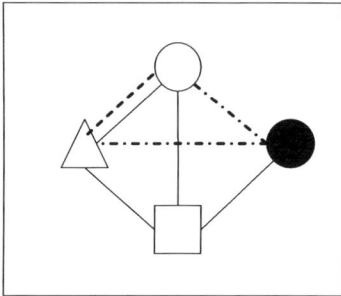

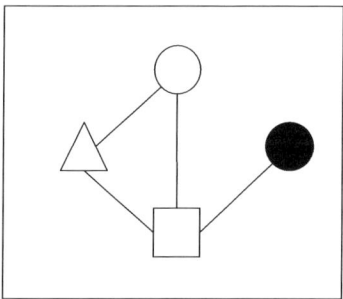
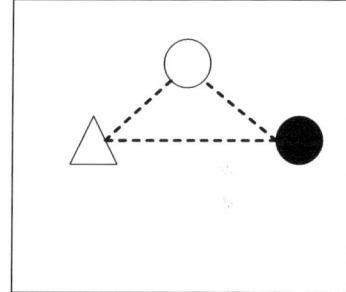

Figure 9.5 The modelling of core relations in the local network of laser applied to restoration

Source: Our elaboration
Note: The triangle represents research centres and universities; the square institutions; the white circle developing firms; the black circle end users; the continuous line indicates the R&D phase in a strict sense; the dotted line the technologic transfer phase of innovation.

environment capable of favouring and implementing innovative process and knowledge transfer.

Discussing the main results according to a theoretical perspective and attempting to identify a potential research trajectory, we can underline the following elements.

A first interesting result emerges from the study of the genesis of the innovation of laser technologies in heritage conservation. With reference to the CCC perspective, this innovation can be classified as an emblematic case of serendipity, initially starting thanks to technological correlation and then developing through cross-fertilization among unrelated clusters/sectors.

The innovation generates and asserts itself thanks to lateral thinking, as this is capable of creating *unusual relatedness* between two apparently distant sectors (health diagnostics and cultural goods). The existence of a cognitive lateral proximity between the main actors plays a key role: the cultural good is treated by scientists as a sort of 'patient' to which medicine-related techniques are applied and whose preservation becomes the object of joint efforts by apparently distant professionals such as technologists, physicists, art historians and architects. Equally, other kinds of proximity, such as physical and institutional, appear to facilitate the interaction. Most of the actors involved are Florentine or Tuscan and most of the nodes identified by the network analysis are locally rooted. Some of them, moreover – such as the Tuscany Region, the Superintendence of Cultural Heritage and the restorers themselves – participate in other cultural clusters, such as the museum and the biomedical regional (e.g. Toscana Life Sciences) clusters, thus increasing the overall level of institutional proximity.

Laser technologies in conservation can be qualified in one way as a 'disruptive innovation' that could be put forward as a candidate to complement (or even replace) existing chemical technologies for cleaning materials.[14]

From these elements, it thus seems appropriate to ascribe this typology of innovation to the category of 'open innovations' originated outside traditional R&D laboratories: a transversal innovation, developed by a creative cluster of economic, non-economic and institutional actors that contribute to defining the city of art as an example of creative milieu.

A second finding to underline is related to the strategic role played by the creative environment. In this sense, the city of art is a candidate to be classified – together with open source communities and industrial districts – among the new types of 'public spaces', informal and creative places whose fundamental contribution to the development of the new 'open innovation' paradigm (Chesbrough 2003) has been identified by Lester and Piore (2004). To this end, we are reminded that the genesis and development of laser technologies for conservation took place in two cities of art, Venice and Florence, which are characterized by a large endowment of cultural heritage. Both cities have been crucial for the development of the innovation, but in different modalities and circumstances. Whereas in the first case the strategic stimulus was represented by the solving of problems generated by a natural catastrophe such as a flood; in the second a pivotal role was played not only by the presence of a cultural heritage to be restored, but also by a system of values shared by the main actors, which acted as a relational 'glue'. In Florence, the path dependence of the place and the actors that dates back to the Renaissance clearly emerges. This is the story of success of a human network capable of starting a virtuous cycle that has then involved institutions.

A crucial question can then be raised: Could this happen in a different place from Florence? Certainly, many of the concepts and instruments used in this case study provide some answers, but these are not sufficient to generalize the hypotheses contained in the model. These first results help us, though, to better identify a new trajectory of study of open innovation phenomena that enters into the analysis of the relationships connecting creativity, cities of art, technology and public space.

Notes

1   The creative economy highlights the role of the human factor and of the creative class and puts creative cities side by side with cultural cities and industries as the main protagonists of the development of the knowledge economy.

2 Serendipity is treated here only as an asset, but it can also be a liability. Both positive and negative outcomes of serendipity can occur, where the case of laser in conservation technologies constitutes a successful example. In addition, the positive effects of 'chance' can also be partly attributed to phenomena of path dependence and resilience in the city of art (Cooke 2010), which is a system capable of both preserving and advancing in a mix of old and new knowledge.

3 'The lateral thinker tends to explore all the different ways of looking at something rather than accepting the most promising and proceeding from that' (De Bono 1971: 10).

4 Cognitive proximity can be found for instance in temporary networks of artists who come into contact for the organization of cultural events (projects, exhibits and festivals) or, on a virtual level, in epistemic communities like open source software.

5 Restoration activities have also become the focal issue of museum exhibitions, such as in the case of Donatello's *David* exhibited at the Museo Nazionale del Bargello of Florence in 2009.

6 For a more detailed analysis we refer the reader to Lazzeretti (2009).

7 The restoration of the Porte del Ghiberti started in 1982 with different technologies, but not until 1999 was a first laser attempt was realized.

8 The main actors interviewed were: Dr Salimbeni (director) and Dr Siano (researcher) of the IFAC-CNR; Professor Masotti (founder and president of the scientific committee of El.En., a group that manufactures and distributes high-tech laser systems); Dr Giusti (Director of the Sector for the Restoration of Stones, Bronzes and Ancient Weapons of the Workshop for Hard Stone – Opificio delle Pietre Dure, OPD); the building surveyor Dr Bianchini of the Duomo Museum and Dr Beatrice Paolozzi Strozzi, Director of the Bargello Museum.

9 Institute of Applied Physics, Centre of National Research.

10 The two projects were Brite-Euram LAMA, 'LAser MAnuporteable for stone conservation' (FP4), which ended in 1996, and Eureka-Eurocare RESTOR (FP5), which ended in 2001.

11 The first European projects gave a substantial financial contribution to laser application for marble and stone (LASERART); soon after, the clearing of paper and vellum (LACLEPA, PARELA, PAPERTECH); then painting cleaning (ENV2C, INART); and finally the application of laser to diagnostics, and holographic records (LASERACT, HISTO-CLEAN, INTAS, PROMET and MULTIENCODE).

12 The actors located in Tuscany constitute 43.2 per cent of the sample, while 3.7 per cent is scattered in the rest of Italy, 50.6 per cent in the rest of Europe, and 2.5 per cent are non-European.

13 This phase has been defined as 'analytic design' (Kline and Rosenberg 1986).

14 This is both a product and a process innovation, basically induced by the end-users. At its discovery stage, the polishing potential on stone materials of laser technologies was revealed in the same process as the making of holograms. Later, its further development was subjected to many subsequent adjustments and finally became a successful product used by restorers as a community of practice. One strategic aspect has been the adaptation of the laser hand-piece to the working conditions of operators (on scaffolding) from the point of view of both the difficult working environment and work ergonomics.

References

Andersson, D.E., Andersson, E.A. and Mellander, C. (2011) *Handbook of Creative Cities*, Cheltenham: Edward Elgar.

Asmus, J.F., Murphy, C.G. and Munk, W.H. (1974) 'Studies on the interaction of laser radiation with art artefacts', in R.F. Wuerker (ed.) *Developments in Laser Technology*

II, Proceedings of the Society of Photo-Optical Instrumentation Engineers, 17th Annual Technical Meeting, 1973, Palos Verdes Estates, CA: SPIE, pp. 19–30.

Belussi, F. and Staber, U. (2011) *Managing Networks of Creativity*, London: Routledge.

Boschma, R.A. (2005) 'Proximity and innovation. A critical assessment', *Regional Studies*, 39(1): 61–74.

Boschma, R. and Martin, R. (eds) (2010) *The Handbook of Evolutionary Economic Geography*, Cheltenham: Edward Elgar.

Burt, R.S. and Minor, M.J. (eds) (1983) *Applied Network Analysis*, Beverly Hills, CA: Sage.

Chesbrough, H. (2003) *Open Innovation: The New Imperative for Creating and Profiting from Technology*, Boston, MA: Harvard Business School Press.

Cooke, P. (2010) *Transversality and Transition: Branching to New Regional Path Dependence*, Papers in Evolutionary Economic Geography No. 10.10, Utrech: Utrech University, Urban and Regional Research Centre Utrech.

Cooke, P., Asheim, B., Martin, R., Schwartz, D. and Todtling, F. (2011) *Handbook of Regional Innovation and Growth*, Cheltenham: Edward Elgar.

Cunha, M.P., Clegg, S.R. and Mendonca, S. (2010) 'On serendipity and organizing', *European Management Journal*, 28(5): 319–30.

De Bono, E. (1971) *The Use of Lateral Thinking*, 1st edn 1967, Harmondsworth, Middlesex: Penguin Books.

Etzkowitz, H. and Leydesdorff, L. (eds) (1998) *Universities in the Global Economy: A Triple Helix of University-Industry-Government Relations*, London: Cassell Academic.

Florida, R. (2002) *The Rise of the Creative Class: And how it's Transforming Work, Leisure and Everyday Life*, New York: Basic Books.

Goodman, L.A. (1961) 'Snowball sampling', *Annals of Mathematical Statistics*, 32(1): 148–70.

Jeffcutt, P. and Pratt, A. (2002) 'Managing creativity in the cultural industries', *Creativity and Innovation Management*, 11(4): 225–33.

Kline, S.J. and Rosenberg, N. (1986) 'An overview of innovation', in R.N. Landau and N. Rosenberg (eds) *The Positive Sum Strategy*, Washington: National Academy Press, pp. 275–306.

Lazzeretti, L. (2003) 'City of art as a HC local system and cultural districtualization processes. The cluster of art restoration in Florence', *International Journal of Urban and Regional Research*, 27(3): 635–48.

Lazzeretti, L. (2009) 'The creative capacity of culture and the new creative milieu', in G. Becattini, M. Bellandi and L. De Propris (eds) *The Handbook of Industrial Districts*, Cheltenham: Edward Elgar, pp. 281–94.

Lazzeretti, L., Capone, F. and Cinti, T. (2011) 'Open innovation in the city of art: The case for laser technologies for conservation in Florence', *City, Culture and Society*, 2(1): 159–168.

Lester, R.K. and Piore, M.J. (2004) *Innovation. The Missing Dimension*, Cambridge, MA: Harvard University Press.

Margheri, F., Modi, S., Masotti, L., Mazzinghi, P., Pini, R., Siano, S. and Salimbeni, R. (2000) 'SMART CLEAN: A new laser system with improved emission characteristics and transmission through long optical fibres', *Journal of Cultural Heritage*, 1(Suppl. 1): S119–23.

Potts, J., Hartley, J., Banks, J., Burgess, J., Cobcroft, R., Cunningham, S. and Montgomery, L. (2008) 'Consumer co-creation and situated creativity', *Industry and Innovation*, 15(5): 459–74.

Pratt, A.C. and Jeffcutt, P. (2009) *Creativity, Innovation and the Cultural Economy*, London and New York: Routledge.

Salimbeni, R., Pini, R. and Siano, S. (2002) 'Thirty years of laser applications in conservation', in A.H. Guenther (ed.) *International Trends in Applied Optics*, Bellingham, WA: SPIE Press, pp. 667–688.

Schreiner, M. and Strlic, M. (eds) (2006) *Handbook on the Use of Lasers in Conservation and Conservation Science*, Brussels: COST Action G7.

Scott, A. (2004) 'Cultural-products industries and urban economic development: Prospects for growth and market contestation in global context', *Urban Affairs Review*, 39(4): 461–90.

Staber, U. (2004) 'Networking beyond organizational boundaries: The case of project organizations', *Creativity and Innovation Management*, 13(1): 30–40.

Storper, M. and Scott, A. (2009) 'Rethinking human capital, creativity and urban growth', *Journal of Economic Geography*, 9(2): 147–67.

Towse, R. (ed.) (2003) *A Handbook of Cultural Economics*, Cheltenham: Edward Elgar.

Vergès-Belmin, V., Wiedemann, G., Weber, L., Cooper, M., Crump, D. and Gouerne, R. (2003) 'A review of health hazards linked to the use of lasers for stone cleaning', *Journal of Cultural Heritage*, 4(Suppl. 1): 33S–37S.

Wasserman, S. and Faust, K. (1994) Social Network Analysis: Methods and Applications, New York: Cambridge University Press.

10 Geographical proximity and new short supply food chains

Leïla Kebir and André Torre

Short supply food chains and innovation?

Short supply food chains (SSFCs) have long existed. Before the mid-nineteenth century, Paris was for example mainly supplied by its surrounding agriculture (Fleury and Donadieu 1997). In the countryside it was (and still is) not unlikely that people bought or exchanged local food products in more or less merchant relations. The reduction of transportation costs, as well as the development of agro-based industries and long anonymous supply chains have loosened, and in most cases broken, the relation between growers and end-users.

A recent but still fuzzy notion

The recent resurgence of SSFCs has come alongside the development of innovative forms of farming by involving new commercial practices (more direct selling). But before analyzing these new forms of food production and commercialization, often named 'alternative food chains' or 'alternative food networks', let us start with a definition of what we mean here by SSFC.

Based on Parker (2005) a supply food chain is considered short when the geographic distance between the farm and the consumer is perceived as low and/ or when the number of intermediaries between the producer and the consumer is reduced (ideally one maximum). The boundaries of such supply food chains vary. In France, for instance, the Ministry of Agriculture (Ministère de l'Agriculture et de la Pêche 2009) has launched an official national definition relying on the number of intermediaries: one, regardless of geographical distance. In this sense, it has privileged the direct relation between producer and consumer rather than the geographical distance between them, that is left unbounded. Moreover Selfa and Qazi (2005) have shown that distance can be perceived quite differently by producers and consumers, in urban and rural areas; nevertheless shortness in our context usually relates to the 'local' scale. Some have given ideal limits: the Canadians Smith and MacKinnon (2007) have for example limited their purchasing area to 160 km (100 miles) in the same chain; a recent French locavore suggested 200 km (Novel 2010). The development of local foodism and the scarcity of local production (in particular when the farming approach is organic) tend to loosen these limits. In the French Community Supported Agriculture (CSA) movement it is not unlikely that a lot of kilometres stand between the producer(s) filling the week box and the consumers' association even though 'geographical proximity' appears to be one of the preoccupations here.

In this respect there are many forms of SSFCs: direct selling schemes (on-farm selling, farmers' market, pick-your-own, producers shop, CSA, box schemes from the farm, etc.), collective points of sale, local school food schemes, catering services by restaurants, supermarkets provisioning, box schemes from retailers, Internet selling, etc. Each involves different and more or less intense geographical proximity and producer–consumer relations.

SSFCs have been mobilizing North Western citizens, activists, policy makers and researchers. The latter have had different agendas according to their social context. According to Goodman (2003), North American literature has been marked by the questions of activism against large agro-industrial corporations. Whilst in Europe, rural development and agriculture competitiveness through agro-innovation have mobilized most attention. Therefore, there are two major sub-issues with SSFCs. First the restoration, after recurrent food crisis, of food quality and trust relations between producers and consumers and through this the restoration of the relation to food: the *relocation issue*. Second the shortening of physical distance between producers and consumers as a mean for the maintenance and development of North Western threatened urban agriculture and rural areas: the *territorial development and agriculture safeguard issues*.

In both issues the 'local' appears as the vehicle of some form of intrinsic quality that can be objectified, described and most of all marketed on the food market (freshness, trust, information, etc.). This 'local' quality provides (or is at least is expected to provide) competitiveness between food products and most of all between *generic* food products, such as carrots, cabbage and leeks whose production does not require the use of specific assets such as *terroir*, tradition and local know-how, etc. As such it challenges the means of regional competitiveness that have indicated the importance of specificity in the paradigm of competition through differentiation and competitive advantages. Local food is in this sense a very different scheme from PGI/PDO (Protected Geographical Indicator/Protected Designation of Origin), Appellation d'Origine Contrôlée (AOC, a label guaranteeing the quality of wine in France) or even slow food movements that tend to valorize specificity and protect *terroir* and know-how (Torre 2006). Of course both can overlap: products sold under PGI are often sold through SSFC (on the farm, at the cellar or farmers' market) – in connection for example with tourism – but their main purpose is exportation from the local area. Both are about quality, but at very different levels. As we mentioned before, SSCF relies on geography regardless of specificity. Geography appears here more alive than ever! It nevertheless still relies on innovation and, as we will see, on the redefinition of the symbolic meaning of food products.

New forms of short supply food chains

Today authors distinguish 'old' forms of short supply chains (farmers' market, buy on farms, etc.) from more innovative ones (box schemes, CSA forms, pick-your-own farms, etc.) (Delfosse and Bernard 2007). Nowadays, the development of these old and new forms are challenging farming production and consumption systems technically (more complex farming due to diversification of production, distribution and commercial extra-organization, know-how and skills development, etc.), socio-institutionally (emergence of new actors, network structure, new forms of contracts – CSAs, etc.) and territorially (scales articulation, proximity/ distance relations, relocation processes, etc.) (Ilbery and Maye 2005a; Aubry *et al.* forthcoming). They give rise to knowledge development (agricultural skills, communication ability, organizational skills, media, organizational structures of the supply chain, consumers' knowledge on food and on their region, etc.) and new forms of organization.

Moreover, SSFCS are also associated in the literature with the studies devoted to 'alternative food networks/food chains' (Renting *et al.* 2003; Winter 2005; Sonnino and Marsden 2006). These alternative farming models have developed in contrast to the industrial, rationalist, distrustful and for many producers unprofitable agriculture (the proportion of land as well as the number of farms has dramatically decreased in the last twenty years). They are characterized by notably more artisanal, quality, organic or sustainable-oriented farming practices, short supplying and embeddedness (Ilbery and Maye 2005b). The relation to space and the re-creation of a proximity relation between producers and consumers is fundamentally structuring (Renting *et al.* 2003). Although, SSFCs appear as an essential piece of these new models of farming it must be noted that all SSFCs are not necessary part of alternative food chains (the conventional, large-scale farmer can sell some of his production on a farmers' market) and also the frontiers between conventional and alternative can be porous (Ilbery and Maye 2005a). It is not unlikely that alternative producers sell part of their production on international markets (Vassor 2007; Aubry and Chiffoleau 2009).

Almost all SSFCs rely on the existence of niche food markets related to hypermodern and multifaceted (Chinese fast food for lunch, organic local salad plus home-baked meat pie with good AOC French wine for dinner) food consumption practices, and are characterized by a demand seeking differentiation (Ascher 2005; Manniche 2007). The symbolic dimension of food products is incorporated in what is called 'value-laden information' (Renting *et al.* 2003), which is the information related to the nature of the product, its provenance, the modes of production and its quality, but also the way one can cook it, the symbolic meaning of buying local food, etc.

The added value of these chains is built upon the information the consumer has. If the latter does not know about the provenance of the product for example, it cannot be valued as 'local'. In Île-de-France (greater Paris region) for instance many producers sell all or part of their production on the nearby international wholesale food Market of Rungis, which is then redistributed through standard supply chains to local supermarkets, restaurants, school canteens, farmers' market suppliers, etc. These 'local' products end up on the plate in the same way as any other non-local product. Therefore, the issue of the constitution and diffusion of the value-laden information, as well as the way it is objectivized and transmitted to the consumer either directly or through cultural artefacts (books, papers, TV reports, etc.) is a central part of the innovation dimension of contemporary SSFCs. Internet websites, newsletters, designed packaging, direct communication or information on the producer or the farm (picture, news on the daily life of, etc.) accompany most of SSFC's new schemes. They are fundamental to the sense building that is needed to objectivize and concretize the proximity relation. These communication channels also exist on the consumer side, from consumers to consumers (websites, blogs, etc.) and constitute powerful relays of dissemination of these new forms of food purchase.

The large number of existing box schemes, initiatives for local food marketing, etc. reveals this creative emulation. These promising and creative forms of commercialization proves to be reactive in the capacity of actors to reinvent forms of supplying and purchasing but most of all of creating sense and building the means to activate proximity relations between consumers and producers. But they have not yet been able to prove their sustainability, be that in environmental, social and/or economical terms (Jarosz 2008; Coley *et al.* 2009).

Finally, many authors have mentioned the importance of the quality turn related to the production practices associated with alternative food chains and thus SSFCs (organic production, attention to taste, *terroir* forms of productions, etc.) (see, for example, Goodman 2003; Sonnino and Marsden 2006; Manniche 2007). The quality turn in question here develops mainly in opposition to tasteless, industrial agriculture. In fact it is not really related to food security or organoleptic superiority, but rather to the idea that this food is of a different kind and is shared between smart people too: the symbolic dimension is crucial here. But as mentioned before the 'quality' is also strongly embodied in the 'local' or 'proximity' dimension of the product. The question being asked is: Which aspect is the most relevant in particular when the question of sustainable agriculture is raised (Ilbery and Maye 2005b)? As explained by Ilbery and Maye (2005a), if geographical proximity is preferred (which seems to possibly be the case), qualities such as organic or more sustainable production processes can be abandoned in favour of local agriculture support and, in the worst case, defensive localism (Winter 2003).

Some basic definitions of proximity relations

The analysis of proximity relations (Boschma 2005; Torre 2008) proves to be a valuable field of research in various disciplines as well as for different topics such as innovation, industrial production and clusters' relations, or land use conflicts. We will show that it can be of great interest for the analysis of SSFCs as well, for at least two reasons:

- The first one is that this approach widely uses the term 'proximity', which is also used at length in local food approaches. Some of these local systems are even nowadays called 'economies of proximity'. This coincidence in the terms reveals the crucial concern for the questions of spatial distances and for the strong involvement of local actors.

- The second and most interesting reason is the fact that the analysis of proximity relations directly relies on the two main features at the basis of SSFCs: short distance between producers and consumers, and a network of people involved in the production or the consumption system.

In keeping with our previous work, we consider that the distinction between two main categories of proximity – 'geographical proximity' and 'organized proximity' (Torre and Rallet 2005) – redefined more precisely on the basis of recent research on the subject (Torre 2011), could be of a great importance in the explanation of the relationships that are set up in SSFCs. These notions of proximity refer, above all, to potentialities given to individuals, groups and human actions in general, in their technical and institutional dimensions. This potential may, or may not exist at a time t, and therefore may or may not be usable or actionable through the actions and representations of the actors (human or non-human). These types of proximity have no moral value and their existence constitutes neither an advantage nor a disadvantage. It is activation through human action that gives this potential its significance and value ('positive' or 'negative') in relation to the economic and social criteria that are relevant in the societies where it is found.

Geographical proximity

Geographical proximity is above all about distance. In its simplest definition, it is the number of metres or kilometres that separate two entities. But it is relative in three ways:

- In terms of the morphological characteristics of the spaces in which activities take place. There can be a 'crow flies' proximity, in the case of a trip by plane for example, but the nature of the terrain also plays a role: travelling from one point to another on a flat surface is not equivalent to climbing up and down a mountain in order to go from point A to point B.
- In terms of the availability of transport infrastructure. The existence of a road or a highway, of a railway or metro network, or of river-borne transport will make access to a place more or less quick and more or less easy. It is in this sense – that of Perroux – that we view functional distance.
- In terms of the financial resources of the individuals who use these transport infrastructures. A high-speed railway line might enable people to travel more quickly to and from two places, but its cost proves prohibitive for part of the population, at least in cases when the individuals have to travel frequently. Therefore, we shall say that the geographical proximity between two people, or between people and places, is partly related to the cost of transport, and to the financial means of individuals.

Geographical proximity is neutral in essence. It is human actions and perceptions that give it a more or less positive or negative dimension, as well as a certain usefulness. It is the way in which actors use it that matters. Thus, the fact that two firms are located in near proximity may or may not be a source of interaction: these two entities may remain indifferent to each other or they may choose to interact; in this latter case we talk of a mobilization of the potentialities of geographical proximity. But this mobilization can have different results depending on the actions undertaken. For example, in the case of innovating firms, it might be the diffusion of scientific or technological knowledge through the geographical spillover effect (Bönte 2008) but it might also lead to firms spying on other firms, or unduly reaping the benefits of an invention that is supposed to be protected by intellectual property right (Boschma 2005; Arend 2009).

Geographical proximity can be activated or mobilized by the actions of economic and social actors. Depending on their strategies or strategic choices, or according to their perceptions of their environment, the behaviours and attitudes of these actors vary and they mobilize geographical proximity differently. More precisely, actors might seek to get closer to or further away from certain people or places, or they might feel satisfied or dissatisfied with the geographical proximity of certain people, places or technical objects. Geographical proximity can be enhanced by the deploying of urban space, by the setting of localized clusters of innovation for example, or by the development of local networks of producers, exchanging knowledge and information through face-to-face contacts.

Organized proximity

Organized proximity too is a potential that can be activated or mobilized. Organized proximity refers to the different ways of being close to other actors, regardless of the degree of geographical proximity between individuals, the qualifier 'organized' referring to the arranged nature of human activities (and not to the fact that one may belong to any organization in particular[1]). Organized proximity rests on two main areas of logic, which do not necessarily contradict each other, and which we shall call the 'logic of belonging' and the 'logic of similarity'. Both can help in the setting of trust relations, because they help to build a set of common references and interpersonal links between participants to a joint project for example.

The *logic of belonging* refers to the fact that two or several actors belong to the same relationship graph or even to the same social network whether their relation is direct or intermediated. It can depend in the sector they are operating in; in this case they share common creative or innovation capital. It can be measured in terms of degrees of connectivity, reflecting more or less high degrees of organized proximity and therefore a more or less great potential of interaction or common action (Bouba-Olga and Zimmermann 2004). The development of interaction between two actors will be facilitated by their belonging to the same tennis club, or Internet knowledge network. Similarly, cooperation will, a priori, develop more easily between researchers and engineers who belong to the same firm, the same technological consortium or innovation network. It includes a common organizational culture between the members of a team for example.

The *logic of similarity* corresponds to a mental adherence to common categories; it manifests itself in small cognitive distances between some individuals. They can be people who are connected to one another through common projects, or share the same cultural, religious, etc. values or symbols. Social norms and common languages contribute to this organized proximity. It can also, however, correspond to a bond that sometimes emerges between individuals without them having had to talk in order to get to know one another. It facilitates the interactions between people who did not know one another before but share similar references. Thus, collaboration is all the easier when it involves individuals who share the same culture. Similarly, researchers who belong to the same scientific community will easily cooperate because they share, not only the same language, but also the same system of interpretation of texts and results.

The logic of similarity possesses two facets. It can develop within a reciprocal relationship, a relationship that shortens the cognitive distance between the actors involved (common project, common education and knowledge circulating within a network, etc.), but it can also emerge from a common basis, facilitating the communication between strangers (see the example of diasporas). It is also the case when actors share the same or similar symbolic attributes and therefore refer to common norms or goals, in terms of way of living or social attitudes towards food or clothes for example. The actors linked by a logic of similarity share certain resources, of a material (diplomas or social status) or cognitive (routines, conventions, etc.) nature, which can be mobilized when the properties described here are activated.

Just like geographical proximity, organized proximity refers to a potential that is neutral in essence. It is the perceptions and actions of individuals that give it a more or less positive or negative dimension, and therefore a certain usefulness. Thus, being connected by a logic of belonging is not a guarantee that interactions will occur, and even less a guarantee of the quality of these interactions. It is human actions that determine whether or not actors are going to start interacting, and the results of the interactions vary in this regard: a firm may enter into a relationship with a laboratory in order to collaborate with the latter or, instead, to try and rob the laboratory of one of its inventions. For the logic of similarity, a common project has as much chance of leading to an industrial or technological success as to end up in a failure resulting in heavy losses for the parties involved. Finally, the logics of similarity and of belonging can also facilitate collaborations that might be immoral in their motivations. For example, Mafia organizations often feed on both the logic of similarity (ethnic origins) and the logic of belonging (strong connection within a network of actors), which can be considered ethically immoral.

Temporary geographical proximity

We should now add to these two original notions the notion of temporary geographical proximity (TGP), which constitutes one form of geographical proximity that enables actors to temporarily interact face to face, whether these actors are individuals or organizations such as firms or laboratories for example (Torre and Rallet 2005; Torre 2008).

The development of information and communication technologies (ICT) nowadays facilitates long-distance exchange, be it for economic reasons between producers, or for day-to-day relations between friends or relatives. Consequently co-location, which has for a long time been considered a necessary condition of cooperation between organizations or individuals, no longer constitutes an absolute necessity. A large part of the information and knowledge that are necessary for production or innovation activities can be transferred from a distance, through telephone or Internet mediated exchanges for example (Walther *et al.* 2005). However, face-to-face interaction are necessary and beneficial in this context. The example of the growing importance of trade fairs (Bathelt and Schuldt 2010), or that of the travelling done by members of research and development (R&D) collaboration projects undertaken by biotech start-ups are good examples of such situations. Face-to-face interaction cannot altogether be eliminated, including in the case of communities of practice, for example (see Torre 2008). As a consequence ICTs cannot be considered as substitutes for face-to-face relations: they are useful tools to support or enhance the interaction between two or several individuals.

Space matters, but in a new way: one that consists of temporary face-to-face contact between two or several individuals. TGP corresponds to the possibility of satisfying the need for face-to-face contact between actors, by travelling to different locations. This travelling generates opportunities for moments of geographical proximity, which vary in duration, but which are always limited in time. TGP is limited to certain times; this form of geographical proximity should not be mistaken for a permanent co-location of firms or laboratories.

The necessity of TGP is embodied in the existence of places that are especially made for TGP-based activities. In the case of private individuals they can be conferences, theme or recreational parks. In the case of firms or laboratories they are specialized venues:

- Trade shows, conferences and exhibitions enable actors to fulfil certain needs related to the processes of production, research or innovation, such as the collection of information, sharing experiences, or speculations about a certain type of production (Entwistle and Rocamora 2006). The 'hub' formula, which enables individuals from different horizons to meet in the same place, enables them to save on transport costs; these hubs are readily viewed as 'temporary' clusters (Maskell *et al.* 2006), a term that highlights the relation with the permanent clusters formed by localized systems of production. But above all, these places respond to a need for face-to-face relations related to the wish to reduce the costs of transactions (North 1991; Norcliffe and Rendace 2003).
- Common 'platforms' of project teams are meant to enable the participants of a project to work together for a period of up to several months, in the framework of a project team. It is also the case for members of a project

undertaken by the geographically dispersed subsidiaries of a firm (Kechidi and Talbot 2010). Once the partners have reached an agreement as to the characteristics of the project, the platform is dismantled and the participants go back 'home'.

But there are two main reasons for the need for TGP: business trips are undertaken in order to reach a common decision or determine the characteristics of a joint project; or they are related to an activity that can only be performed in a place other than the individual's usual workplace. These meetings are needed at regular intervals during the coordination process. Their frequency and regularity are the cause of most business trips. The face-to-face interactions do not, in this case, occur in places exclusively dedicated to meetings, but in 'ordinary' places, i.e. in the participants' usual workplaces, firms or laboratories.

Discussion: proximities as a tool to understand the rationale of short supply chains

The use of the theoretical apparatus of the so-called 'school of proximity' can help in clarifying the debates about food supply chains, and most of all about the complex and sometimes fuzzy definition of SSFCs. In particular it provides arguments that enable the disentangling of the two major types of relations at work in food supply chains and especially SSFCs: namely, distance relations on the one hand and economic and social interactions (be they network relations or relations between producers and consumers) on the other hand.

The analysis of economic and social interactions deserves special attention in the framework of food supply chains and SSFCs because of its intrinsic complexity. As a matter of fact, it involves not only relations between producers and consumers, but also production relations and sometimes links with the distribution sector, as well as symbolic references to shared social norms and values, between all the actors of the supply chain. In order to better understand this complex set of relations, let us try to isolate each block of interactions (horizontal and vertical productive relations, relations between production and distribution, and relations between producers and consumers) and to shed light on their main peculiarities. We will first examine organized proximity relations and geographical proximity relations thereafter.

Organized proximity relations

The first set of interactions within supply food chains is directly related to the relations between the various actors involved in the process of production. It is first concerned with the horizontal relations between different types of producers: for example, a farmer who produces lettuces may have close interactions with other producers of the same type of products, or with people who help him to bring some natural fertilizers or chemical components into the process of cultivation. But one may be aware of the existence of a second type of interaction, all along the production chain. Even if we are mainly concerned with SSFCs, these latter interactions should not be reduced to a one-stage process. As described at the beginning of this chapter, there are various forms of production chains, and some of them can correspond to successive stages: for example the packaging of agricultural products into boxes or trays can be performed by another small entrepreneur, just before bringing them to a local market. Given all these network relations, we can assume that there are various types of organized relations at work within a food production chain and that their study should be valuable in terms of organized proximity relations.

There exists a second type of set of interactions within a food production chain, that of the link between production and consumption and also production, distribution and consumption (when there is an intermediary). This link does not always exist and often disappears in most of supply chains. It is nevertheless of great importance, in short or alternative food chains such as direct selling in supermarkets or organic canteens. This indicates that there are organized proximity relations between the links in the chain, and that organization models of production apply as well, be they at the local level or based on remote relations. For example, organization of producers who gather (sometimes across space) in order to be able to supply their customer with diversified products and regularity, mobilize a complex set of organized proximity relations and share the common goal of bringing food products to local citizens, be they acting upstream or downstream of the value chain. The same exists for groups of consumers as well (CSAs for example). We mostly find here the adhesion to common norms or shared values: for example the participants of a SSFC, be they consumers or producers, mainly subscribe to the same idea of an organic agriculture, or to the will to promote social mixing through their action. At the same time, these behaviours are rather innovative and demonstrate the creative character of the local actors involved in SSFCs. The development of SSFCs in other cases is associated with the development of networks (many authors highlight alternative food networks). In France for example most of the SSFCs' initiatives by producers, consumers or public bodies consist of networks that are often interconnected across space and across activities. The logic of belonging appears structuring and necessary for the creation of new ways of supplying food. One can even recognize here forms of innovative networks common to typical industrial innovation described in the 1990s (see e.g. Camagni 1991). The logic of similarity complements belonging as it helps to build common sense, objectives, shared values and, by this, trust. It contributes to the information-laden value of the products that differentiate these products from others on the market. As such it appears as a cornerstone of today's SSFCs' development. Not only media (through advertisements), but consumer associations have also played (and are still playing) an important role in creating and diffusing this logic of similarity: first in underground and confidential networks and more recently in wider and even standard channels. By this approach, not only the creative character of these organizations is assessed but it is also displayed and publicized, especially through media coverage.

Geographical proximity relations

The question of geographical proximity within food production chains directly refers to the spatial distance between producers, or between producers and consumers. The case of a short distance between producers, or even between producers and distributors, is well known in the proximity literature and has provided the opportunity to produce a great number of papers, especially in the field of industrial economics or innovative behaviours. These approaches can be directly derived at the level of food processing. Let us just point out the fact that geographical proximity between producers must not only be related to the existence of short distances between producers but mainly to the presence of transportation devices and to the accessibility of the different actors. In this respect, the question of congestion in large urban areas could be an interesting field to explore in future research, given the fact that it could lessen or even impede the possibility of daily interactions between local actors (be they producers or consumers). One has also to notice that the question of distance is severely at stake with respect to this question: How many kilometres does a short supply chain have to be to become long?

The second case, the one of the relation between producers and consumers, is by far the most innovative in the field of proximity analysis. Most of the studied relations between close or remote actors are bounded to the case of producers, or to the study of interactions between inhabitants in terms of local planning. But the interaction between producers and consumers is a truly new issue and deserves very special attention. It paves the way for future development of research on the question of proximity between production and consumption (and not only on the spatial side) and on the types of face-to-face interactions between these two groups of social and economic actors.[2] Let us just add for the moment that this case also refers to the issue of the mobility of people and goods. On the one hand it raises the concern for the logistics of the transportation itself (time and means of transportation by train, plane, car, etc.) as well as their carbon footprint (the opportunity of carbon footprint reduction of SSFCs is at the centre of a very strong and still unclosed debate: Carlsson-Kanyama 1997; Pirog and Benjamin 2003; Pretty *et al.* 2005). The notion of food miles is of crucial concern. On the other hand it is directly related to the question of 'costs' of TGP and opens the agenda to the study of the reasons why and the ways consumers and producers meet. But it also raises several specific questions. Given a geographical distance between the producers and consumers of an agricultural commodity, does the mobility of people replace the necessity to be located together in the same place, and at what distance (in the literature, this rather flexible concept goes from 140 to 200 km)? In the same way, what is the role played by farmers' markets, or by places like canteens in the setting of new food consumption behaviours? Their central situation can be clearly related to the platform role of the fairs of the *équipes plateaux* (common platforms of project teams) in the building of new industrial goods (Torre 2011).

To summarize, geographical proximity is at the heart of the concept of SSFC, because the spatial distance between actors involved is crucial, be they producers or consumers; it must be explored in a thorough way, not only in terms of mobility or transportation, but most of all because geographical proximity carries an opportunity for the differentiation of goods in the market (local versus non-local food) and consequently offers advantages to certain types of production in terms of competitive advantage. It is also valuable as it offers a chance to raise social progress by means of social interactions and discussions as well as shared projects and joint social or economic constructions.

However, these types of innovative and very creative behaviours are strongly linked to the ability to activate the latent potentials of geographical proximity. Briefly speaking, and to give a very stylized example, SSFCs are based upon the idea of an activation of the geographical proximity potential by means of socio-economic behaviours, performed mostly by local actors involved in an intensely creative activity, resulting in the setting of new institutional and organization forms of social interaction. This activation follows two main channels:

- First, the potential of geographical proximity is activated through the market and the relation between producers and consumers. This innovative behaviour reveals a great amount of creativity and involves mainly urban consumers into a process of change of usages. The social inventiveness of local actors gives birth to new types of relations thanks to the activation of the potential of geographical proximity (great change and creativity: geographical proximity between producers and consumers – mainly urban ones). The parallel with the industrial forms of 'co-production' (von Hippel 1976) between producers and competent users is obvious, because consumers can be very active in the development of the production process (at the different stages of the short supply chain, from work on the farm to production choices to land purchase). One can clearly see the very creative character of this type of organization, given the common way of goods exchange in agribusiness, usually mediated by market relations and mass-market retailing to stores.
- Second, this potential is also activated through other forms of alternative merchandization, such as CSAs, subscription and contracts. This type of activation of 'geographical proximity' potentials is also very creative and is not only based on relations between producers and consumers but on internal relations in the network of local producers or eventual distributors as well.

Supply chains through the lens of proximity analysis

As the previous developments have shown, there are multiple forms of supply chains, combining geographical proximity with organized proximity in different ways. Aubry *et al.* (forthcoming) have proposed a typology of the forms of supply chains for agricultural products in urban regions based on a simplified distinction between weak or strong geographical or organized proximities assuming, however, that the scope of various forms and measures of proximity is far more complex and intricate (see Figure 10.1). Note that in this case the study only relies on interactions between producers and consumers, without considering inter-industrial relations.

Table 10.1 Various types of supply chains and proximity relations between producers and consumers

		GEOGRAPHICAL PROXIMITY	
		Weak	Strong
ORGANIZED PROXIMITY	Weak	Case I Supply chains with loose relations • Selling on international markets • Selling to supply platforms LONG SUPPLY CHAINS	Case II Local supply chains with indirect relations • Collective point of sale • Selling to local supermarkets[a] • Selling to local professionals[a] • Box schemes sold by intermediaries SHORT SUPPLY CHAINS
	Strong	Case III Supply chains with distance relations • Direct online selling[a] • Direct mail order selling [a] • Box schemes sold by mail-order catalogue[a] SHORT SUPPLY CHAINS	Case IV Local supply chains with direct relations • Farmer's markets[a] • AMAP/CSA[a b] • On-farm selling[a] • Box schemes, excl. AMAP/CSA[a b] • Fairs[a] SHORT SUPPLY CHAINS

Source: Aubry, Kebir and Pasquier (forthcoming)

[a] Direct selling: producers sell their produce themselves.
[b] AMAP (Association for the maintaining of a farming agriculture) corresponds to the French Community Supported Agriculture movement.

Supply chains with loose relations correspond to classical long supply chains. Geographical and organized proximity relations are very low. The chain comprises inter-industrial relations between producers (growers, transformers/assemblers, deliverers, etc.). The producer–consumer relation is considerably diluted along the chain. The only remaining link are traces of provenance taking the form of traceability codes (mandatory by law) or labels for product quality (AOCs, organic, slow food, etc.).

Supply chains with indirect relations (producer's shop, supermarket selling local products) correspond to the cases where local products are sold to local consumers without a direct relation between producers and consumers. Geographical proximity is high but organized proximity is low between producers and consumers. Intermediaries such as producers' shops, supermarkets and restaurants act as a link – they guarantee the relationship. Some of the value-laden information of the products needs to be objectivized (photos, farm's address, etc.). 'Local' guarantees quality.

Supply chains with distance relations (direct Internet selling, box schemes) do not imply the co-localization of producers and consumers; geographical proximity is rather weak, but organized proximity strong and is based on the logic of similarity. Producers and consumers share a common set of values and confidence (quality, modes of production, common objectives for agriculture development, etc.). Through these chains, producers of specific goods (wine, local traditional products) expand their markets while consumers find the opportunity to continue buying their purchase over time (a consumer that tastes and buys good wine on vacation may keep on buying the product afterwards on the Internet) and also buy products that they do not find at home (or at a similar price).

Supply chains with direct relations corresponds to the canonical SSFC in that is local direct selling (farmers' markets, on-farm selling, CSAs). Here geographical and organized proximities are strong. Producers and consumers meet. The relational potential is high. Both belong to the same 'local' area and also share views on food quality, in the sense given to their relation.

Apart from the first 'loose relation' case, the SSFCs detailed here rely on and mobilize TGP in different ways. Supply chains with indirect relations rely on the permanent collocation of producers and consumers (both are local) and on the existence of intermediary places where a connection between producer and consumer can take place temporarily even if the producer is absent. These places act as platforms for organized proximity building and consolidating. Both the producer and the consumer commit themselves when they deliberately decide to deliver/buy products on these platforms. The third case, SSFCs with distance relations are, most of the time, the result of a former TGP relation between the producer and the consumer (tourist visiting a region and buying some *terroir* product) that is continued afterwards through a distance relation. The meeting can also happen during delivery, for example box schemes. It is rare, as far as we know, that such a chain develops without direct, face-to-face relation between the producer and the consumer at some point or another. The last form of SSFCs, that is with direct relation, relies on both permanent and temporary proximity. TGP is crucial because it gives the opportunity for producers and consumers to meet together for brief moments in the same place, and to frequently repeat these interactions. By doing this, they can build trusting relations, especially concerning the quality of the products, as well as to establish friendly behaviours. It is permanent proximity (collocation in the area) that makes this form of supply possible (one may not want to drive three hours every week to buy carrots when other suppliers are closer).

Conclusion

The development of SSFCs relies on two main types of proximities between actors, and in particular producers and consumers. The challenge for actors wishing to develop such a supply chain, be they producers, consumers or policy makers, etc., is the construction of organized proximity and the structuring of geographical proximity. The construction of organized proximity can be expressed by the emergence of a new paradigm of food consumption (local is beautiful) built upon shared values (importance given to food quality and traceability), trust building, common project (save/keep agriculture nearby, support alternative agriculture), symbolic shared values, etc. It relies on regular or temporary face-to-face relations (farmers' market, on-farm buying) and more broadly on information circulation and diffusion across society. The value-laden information held by the products, the mobilization of policy makers to support SSFCs, strongly relayed by the media (eating organic today is trendy rather than odd) participates to the development of the demand and production for local/organic food supply chains. More work should be done to understand the processes by which this organized proximity is built, by whom, how and across what type of relationship. This would help understand the degree of involvement of actors in the common project, their attachment to the common value (be it just business and trendy consumption), etc. and by this the strengthen and sustain the SSFC model.

Geographical proximity is structurally fundamental to SSFCs. Its activation[3] is nevertheless far from easy. In other words it is not because producers are close to your house that you will buy their products (or because producers are not close to your house that you won't buy their products). SSFCs demand organization and structuration at the micro level (organization of farming and marketing activities) and also at the meso level (networks of producers, networks of groups of consumers, etc.) in order to meet requirements (creation of organizations of producers to provide regularly and with product diversity groups of consumers, school canteens, multi-products box delivery, etc.). Geographical proximity activation stimulates the territorial actor's dynamics and gives rise to forms of innovation in the local production system. Of course, the capacity of the system to mobilize is very important here as is the mobilization of policy makers. The recent legal prescription of organic and low environmental impact food procurement in French public canteens (20 per cent in 2012) has brought a general mobilization of the local actors concerned with these issues (canteen managers, procurement officers, groups of producers, agriculture chambers, etc.). The future of SSFCs will in a large part depend on the capacity of willing actors to activate geographical proximity, that is to organize and to stabilize the chain that is making it socially and economically sustainable. It will also depend on the way the value system and common project associated with SSFCs will hold in time.

Notes

1 One may be organized or one may organize an activity without necessarily refer to or belong to an organization, in the strict sense of the term.
2 A wide literature on producer–consumer relations has been developed in marketing and innovation studies without particularly questioning spatial aspects. Geography of consumption (Goss 2004, 2006) has tackled the subject but not much has been developed in economic geography and in territorial innovation systems. Both have remained centred on production issues, and there is a need to develop this emerging

research agenda (Power and Scott 2005; Coe, Dicken and Hess 2008; Grabher *et al.* 2008; Jeannerat and Kebir 2010).

3 We speak here of activation, because de facto the producer and the consumer are located in the same area, the need being to build the channels/tools by which they will meet and eventually interact.

References

Arend, R.J. (2009) 'Defending against rival innovation', *Small Business Economics*, 33(2): 189–206.

Ascher, F. (2005) *Le mangeur hypermoderne. Une figure de l'individu éclectique*, Paris: Odile Jacob.

Aubry, C. and Chiffoleau, Y. (2009) 'Le développement des circuits courts et l'agriculture périurbaine: histoire, évolution en cours et questions actuelles', *Innovations Agronomiques*, 5: 41–51.

Aubry, C. Kebir, L. and Pasquier, C. (forthcoming) 'Le raccourcissement des circuits alimentaires: une nouvelle ruralité en périphérie des villes?', in F. Papy and N. Matthieu (eds) *Habiter les campagnes. Institutions et gens face au 'bon usage' des ressources naturelles*, Paris: Quae.

Bathelt, H. and Schuldt, N. (2010) 'International trade fairs and global buzz, Part I: Ecology of global buzz', *European Planning Studies*, 18(12): 1957–74.

Bönte, W. (2008) 'Inter-firm trust in buyer–supplier relations: Are knowledge spillovers and geographical proximity relevant?', *Journal of Economic Behavior and Organization*, 67(3–4): 855–70.

Boschma, R. (2005) 'Proximity in economic interaction, special issue', *Regional Studies*, 39(1): 61–74.

Bouba-Olga, O. and Zimmermann, J.-B. (2004) 'Modèles et mesures de la proximité', in B. Pecqueur and J.-B. Zimmermann (eds) *Economies de proximité*, Paris: Hermès.

Camagni, R. (ed.) (1991) *Innovation Networks, Spatial Perspectives*, London: Belhaven-Pinter.

Carlsson-Kanyama, A. (1997) 'Weighted average source points and distances for consumption origin-tools for environmental impact analysis?', *Ecological Economics*, 23(1): 15–23.

Coe, N.M., Dicken, P. and Hess, M. (2008) 'Global production networks: Realizing the potential', *Journal of Economic Geography*, 8(3): 271–95.

Coley, D., Howard, M. and Winter, M. (2009) 'Local food, food miles and carbon emissions: A comparison of farms shop and mass distribution approaches', *Food Policy*, 34(2): 150–55.

Delfosse, C. and Bernard, C. (2007) 'Vente directe et terroir', *Méditerranée*, 109: 23–9.

Entwistle, J. and Rocamora, A. (2006) 'The field of fashion materialized: A study of London Fashion Week', *Sociology*, 40(8): 735–51.

Fleury, A. and Donadieu, P. (1997) 'De l'agriculture périurbaine, à l'agriculture urbaine', *Le Courrier de l'environnement*, 31: 45–61.

Goodman, D. (2003) 'The quality "turn" and alternative food practices: Reflections and agenda', *Journal of Rural Studies*, 19(1): 1–7.

Goss, J. (2004) 'Geography of consumption, I: Progress reports', *Progress in Human Geography*, 28(3): 369–80.

Goss, J. (2006) 'Geography of consumption: The work of consumption, Progress reports', *Progress in Human Geography*, 30(2): 237–49.

Grabher, G., Ibert, O. and Flohr, S. (2008) 'The neglected king: The customer in the new knowledge ecology of innovation', *Economic Geography*, 84(3): 253–80.

Ilbery, B. and Maye, D. (2005a) 'Food supply chains and sustainability: Evidence from specialist food producers in the Scottish–English borders', *Land Use Policy*, 22(4): 331–44.

Ilbery, B. and Maye, D. (2005b) 'Alternative or conventional? An examination of specialist livestock production systems in the Scottish–English borders', in S. Essex, A. Gilg and R. Yarwood (eds) *Rural Change and Sustainability: Agriculture, the Environment and Communities*, Wallingford: CABI, pp. 85–106.

Jarosz, L. (2008) 'The city in the country: Growing alternative food networks in Metropolitan areas', *Journal of Rural Studies*, 24(3): 231–44.

Jeannerat, H. and Kebir, L. (2010) 'Economic system of knowledge and regions: A typology based on the analysis of producer–consumer relation', paper presented at the DRUID Summer Conference, London, 16–18 June.

Kechidi, M. and Talbot, D. (2010) 'Institutions and coordination: What is the contribution of a proximity-based analysis? The case of Airbus and its relations with the subcontracting network', *International Journal of Technology Management*, 50(3–4): 285–99.

Manniche, J. (2007) *Knowledge Dynamics and Quality Conventions in the Food and Drink Sector*, Framework Programme EURODITE. Available at http://www.crt.dk/media/EURODITE%20WP3_Food%20sector%20report_CRT.pdf

Maskell, P., Bathelt, H. and Malmberg, A. (2006) 'Building global knowledge pipelines: The role of temporary clusters', *European Planning Studies*, 14(8): 997–1013.

Ministère de l'Agriculture et de la Pêche (2009) *Rapport du groupe de travail 'Circuits courts de commercialization'*, March, Paris.

Norcliffe, G. and Rendace, O. (2003) 'New geographies of comic book production in North America: The new artisan, distancing, and the periodic social economy', *Economic Geography*, 79(3): 241–63.

North, D.C. (1991) 'Institutions', *Journal of Economic Perspectives*, 5(1): 97–112.

Novel, A.-S. (2010) *Le guide du Locavore pour mieux consommer local*, Paris: Eyrolles.

Parker, G. (2005) *Sustainable Food? Teikei, Cooperatives and Food Citizenship in Japan and in the UK*, Working Paper in Real Estate and Planning, no. 11/05. Available at http://www.reading.ac.uk/REP/fulltxt/1105.pdf

Perroux, F. (1961) *L'économie du XXe siècle*, Grenoble: Presses Universitaires de Grenoble.

Pirog, R. and Benjamin, A. (2003) *Checking the Food Odometer: Comparing Food Miles for Local versus Conventional Produce Sales to Iowa Institutions*, Ames, IA: Leopold Center for Sustainable Agriculture.

Power, D. and Scott, A.J. (eds) (2005) *Cultural Industries and the Production of Culture*, London: Routledge.

Pretty, J.N., Ball, A.S., Lang, T. and Morison, J.I.L. (2005) 'Farm costs and food miles: An assessment of the full cost of the UK weekly food basket', *Food Policy*, 30(1): 1–19.

Renting, H., Marsden, T.K. and Banks, J. (2003) 'Understanding alternative food networks: Exploring the role of short food supply chains in rural development', *Environment and Planning A*, 35(3): 393–411.

Selfa, T. and Qazi, J. (2005) 'Place, taste, or face-to-face? Understanding producer–consumer networks in "local" food systems in Washington State', *Agriculture and Human Values*, 22(4): 451–64.

Smith, A., and MacKinnon, J.B. (2007) *The 100 Mile Diet: A Year of Local Eating*, Toronto: Vintage Canada.

Sonnino, R. and Marsden, T.K. (2006) 'Beyond the divide: Rethinking the relationships between alternative and conventional food networks in Europe', *Journal of Economic Geography*, 6(2): 181–99.

Torre, A. (2006) 'Collective action, governance structure and organizational trust in localized systems of production. The case of the AOC organization of small producers', *Entrepreneurship and Regional Development*, 18(1): 55–72.

Torre, A. (2008) 'On the role played by temporary geographical proximity in knowledge transfer', *Regional Studies*, 42(6): 869–89.

Torre, A. (2011) 'The role of proximity during long-distance collaborative projects. Temporary geographical proximity helps', *International Journal of Foresight and Innovation Policy*, 7(1–2–3): 213–30.

Torre, A. and Rallet, A. (2005) 'Proximity and localization', *Regional Studies*, 39(1): 47–60.

Vassor, R. (2007) 'Diagnostic de l'agriculture spécialisée de la Plaine de Versailles et du Plateau des Alluets. Production/commercialization', Mémoire de stage de césure, Paris: INA PG.

Von Hippel, E. (1976) 'The dominant role of users in the scientific instrument innovation process', *Research Policy*, 5(3): 212–39.

Walther, J.B., Loh, T. and Granka, L. (2005) 'Let me count the ways: The interchange of verbal and nonverbal cues in computer-mediated and face-to-face affinity', *Journal of Language and Social Psychology*, 24(1): 36–65.

Winter, M. (2003) 'Embeddedness, the new food economy and defensive localism', *Journal of Rural Studies*, 19(1): 23–32.

Winter, M. (2005) 'Geographies of food: Agro-food geographies. Food, nature, farmers and agency', *Progress in Human Geography*, 29(5): 609–17.

11 Product category dynamics in cultural industries

Spaghetti Westerns' renewal of the Hollywood Western movie genre

Gino Cattani and C. Moritz B. Fliescher

Introduction

The processes by which creativity and innovation can renew mature products, particularly the question of how cross-fertilization between products takes place, are currently not always well understood. In this chapter, we analyze a case of product innovation from one European creative industry and its impact on the renewal of a mature product in the same industry in the US. Based on our case study we develop a theoretic argument that builds on the extensive literature on (product) categories and combine it with insights from cognitive psychology to provide a framework that can be used to explain how and when creativity and innovation in one product can be more or less impactful for other products.

Categories are a relevant unit of analysis to study the impact of creativity and innovation in cultural industries. Categories are key elements of classification systems that segregate things into groups and impose coherence, therefore creating shared understandings (Rosch 1978; Porac and Thomas 1994; Bowker and Star 1999; Murphy 2004). They structure cognition and behaviour by influencing expectations and evaluations (Osherson and Smith 1982), but also establish boundaries around similar kinds of entities such as objects, people, practices or organizational forms (DiMaggio 1987; Lamont and Molnár 2002). In his work 'Classification in art' DiMaggio (1987) looked at how genres are socially constructed organizing mechanisms used to categorize similar artistic products, providing evidence that categories are also relevant in creative industries. At the product level, categories help producers and consumers to understand each other's demands in product markets (Rosa *et al.* 1999), and product category prototypes can be the bases for evaluation of products by consumers (Lounsbury and Rao 2004).

To explain how and when creativity and innovation in one product can be more or less impactful on other products in cultural industries it is necessary to look at the dynamic aspects of categories. Despite a large body of research on the role of categories and their saliency in shaping action and behaviour, the conditions under which categories are durable and the mechanisms that are responsible for their evolution have remained relatively underexplored (DiMaggio 1987; Clemens and Cook 1999). Recently, some scholars have begun to go beyond the focus on established categories by investigating more systematically how categories emerge and gain legitimacy. Yet the creation of a new category is but one possible outcome of category dynamics. Categories can also evolve through adaptive change without being replaced. Even though the label that identifies a category may not change, the meaning of that label might change with changes in some of the features subsumed by that label. The interaction among cognitively related categories might indeed change their meaning but without resulting in the creation of new categories. Accordingly, the following questions deserve more careful consideration: How and when do creativity and innovation revitalize mature products in cultural industries? How and when do they stimulate innovation in other existing products or across different countries?

We address these questions by looking at the interaction of two product categories. Specifically, we look at the product category 'movie genre' (Altman 1999) and investigate the influence of the so-called 'Spaghetti Western' (also known as 'Westerns Italian Style') on the evolution of the Hollywood Western movie genre. The Western as a feature film experienced its most successful years in the US after the silent period in the 1940s and early 1950s. From 1958 onwards, however, the Hollywood Western faced a sharp decline in popularity – as indicated by the drop in both the number of Western movies produced and distributed in the US and their box office receipts. As Western genre experts have argued, the influx of Spaghetti Westerns into the US, starting in 1961 and through the early 1970s, was 'a prime influence on the form and shape of Hollywood Western from the mid-1960s onwards' (Frayling 2006: 286), and also spurred the resurgence in popularity of Hollywod Westerns (Lenihan 1980; Cawelti 1984; Frayling 2006).

This case study sheds light on the processes that revitalize mature products in creative industries. While Spaghetti Westerns were originally spawned from the classic Hollywood Western genre, they ended up shaping its evolution later on. Tracing this influence reveals how creativity and innovation can stimulate the renewal of mature products (e.g. Hollywood Western movies) through the recombination of features from other products (e.g. Spaghetti Westerns) developed in other socio-economic contexts. The analysis further demonstrates how processes of cross-fertilization might span geographical boundaries (Florida 2005) – thereby promoting innovation (through the renewal of existing product categories) across countries (here Europe and the US).

Our empirical analysis is premised on the basic intuition that the cognitive relationship between categories is critical for understanding whether categories interact to stimulate innovation in existing product categories by changing their meaning. According to research in cognitive psychology on the hierarchical structure of categories (Rosch 1978; Porac and Thomas 1994; Murphy 2004), the three main levels of a cognitive taxonomy are: the *superordinate* (the highest and most general), the *basic* (the intermediate) and the *subordinate* (the lowest and more specific) levels. In our context, these levels correspond to the form of entertainment (e.g. movie, television, opera), the movie genre (e.g. Western, comedy, musical) and the various movie subgenres (e.g. Classic Western, Spaghetti Western, Western Comedy, etc.), respectively (see Figure 11.1). Building on this

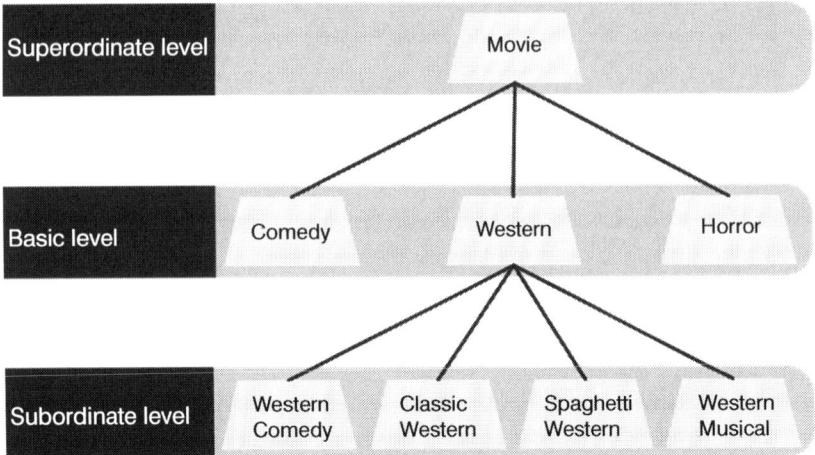

Figure 11.1 Cognitive taxonomy: category levels in the movie industry

Source: Our elaboration

research, we argue that subordinate categories that are vertically related to the same basic-level category, and hence are cognitively linked to it and share with it a set of clearly identifiable traits or features, are more likely to interact with each other.

Theoretical background

Research on categories has developed primarily along one of the following three theoretical perspectives: neo-institutionalism, organizational ecology and sociological theories of markets. Neo-institutionalists have studied how categories shape action in a variety of contexts. On the premise that the patterning of 'social life is not produced solely by the aggregation of individual and organizational behaviour but also by institutions that structure action' (Clemens and Cook 1999: 442), categories represent a source of enduring constraint as they become institutionalized, namely taken-for-granted, rule-like models or schemas that provide substantive guidelines for practical action through socialization, interaction (e.g. Berger and Luckmann 1966; DiMaggio and Powell 1991) or legitimation (e.g. Meyer and Rowan 1977; Hannan *et al.* 2007). Once categories are in place, the behaviour of actors (whether individuals or organizations) is expected to increasingly conform to them as categories become default mechanisms to make sense of the world.

In the field of organizational ecology, recent studies stress how legitimacy depends on the consensus among relevant audiences that the features and activities of organizations are appropriate and desirable within a widespread, taken-for-granted system of norms or social codes (Zuckerman 1999; Hannan *et al.* 2007). Audiences consider the features and activities of organizations in relation to what they expect organizations can or should do. Social codes originate from this set of expectations, generating approval and advantages when respected, but also constraining action due to implied sanctions if expectations are violated. Categories help in this process of evaluation because audiences can use them to classify organizations based on their degree of membership within existing categories.

In sociological theories of markets, researchers have advanced cognitive models of markets that are stabilized by the shared assumptions and frames of reference of consumers and producers (White 1981; Fligstein 1996; Rosa *et al.* 1999). From this perspective, categories help producers and consumers understand each other's demands, provide a basis for the evaluation of products and influence who producers perceive as their rivals (Porac and Thomas 1994; Porac *et al.* 1995). In these approaches categories are considered to be commonly understood and taken for granted, nonetheless they are also understood to be flexible manifestations of an interactive system.

Although sociological theories of markets recognize that categories are flexible, the limited work looking at category dynamics has essentially focused on the emergence of new categories. In the neo-institutional and ecological literatures research on category dynamics is even more limited, as they both share the idea that categories must remain relatively stable to function as rule-like models for action. Both strands of research have been more concerned with reliable reproduction and the constraining aspects rather than the dynamic aspects of categories (e.g. North 1990; Clemens and Cook 1999; Lounsbury and Rao 2004). Most of the studies building on this literature thus provide little guidance about *when* and *why* categories will change, which is the basis for examining the impact of creativity and innovation on other existing products. While increased attention has been lately devoted to the emergence of new categories and their change over time (for a recent comprehensive review, see Negro *et al.* 2010), other aspects of category dynamics beyond new category formation have received very little attention. Two exceptions are the study by Kennedy *et al.* (2010), who develop a classification system of eight different alternative mechanisms for category dynamics, and the study by Karthikeyan and Wezel (2010), who look at how the recombination of social codes allowed the British Liberal Democrats to reposition their identity.

From extant research on new category creation two major findings emerge: ambiguity in existing categories eventually leads to their replacement with newly created categories, and new categories are created to seize untapped opportunities (e.g. a new market niche), regardless of the level of ambiguity in existing categories. Despite their common focus on category creation, the two cases are quite different: in the first case, new categories are substituted for existing categories, which then disappear due to their poor fit with the new features of the environment; in the second case, new categories are perceived as qualitatively distinct from other categories from which they originated.

Across the multiple literature categories have been used with different terminology. In this chapter, we follow previous research in cognitive psychology and conceptualize categories as cognitive orderings of features that are embedded in a cognitive taxonomy (Rosch 1978; Porac and Thomas 1994). Specifically,

Rosch (1978) defines a category as encompassing a number of objects that are considered equivalent because they share some basic features. Categories are generally designated by names or labels (e.g. dog, animal, tree, furniture) and are related to one another by means of class inclusion. The system by which categories are related constitutes a taxonomy: each category in a taxonomy is entirely included in one other category (unless it is the highest level category), but is not exhaustive of that more inclusive category.

The internal structure of a cognitive taxonomy has both vertical and horizontal aspects (Rosch *et al.* 1976). Vertically, categories that are at different taxonomic levels vary in both the abstractness and the restrictiveness of their identity. At higher levels in the taxonomy, categories are broad and general, with only a few features that define them; at lower levels, on the contrary, categories are narrow and specific, with a larger set of features that define them. A lower-level category has all the features of the higher-level category to which it is related and some other features that distinguish it from the higher-level category (Murphy 2004). Categories are vertically related to one another through class inclusion, with more specific (lower-level) categories being members of broader and more inclusive (higher-level) categories.

Among the multiple levels of a cognitive taxonomy, the *basic level* is the conceptual centre around which descriptions of the environment are usually organized. The basic level is the most inclusive level at 'which there are features common to all or most members of the category' (Rosch 1978: 31). Categories one level higher (lower) will be superordinate (subordinate) categories whose members share only a few (many) features among each another. Utilizing the movie genre as an example (see Figure 11.1), a 'Western' is the basic-level category while 'Movie' is the superordinate category and 'Spaghetti Western' or 'Western Comedy' is the subordinate category. The middle taxonomic or basic levels are most informative 'because they strike a balance between being too inclusive and too specific' (Porac and Thomas 1994: 56). As this example suggests, superordinate categories are very distinctive ('Movie' is very different from 'Sports game'), but not very informative (there are indeed many types of movies as there are many types of sports game); while subordinate categories are very informative but not very distinctive (a Spaghetti Western is not too different from a Classic Western); a basic-level category, on the contrary, is both informative and distinctive.

Horizontally, distinctions must be made among categories at the same level of abstraction. In the case of Western movies, Spaghetti Western, Classic Western and Western Musical are all instances of a Western movie and as such they share some common features, while also presenting unique features that define the particular category they belong to. Yet horizontal distinctiveness can be fuzzy. As they share a set of common features, categories belonging to the same higher-level category by definition overlap to some degree. Specifically, the horizontal distinctiveness of each category depends on how many features it shares with other categories at the same level of abstraction. This implies that an object is categorized more easily when the degree of feature overlap among categories is low, and that the categorization into one category can be difficult when such overlap is high. The distinction between a Spaghetti Western and a Classic Western can thus be fuzzy, as both those Western movies tend to share a large set of features. The distinction between a Classic Western and a Western Musical, on the other hand, is easier as they share a smaller set of features while still both belonging to the higher-level Western movie category. Building on research on the cognitive taxonomy of categories, the next section examines a case where one subordinate category (Spaghetti Western) interacts with other subordinate categories (the Hollywood Western categories) sharing the same basic-level category resulting in the change of the meaning of those categories, and describes the empirical evidence on which our theoretical arguments are built.

Empirical setting

We explore how innovation and creativity in one product category can impact another already existing product category by looking at the impact of Spaghetti Western on the Hollywood Western movie genre. We focus on the movie genre because a genre is a fitting empirical case to study categories in general (DiMaggio 1987) and because previous empirical research (e.g. Hsu 2006; Jensen 2010) has utilized movie genres to further our understanding of categories. Additionally, movie production in Italy taking place in Cinecittà (the hub of Italian cinema in Rome) is a relevant cultural industry to study. The American Film Institute (AFI) offers a rather extensive definition of Western movies. In particular, the 'Western' genre identifies those movies that are set in the American West and that embody the spirit, the struggle and the demise of the new frontier. Under the broader Western category, the term 'Spaghetti Western' refers to Western movies produced in Europe, the majority of which were made between the years 1963 and 1970. These movies are generally referred to as Spaghetti Westerns due to the prominence of Italians in the production of Westerns in Europe. Following the initial, often derogatory, use of the term by critics, Spaghetti Westerns are now widely studied in scholarly work on cinema history and movie genres (López 1993; Frayling 2006; Fridlund 2006). The influence of the Spaghetti Western on the Hollywood Western is situated at the tail of a sharp decline in popularity of the Western movie genre in the US at the end of the 1950s and early 1960s. Researchers have attributed this decline to a combination of social and generational changes as reflected in a different audience taste and in the uninventive application of the Western formula in movie production (Hardy 1994).

The introduction of the Spaghetti Western to American audiences at the end of this period of decline sparked a significant revitalization in the popularity of Hollywood Westerns due to the success of Spaghetti Westerns with the American audiences (Cawelti 1984). Film critics and cinema historians have also discussed how the Spaghetti Westerns had a direct influence on the 'formula' of the Hollywood Western, indicating that the innovation of Spaghetti Westerns impacted the established product category of the Western in another country. We first identify the three important levels of a cognitive taxonomy – superordinate, basic and subordinate (Rosch 1978) – which in our context roughly correspond to movie, movie genre (e.g. Western) and the various movie genre subcategories (e.g. Classic Western, Spaghetti Western, Western Comedy, etc.), respectively (Figure 11.1). The genre can be viewed as the *basic level* because it is the genre of a movie that is used by audiences and critics to categorize a movie. We now describe the data, present the empirical case analysis, and offer a brief historical account of how Spaghetti Westerns emerged in Europe and their subsequent success in the US.

Data

In our data collection for this case study we relied on academic work, original sources and two movie databases. The academic work on the Spaghetti Western and the Hollywood Western provided us with a better understanding of the phenomenon as experts of the field see it and as a launching point for studying the evolution of the genre. The academic work we relied on includes work by Staig and Williams (1975), Wright (1975), Cawelti (1984) and Frayling (2006). We identified all Spaghetti Westerns by looking at Paul Bruckner's (2006) filmography, which is arguably the most comprehensive filmography on European Westerns in general, and on Spaghetti Westerns in particular. To identify all Hollywood Westerns, we relied on genre attributions made by the AFI – for the years 1974 and 1975 we used genre classification from the Internet Movie Database (IMDB) as AFI data is not available after 1973 – and the country attributions of the IMDB. By identifying the whole set of relevant movies that were produced between 1950 and 1975, we ended up with a list of 601 Spaghetti Westerns – of which 129 were released in the US – and 985 Hollywood Westerns.

For those movies, whenever available, we collected from IMDB or the AFI the following data, which we then used to create our variables of theoretical interest: production year, Spaghetti Western release year in the US and individuals involved in making the movie. With this data we hoped to trace the evolution of the Hollywood Western genre through the incorporation of novel elements from Spaghetti Westerns. In particular, we traced the development of movie production and box office, variations in the themes and Western movies' production members – i.e. the key areas in which, according to film critics and cinema historians, the influence of Spaghetti Westerns manifested itself. Whenever possible, we performed content analysis of original film reviews to corroborate the other measures and enhance our understanding of the phenomenon. We looked at reviews from the major sources of film reviews during the 1960s and the 1970s, such as the *New York Times*, *Washington Post* and the *Christian Science Monitor*.

The birth of Spaghetti Westerns in Europe

The cultural industry producing Westerns in Europe was already well established by the time production numbers of movies skyrocketed in the 1960s. Movie historian Frayling (2006) stresses the popularity of the Western genre in Europe from the beginning of the film industry. The Germans sparked a frenzy of Western production in Europe in 1962, when German produced Westerns were box office successes in Germany and all across Europe. The Italians quickly picked up on this, making their own Westerns shortly thereafter and soon surpassed the German productions in volume and popularity. The Westerns produced in Europe were originally influenced by Hollywood Westerns, as the Hollywood Western provided a definition for the genre that was accepted and known by European audiences, who were familiar with them and enjoyed them. Rather than copying the established Hollywood Westerns exactly, European producers adapted those movies to better fit with the taste of European audiences. Frayling states that Spaghetti Westerns were 'part critique of Hollywood originals, part attempt to get Italians to the Cinema' (2006: 49). It is these innovations that European producers made to the Hollywood Western that allow us to trace the later influence of the Spaghetti Western on the Hollywood Western when they were released in the US.

Although Spaghetti Westerns and other European Westerns shared the same heritage in the Hollywood Western, they developed into different forms to adjust to local tastes and movie production traditions. Spaghetti Westerns were influenced by both Italian society and the tradition of Epics produced in Cinecittà prior to Westerns' popularity. They also were 'able to retain some vestiges of a cultural identity, and to criticize what had up till then been accepted internationally as *the* context within which to make Westerns, and *the* Protestant–liberal tradition which Westerns were expected to represent' (Frayling 2006: 115–17). Spaghetti Westerns were also heavily influenced by the style of Sergio Leone, the most successful director of this genre. His film *A Fistful of Dollars* was the first widely popular Cinecittà Western production, and it influenced other directors of Spaghetti Westerns who tried to emulate its success. Other European Westerns remained closer to the tradition of the Hollywood Western and did not provide as much of a critique of their American predecessors. The German-produced Westerns that kick-started the production of European Westerns in 1962 were produced specifically with international audiences in mind. Frayling points out that this led to 'bland, non-committal adaptations of the "Winnetou" stories' – originally written by German author Karl May in the late nineteenth century – and resulted in the movies being only a diluted 'culmination of a specifically German tradition of attitudes towards the Western' (2006: 115).

The rise of Spaghetti Westerns in the US

Even though initially it took a while for European Westerns to be released in the US – the popular German Westerns produced in 1962 were released in the US in 1965 – the production of Westerns in Europe began to attract American audiences' interest early on. The ABC programme *Scope*, which looked at important political, economic and social issues around the world, dedicated the episode 'Westerns, European Style' aired on 28 July 1965 to the 'examination of the current big fad in European film making' (*Los Angeles Times*, 28 June 1965: C12). The interest was also reflected in newspaper articles, such as the article 'Italian Westerns getting the hang of it', published in the *Los Angeles Times* on 3 July 1966. The interest in

Westerns produced in Europe and the growing number of those movies released in the US after 1965 led to their initial categorization as 'European productions' or 'Italian made Westerns'. However, in 1966 Judith Crist – a film critic working for the *New York Herald Tribune* – started using the term 'Spaghetti Western' as a derogatory term for Westerns made in Italy.[1] The term was also adopted by other critics, and by 1968 news outlets across the country utilized the term, including *The New York Times* (e.g. in 'The screen: Zane Grey meets the Marquis de Sade', *The New York Times*, 25 January 1968) or the *Village Voice* (e.g. in 'Spaghetti & Sagebrush', *Village Voice*, 26 September 1968). In the following years, the term 'Spaghetti Western' became an accepted label for a new category of Western movies produced in Europe that was meaningful to the American audience.

Analysis

The enduring impact of Spaghetti Westerns on the Hollywood Western

According to film critics and cinema historians Spaghetti Westerns had direct influence on the 'formula' of the Hollywood Western, which manifested itself in: (a) the revitalization of the genre; (b) the borrowing from and copying of themes and plot lines; (c) the utilization of Spaghetti Western actors and their image; (d) the incorporation of typical style elements; and (e) the increased violence of the Hollywood Westerns (Frayling 2006). There is broad evidence that it did occur, and thus that the innovation in the cultural industry in Italy revitalized and stimulated innovation in a mature category in the US. The influence has not just been discussed by scholars in retrospect, but was also recognized by film critics at the time. For example, the critic Gary Arnold mentions this influence in his review of *A Bullet for the General* published on 25 April 1969 in *The Washington Post*, where he concludes that: 'On its own, "Bullet" can be written off as another awful but harmless Spaghetti Western. The troublesome thing is that its "style" has begun to influence American-made Westerns as well.' Arnold points to the movie *100 Rifles* as an example of a Hollywood Western that was impacted by the typical Spaghetti Western, leading to the action being 'fast, furious and pointless'.

Since the Western genre, like all movie genres, is fuzzy and its definition might change over time, in our empirical analysis we decided to focus on those movies that were considered to be part of the Western genre at the time of release. We used the AFI genre classification, which is attributed shortly after the release of a movie and allows for (at most) two genres to be attached to each movie, thereby ensuring a clearer classification. In contrast, genre classifications in the IMDB are attributed in retrospect by current audiences, and multiple genres are usually attached to each movie. This implies that movies may be classified as Westerns even when they share only one or a few minor features with real Western movies.

To document the evolution of the Hollywood Western and the influence the Spaghetti Western had on it in each of the four areas mentioned before we use some descriptive statistics of movies produced, top box office earned and the number of shared professionals in the movies. We also complement this analysis

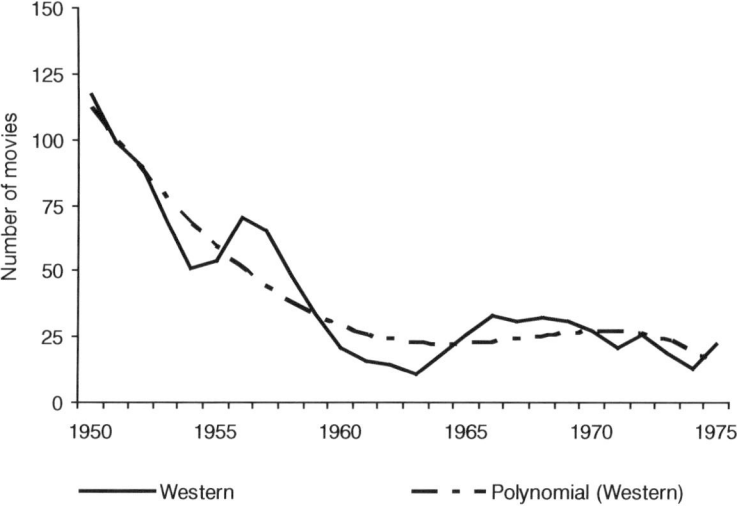

Figure 11.2 Number of Hollywood Westerns produced per year

Source: Our elaboration based on AFI and IMDB

with quotes and commentaries from industry insiders (e.g. movie directors), cinema historians and movie critics.

Revitalization

To trace the popularity of the Hollywood Western we look at (a) the number of Western movies produced in the US; and (b) their box office rental income from 1950 to 1975. The goal is to capture variations in the relative importance (number of movies) and market share (box office receipts) of Western movies in the US film industry. With both outcome measures we consider the development of the absolute numbers and the relevant shares of overall movies.

To better trace the popularity trend of the Hollywood Western, we also included a fifth order polynomial trend line in the graphs. From these it is clear that during the 1950s and early 1960s, the popularity of the Western genre declined sharply in the US in both the number of movies produced and box office receipts. After this sharp decline, Hollywood Western movie production resurged in 1964 (see Figure 11.2), resulting in higher movie production into the early 1970s. This increase in the number of productions can be explained by a general resurgence of movie production in the US rather than the influence of the Spaghetti Western: in fact, the share of Hollywood Westerns relative to all non-Western movies produced in the US increases slightly for the years 1965 through 1967, but otherwise remains at a very low level (see Figure 11.3).

The development of the box office, which is based on *Variety*'s list of the previous year's top grossing movies,[2] in turn provides a very different picture. The fifth order polynomial trend line for the Hollywood Western included in Figures 11.4 and 11.5 shows a significant resurgence in the popularity of Westerns

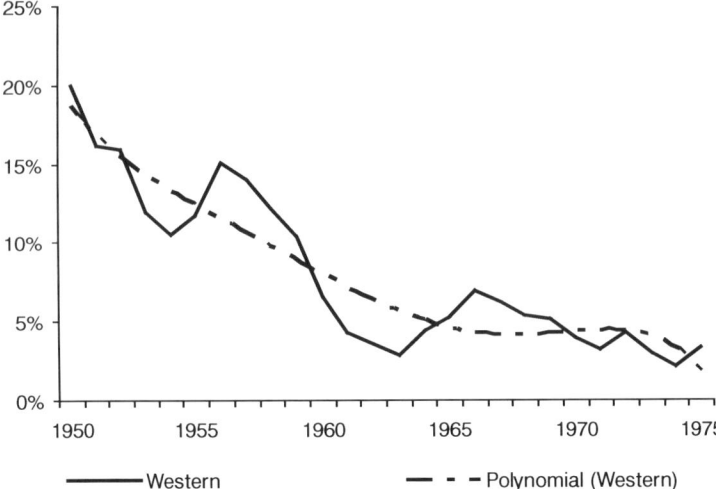

Figure 11.3 Share of Hollywood Western production of all non-Western American movie production

Source: Our elaboration based on AFI and IMDB

in the US. This increase in popularity of Hollywood Westerns is clearly observed in the top box office performers list for both total box office volume, displayed in 1967 US dollars using the consumer price index (see Figure 11.4), and share of the total box office in the list (see Figure 11.5). In his *The Six-Gun Mystique*, Cawelti (1984) proposes a causal link between Spaghetti Westerns and the success of Westerns in the US when he concludes that particularly the Leone-made Spaghetti Westerns 'brought about a significant resurgence in [the] popularity of the Western film' (1984: 31).

Themes and plots

The success of Spaghetti Westerns inspired the inclusion of general themes and specific plot lines in American-made movies. First, Spaghetti Westerns played an important role in shaping a shift of typical characters employed in Westerns at that time. This shift introduced an increased focus on Mexican rather than traditional American Indian characters as the opponents of the main character – an adjustment in which 'the expendable Mexican has taken the place of the expendable Indian' (Calder 1977: 141). Similarly, Austen stated that the Spaghetti Westerns 'have given the world of the Western a "new look", peopled it with the characters of unshaven bounty-hunting anti-heroes and sadistic Mexican outlaws' (1971: 36). At a more content-specific level the Spaghetti Westerns introduced a different style of hero, who is driven mainly by self-interest and is not integrated into society. This is a break from the Hollywod Western where the hero is a good character that brings order and justice to society. Frayling describes this change as: 'The parochialism of the American hero (civic consciousness divorced from political consciousness) becomes the "amoral familism" of the Italian hero

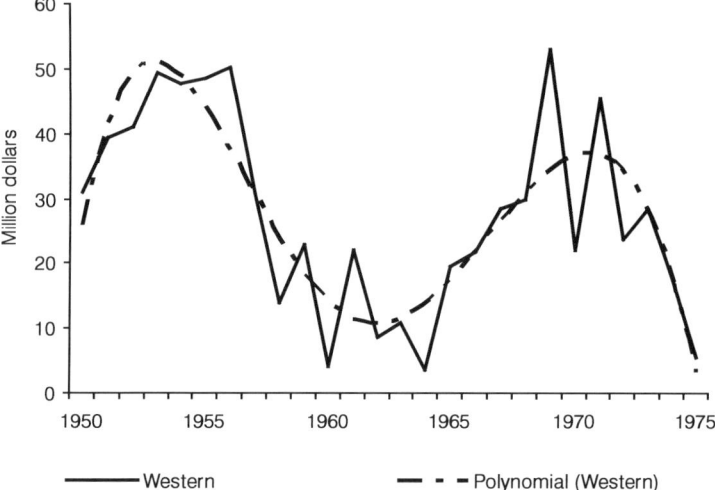

Figure 11.4 Box office of Hollywood Westerns in *Variety*'s top box office list (1967 dollars)

Source: Our elaboration based on AFI, IMDB and *Variety*

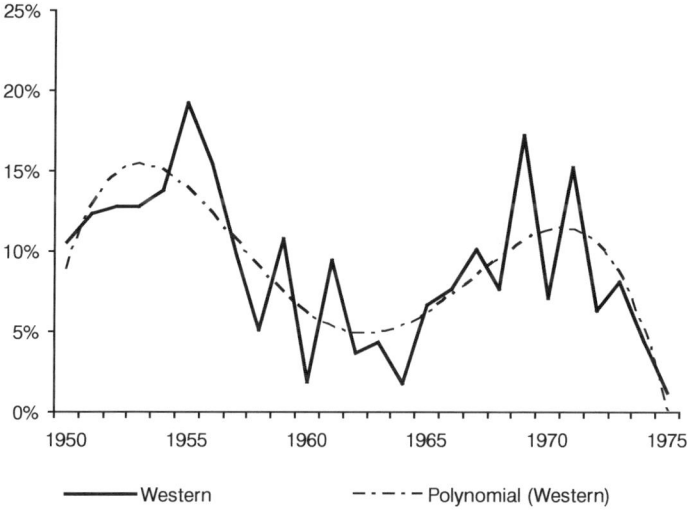

Figure 11.5 Share of box office of Hollywood Westerns of total box office in *Variety*'s top box office list

Source: Our elaboration based on AFI, IMDB and *Variety*

(revenge, or playing one side off against the other, without any reference to the role of the state or central government)' (Frayling 2006: 79).

Second, the plot of Hollywood Westerns adopted innovations from Spaghetti Western movies. There were some specific plot elements from Spaghetti Westerns that were incorporated in American productions – e.g. the utilization of the gag of the gun in the bathtub from Sergio Leone's *The Good, the Bad and the Ugly* in John Wayne's *Big Jake* or the climax of a train driving through a saloon from Harald Reinl's *Winnetou the Warrior* in John Sturge's *Joe Kidd*. But the impact on the plot has also been broader. The foundational and traditional plots of Spaghetti Westerns identified by Frayling (2006) – which are centred around an outsider who plays opposing factions against each other for his own benefit and potentially also struggles with a juxtaposition of self-interest and a set of values – were reflected in the narrative of some later Hollywood Westerns.

Spaghetti Western actors' involvement

The involvement of actors in American productions after their successful roles in Spaghetti Westerns indicates another type of direct influence. The images associated with actors' characters from Spaghetti Westerns could be carried over into later American productions. The most notable case of this direct impact is Clint Eastwood, who played the *Man with No Name* in the very popular trilogy of movies directed by Sergio Leone. The combination of repeatedly playing the same character in three very popular movies made it possible to exploit Eastwood's image in later productions. This effect is discussed by Frayling, who states that 'many of the films [Clint Eastwood] made with [Don] Siegel were explicitly intended to explore the "image" he had presented in the Spaghetti Westerns' (2006: 281).

One also can consider the involvement of individuals to be indirectly indicative of an influence, as individuals who were involved in Spaghetti Westerns took their skill sets to Hollywood Western productions. The employment of a cinematographer or director who was previously involved in Spaghetti Westerns suggests that the camera technique and direction style of the Spaghetti Western was adopted by the Hollywood Western. We thus think that the involvement of individuals previously involved in the making of Spaghetti Westerns is also indicative of the influence the Spaghetti Western had on the Hollywood Western. The data we collected from the IMDB indicates that indeed some individuals who worked on Spaghetti Westerns were later hired to work on Hollywood Westerns (see Figure 11.6).

Our data indicates that from 1970 to 1975, on average about 6 per cent of individuals involved in making Hollywood Westerns were previously involved in making Spaghetti Westerns. During this period, 9 per cent of Hollywood Western composers – and, even more significantly, 10 per cent of the directors – were previously involved with Spaghetti Westerns. Even though these percentages might seem low, we think that the number of individuals is significant enough to indicate an influence. The involvement of those individuals was also fairly widespread; on average, more than 60 per cent of the Hollywood Westerns produced from 1965 to 1975 included at least one individual who previously was involved in making Spaghetti Westerns.

Violence of Westerns

The impact of Spaghetti Westerns on the violence in Westerns produced in the US has been qualitatively traced by multiple scholars. For instance, Frayling states

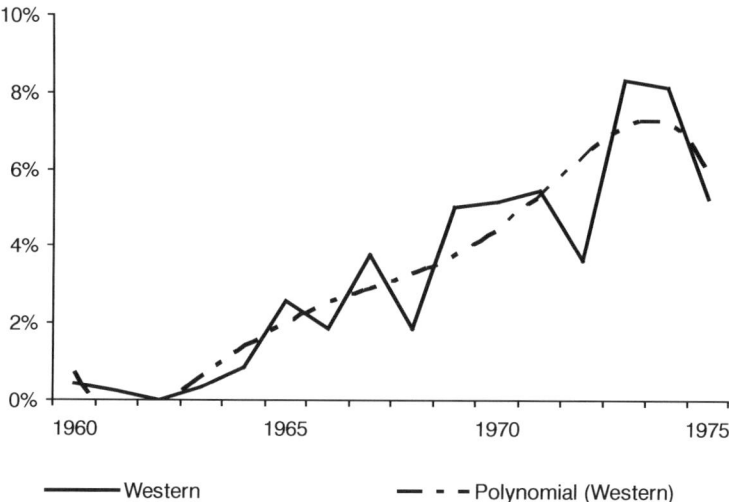

Figure 11.6 Share of individuals in Hollywood Westerns that were previously involved in Spaghetti Westerns

Source: Our elaboration based on AFI and IMDB

that the success of the Spaghetti Westerns 'may have created a context within which Peckinpah was permitted not only to film the opening and closing sequences of *The Wild Bunch*, but also to include them in the final version virtually uncut' (2006: 280). In regard to the direct influence Sergio Leone had on Sam Peckinpah, Sergio Leone was quoted by Frayling as saying:

> In retrospect, I can see that a Fistful of Dollars heralded the beginnings of a new cinema: Clockwork Orange, for example, would never have been filmed in the way it was. And Sam Peckinpah would have hesitated before shedding so much blood. He told me himself, 'Without you, I would never have thought of making the films I have made…'
>
> (Frayling 2006: 280)

Likewise, in his book *Violence in the Arts*, Fraser (1974) pointed out how the use of violence in *For a Few Dollars More* by Leone and *Django* by Corbucci was similar to the use of violence by Peckinpah in *The Wild Bunch* – which was not only Peckinpah's first Western after the release of Leone's movies in the US, but also much more violent than his previous productions. Fraser states that the filmed violence in all three movies is 'cathartic because the shocking parts provide climaxes to certain movements or phases in them and permit certain formal anticipations to be fully satisfied' (1974: 179). Interestingly, one of the first systematic studies on Spaghetti Westerns by Lawrence Staig and Tony Williams was published in 1975 with the title *Italian Western. The Opera of Violence* (Staig and Williams 1975).

It is worth noting that in the 1950s and early 1960s movies across all genres displayed an increasing level of graphic violence that reflected a more general and profound change within American society. The traditional ideals of triumphalism vanished from the Western, defeated by the racial and political turmoil that was engulfing the nation and seen in every home with a TV set. The commercial success of the Spaghetti Westerns simply 'galvanized this trend, leading to more explicit depictions of violence and a darker moral tone focused on frontier greed rather than romantic notions of law and civilization' (Block 2006: 100). As Coyne (1997: 125) wrote: 'In the mid-1960s, violence became ensconced as a high-profile and hugely profitable cinematic theme, a cornerstone rather than a condiment.'

Discussion

As similar artistic products are categorized in genres it is important for us to understand the process of category evolution in order to understand how creativity and innovation in one creative product can impact other existing products. Previous work on category dynamics has been mute on this point and has mainly focused on the process by which new categories are being created. In this section, we elaborate on the key theoretical mechanisms responsible for category evolution. To this end, we build on the previously discussed research in cognitive psychology on categorization, and particularly on the seminal work by Rosch and her colleagues on the internal structure of a cognitive taxonomy.

The distinction between vertical and horizontal dimensions of a cognitive taxonomy is important for identifying what facilitates the interaction between categories. Vertically, the relation of multiple lower-level categories to the same higher-level category results in a shared set of features among those lower-level categories and it provides a cognitive link among them. Whether categories share a higher-level category or not thus impacts whether two categories have a simple overlap in features or an overlap in features based on a cognitive link. We propose that the variance between different categories in whether they share a higher-level category and the degree of similarity based on a cognitively linked overlap between them is relevant in understanding category interactions.

Horizontally, categories are significantly more or less distinctive from other categories at the same level in the taxonomy depending on how different their features are from those of other categories. Categories at one horizontal level can become fuzzy when they share a large part of the features attributed to them with another category – and, therefore, it is increasingly difficult to distinguish between them. The distinctiveness of categories at the horizontal level is a further dimension we surmise to be relevant in understanding category interactions.

As we mentioned before, in our context the three important levels of the taxonomy – superordinate, basic and subordinate – roughly correspond to the levels of movie, movie genre and the various movie genre subcategories. We also assume that the genre is the *basic level* or conceptual centre, as it is the genre of a movie that is used broadly by audiences and critics to categorize a movie. The basic-level role of the genre is evident in movie reviews of the time of the Spaghetti Western, which in general begin with categorizing the movie into a genre before going into the plot of the movie in greater detail. The assumption is further supported by evidence that the AFI decided to utilize the genre level for classification when it established its *Catalog of Feature Films*. Furthermore, research on movies and movie genre points to typical features of movies in a genre, such as Wright's *Sixguns and Society* (1975), which reviews the typical plot elements of Western movies. These works on features most representative of that genre as well as features least representative of that genre indicate that the genre is being used as a conceptual centre in the marketplace for feature films.

From a large body of research on innovation that goes back to Schumpeter's (1934) seminal work, we know that innovations often originate from the recombination of existing elements or knowledge. Similarly, we expect creativity and innovation in one product category to be a viable source of change in other existing categories. From this perspective, the process through which innovation in one product category impacts another product category is not random, but reflects the internal structure of a cognitive taxonomy. The level of a category in the taxonomy and the relationships of that category with other categories are critical for understanding category dynamics.

If categories are vertically related they share the same basic-level category and they are cognitively linked through their taxonomic connection. This cognitive link facilitates the acceptance of features from one category into the meaning of another vertically related category as audiences have already established a meaningful link between the two categories. As a subordinate category of the Western genre, *Spaghetti Western* influenced the other subordinate categories of that genre, even across geographic boundaries. If two categories belong to the same basic-level category, by definition, those categories also share the set of features that defines their common basic-level category. This transitive property of a cognitive taxonomy may prevent the recombination of features from categories that do not share the same higher-level category. By contrast, having *different* higher-level categories is likely to result in the creation of a new intermediate (hybrid) category. This was the case, for instance, in the creation of a new genre of feature films that combined aspects from comedy and pornography following the legalization of picture pornography in Denmark in 1969 (Jensen 2010). Comedy and pornography are distinct movie genres, and as such they represent two separate basic-level structures of the same general (superordinate) movie category. In all these cases, the blending or recombination effort involve borrowing features of categories included in different superordinate categories, thus fostering the emergence of a new category.

Horizontally, the difference in features of categories that are subordinate to the same basic-level category impacts their individual distinctiveness. Most, if not all, categories do not have clear-cut or sharp boundaries. This is particularly true for lower-level categories, whose boundaries become fuzzy when they share a large set of features, making it harder to distinguish between them. As subordinate categories usually contain many features that overlap with other categories related to the same basic-level category, we would expect them to interact more easily and maybe even without much consideration. Our case study illustrates an instance where two categories that had a strong feature overlap – the Spaghetti Western and the Hollywood Western – interacted with each other.

Conclusions

Our case study showed how an innovation in the movie industry in Italy not only revitalized the mature product category of Western movies in the US, but also how it changed the meaning of the existing category and stimulated innovation to take place in the existing category. We then proposed that the cognitive links between two categories, established through their vertical and horizontal relations in a cognitive hierarchy, are important to understand whether and through which processes innovation in one category can impact another existing category even across national boundaries. We also show that an existing category can in fact evolve by incorporating features from other categories sharing the same basic-level.

Despite a growing body of research on categories only a few studies have begun to investigate category dynamics more systematically. These studies have mostly focused on how new categories are created (e.g. Rosa *et al.* 1999; Lounsbury and Rao 2004; Jensen 2010; Pontikes 2010). To date, in fact, virtually no study (except Karthikeyan and Wezel 2010; Kennedy *et al.* 2010) has explicitly examined how existing categories evolve through adaptive change. This study is among the first to demonstrate that product categories can evolve over time as well as elaborate the theoretical foundations for understanding when and why one should expect categories to evolve. The distinction between vertical and horizontal dimensions of a cognitive taxonomy is important for identifying the theoretical mechanisms responsible for category evolution through adaptive change, and for distinguishing between this case and the case when new categories emerge.

Category evolution also suggests that the meaning of a category is likely to change over time. Different periods might use the same category term, but the meaning of this term may not be identical in each period. For instance, within the context of movie genres, 'film noir' has been defined in several ways since its original usage in the late 1940s. The term 'film noir' 'had very different meanings in the late 1940s from those it acquired by the late 1950s [and] in these distinct historical periods, different films or groups of films were privileged as canonical texts within the genre, or were excluded from the category all together (Geraghty and Jancovich 2008: 2).

Similarly, the resurgence of the Hollywood Western in the mid-1960s was largely due to the efforts of revisionists who revived Hollywood Westerns through the incorporation of new features (primarily) from Spaghetti Westerns, and the reinterpretation of those features by assigning them different values. These values mirrored broader societal changes, and their embodiment helped the genre regain appeal among audience members.

Like other categories, movie genres are not static classification schemes but evolve over time (Lenihan 1980; Cawelti 1984; Altman 1999). This evolution can best be explained by looking at the cognitive taxonomy's internal structure. The vertical and horizontal dimensions through which categories are cognitively related are indeed critical for elaborating theoretically grounded explanations that distinguish between category evolution and category creation.

Notes

1 The *Christian Science Monitor* attributes the name to Judith Crist in its article 'TV and films move to mop up violence' (*Christian Science Monitor*, 06/21/1968: 1).
2 This list captures all movies with a box office rental income above a certain level, which varies slightly over the years but is close to $1 million. It thus excludes the majority of movies counted in the number produced. The list on average includes 92 movies each year.

References

Altman, R. (1999) *Film/Genre*, London: British Film Institute.

Austen, D. (1971) 'Continental Westerns', *Films and Filming*, 17(10): 36–42.

Berger, P.L. and Luckmann, T. (1966) *The Social Construction of Reality: A Treatise in the Sociology of Knowledge*, Garden City, NY: Doubleday.

Block, A. (2006) *Deconstructing the American Mythology: Revisionist Westerns and US History*, Williamstown, MA: Williams College.

Bowker, G.C. and Star, S.L. (1999) *Sorting Things Out: Classification and its Consequences*, Cambridge, MA: MIT Press.

Bruckner, U.P. (2006) *Für ein paar Leichen mehr: Der Italo-Western von seinen Anfängen bis heute (Stark erweiterte und aktualisierte Neuausgabe des Standardwerkes)*, Berlin: Schwarzkopf & Schwarzkopf.

Calder, J. (1977) *There Must be a Lone Ranger: The American West in Film and in Reality*, New York: McGraw Hill.

Cawelti, J.G. (1984) *The Six-Gun Mystique*, 2nd edn, Bowling Green, OH: Bowling Green University Popular Press.

Clemens, S.E. and Cook, J.M. (1999) 'Politics and institutionalism: Explaining durability and change', *Annual Review of Sociology*, 25: 441–66.

Coyne, M. (1997) *The Crowded Prairie: American National Identity in the Hollywood Western*, New York: St Martin's Press.

DiMaggio, P.J. (1987) 'Classification in art', *American Sociological Review*, 52(4): 440–55.

DiMaggio, P.J. and Powell, W.W. (1991) 'Introduction', in W.W. Powell and P.J. DiMaggio (eds) *The New Institutionalism in Organizational Analysis*, Chicago, IL: Chicago University Press, pp. 1–38.

Fligstein, N. (1996) 'Markets as politics: A political–cultural approach to market institutions', *American Sociological Review*, 61(4): 656–73.

Florida, R. (2005) *The Flight of the Creative Class*, New York: Harper Collins.

Fraser, J. (1974) *Violence in the Arts*, Cambridge, UK: Cambridge University Press.

Frayling, C. (2006) *Spaghetti Westerns: Cowboys and Europeans from Karl May to Sergio Leone*, Revised paperback edn, New York: I.B. Taurus.

Fridlund, B. (2006) *The Spaghetti Western: A Thematic Analysis*, Jefferson, NC: McFarland.

Geraghty, L. and Jancovich, M. (2008) *The Shifting Definitions of Genre*, Jefferson, NC: McFarland.

Hannan, M.T., Pólos, L. and Carroll, G.R. (2007) *Logics of Organization Theory: Audiences, Codes and Ecologies*, Princeton, NJ: Princeton University Press.

Hardy, P. (1994) *The Overlook Film Encyclopedia. The Western*, Woodstock, NY: Overlook Press.

Hsu, G. (2006) 'Jacks of all trades and masters of none: Audiences' reactions to spanning genres in feature film production', *Administrative Science Quarterly*, 51(3): 420–50.

Jensen, M. (2010) 'Legitimizing illegitimacy: Identity spaces and markets for illegitimate products', in G. Negro, Ö. Koçak and G. Hsu (eds) *Categories in Markets: Origins and Evolution*, (Research in the Sociology of Organizations, Vol. 31), London: Emerald Group Publishing, pp. 39–80.

Karthikeyan, S.I. and Wezel, F.C. (2010) 'Identity repositioning: The case of liberal democrats and audience attention in British politics, 1950–2005', in G. Negro, Ö. Koçak and G. Hsu (eds) *Categories in Markets: Origins and Evolution* (Research in the Sociology of Organizations, Vol. 31), London: Emerald Group Publishing, pp. 295–320.

Kennedy, M.T., Lo, J. and Lounsbury, M. (2010) 'Category currency: The changing value of conformity as a function of ongoing meaning construction', in G. Negro, Ö. Koçak and G. Hsu (eds) *Categories in Markets: Origins and Evolution* (Research in the Sociology of Organizations, Vol. 31), London: Emerald Group Publishing, pp. 369–97.

Lamont, M. and Molnár, V. (2002) 'The study of boundaries in the social sciences', *Annual Review of Sociology*, 28: 167–95.

Lenihan, J.H. (1980) *Showdown. Confronting Modern America in the Western Film*, Urbana, IL: University of Illinois Press.

López, D. (1993) *Films by Genre: 775 Categories, Styles, Trends and Movements Defined, with a Filmography for Each*, Jefferson, NC: McFarland.

Lounsbury, M. and Rao, H. (2004) 'Sources of durability and change in market classifications: A study of the reconstitution of product categories in the American mutual fund industry, 1944–85', *Social Forces*, 82(3): 969–99.

Meyer, J. and Rowan, B. (1977) 'Institutionalized organizations: Formal structure as myth and ceremony', *American Journal of Sociology*, 83(2): 340–63.

Murphy, G.L. (2004) *The Big Book of Concepts*, Cambridge, MA: MIT Press.

Negro, G., Koçak, Ö. and Hsu, G. (2010) 'Research on categories in the sociology of organizations', in G. Negro, Ö. Koçak and G. Hsu (eds) *Categories in Markets: Origins and Evolution* (Research in the Sociology of Organizations, Vol. 31), London: Emerald Group Publishing, pp. 3–35.

North, D.C. (1990) *Institutions, Institutional Change and Economic Performance*, New York: Cambridge University Press.

Osherson, D. and Smith, E. (1982) 'Gradedness and conceptual combination', *Cognition*, 12: 299–318.

Pontikes, E. (2010) 'Fitting in or starting new? Invention, ambiguity and category emergence in the software industry, 1990–2002', Working paper invited for revision and resubmission at *American Sociological Review*.

Porac, J.F. and Thomas, H. (1994) 'Cognitive categorization and subjective rivalry among retailers in a small city', *Journal of Applied Psychology*, 79(1): 54–66.

Porac, J.F., Thomas, H., Wilson, F., Paton, D. and Kanfer, A. (1995) 'Rivalry and industry model of Scottish knitwear producers', *Administrative Science Quarterly*, 40(2): 203–27.

Rosa, J.A., Porac, J.F., Runser-Spanjol, J. and Saxon, M.S. (1999) 'Sociocognitive dynamics in a product market', *Journal of Marketing*, 63(special issue): 64–77.

Rosch, E. (1978) 'Principles of categorization', in E. Rosch and B. Lloyd (eds) *Cognition and Categorization*, Hillsdale, NJ: Erlbaum, pp. 27–48.

Rosch, E., Mervis, C., Gray, W., Johnson, D. and Boyes-Braem, P. (1976) 'Basic objects in natural categories', *Cognitive Psychology*, 8(3): 382–439.

Schumpeter, J.A. (1934) *The Theory of Economic Development*, Cambridge, MA: Harvard University Press.

Staig, L. and Williams, T. (1975) *Italian Western. The Opera of Violence*, London: Lorrimer.

White, H. (1981) 'Where do markets come from?', *American Journal of Sociology*, 87(3): 517–47.

Wright, W. (1975) *Sixguns and Society: A Structural Study of the Western*, Berkeley, CA: University of California Press.

Zuckerman, E.W. (1999) 'The categorical imperative: Securities analysts and the illegitimacy discount', American Journal of Sociology, 104(5): 1398–438.

12 Cultural activities in territorial development

The case of cultural and creative enterprises in the Swiss watchmaking industry

Hugues Jeannerat and Olivier Crevoisier

Introduction

The place of culture in economic development has progressively become a critical issue in the analysis of regional and urban competitiveness. In European countries, where traditional industries face competition from new developing countries, companies and policy makers increasingly regard culture and creativity as strategic resources to develop market distinction and value added. In this context, increasing literature has recently emphasized the importance of cultural resources in local production activities. In this chapter, we propose to address the general question of the commercial and territorial forms that culture takes when integrated in various types of economic activity.

This contribution proposes not restricting cultural activities to the question of production and of commodification of culture but addressing the broader question of culture in market construction. Two important issues are here emphasized. The first one relates to the way culture is commercialized within different forms of business models. Is culture always commercialized as an ordinary industrial commodity or should it be rather considered as a particular input within a broader economic value chain? What are the business models of cultural and creative enterprises? The second issue relates to the territorial organization of production and consumption in markets. How do cultural activities participate to the attraction of consumers or to the export of particular products? How do they integrate with other productive activities and consumption channels? In this chapter, we assume that the way cultural activities are commercialized, produced and consumed mirrors different approaches regarding territorial development itself but also regarding different conceptual perspectives in regional studies or economic geography at large.

The first part of the chapter proposes distinguishing four typical approaches considering the place of cultural activities in regional development. The first places the commodification of cultural activities and the attraction of temporary visitors at the centre of regional growth. The second perceives culture as an input for local creativity or for residential economy and is mostly based on the attraction of permanent residents. The third considers cultural activities as an ordinary productive activity that is carried out locally, or partially locally, through regional competences and exported as a commodity to a global market. The fourth regards cultural activities as an additional input to exported goods or services. In this last case, cultural activities participate in the broader commercialization and the general export process of particular culturized products.

The second part of this chapter presents the cases of two cultural/creative enterprises that recently developed in the changing contexts of fine watchmaking, luxury and media activities in Switzerland and abroad. The first case emphasizes how a traditional Swiss media company seeks to exploit its proximity to traditional watchmaking companies to develop a new market niche dedicated to luxury multimedia services. The second case relates to the creation by several luxury watch brands of a particular foundation whose mission is to promote, legitimate and diffuse the specific cultural and technical value of *haute horlogerie* towards increasingly knowledgeable consumers.

Following the distinction proposed by Cooke and Lazzeretti (2008b), the first case could be regarded as a typical for-profit creative enterprise, while the second would be more perceived as a traditional non-profit cultural enterprise. However, beyond a restrictive comparison of those two cases, we assume that both enterprises participate in a common process of cultural co-production, diffusion and legitimation of Swiss watchmaking at local and international scales. We finally underline that they contribute to the establishment and reinforce the position of the city of Geneva as a territorial bridge between the local production milieu of watchmaking and its international market.

Production and consumption of cultural/creative activities in a territorial perspective

The rise of the creative economy as a progressive commercialization of culture and cultural spaces

The place of culture and creativity in economic development has progressively become a critical issue in the analysis of regional and urban competitiveness. In European countries, where traditional industries face increasing competition on technological development and on production costs, culture and creativity are increasingly regarded by companies, by policy makers and by scholars as strategic resources to create new distinctive products and to boost economic added value. Considering culture as an economic resource leads to the discussion of the link between markets and culture, i.e. the general question of commercializing culture in the market.

As emphasized by Scott and Leriche (2005), conversely to earlier theories considering cultural creation as a fundamentally non-market activity, culture is today often theorized as a determinant resource for economic development and for competitiveness. For numerous scholars, culture and market transactions are not now perceived as fundamentally contradictory, mutually exclusive or just separate. The increased scientific attention paid to cultural and creative industries is particularly illustrative of such an evolution (Power and Scott 2004; Cooke and Lazzeretti 2008a; Leriche and Daviet 2010).

Over the last years, the concept of *creative economy* has progressively encompassed that of *cultural economy* in most policy and academic discourses. For different researchers, the substitution of the concept of culture with the concept of creativity reflects the achievement of a perspective where cultural production has become an ordinary economic and marketable activity (Pratt 2005). While cultural activities were earlier seen as inspiring 'public conditions' for local entrepreneurs, creative activities are now generally considered as activities that directly 'make money' (Cooke and Lazzeretti 2008b). Furthermore, with such an economic interest in creativity, policy makers and scholars have mainly focused their attention on the supply-side of cultural economies (Garnham 2005).

In economic geography and regional studies, the question of articulating cultural and economic development also stimulated various theories (Costa 2008; Leriche and Daviet 2010; Liefooghe 2010). Different studies have analyzed particular localized 'districtualization' or 'clustering' processes around the development of cultural activities. In particular, urban areas have been pointed out as privileged and innovative contexts for cultural and creative activities (Scott 1997; Lazzeretti 2003, 2008; Cinti 2008; Lorenzen and Frederiksen 2008).

These recent studies advocate the importance of culture as a crucial non-technological issue for regional competitiveness, while previous territorial innovation models mainly pay attention to technological development (Moulaert and Sekia 2003; Lagendijk 2006). For instance, they address the place of culture and creativity for the development or the regeneration of urban (Miles and Paddison 2005; Cooke 2008), peripheral (Scott 2010) or traditional industrial regions (Kebir and Crevoisier 2008). The aim of the present article is not to provide a complete review of those approaches. Rather it is to highlight some differences in the way territorial development is perceived in relation to cultural activities and to market construction. A first distinction can be made around the place that culture occupies in the general process of market commercialization. A second distinction can be based on the territorial organization that the production and the consumption of cultural activities take in the market. Based on these two fundamental distinctions, different theoretical insights on territorial development can be highlighted.

The commercialization of culture: culture as an economic output or input

The increased importance of cultural industries in today's economy such as the film, the tourism or the leisure industries can be regarded as a commodification of culture. However, such industries are far from covering all economic activities by which culture becomes of market value. For instance, in cases such as branding, fashion or design, culture itself is not necessarily what is directly paid for. In such cases, culture participates in boosting the economic value of a particular market good or service. Therefore, the place of culture in economic processes has to be considered in a broad view of commercialization. This is particularly relevant in today's economy where information and communication technologies (ICT) and new media have given rise to extremely complex, immaterial and potentially ubiquitous pricing and revenue models (Ng 2010).

The general question of commercialization encompasses the more particular question of commodification. Commodification is the specific process of commercialization 'whereby a produced thing or activity *itself* is given a consumptive market value' (Kaul 2007: 706). In this case, particular market counterparty (e.g. a payment) is given to a good or a service and substitutes – temporary or definitely – the interpersonal relations of actors in market (Weber 2000; Testart 2001). Commercialization refers more broadly to the different transactions, interdependencies and complementarities that market actors develop when establishing a particular equivalency between a consumed good and its payment. For instance, traditional folk music in Irish pubs is not directly commodified as the audience does not primarily pay for the musical performance but for their drinks in the pub. In such a case, commercialization implies particular forms of control and of interdependencies between musicians, publicans and tourists (Kaul 2007).

In other words, cultural activities participate in particular commodification processes as well as in more general commercialization processes. While commodification primarily places the emphasis on culture as an economic *output*, commercialization places more considerations on culture as an economic *input* (Lefèbvre 2008; Leriche and Daviet 2010). The first perspective often reflects an 'industrialization process of culture' (for instance in Scott 2005), while the second often mirrors a 'culturization processes of industry' (for instance in Crevoisier and Kebir 2009).

Territorial market forms of production–consumption

A second fundamental market distinction relates to the way the production and the consumption of cultural activities organize at territorial level. To address this second perspective, Scott and Leriche (2005) propose differentiating between *non-mobile* and *mobile* cultural products. On the one hand, mobile cultural products are produced locally – or at least partially – and are dedicated to a distant market. Hollywood film production is often presented as the most illustrative case of a mobile cultural production. However, this category should also consider 'globalized advanced services' (Pratt 2008) such as advertising services or, more generally, all the traditional industrial products, such as fashion or luxury products, whose economic value relies on an important cultural base. This last category of cultural activities probably represents the main part of mobile cultural products.

On the other hand, non-mobile cultural products – produced locally or at least partly locally – are dedicated to be consumed where they are produced, for example the increasing 'eventification' (e.g. festivals, sport events) of urban and rural areas (Richards and Wilson 2004). Tourism activities are certainly among the most studied non-mobile cultural activities. Nevertheless, non-mobile cultural

Territorial form of production–consumption Form of commercialization	Co-localized production–consumption (non-mobile cultural products)	Distant production–consumption (mobile cultural products)
Culture as an economic output (commodification of culture)	VISITOR-BASED CULTURAL ECONOMY (tourism spaces, urban destinations) Case 1	EXPORT-ORIENTED CULTURAL ECONOMY (film production clusters, advanced cultural services) Case 3
Culture as an economic input (culture in commercialization)	Case 2 CULTURIZED RESIDENT-BASED ECONOMY (creative class, residential economy)	Case 4 CULTURIZED EXPORT-ORIENTED ECONOMY (fashion/luxury industries, brand channels, cultural retail places)

Figure 12.1 Four perspectives on cultural activities and territorial development

Source: Our elaboration

products should be regarded as attractions not only for intermittent visitors but also for permanent residents. With the increasing importance of the experience economy (Pine and Gilmore 1999), the attraction of end consumers is considered as a crucial challenge for urban/regional development (Richards 2001; Stamboulis and Skayannis 2003; Lorentzen 2009). For instance, urban cultural amenities are increasingly considered as key resources to attract creative workers (Florida 2002) or to develop a residential-based economy (Markusen 2007; Markusen and Schrock 2009; Davezies 2009).

In brief, the fundamental difference between mobile and non-mobile cultural products is that the former supposes a local capacity to make a cultural product mobile toward distant consumers while the latter focuses on the local capacities to exploit the mobility of consumers (visitors or residents) through a cultural attraction.

Various forms of territorial development through cultural activities

Based on the two market distinctions described above, four differentiated types of territorial development can be identified. Each one presents particular regional issues and can be associated with different theoretical insights emphasized in economic geography or regional studies (Figure 12.1).

In the first type of territorial development, culture is considered as an economic market commodity, or market output, co-locally produced and consumed. In such a case, regional development strongly relates to a *visitor-based cultural economy* whereby cultural resources are used to generate additional revenue for the region (Case 1). For instance, this particular approach to cultural activities has often been applied in recent strategies of urban regeneration (Miles and Paddison 2005). On the one hand, regional development relates here to the local capacity to turn specific resources into particular cultural attractions or to facilitate the establishment of global cultural stakeholders. Cooke (2008) speaks in this latter case of a 'Wimbledonization' of cultural assets. On the other, regional development also relates to the capacity to organize the attraction of end consumers through transport facilities or acknowledge their cultural assets through supra-regional labels such as the nominations for Capital of Culture (Garcìa 2005; Cooke 2008).

A second form of territorial development also relates to co-localized production and consumption processes but considers cultural activities rather as an input within a broader commercialization context. In this case, cultural resources contribute to the general regional conditions of living and of creativity. In Florida's (2002) perception of creativity, culture is not primarily seen as a commodity. It is primarily considered as an element of an attractive 'people climate' for 'talents' involved in various competitive economic activities. Nowadays, scholars and policy makers perceive cultural inputs as a crucial issue for urban/regional competitiveness in a knowledge-based economy (Asheim and Hansen 2009). In such an approach, cultural activities and cultural amenities are not primarily seen as end products in market. They are factors of attraction fuelling local residential-based activities (Markusen 2007, 2010; Davezies 2009) or globally valuable economic activities (Florida 2002). We can speak here of a *culturized resident-based economy* (Case 2).

A third approach considers cultural production as a particular industrial activity. Culture is regarded here as a resource mobilized within a particular localized production process in order to produce a particular market commodity. This reflects an *export-oriented cultural economy* whereby culture is commodified as an end product and is exported to a distant market (Case 3). Here regional development and competitiveness are mainly based on the capacity to specify and specialize local productive activities (cultural goods and related services), to reach global market standards and distribution channels. Two examples are particularly illustrative of such territorial development. The first is the famous case of the Hollywood film industry that reflects a local production of cultural commodities exported to a global market (Scott 2005). The second example is the case of cultural 'advanced productive services' that are partially detached from local consumption and that are largely exported (e.g. advertising or new media activities concentrated in particular cities) (Pratt 2008).

Finally, a fourth form of territorial development relates to the situations where culture is not directly produced and consumed as a commodity but as the valuable added component of an exported good or service. Such a case characterizes what can be called a *culturized export-oriented economy* (Case 4). In Europe, where traditional industries face important competition on production costs, cultural resources are increasingly mobilized to create additional economic value. For instance, design and fashion activities are usually not sold as such on end markets. They are intermediary activities that participate in the value of industrial products. Branding activities are particularly illustrative examples of cultural activities achieved within a broader commercialization process (Power and Hauge 2008; Pike 2009). In such a context, two main territorial issues can be identified. On the one hand, a local production system has to be able to mobilize and combine local or global cultural resources with original local productive competences. On the other hand, the mobility and the tradability of the culturized products in a distant consumption context take place within complex multi-local relations and interdependencies (Jeannerat and Crevoisier 2011). Such relations do not only imply cultural activities within original production areas but also within particular cultural retailing contexts (Crewe 2003) or particular brand channels (Jansson and Power 2010).

Of course, these different stylized forms of territorial development related to cultural activities should not be considered as mutually exclusive. Most often, they intertwine and are interdependent. For instance, the cultural attraction of creative residents may induce the development of new attractions for visitors or of new advanced productive services (Florida 2002, 2005). However, our contention is that such a distinction illustrates particular analytical and theoretical issues regarding how culture becomes commercialized and how it is produced and consumed in various territorial forms. Not only does this framework enable a comparison of different types of cultural activities, it also emphasizes how those various forms of territorial development may overlap within a given region.

The next section analyzes two cases of cultural/creative enterprises that have developed in the culturized export-oriented economy of the Swiss watchmaking industry. They illustrate how new cultural and creative activities participate in the broader commercialization of luxury and high-end watches. Although these two cultural/creative enterprises represent very different development and business trajectories, it appears that both offer very similar support to watch brands: the co-production, the diffusion and the legitimation of their cultural value.

Cultural and creative enterprises in Swiss watchmaking

Since the 1980s, facing the increased international competition in the market of electronic watches, the Swiss watchmaking industry has been the subject of an intense culturization (Kebir and Crevoisier 2008; Jeannerat and Crevoisier 2011). Progressively, Swiss watchmaking companies singularized their products by increasing their aesthetical and cultural value. Production and communication strategies became more focused on the social distinction and on the cultural values of consumers (e.g. sport watches, fashion watches or luxury watches). In parallel, original French and Italian fashion or luxury companies set up in the Jura region in order to produce their own branded watches (Crevoisier 1993).

This increasing culturization of Swiss watches reached a new stage with the general revival of mechanical watches started in the mid-1990s. Today, mechanical watches represent the technical and cultural authenticity of Swiss watchmaking and constitute the major export value of this industry. In this context, Swiss or foreign watchmaking companies established in the Jura region face new business challenges (Jeannerat and Crevoisier 2011).

- First, as well as their traditional technical productive competences, watchmaking companies increasingly rely on additional cultural activities dedicated to the *co-production* of image and of communication content (e.g. film production, event organization, exhibitions, websites, magazines, etc.).

- Second, as a mostly exporting industry, watchmaking companies cannot only distribute their products in an industrial way but have also to *diffuse* their cultural specificity and make it understandable to distant consumers.
- Third, by increasingly basing their value added on cultural and technical authenticity, watchmaking companies have to rely on particular intermediaries (journalists, experts, etc.) and technical devices (auctions, awards, etc.) in order to *legitimate* their cultural and technical particularities.

To address these different issues, watchmaking companies have consequently developed new internal competences and diffusion channels. For instance, marketing and communication departments or mono-brand shops have quickly and widely expanded during the last ten years. Furthermore, particular cultural or creative enterprises have developed dedicated services to support the cultural co-production, the cultural diffusion and cultural legitimation of authentic watchmaking. Here a *cultural or creative enterprise* is regarded as a general organization that *undertakes* particular projects and activities through which social or economic value is created from cultural resources. Such enterprises may undertake profit as well as non-profit-making activities. In this view, they should not exclusively be defined as business companies.

The next sections present the recent development in Switzerland of two cultural/ creative enterprises dedicated to the promotion of high-range watchmaking. The first one emphasizes how an important media company headquartered near Geneva has repositioned its business strategy to enter the market niche of multimedia services dedicated to luxury and high-end watchmaking. The second case describes the creation by several watchmaking brands of a foundation dedicated to the promotion of the authentic *haute horlogerie* (which translates in English as 'fine watchmaking').

The analysis of these two cases is based on particular empirical observations made in the broader context of the European FP6 project called 'EURODITE'.[1] The aim of this project was to analyze how learning processes organize within and across regions, firms or sectors (MacNeill and Collinge 2010). The two empirical cases presented were studied as particular *knowledge biographies* (Butzin 2009; Larsson and Butzin 2010) illustrating the general evolution of Swiss watchmaking during the last ten years.

Two types of data were gathered. On the one hand, an intensive data collection was carried out on websites, press releases and specialized magazines to understand the general context in which the two cases emerged. On the other hand, in each case, ten semi-directional interviews were obtained with people involved in the creation or the development of the studied enterprise. Those interviews were about the kind of competence and of actors engaged in the development of the enterprise, the context in which the project was undertaken and its territorial organization.

The empirical analysis proposed here points to the crucial importance of cultural and creative activities for a traditional European industry such as Swiss watchmaking. First, a particular emphasis is placed on the economic model of each enterprise and on the context in which each one emerged. Then, the particular innovation and learning processes involved in their development are described from a territorial perspective.

'Edipresse Luxe': a business niche between local specification and global diffusion

With the increasing importance for the Swiss watchmaking companies of new international markets (especially in Asia), new dedicated activities and knowledge are needed to communicate and diffuse in an appropriate way the semantic codes of quality and the authenticity of Swiss watches. This economic change is illustrated here through the decision of Edipresse, an important Swiss media group, to create a specific subsidiary company dedicated to luxury and watches. As well as the evolution of the Swiss watchmaking context described above, this change also appears in the challenging evolution of the media sector.

Edipresse Luxe and the Edipresse Group

According to several interviewees, the traditional media sector faces new, crucial challenges. First, traditional business models have changed with the centrality of advertisement and with the rise of free newspapers. Second, the development of ICT leads traditional media companies to adapt their traditional competences to benefit from the opportunity provided by new social media and to defend their market position towards new Internet competitors (e.g. Google, Twitter, Facebook). More and more, media companies have to become multi-support companies providing services in traditional publishing, in web publishing, web television or event production. Third, the globalization of trade has increased the need for communication campaigns to new foreign markets and provides new opportunities for new advertisement campaigns. Fourth, these new challenges ask for important organizational and financial capacities. The media industry has progressively concentrated into large national or multinational companies. In Switzerland, the media sector is mainly controlled by large media groups mainly established in the Zurich area. In this context, Edipresse, which is the only large media company established in the French-speaking part of Switzerland, has progressively repositioned its business strategy around two axes (Figure 12.2).

On the one hand, the Edipresse Group has intensified its international activities in foreign markets where initial investment is modest but presents a high potential for development in particular niches such as lifestyle media. During the last five years, this internationalization has been particularly strong in Eastern Europe and in Asia. For instance, Edipresse Asia, a subsidiary headquartered in Hong Kong, was created in 2005 to manage the various magazines and web activities of the Group in China and Asian-Pacific countries. Such international expansion was generally achieved through the acquisition of strategic publishers or through strategic publishing licences.

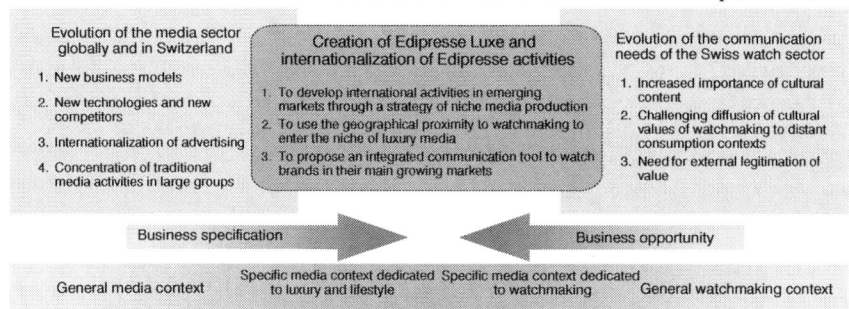

Evolution of the media sector globally and in Switzerland	Creation of Edipresse Luxe and internationalization of Edipresse activities	Evolution of the communication needs of the Swiss watch sector
1. New business models 2. New technologies and new competitors 3. Internationalization of advertising 4. Concentration of traditional media activities in large groups	1. To develop international activities in emerging markets through a strategy of niche media production 2. To use the geographical proximity to watchmaking to enter the niche of luxury media 3. To propose an integrated communication tool to watch brands in their main growing markets	1. Increased importance of cultural content 2. Challenging diffusion of cultural values of watchmaking to distant consumption contexts 3. Need for external legitimation of value

Business specification → ← Business opportunity

| General media context | Specific media context dedicated to luxury and lifestyle | Specific media context dedicated to watchmaking | General watchmaking context |

Figure 12.2 The strategic repositioning of the Edipresse Group

Source: Our elaboration

On the other hand, as well as its internationalization, Edipresse has repositioned its business strategy in Switzerland towards the niche of multimedia activities dedicated to luxury and high-end watchmaking. This local strategic development has been institutionalized by the creation in 2007 of the subsidiary named 'Edipresse Luxe'. This new entity was developed to provide integrated multimedia services dedicated to high-end watchmaking and luxury companies. Through magazines, Internet platforms and particular events, Edipresse Luxe provides a multi-support service of diffusion for the Swiss watchmaking brands in their principal export markets.

This new business orientation was largely induced by the geographical proximity of Edipresse to the traditional watchmaking industry. While Edipresse Group's headquarter was established in Lausanne, Edipresse Luxe's headquarter was established in Geneva to reinforce its proximity with a long and legitimate cultural heritage in watchmaking and with international facilities (international tourism and events). This was underlined by the chief executive officer (CEO) of Edipresse Luxe: 'Established in Geneva, the cradle of luxury watchmaking, Edipresse Luxe is proud to be present in the success of one of the most important industries of the Swiss economy, and for which, thanks to an integrated approach, we will be able to develop tailor-made products (Edipresse 2007).

However, the Edipresse Group's strategy did not only seek to propose a dedicated service to watchmaking brands but also international channels of diffusion. This was emphasized by the CEO of the Group: 'In collaboration with the various Group subsidiaries in rapidly expanding markets, such as Asia and Russia, Edipresse Luxe offers advertisers and consumers a range of perfectly complementary products, from online to event, from print to marketing and advertising' (Edipresse 2007). In other words, this evolution of the Edipresse business strategy does not merely illustrate a strategic positioning in the market of new media. It also relies on a territorial coupling between the localized creative activities of Edipresse Luxe, anchored in the region of watchmaking production, and the creative activities of the foreign subsidiaries anchored in the consumption context of Swiss watches, mostly in Asia.

Edipresse's move towards the production and the diffusion of cultural multimedia content dedicated to luxury and high-end watchmaking involved a change not only in the business strategy of the company but also in its knowledge base. Before the creation of Edipresse Luxe, Edipresse was an important player in Switzerland mostly through various local magazines and newspapers and abroad mostly through particular magazines. The particular niche of media activities dedicated to watchmaking (specialized magazines, dedicated websites) was predominantly occupied by heterogeneous small companies and specialized freelancers. Edipresse's strategy was to exploit its greater investment capacity and its established international network rapidly to become a central player in media activities dedicated to high-end watchmaking.

In addition to a local magazine dedicated to arts and an international fashion magazine already owned by the Group, three strategic companies established in Geneva were purchased to constitute the core of Edipresse Luxe activities. The first was the magazine *GMT*, dedicated to watchmaking, the second was a famous French language watchmaking website called 'Worldtempus' and the third was the award-giving body called the 'Geneva Watchmaking Grand Prix'. Moreover, a journalist specialized in watchmaking was hired as chief editor of Worldtempus. While the first two activities were clearly dedicated to profit-making (mostly based on advertisement), the third one was conceived as a complementary non-profit tool. On the one hand, the Geneva Watchmaking Grand Prix, which is an independent institution awarding the most prestigious watches every year, was perceived by Edipresse as an opportunity to establish its credibility with strategic watch producers and other connoisseurs. On the other hand, this event was also seen as a 'glamorous show' giving the opportunity to produce particular multimedia content (dedicated videos and articles). With more modest ambitions, this event was compared by the CEO of Edipresse Luxe as a potentially future 'Cannes Festival for watchmaking'.

As well as anchoring its local activities through Edipresse Luxe, the Edipresse Group also mobilized its international subsidiaries to 'assist watchmakers in their various needs and in their key markets' (Edipresse 2008). Most of Edipresse Luxe activities (magazines, website and events) were internationalized through the Group's global channels. The internationalization of magazines was mainly achieved through licensing agreements and was launched by Edipresse subsidiaries or partners established in localized international markets. In distant markets, local editorial teams were created to adapt and to contextualize the original magazines in the local consumption context. A spin-off of the Geneva Watchmaking Grand Prix was also launched in Singapore through the local subsidiary and the local partners of Edipresse. Recently, a Chinese version of the website Worldtempus has been created. It is managed by the Shanghai office of Edipresse Asia. Finally, Edipresse achieved a licensing agreement to launch a famous Singaporean watchmaking magazine in Europe and Russia.

Edipresse Luxe: a creative or a cultural company?

When analyzing the particularities of this case, the creation of Edipresse Luxe relates more to the concentration and to the new organization of dispersed localized knowledge within an integrated business model than to the creation of fundamentally new knowledge. It also illustrates how cultural activities related to the promotion of watchmaking can be commercialized by a multinational media company. This intensive commercialization of culture, for instance through the trade of publication licences, could also reflect the conceptual turn from cultural to creative economy.

However, the case also shows that this cultural/creative enterprise in not based on a simple commodification of culture. Even though Edipresse Group uses its proximity to watchmaking as a resource to enter a niche market within the global media industry, it remains an intermediary activity making profit mainly from advertising watchmaking. In other words, the case of Edipresse Luxe cannot be considered as the development of an 'advanced productive service' as described by Pratt (2008). Furthermore, profit and non-profit activities intertwine within the business model of this creative enterprise. For instance, the organization of the Geneva Watchmaking Grand Prix is not primarily considered as a direct profit-making activity but rather as a service that consolidates Edipresse legitimacy as a credible intermediary between watchmaking brands and end consumers.

Nevertheless, the activities of Edipresse Luxe are not restricted to the co-production of cultural content dedicated to watchmaking. Of course, cultural co-production is part of the value created by the company through the organization of glamorous events, through the edition of original articles on watches or brands and through original image production (films or photo shootings). However, the diffusion and the legitimation of the cultural and technical value of the Swiss watches is seen by Edipresse as a strategic service for watchmaking brands as illustrated by the coupling of Edipresse Luxe activities with the international subsidiaries of Edipresse Group. Edipresse seeks also to play a significant role as a 'legitimizing third party' (Jeannerat and Crevoisier 2011), an actor with cultural authority and not directly involved in business, through its awarding activity in Geneva or abroad.

In brief, the case of Edipresse Luxe, and of Edipresse Group at large, should not be understood through the restrictive lens of the local production and commodification of a cultural product. It is through its capacity to anchor within the local milieu of watchmaking and to diffuse within particular distant consumption contexts that this company has built its business strategy.

The Fondation de la Haute Horlogerie: a cultural enterprise initiated by watch brands

The second case study provides a different but complementary perspective to the case of Edipresse Luxe. It deals with the creation and the development of a cultural enterprise directly initiated by various watchmaking companies. In 2005, the Richemont Group, one of the major world leading companies in the sector of luxury, owner of the famous French brand Cartier and also of some traditional Swiss watch brands, announced with two other Swiss independent manufacturers (Audemars Piguet and Girard Perregaux) the creation of a foundation whose aim will be to promote the value of *haute horlogerie* across the world. The appellation of *haute horlogerie* was established in reference to the original concept of 'haute couture' to designate particular brands or watches that represent a high cultural, technical and innovative heritage in high-end watchmaking (e.g. a sophisticated mechanical movement, fine jewellery components, or a long historical tradition of watchmaking). In English, 'fine watchmaking' is the best translation of the concept of *haute horlogerie*.

The Fondation de la Haute Horlogerie and the development of haute horlogerie

As expressed by its founders, the Fondation de la Haute Horlogerie (FHH) mirrors an important evolution of the watchmaking sector, of the luxury sector, of the media and communication sector as well as of consumption practices:

- The world of watchmaking has changed, and is continuing to change with increasing rapidity: increase in the number of products and brands; opening up of formerly reserved and legitimate territories (its seems any brand can launch Fine Watch models); increasing public and media interest in watchmaking (the role of providing information and guidance is transferred from watchmaking specialists to the press); the Internet's developing role as a preferred source of information.
- Luxury has evolved from a 'social aspiration' into a 'cultural aspiration': history, culture and expertise are source of legitimacy for 'true luxury'; instruction, education and attitudes determine social status.
- Younger generations are growing up in a completely different technological environment from that of their elders (Internet chat rooms, blogs, cell phones, MP3 players, etc.) and different ideas of what constitutes groups, time, space, and reality.

(Fondation de la Haute Horlogerie 2008)

In such a context, watch luxury brands face two main issues. On the one hand, they need to prevent a trivialization of watchmaking and luxury by promoting and defending the cultural and technical authenticity of fine watchmaking and of 'true luxury'. On the other hand, the new challenges and the new opportunities induced by IC technologies and new media tools require communicating the value of fine watchmaking to their audience (intermediaries or end consumers) in new ways. The FHH was created as a non-profit-making enterprise whose aim would be to develop innovative actions to answer these new challenges (Figure 12.3).

One of the first actions undertaken by the Foundation was to institutionalize the legitimate 'perimeter' of *haute horlogerie*. This was done through the establishment of an independent *cultural council* composed of prominent people within the field of watchmaking (e.g. distributors, journalists, experts or collectors). This council wrote a 'manifesto' pointing out the fundamental cultural and technical principles against which a watch or a watch brand should be evaluated. Based on this document, the Cultural Council designates the legitimate brands of *haute horlogerie* every year. The designated brands can choose to become partners of the Foundation. By institutionalizing the perimeter of *haute horlogerie*, the aim

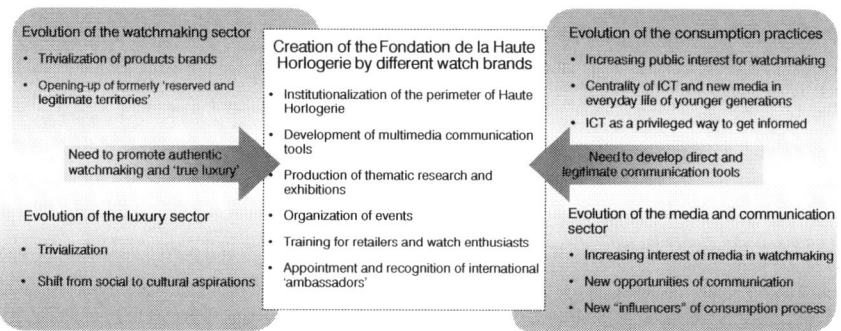

Figure 12.3 The context of the creation of the Fondation de la Haute Horlogerie

Source: Our elaboration

is not only to prevent competition from non-legitimate brands. It is also to create an integrative framework to undertake a joint enterprise above the individual strategy of each brand. Today, the FHH is supported by more than thirty partners, among which most are watch brands but also local museums and other collective organizations. The manifesto is updated every year by the Cultural Council.

As well as the creation of the perimeter of *haute horlogerie*, the FHH developed specific activities dedicated to the education, the selection and the appointment of a knowledgeable audience for *haute horlogerie* (intermediaries or enthusiastic end consumers). This meant the organization of training programmes, initiation courses or conferences. Subsequently, particular prizes and certificates were given to acknowledge official 'ambassadors' and retailing staff in each national/local market.

In addition, different cultural activities were dedicated to the creation of credible and well-documented multimedia materials communicating the technical, cultural and historical particularities of fine watchmaking (online journal, online encyclopaedia, film documentation, travelling exhibitions). In addition to the multimedia tools, specific activities have been developed to create travelling exhibitions and events that present the cultural value of fine watchmaking. Recently, the FHH also developed a multimedia 'touch screen tablet' to be used as an interactive information and communication tool by retailers and customers to access the informational and training content provided by the Foundation. Those various actions of cultural co-production and diffusion mean the involvement of historians, journalists, retailers, film producers and IT developers, mostly based near the original region of watch production.

The Fondation de la Haute Horlogerie: a cultural enterprise?

As its activities are mostly funded by the annual fees paid by the partner brands, the FHH could be considered as a 'non-profit' cultural enterprise rather than as a 'for-profit' creative enterprise. However, the Foundation also sells additional services to watchmaking companies. For instance, the FHH has developed competences in event organization and sells these competences to watchmaking companies at various occasions (e.g. during the Salon de la Haute Horlogerie that takes place in Geneva). Even though such additional revenue is used to develop other non-profit activities, in such cases the FFH works as a normal for-profit company. As in the case of Edipresse Luxe, distinguishing a creative from a cultural enterprise according to its business model seems to be too limited, as profit and non-profit activities often overlap.

Also, similar to the case of Edipresse, the cultural activities of the FHH should not only be analyzed within the local production context of watchmaking but also within its international context of consumption. This is underlined by the chairman of the Foundation: 'As a Foundation established in Geneva, the Fondation de la Haute Horlogerie is ingrained in the Swiss landscape. But not only. Its vocation is also to conquer the world and explore new territories as they open up to fine watchmaking' (Fondation de la Haute Horlogerie 2011). This internationalization is supported through three different channels. The first is based on the use of new media and ICT technologies. The Foundation considers its website as its fundamental resource. This website is translated into French, English, Chinese and Japanese and is the referential platform used to communicate interactively the cultural and technical content of *haute horlogerie* to an international audience. Virtual platforms such as Twitter, Facebook or YouTube are now increasingly used to provide short interviews, technical explanations or live lectures about watchmaking.

In addition to virtual channels, the Foundation uses the international distribution network of its partners (watch brands) to establish local delegates. The latter assist the Foundation in the local organization of events, exhibitions and training programmes. Furthermore, the Foundation relies on local retailers appointed as ambassadors to relay its campaigns and to promote its cultural commitments. Conversely to Edipresse Luxe, which has developed its own diffusion channels, the Foundation utilizes the existing international distribution and retailing networks of its brand partners.

To sum up, as in the case of Edipresse Luxe, the cultural activity of the FHH cannot be restricted to an activity of cultural production and commodification. Co-production of cultural content (e.g. multimedia production, exhibitions) intertwines with activities of diffusion within distant consumption contexts (IT tools, local delegates/ambassadors, travelling exhibitions). Moreover, cultural legitimization appears as a central issue for the FHH through its activities of authentication dedicated to the perimeter of *haute horlogerie* (establishment of the Cultural Council, appointment of official representatives of *haute horlogerie*).

Discussion and conclusion

In different ways, cultural activities play a central role in today's European regional development. In this context, creativity is often regarded as the economic side of culture. However, it was argued that such a distinction is too restrictive as culture integrates in various forms of market organizations. It can be commodified and sold as such as an economic output or be more broadly commercialized as an economic input. It can be produced and consumed in the same location or between distant places.

Through the cases of Edipresse Luxe and FHH, the importance of culture in economic development was underlined within the wider context of industrial watchmaking. In both cases, cultural and creative activities cannot be decoupled from the industrial activity of watchmaking. Also, it was emphasized that the distinction between 'profitable creative enterprises' and 'non-profitable cultural enterprises' is often difficult to establish, as economic and non-economic processes often intertwine within complex market interdependencies.

As well as advocating the importance of the co-production of additional cultural inputs for existing products, these two cases also reveal the importance of cultural diffusion and of cultural legitimation in the market. Edipresse, as well as the FHH, do not only seek to produce cultural content for watchmaking companies. On the one hand, they provide dedicated and specialized diffusion channels towards particular consumption contexts. On the other hand, they have developed socio-technical devices (Callon *et al.* 2002) to control and establish the cultural and technical legitimacy of fine watchmaking toward initiated consumers. In such cases, cultural resources and activities cannot only be understood from a localized and productive perspective.

Both cases point out the important coupling processes occurring between multi-local production–consumption milieux. On the one hand, Edipresse and the FHH anchor and justify their original activities within the historical context of Swiss watch production. On the other hand, they anchor within particular distant consumption contexts through the existing channels of the watchmaking companies, through interpersonal acknowledgment (e.g. ambassadors), publishing licences, local subsidiaries, local partnerships or virtual channels.

In this territorial interplay, the city of Geneva appears as a bridge between local anchoring and international market diffusion and as a hub for the global channels of luxury goods. Even though the creation of Edipresse Luxe and of the FHH in Geneva is only a part of the evolution of the Swiss watchmaking industry, it consolidates the role of this city as a multi-local platform.

Notes

1 EURODITE ('Regional Trajectories to the Knowledge Economy: A Dynamic Model') was supported by the European Commission under its sixth Framework Programme, contract no. 006187.

References

Asheim, B. and Hansen, H.-K. (2009) 'Knowledge bases, talents and contexts: On the usefulness of the creative class approach in Sweden', in P. Cooke and D. Schwartz (eds) *Creative Regions. Technology, Culture and Knowledge Entrepreneurship*, London: Routledge, pp. 23–39.

Butzin, A. (2009) 'Innovationsbiographien als Methode der raum-zeitlichen Erfassung von Innovationsprozessen', in P. Dannenberg, H. Köhler, T. Lang, J. Utz, B. Zakirova and T. Zimmermann (eds) *Innovationen im Raum – Raum für Innovationen*, Hanover: Akademie für Raumforschung und Landesplanung, pp. 189–98.

Callon, M., Méadel, C. and Rabeharisoa, V. (2002) 'The economy of qualities', *Economy and Society*, 31(2): 194–217.

Cinti, T. (2008) 'Cultural clusters and districts: The state of the art', in P. Cooke and L. Lazzeretti (eds) *Creative Cities, Cultural Clusters and Economic Development*, Cheltenham: Edward Elgar, pp. 70–92.

Cooke, P. (2008) 'Culture, clusters, districts and quarters: Some reflections on the scale question', in P. Cooke and L. Lazzeretti (eds) *Creative Cities, Cultural Clusters and Economic Development*, Cheltenham: Edward Elgar, pp. 25–47.

Cooke, P. and Lazzeretti, L. (eds) (2008a) *Creative Cities, Cultural Clusters and Local Economic Development*, Cheltenham: Edward Elgar.

Cooke, P. and Lazzeretti, L. (2008b) 'Creative cities: An introduction', in P. Cooke and L. Lazzeretti (eds) *Creative Cities, Cultural Clusters and Economic Development*, Cheltenham: Edward Elgar, pp. 1–22.

Costa, P. (2008) 'Creativity, innovation and territorial agglomeration in cultural activities: The roots of the creative city', in P. Cooke and L. Lazzeretti (eds) *Creative Cities, Cultural Clusters and Economic Development*, Cheltenham: Edward Elgar, pp. 183–210.

Crevoisier, O. (1993) 'Spatial shifts and the emergence of innovative milieux: The case of the Jura region between 1960 and 1990', *Environment and Planning C: Government and Policy*, 11(4): 419–30.

Crevoisier, O. and Kebir, L. (2009) 'Culture as a productive resource, international networks and local development', in G. Becattini, M. Bellandi and L. De Propris (eds) *A Handbook of Industrial Districts*, Cheltenham: Edward Elgar, pp. 307–20.

Crewe, L. (2003) 'Geographies of retailing and consumption: Markets in motion', *Progress in Human Geography*, 27(3): 352–62.

Davezies, L. (2009) 'L'économie locale résidentielle', *Géographie, économie, société*, 11(1): 47–53.

Edipresse (2007) *Official Press Release*, 7 June.

Edipresse (2008) *Official Press Release*, 18 November.

Florida, R. (2002) *The Rise of the Creative Class: And How it's Transforming Work, Leisure and Everyday Life*, New York: Basic Books.

Florida, R. (2005) *Cities and the Creative Class*, New York: Routledge.

Fondation de la Haute Horlogerie (2008) *Official Presentation File and Press Release of the Fondation de la Haute Horlogerie for the Year 2008*, Geneva: Fondation de la Haute Horlogerie.

Fondation de la Haute Horlogerie (2011) *Official Presentation File and Press Release of the Fondation de la Haute Horlogerie for the Year 2008*, Geneva: Fondation de la Haute Horlogerie. http://www.hautehorlogerie.org/en/fondation/about/fondation-de-la-haute-horlogerie (accessed 20 September 2011).

Garcìa, B. (2005) 'Deconstructing the city of culture: The long-term cultural legacies of Glasgow 1990', *Urban Studies*, 42(5–6): 841–68.

Garnham, N. (2005) 'From cultural to creative industries', *International Journal of Cultural Policy*, 11(1): 15–29.

Jansson, J. and Power, D. (2010) 'Fashioning a global city: Global city brand channels in the fashion and design industries', *Regional Studies*, 44(7): 889–904.

Jeannerat, H. and Crevoisier, O. (2011) 'Non-technological innovation and multi-local territorial knowledge dynamics in the Swiss watch industry', *International Journal of Innovation and Regional Development*, 3(1): 26–44.

Kaul, A.R. (2007) 'The limits of commodification in traditional Irish music sessions', *Journal of the Royal Anthropological Institute*, 13(3): 703–19.

Kebir, L. and Crevoisier, O. (2008) 'Cultural resources and regional development: The case of the cultural legacy of watchmaking', in P. Cooke and L. Lazzeretti (eds) *Creative Cities, Cultural Clusters and Economic Development*, Cheltenham: Edward Elgar, pp. 48–69.

Lagendijk, A. (2006) 'Learning from conceptual flow in regional studies: Framing present debates, unbracketing past debates', *Regional Studies*, 40(4): 385–99.

Larsson, A. and Butzin, A. (2010) 'Time–space dynamics of knowledge processes: Analysis of knowledge biography case-studies in four sectors', paper presented at the Annual Conference of the Regional Studies Association, Pécs, 24–26 May.

Lazzeretti, L. (2003) 'City of art as a high culture local system and cultural districtualization processes: The cluster of art restoration in Florence', *International Journal of Urban and Regional Research*, 27(3): 635–48.

Lazzeretti, L. (2008) 'The cultural districtualization model', in P. Cooke and L. Lazzeretti (eds) *Creative Cities, Cultural Clusters and Economic Development*, Cheltenham: Edward Elgar, pp. 93–120.

Lefèbvre, A. (2008) 'L'économie culturelle au risque de l'économie de la création', in F. Leriche, S. Daviet, M. Sibertin-Blanc and J.-M. Zuliani (eds) *L'économie culturelle et ses territoires*, Toulouse: Presses Universitaires du Mirail, pp. 345–54.

Leriche, F. and Daviet, S. (2010) 'Cultural economy: An opportunity to boost employment and regional development?', *Regional Studies*, 44(7): 807–11.

Liefooghe, C. (2010) 'Economie créative et développement des territoires: enjeux et perspectives de recherche', *Innovations*, 1(31): 181–97.

Lorentzen, A. (2009) 'Cities in the experience economy', *European Planning Studies*, 17(6): 829–45.

Lorenzen, M. and Frederiksen, L. (2008) 'Why do cultural industries cluster? Localization, urbanization, products and projects', in P. Cooke and L. Lazzeretti (eds) *Creative Cities, Cultural Clusters and Economic Development*, Cheltenham: Edward Elgar, pp. 155–79.

MacNeill, S. and Collinge, C. (2010) 'The rationale for EURODITE and an introduction to the sector studies', in P. Cooke, C. De Laurentis, S. MacNeill and C. Collinge (eds) *Platforms of Innovation: Dynamics of New Industrial Knowledge Flows*, Cheltenham: Edward Elgar, pp. 38–52.

Markusen, A. (2007) 'A consumption base theory of development: An application to the rural cultural economy', *Agricultural and Resource Economics Review*, 36(1): 9–23.

Markusen, A. and Schrock, G. (2009) 'Consumption-driven urban development', *Urban Geography*, 4: 344–367.

Miles, S. and Paddison, R. (2005) 'Introduction: The rise and rise of culture-led urban regeneration', *Urban Studies*, 42(5–6): 833–39.

Moulaert, F. and Sekia, F. (2003) 'Territorial innovation models: A critical survey', *Regional Studies*, 37(3): 289–302.

Ng, I.C.L. (2010) 'The future of pricing and revenue models', *Journal of Revenue and Pricing Management*, 9(3): 276–81.

Pike, A. (2009) 'Brand and branding geographies', *Geography Compass*, 3(1): 190–213.

Pine, B.J. II and Gilmore, J.H. (1999) *The Experience Economy. Work is Theatre and Every Business is a Stage*, Boston, MA: Harvard Business School Press.

Power, D. and Hauge, A. (2008) 'No man's brand. Brands, institutions, and fashion', *Growth and Change*, 39(1): 123–43.

Power, D. and Scott, A.J. (eds) (2004) *Cultural Industries and the Production of Culture*, London: Routledge.

Pratt, A. (2005) 'Cultural industries and public policy', *International Journal of Cultural Policy*, 11(1): 31–44.

Pratt, A. (2008) 'L'apport britannique à la compréhension des fonctions créatives dans les villes globales', in F. Leriche, S. Daviet, M. Sibertin-Blanc and J.-M. Zuliani (eds) *L'économie culturelle et ses territoires*, Toulouse: Presses Universitaires du Mirail, pp. 257–67.

Richards, G. (2001) 'The experience industry and the creation of attractions', in G. Richards (ed) *Cultural Attractions and European Tourism*, Oxon: CABI, pp. 55–69.

Richards, G. and Wilson, J. (2004) 'The impact of cultural events on city image: Rotterdam, cultural capital of Europe 2001', *Urban Studies*, 41(10): 1931–51.

Scott, A.J. (1997) 'The cultural economy of cities', *International Journal of Urban and Regional Research*, 21(2): 323–39.

Scott, A.J. (2005) *On Hollywood: The Place, the Industry*, Princeton, NJ: Princeton University Press.

Scott, A.J. (2010) 'The cultural economy of landscape and prospects for peripheral development in the twenty-first century: The case of the English Lake District', *European Planning Studies*, 18(10): 1567–89.

Scott, A.J. and Leriche, F. (2005) 'Les ressorts géographiques de l'économie culturelle: du local au mondial', *L'Espace géographique*, 34(3): 207–22.

Stamboulis, Y. and Skayannis, P. (2003) 'Innovation strategies and technology for experience-based tourism', *Tourism Management*, 24(1): 35–43.

Testart, A. (2001) 'Echange marchand, Echange non marchand', *Revue française de sociologie*, 42(4): 719–48.

Weber, F. (2000) 'Transactions marchandes, échanges rituels, relations personnelles', *Genèses*, 4(41): 85–107.

13 Putting creativity in place

A relational and practice perspective

Udo Staber

This is what city life is. It's verbal communication. City life is cerebral.
You're not up in the morning like the Tolstoy peasant cutting the hay.

> (Woody Allen, quoted in Björkman 2004: 79)

The country existence hasn't offered anything as yet in the way of subject.
Probably it never will and I should get the hell out.

> (Roth 2001: 138)

Introduction

'Creative places', variably referred to as 'creative clusters' (Cooke and Lazzeretti 2008), 'creative cities' (Scott 2006a) or 'creative fields' (Scott 2006b), are typically characterized as locations where the talents of creative workers, the productive assets of enterprises, a rich tissue of institutional rules and conventions, and a local social milieu consisting of cultural diversity and bohemian lifestyle come together to produce an environment in which creativity can flourish (Florida 2002: 22). A key argument in this literature is that the symbolic currents of location are vital for the economic success of cultural artefacts and goods (Molotch 2002), and that creative workers use locality as a source of signs, symbols and cues for making their decisions about products and location (Drake 2003). In the present study, I explore the role of place in the identity of artists as creative workers. Identity is vital to artists' efforts to make sense in and of place in ways that support their decisions. Place refers to a territorial entity (e.g. a work studio, neighbourhood, trade fair, park) that has a material form (natural or artificial) and is subjectively interpreted, experienced and narrated (Gieryn 2000). The objective of this study is to understand the various meanings artists assign to place as they construct their identity as creative workers.

Many researchers have adopted an embeddedness perspective (Zukin and DiMaggio 1990), treating place as if it provided a single and stable source of identity. By embeddedness I mean the strong sense of identification that individuals feel with the place in which they work or live (Relph 1976; Lippard 1997), without implying anything a priori about the mechanisms by which they feel bound to the place. This embeddedness perspective is useful for drawing attention to the importance of place as a constituent element of social and economic life, but it tells only half the story. The other half of the story concerns the way in which individuals actually form their identity based on their particular interpretation of place. Creative workers can find different meanings in different kinds of places, even in the same geographic setting, and an analysis of how and why this happens should show how they construct and reconstruct these meanings, which are not just residues of past experiences. The conventional focus on place as a location *where* things happen can be misleading if it ignores *how* they happen. Places are not primarily locational and abstract, but are contestable, provisional and socially constructed.

In the present study, I argue for a broader, more encompassing construct of place-based identity, one that takes into account the variable nature of identity and does not assume that the relationship between place and identity is fixed. I adopt a practice perspective to achieve two objectives. First, the practice perspective highlights the fact that when people assign meaning to place, they do not merely perceive images, symbols and signs, but engage in activities. They communicate with others, evaluate objects and behaviours, imitate what others do, and develop strategies for differentiating their output from competitors. The embeddedness view says little about how the categories and understandings that shape identity are constructed. The practice perspective adds a more action-oriented and processual framework, by emphasizing the activities individuals engage in as they make sense of place and their identification with place. A person's identity can be understood only in relation to the practices that sustain it. Second, in contrast to the social embeddedness view of place as a location to which creative workers are more or less firmly bound, the practice perspective draws attention to the possibilities for variation and differentiation. It highlights the relational nature of identity as a set of complementary or conflicting attributes, reflecting the fact that individuals have multiple affiliations in a range of domains. Identity construction combines practice and identity aspects, indicating that the material world of creative workers (the world of action) and the world of creative identity (the world of meaning) interpenetrate and are mutually constituted. The relation between the structure of identity attributes and the structure of practices is problematic in ways that are highly productive for the analysis of creative places. Using data on the identity constructions of self-employed visual artists in two urban creative fields, I employ correspondence analysis as a technique to explicate the co-constitution of identity attributes at the cognitive level of perception and the structural level of association.

Theorizing place-based identity

Much of the research on creative places has adopted, often implicitly, an embeddedness perspective, to highlight the role of institutions and social networks in supporting creative people working in close vicinity (Montgomery and Robinson 1993). A central insight of this perspective is that identity is shaped by the structure of social relationships. Individuals derive their identity from the various domains in which they are embedded, such as education (Burke and Franzoi 1988), workplace (Bain 2005), and profession (Abbott 2005). In research on 'creative clusters', it is often argued that producers align themselves closely with the images that external audiences hold about the distinctiveness of a place, as when customers attribute innovativeness to fashion designers in Milan, tradition mindedness to musicians in Nashville, or an identity of social deviance to artists in the Soho district of New York City in the 1960s. In each case, it is argued that distinctive identities emerge through location in 'local art worlds' and that creative workers tend to migrate to such places to derive social, economic or political value from their image (Molotch 2002). Creative workers bring to creative places a personal history of involvement in different aspects of a cultural industry that may complement or conflict with one another, thus contributing to the diversity and fluidity of creative places (Scott 2006a).

Despite the growth of empirical research based on an embeddedness view, this perspective has been critiqued for lacking theoretical depth. While the embeddedness concept is useful for extending analysis beyond neoclassical models of economic action to include social considerations, 'it suffers from theoretical vagueness', when used to formulate concrete propositions (Portes and Sensenbrenner 1993: 1321). Embeddedness has its effects on action partly by shaping identity through social interaction (White 1992: 5). According to social network theory, an individual's identity is based on his or her involvement in multiple role settings. A role indicates the points of contact and interaction between actors occupying different positions in different domains (Burt 1992). Hence, knowledge of a person's social ties helps predict the person's understandings and orientations. But beyond this general argument, the concept of embeddedness sidesteps the issue of *how* individuals derive their identity from participation in particular domains. This issue may be framed in terms of the interplay of identity attributes, relations and practice.

Place and identity

Identity concerns questions about 'Who am I?' and 'How do others see me?', which individuals must answer as a basis for interaction with others. The power of identity derives from its integrative, generative and status enhancing capacity, based on social categorizations of similarity and distinctiveness. Place is an integral part of a creative worker's identity, by providing ontological security and emotional well-being, embodying personal history, and inspiring social action and interaction (Giddens 1991). A given place can have multiple meanings. The meaning of places like incubation centres, artist studios and training workshops contains ambiguity, in that they can be taken to say different things about the artist. For example, place can say something about the artist as a person deriving pleasure from being in a particular location, or it can indicate something about artistic labour involving solitary learning. Artists may identify with a building because it is the place where they first conceived an original idea or because it gives them the sense of emotional security. Place may imply image, as when artists identify with a landmark located near their workshop, or it may imply power, as when location helps them gain access to financial support. Or, when thinking about the commercial value of creativity, place may signal agglomeration economies, whereas when thinking about the cultural value of creativity, place may indicate tradition.

A place may be a singular location at any given time, but the actors may have many different stories to tell about this location and they may change their stories as they move into different situations (Burke and Franzoi 1988). Woody Allen, for example, considers the city a place of inspiration. The introductory vignette describes him as an individual who loves New York as a place that gives him opportunities to learn, a place where he can 'walk out of my house and have the whole city around me, pavement to walk on and stores and places to go to' (Woody Allen, quoted in Björkman 2004: 90). By contrast, Philip Roth (2001: 139) prefers places that drive him 'crazy', because 'a writer *has* to be driven crazy to help him *see*' (emphasis in original). While Woody Allen and Philip Roth might both be drawn to New York as a place of intellectual sophistication and American–Jewish identity, they construct distinctly different identity maps with which they orient themselves. Places are not only physically carved out. They are also negotiated, communicated and imagined. The theoretical openness of the concept of place raises the empirical question: How does inserting an artist's identity into a particular space structure the constitution of place? The analytical task is to discover how the attributes that make up a place-based identity are related to one another.

'Being there' should not be thought of as a fixed state, embedded in a well-bounded physical, occupational, organizational or social location. The position of place in identity is not 'totalizing' in the sense that a single category of experience or imagination will fully determine any number of intersecting differences between the elements involved. This seems especially true for creative work in the arts sector. In production settings serving a variety of potentially competing functions (e.g. utilitarian and expressive, material and sensory, private and public), one would expect identity to challenge any category that puts forth an essentialist feature as the sole and unique property of any given individual. Art may have a highly personal and subjective character, but something is recognized as a piece of art only if there is an audience (e.g. art critics, consumers, investors) labelling it and celebrating it as such. The meaning of a piece of art depends not only on the reception by audiences. It also depends on its position in relation to other pieces of art and non-art with which it competes for attention, and the dynamics of markets (e.g. galleries, fairs, publishing) through which it is diffused, institutionalized or replaced by something else. In creative places, where specialized competencies come together in a diverse set of individuals, organizations and institutions, it would be difficult to argue that the identity of any given individual artist is fully and exclusively inscribed in a particular cultural product or a place, or that there is a single relationship between a particular identity attribute, such as autonomy or professionalism, and the place where this attribute makes a difference. The very meaning of artistic identity is in tension with itself, and not simply with other identities, in a place that is constructed out of identity, while at the same time giving meaning to identity.

Relations between identity attributes

The research challenge is to model this tension in a way that captures both similarities and differences in identity attributes. I suggest that this can be accomplished, and with potentially counter-intuitive results, by mapping clusters of identity attributes to reveal how artists categorize them in terms of a limited number of salient dimensions. Identity includes multiple aspects, made salient by different roles and contexts (Burke and Franzoi 1988). Some of these aspects may be more central and enduring than others, regardless of contexts, whereas others become salient only in particular circumstances. A visual artist, for example, may see herself primarily as a graphic designer, but in the company of an advertising executive she may define herself as an advertiser, whereas in an arts gallery she may identify with the traditions of art collection. The crossing of categories suggests a characterization of identity as a set of interrelated attributes, not all of which need to be active at any particular time. Identities are not given essentials but are constantly formed and reformed as a consequence of a variety of influences on the individual, creating new combinations of identity attributes in different domains (White 1992; Fuchs 2001). There is no presumption of coherence, and the data discussed below confirm this. The emphasis is on distinctions (Zerubavel 1991; Bourdieu 1993: 106–111) rather than essence.

Practice and identity construction

To explicate the diversity of identity attributes, one must specify not only the individual attributes of identity but also the connections that the actors are making to give meaning to them. It is difficult to predict the position of place in creative identity without knowing something about how individuals construct their self-conception through practice. Practice theory has its origins in various writings of scholars like Bourdieu, Giddens, and Geertz who think of objects of knowledge as being grounded in concrete human activity. The theory of practice is based on the understanding that objects of knowledge and meaning are socially constructed, driven by some underlying generative principle or logic, which Bourdieu (1993) referred to as 'habitus'. Habitus indicates neither programmed nor spontaneous action, but refers to a set of predispositions that enables actors to cope with emerging situations. Practice does not mean actions that people engage in to merely accomplish some task. Practice refers to activities that are infused with broader meaning and that provide a foundation for social order, such as classifying works of art (DiMaggio 1987) or typecasting film actors to obtain robust understandings of personal style like hero, lover or family man (Zuckerman *et al.* 2003). Practices are located in cultural frameworks that people use to evaluate, differentiate and integrate (Bourdieu 1993). When artists position themselves and their work in relation to others and different kinds of work, they do so, for example, by sharing or withholding technical expertise, lobbying media people, displaying their products or providing feedback about other people's artwork. 'Having an identity requires continually reproducing consistent joint construction out of actions from distinct settings' (White 1992: 7–8).

The concern for practice adds a distinct approach to the study of place and identity, one that concentrates less on the attributes and more on their construction. Practice functions as a linchpin connecting the attributes of identity and, in the context of this study, relating them to place. Conversely, identity gives meaning to place by connecting it to action. The enactment of place shapes identity by providing behavioural frames for its manifestation. Practice provides identity with movement, on a day-to-day basis, either creating something new or institutionalizing something old.

Methodology

The research sites for this study are the visual arts industries in Munich (Germany) and Christchurch (New Zealand). Both cities have an international reputation as 'creative centres' and possess the essential features of 'creative cities' (Scott 2006a; Stolarick and Florida 2006): infrastructures equipped with cultural, educational and research facilities; a broad range of knowledge-intensive industries and creative professions; an institutional governance system oriented to the needs of cultural production, image management and place marketing; and a general atmosphere of openness and receptivity to cultural diversity and consumption. The creative sector in Munich constitutes about 15 per cent of the city's labour force, with the visual arts community comprising the largest contingent (Streit 2007). Christchurch has an international reputation in Australasia as a 'vibrant arts community' (Creative New Zealand 2003).

The sample in both locations was restricted to self-employed individuals working in the arts sector. The respondents were selected using convenience and theoretical sampling methods to obtain access to as diverse a group of visual artists as possible. Given the absence of clear sampling frames in cultural industries (Markusen *et al.* 2008), complete enumeration and standard population-sampling methods were not practical. The respondents were drawn randomly from a range of information sources, including arts directories, yellow pages, promotional materials and stories in newspapers. Eighty-one individuals contacted in Munich and thirty-four individuals contacted in Christchurch agreed to be interviewed in 2007 and 2008. The individuals included artists from a wide variety of fields, such as sculptors, photographers, graphic and textile designers, weavers, illustrators and painters. The primary criterion for inclusion in the (not necessarily representative) samples was a genuine commitment to art as a central life activity, irrespective of whether it was the main source of income.

To minimize disruption, given that the respondents were approached at their workplace, exhibitions or street fairs, the interviews were kept short, lasting about fifteen minutes on average. The interview situation was focused narrowly on questions related to place and identity but structured loosely to allow the respondents to reflect on their identity as they saw themselves in situ (Alvesson 2003). The central interview question asked them to describe themselves as creative workers: 'Thinking about the work you do, please tell me if and how you see yourself as a creative worker. In two or three sentences, what kinds of ideas come to your mind when you think of yourself doing creative work?' I took extensive notes both during and immediately after the interview to preserve the full wording of the responses to this question, focusing on the artists' identification with place.

Based on the responses, I constructed a data set consisting of thematically bounded statements that could be analyzed using semantic techniques. I studied statements as syntactically closed units of analysis, defined as semantic relationships between proximate concepts (Carley and Palmquist 1992). For example, in the statement 'I immerse myself in my neighbourhood to get recognition', the concepts 'immerse', 'neighbourhood' and 'recognition' are proximately related. In an iterative process, the interview narratives were read first to identify statements. The texts were recoded again and again until the set of statements was sensitive enough to reproduce non-redundant statements and to arrive at a parsimonious set without the loss of information. This resulted in a data set containing 611 statements for the Munich sample and 332 statements for the Christchurch sample. The aim of the analysis was to identify relationships between the narrative fragments at the level of concepts rather than words, in order to derive semiotically coherent place-related attributes of identity.

I employed correspondence analysis to map associations between identity attributes, in much the same way in which previous semiotic studies have examined associations between concepts in cultural fields (De Nooy 2003). Regarding the technical procedures of correspondence analysis, I limit the discussion to the essentials (for details, see Clausen 1998). The distinct advantage of this technique derives from the ability to portray several categories in the same space. The aim of the present study was to discover which combinations of concepts occur and which do not. Using the logic of weighted least squares, the analysis finds the plane that captures as much of the distribution in multidimensional space as possible, relative to what one would expect if the distribution were completely random. The analysis produces a two-dimensional graph that visually represents the distribution. Points that co-occur relatively often appear in the map as clusters, whereas points that exclude one another are drawn apart. The map represents the distance of the concepts from each other, interpreted as the probability of their co-occurrence on the map, as well as the relationship between the clusters as given by their relative distance from the concepts contained in the clusters. The adequacy of the map is measured by the proportion of variance the two dimensions represent of the original variance in the distribution of concepts.

Empirical analysis and results

The interview context specified place as the core category of artists' identity embedded in a web of identity attributes tied to artists' specific circumstances and orientations. Correspondence analysis organizes these attributes into recognizable 'conceptual webs' (Gabora *et al.* 2008). In a first step, using AutoMap (Carley and Palmquist 1992), I content analyzed the statements collected in the interviews to glean the concepts related to place-based identity and to construct a 'profile' (Han 2003; Popping 2003) for each respondent. Based on semiotic conventions (Weber 2005), I distinguished between aspects of identity (conceptual representations of attributes) and practices (conceptual representations of actions) that enact these identity aspects. For example, in the statement 'I immerse myself in my neighbourhood to get recognition', the concepts 'neighbourhood' and 'recognition' were coded as attributes, and the concept 'immersing' was coded as a practice through which the individual seeks recognition. The attributes 'neighbourhood' and 'recognition' are linked through the individual's practice of using the neighbourhood as a place to obtain recognition. In the present research context, the objective of using the neighbourhood is to gain recognition. In another context, the objective of immersion in the neighbourhood might be to seek a marriage partner. The coding exercise produced a practice-by-attribute matrix for each sample, which I reduced in size to enhance visual representation. Using a filtering procedure, I removed redundant concepts consistently across all cases, generalizing concepts to broader categories with a common connotation. The resulting repertoire of attributes and practices was confirmed by the correspondence analysis of the original matrix containing all concepts identified in the first step.

In a second step, I subjected the data matrix to a correspondence analysis to reveal the similarities and distinctions contained in the statements. The analytic strategy was to decompose the matrix to uncover a parsimonious low-dimensional summary of the structure of identity, which is visually represented as distances between row and column points. In a correspondence analysis plot, such as those shown in Figures 13.1 and 13.2, the centre is uniquely defined as the arithmetic mean of all row and column scores. The mean is the point that minimizes the sum of the squared distances to all points. The interpretation of the overall configuration of the row and column points is based on the chi-square distances between the points. In Figure 13.1, for example, the matrix cell representing 'COMMUNICATE/ambition' includes more observations than what would be expected from its marginal distribution. Points that lie close together in the map have similar the profiles. The two dimensions account for 86 per cent of the total variation explained in the Munich sample (Figure 13.1) and 84 per cent in the Christchurch sample (Figure 13.2).

The structural profiles of the samples show similarities in the attributes and practices the respondents emphasized as well as the relative position of these elements on the map. This similarity suggests that, in these two cases, there is a common underlying logic in the interpretation of place. This is all the more noteworthy as the two urban centres studied here differ widely in size. The much larger population size of Munich and its central location in Europe may reflect the kind of cultural diversity and cosmopolitanism that is often seen as a vital ingredient of entrepreneurial creativity and urban growth (Florida 2002). However, research has shown that smaller cities also can be disproportionately

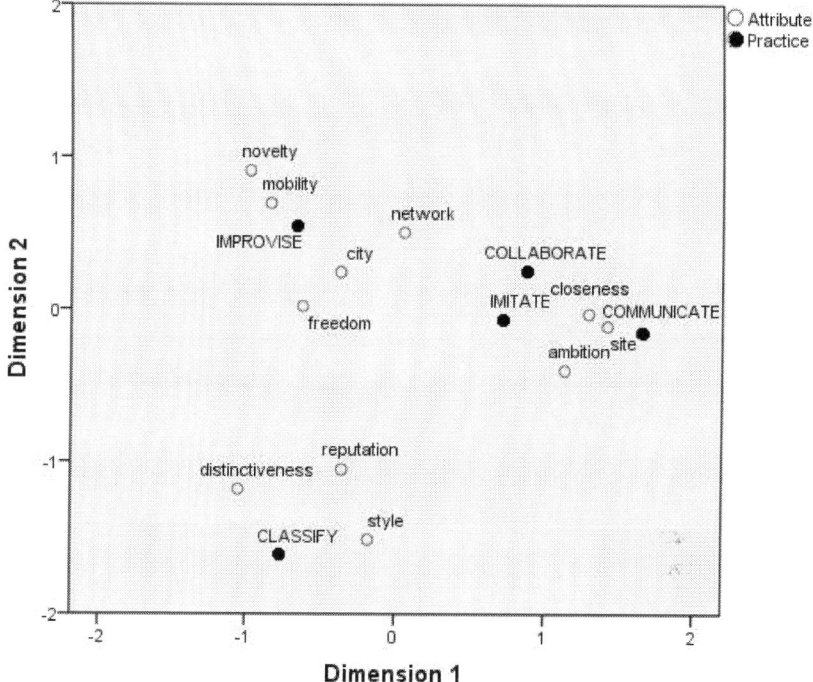

Figure 13.1 Correspondence analysis solution of reduced practice-attribute matrix for the Munich sample (practices are shown in capital letters, ideas are shown in lower case letters)

Source: Our elaboration

populated by a large number of diverse cultural organizations and knowledge-intensive industries attracting creative talent, net of the influence of population size (Ottaviano and Peri 2006).

The structurally best solution (based on a chi-square logic) yielded a set of associations between artists' identity attributes that emphasized practices related to improvisation, imitation, communication, collaboration and classification. Given space restrictions, I focus in the discussion below on the practices with which the artists constructed an identity centred on reputation and distinctiveness. Reputation and distinctiveness are main aspects of creative identity in both samples, but they are located differently vis-à-vis each other and are enacted by different practices. The Munich artists tended to classify art and themselves to obtain both reputation and distinctiveness. By contrast, the artists in the Christchurch sample were more likely to use classification to achieve reputation. To achieve distinctiveness they tended to practice improvisation.

Classification means that the artists organized their judgments about differences (e.g. between art and non-art, personal and impersonal, central and marginal, profane and sacred, traditional and avant-garde) into 'conceptual grids' (Fuchs 2001). For example, a painter in Munich saw herself as 'different' by pursuing 'elitist art' as opposed to 'doing everyday art'. She said that 'I do what I can to get

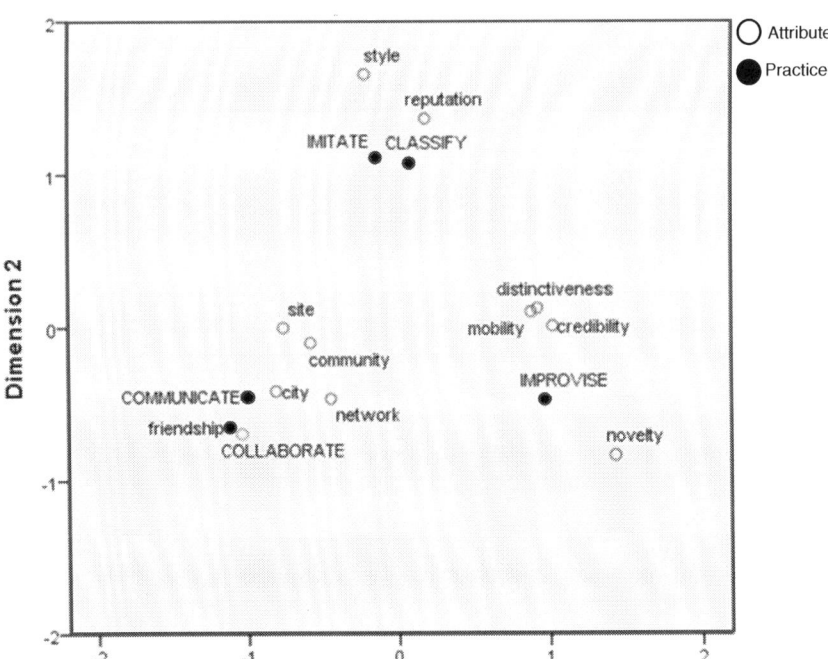

Figure 13.2 Correspondence analysis solution of reduced practice-attribute matrix for the Christchurch sample (practices are shown in capital letters, ideas are shown in lower case letters)

Source: Our elaboration

a solid reputation as being unique. I see myself as a different person through my paintings. I know, I am quite elitist in this. I don't want to be like everyone else.' An illustrator in Christchurch referred to the difference between 'commercial' and 'mystical' as an important aspect of her identity as a creative worker. 'My distinctiveness lies in the idea of mysticism', she commented. Classifying things often involves conflict and controversy, as artists compete among each other and with audiences over appropriate criteria. Sorting, ranking, subsuming and dissecting meanings takes place in fora like arts catalogues, newsletters and workshops, which a Christchurch designer referred to as 'places in the making': 'When I classify my art, I sometimes use an arts catalogue, depending where I am at the moment. In a different place, like a workshop, I talk with others about our differences. So it all depends on the place where I am.'

Classifying involves setting boundaries around things. Identities are more or less strongly bounded, internally as well as externally. The more bounded identities are more selective in what they include and exclude. 'I feel very distinct as an artist', a textile designer in Christchurch said, 'because I focus my entire energy, my entire self, on this one technique.' Other identities are more ambiguous. 'I'm still searching for my place in the arts', a Munich designer said. 'There are so many criteria that I could use to build a distinct reputation for myself. Last month, for example, I was at an exhibition where I got new ideas about what I am doing, or might be doing, which helped me see myself in a completely different light. But who knows where I will be in two years. I might be doing different things with my talents.' When an artist sees himself as a member of a particular group, such as a genre or style, that group becomes related to images that are already in the web of identity attributes. Classifying oneself as an artist then becomes a way of establishing some coherence in this web, based on a high degree of connectivity among the elements rather than by definitional agreement. In both samples, the respondents talked about classifying themselves in terms of 'style' as a condition for achieving reputation. A painter in Munich said that 'you can only have a reputation if people know you for what you are. You got to have style. That's how you get rated in this business.' Classifying leads to boundaries as outcomes, rather than starting points. Identity boundaries change with new discoveries and breakthroughs. A graphic designer in Munich commented: 'I didn't even realize how distinctive my art is until I met my current partner, who comes from a completely different place in the art world. ... He showed me the way to become even more different.' Comments like these indicate that identity boundaries are not fixed in a particular place but are open to intrusion from other places (Bain 2005; Sunley *et al.* 2008). The boundaries are more permeable with artists who see themselves as mobile and adaptable. Artists in both samples used improvisation to construct an identity that values mobility. In the Christchurch sample, however, improvisation was also practiced to gain a distinctive identity, thus relating mobility to distinctiveness.

Much of what artists do is by way of improvisation. Jazz musicians improvise by playing with melodies in new combinations, stage actors improvise by playing with words and gestures, and visual artists experiment with new techniques of production or with new materials. In the Munich sample, improvisation was seen more as a practice to benefit from working in a city that offers a sense of freedom and allows them to feel special and exercise choice. As a sculptor there suggested, 'I'm here because it makes me feel free to do what I want. You know the saying, "city air makes you free". Well, that's it exactly.' In the Christchurch sample, by contrast, 'being in this city' was associated more with the opportunity to collaborate with like-minded others. As a fabric designer suggested: 'I am in this place so I can feed on the ideas of others around me. Being in this city, you can make close friends, and that's really important to who I am as a person. ... But that doesn't mean that I can't be different when circumstances call for it.'

The artists also drew attention to reputation as something provided by external audiences. A photographer in Christchurch asked: 'How would I know who I am unless my customers tell me?' Reputation is not a property of individual artists but belongs to the place in which audiences can recognize it. Artists do not carry their reputation around with them as if it made no difference whether they communicate with audiences in a street fair or in a workshop. 'I use this place to display myself, not just my work', a weaver in Christchurch said, referring to her studio as a 'public place to show and tell'. Reputations are made, not possessed. As such, they can be contested, by audiences using different criteria of authenticity, or by associates claiming that an idea originated somewhere else. 'Creativity means uniqueness, but that is a sore point in this place', a photographer in Munich said. 'We argue constantly over who should get credit for this or that idea … if it's really that different from what the other guy does.' Such disputes lead to reputations that evolve together with other aspects of identity.

In sum, although the artists in both samples expressed similar ideas about the meaning of place in their self-identity as creative entrepreneurs, the correspondence analysis revealed several noteworthy differences in the way they enacted these ideas in practice. 'Being there' does not necessarily mean that the artists collaborate closely and communicate frequently. They may build networks for different reasons and may seek reputation and distinctiveness through different practices, which are themselves connected differently in different combinations of identity attributes. The analysis shows that artists' identities as creative workers involve diverse attributes and different ways of enacting them, depending on the places in which they are active.

Further research and conclusion

It is often assumed, especially when taking an embeddedness perspective, that the place where artists work structures their identity unambiguously, for example by leading them to develop certain 'feelings' for place, to which they are then permanently bound. On the other hand, there is also the expectation that to be successful in this volatile sector, artists need to be constantly 'on the move'. Insisting on a singular and robust identity is considered a hindrance in this regard. The aim of this study was to add substance to the argument that place, while central to identity, is not an essentialist feature of identity. To obtain meaning and force, place must be enacted, in the sense that the artists have to *act* beyond cognitive engagement. The artists interviewed in this study bring their identity to places, but they also bring places to their identity. The data reveal considerable variability in the meaning of place, even in the same urban environment. Based on the meaning-in-use of different ideas about place, artists patch together a particular representation of place in their identity as creative workers. The discipline of formal correspondence analysis helps the investigator uncover the connections that individuals are making between the various meanings of place. The analysis makes these connections transparent in a way that the artists themselves may not be aware of.

The observation that different actors employ different constructions of place raises some doubt about the value of studying place as a singular entity in 'creative places'. Lumping all such constructions into a single meaning of place is at the peril of misunderstanding the reasons why enterprises in cultural industries tend to be spatially clustered, such as the sheer diversity of institutions and the knowledge spillovers that co-location enables. The implication for comparative research on cultural clusters and creative cities is that any observed differences are not merely the result of variations in cultural values, consumer tastes and institutional infrastructures. Comparative studies must also attend to the question of how the actors in the places they occupy manage their embeddedness when they *construct frames of meaning* for what they do and how they see themselves. Identity construction requires actors to *make* connections between ideas in an ecological space of actors, knowledge and conventions that would otherwise appear empty.

This study offers some ideas for research in new directions. First, it extends research on entrepreneurship by focusing not so much on individual actors and social networks than on the connections between the ideas underpinning identity and creativity. If one conceives of entrepreneurial creativity in terms of categories that include various kinds of ideas and orientations, both novel and mundane, old and new, and central and peripheral, then one can better understand the processes involved and the variety of outcomes generated. Singular notions of place should be avoided if investigators want to understand how place figures in products, production and flows of knowledge, thus moving research beyond assumptions of 'location' as a single and fixed scale.

Second, the logic of relational analysis, as in correspondence analysis, forces attention to the interdependence of identity attributes and practices, as opposed to the linear logic in perspectives that view creativity and innovation as a unidirectional sequence of steps. Distinctions – in meanings, interests, perspectives, behaviours and so on – are critical to creativity and innovation, while interdependencies between the elements reveal both differentiation and integration. An interesting question for further research concerns the mechanisms by which entrepreneurs and creative workers balance the maintenance of distinctions to preserve identity on the one hand, and the creation of new connections to explore new sources of knowledge on the other hand. While individuals tend to interact most comfortably with others who are similar in attitudes, preferences and social status, as entrepreneurs they also need to break away from existing knowledge and form linkages with individuals in different domains and outside the local creative field. Mechanisms to maintain identity distinctions include skill specialization, institutional regulation and geographic isolation. Mechanisms to explore new domains include imitation, experimentation and creative partnerships. Studies that explore the dynamic mix of such mechanisms in creative clusters could yield new insights concerning the flow of knowledge across organizational, community and cluster boundaries.

Third, further research should look more closely into the context dependence of shifting identity boundaries. When comparing identities across contexts, the same attribute may be employed across different identities but with very different results, since the attribute may be connected to different patterns of other elements. Different connections can produce different ideas about identity and place, transforming the context and, in turn, shaping the meaning of the interrelated ideas. Thus, research must also pay attention to the ephemeral side of place. The culture of place is not a self-perpetuating tradition determining current behaviours but is continually reconstructed or transformed through action and social interaction. Creating new social relations with ideas across an identity boundary may lead to a reconfiguration of the social milieu. Relocation across places may alter existing identity boundaries, activate new ones and dissolve outdated ones. As the data in this study show, the identities of artists have strong place-based elements, but these elements are not place-bound in the conventional sense of embeddedness.

The study of identity and creativity in cultural industries offers insights into other domains as well, in particular those parts of the economy in which knowledge creation is key. All entrepreneurship involves identity, however unstable, incoherent or unrealizable. Identity makes it difficult for entrepreneurs to consider their actions as something apart from themselves. Their challenge is to engage in the sort of discourse and interaction through which identification with place becomes not so constraining that it stifles creativity, and not so disjointed that it loses its grip. Woody Allen knows this all too well when he insists on 'placing' his identity and creative energy in New York, 'the city that never sleeps'.

Acknowledgements

Thanks go to two anonymous reviewers for their comments and suggestions.

References

Abbott, A. (2005) 'Linked ecologies: States and universities as environments for professions', *Sociological Theory*, 23(3): 245–74.

Alvesson, M. (2003) 'Beyond neopositivists, romantics, and localists: A reflexive approach to interviews in organizational research', *Academy of Management Review*, 28(1): 13–33.

Bain, A. (2005) 'Constructing an artistic identity', *Work, Employment and Society*, 19(1): 25–46.

Björkman, S. (ed.) (2004) *Woody Allen on Woody Allen*, London: Faber and Faber.

Bourdieu, P. (1993) *The Field of Cultural Production*, New York: Columbia University Press.

Burke, P. and Franzoi, S. (1988) 'Studying situations and identities using experiential sampling methodology', *American Sociological Review*, 53(4): 559–68.

Burt, R. (1992) *Structural Holes: The Social Structure of Competition*, Cambridge, MA: Harvard University Press.

Carley, K. and Palmquist, M. (1992) 'Extracting, representing and analyzing mental models', *Social Forces*, 70(3): 601–36.

Clausen, S. (1998) *Applied Correspondence Analysis*, Thousand Oaks, CA: Sage.

Cooke, P. and Lazzeretti, L. (eds) (2008) *Creative Cities, Cultural Clusters and Local Economic Development*, Cheltenham: Edward Elgar.

Creative New Zealand (2003) *Portrait of the Artist: A Survey of Professional Practising Artists in New Zealand*, Wellington: Creative New Zealand.

De Nooy, W. (2003) 'Fields and networks: Correspondence analysis and social network analysis in the framework of field theory', *Poetics*, 31(5–6): 305–27.

DiMaggio, P. (1987) 'Classification in art', *American Sociological Review*, 52(4): 440–55.

Drake, G. (2003) '"This place gives me space": Place and creativity in the creative industries', *Geoforum*, 34(4): 511–24.

Florida, R. (2002) *The Rise of the Creative Class: And How it's Transforming Work, Leisure and Everyday Life*, New York: Basic Books.

Fuchs, S. (2001) *Against Essentialism: A Theory of Culture and Society*, Cambridge, MA: Harvard University Press.

Gabora, L., Rosch, E. and Aerts, D. (2008) 'Toward an ecological theory of concepts', *Ecological Psychology*, 20(1): 84–116.

Giddens, A. (1991) *Modernity and Self-Identity*, Stanford, CA: Stanford University Press.

Gieryn, T. (2000) 'A space for place in sociology', *Annual Review of Sociology*, 26: 463–96.

Han, S. (2003) 'Unraveling the brow: What and how of choice in musical preference', *Sociological Perspectives*, 46(4): 435–59.

Lippard, L. (1997) *The Lure of the Local: Senses of Place in a Multicentered Society*, New York: Free Press.

Markusen, A., Wassall, G., DeNatale, D. and Cohen, R. (2008) 'Defining the creative economy: Industry and occupational approaches', *Economic Development Quarterly*, 22(1): 24–45.

Molotch, H. (2002) 'Place in product', *International Journal of Urban and Regional Research*, 26(4): 665–88.

Montgomery, S. and Robinson, M. (1993) 'Visual artists in New York: What's special about person and place?', *Journal of Cultural Economics*, 17(2): 17–39.

Ottaviano, G. and Peri, G. (2006) 'The economic value of cultural diversity: Evidence from US cities', *Journal of Economic Geography*, 6(1): 9–44.

Popping, R. (2003) 'Knowledge graphs and network text analysis', *Social Science Information*, 42(1): 91–106.

Portes, A. and Sensenbrenner, J. (1993) 'Embeddedness and immigration: Notes on the social determinants of economic action', *American Journal of Sociology*, 98(6): 1320–50.

Relph, E. (1976) *Place and Placelessness*, London: Pion.

Roth, P. (2001) *Reading Myself and Others*, New York: Vintage International.

Scott, A. (2006a) 'Creative cities: Conceptual issues and policy questions', *Journal of Urban Affairs*, 28(1): 1–17.

Scott, A. (2006b) 'Entrepreneurship, innovation and industrial development: Geography and the creative field revisited', *Small Business Economics*, 26(1): 1–24.

Stolarick, K. and Florida, R. (2006) 'Creativity, connections and innovation: A study of linkages in the Montréal region', *Environment and Planning A*, 38(10): 1799–1817.

Streit, A. (2007) *The Creative Knowledge Sector in the Munich Region: Workers, Firms, Turnover*, ACRE report no. 47, Amsterdam: University of Amsterdam.

Sunley, P., Pinch, S., Reimer, S. and Macmillen, J. (2008) 'Innovation in a creative production system: The case of design', *Journal of Economic Geography*, 8(5): 675–98.

Weber, K. (2005) 'A toolkit for analyzing corporate cultural toolkits', *Poetics*, 33(3–4): 227–52.

White, H. (1992) *Identity and Control: A Structural Theory of Social Action*, Princeton, NJ: Princeton University Press.

Zerubavel, E. (1991) *The Fine Line: Making Distinctions in Everyday Life*, Chicago, IL: University of Chicago Press.

Zuckerman, E., Kim, T., Ukanwa, K. and von Rittmann, J. (2003) 'Robust identities or nonentities? Typecasting in the feature-film labor market', *American Journal of Sociology*, 108(5): 1018–74.

Zukin, S. and DiMaggio, P. (1990) 'Introduction', in S. Zukin and P. DiMaggio (eds) *Structures of Capital: The Social Organization of the Economy*, Cambridge, UK: Cambridge University Press, pp. 1–36.

14 Design at work

The interwoven effect of territorial embeddedness, social ties and business networks

Marco Bettiol and Silvia Rita Sedita

Introduction

The chapter aims to shed light on the modalities by which creative outputs in the design sector are organized. Special attention has been dedicated to the interwoven effect of territorial embeddedness, social ties and business networks and how it shapes creative projects within a community of practice (CoP). As Richard Florida (2002) pointed out, the relationships between design professionals are based on 'weak ties' and are motivated by the search for novelty and diversity more than for identity and shared views. Creative people easily switch teams and leave one project behind to embrace another (Grabher and Ibert 2006) as they pursue new visions and ideas. The advent of digital technologies has fuelled relational proximity without spatial proximity (the 'buzz without being there' (Gertler 2008)) and extended the geographical boundaries of situated practices and learning systems (Amin and Roberts 2008). That activity can be facilitated by appropriate 'socio-technical devices' (Callon *et al.* 2002) and communication bridges, such as trade fairs or virtual platforms (as in the case of the most well-known industrial cluster of apparel companies in Hong Kong; see Ho *et al.* 2003).

Even if spatial proximity is less relevant when creative output is being organized, it still plays an important role. Metropolitan areas (Florida 2002) and clusters, where serendipity may occur and long-distance collaboration can be reinforced, are important meeting places for design professionals. The local context is also important because it allows experimentation, facilitates contact networks and tests ideas. Amin and Roberts (2008) pointed out that creative communities utilize face-to-face and localized interactions as well as those struck at a distance. More than on practice, which is constantly evolving, creative communities rely on shared codes (Amin and Roberts 2008) that support communication both at the local and global levels.

Design, considered a variety of creative practices and skills, is not entirely codified and classified. Its body of knowledge is subject to rapid change and obsolescence. In this perspective, the CoP is a fundamental learning environment by which members can exchange professional experience and knowledge and explore new opportunities. As far as we can discern, this process takes place in a spirit of cooperation and competition. Although professionals belong to the same

CoP, they are often but not necessarily competitors in the same market in which they offer similar services. In addition, when members of a CoP have complementary competences, they may collaborate to develop complex professional services. It is interesting that cooperation and competition are not necessarily contradictory but are the way real people interact and exchange knowledge. Business and learning intersect one other. The glue that keeps a CoP together is made up of two elements: on the one hand there is the intention to improve professional skills through knowledge and experience sharing, on the other there is the determination to exploit opportunities.

Turn, a community of designers founded and based in Turin, is a concrete example illustrating the importance of territorial embeddedness and the role of social and business networks in designing and implementing design projects. The local context proved to be a fruitful terrain for the design community that nurtured the opportunity for knowledge sharing and for selecting business partners.

Theoretical background and research questions

Strongly influenced by the theory of shared practices (Suchman 1987), Lave and Wenger (1991) first introduced the concepts of CoPs and of mutual engagement and developed a 'situated' social theory of learning. They described a CoP as 'a set of relations among persons, activity, and the world, over time and in relation with other tangential and overlapping communities of practice' (Lave and Wenger 1991: 98). Seven years later, Wenger (1998) took the concept of the CoP a step further calling it the preferred locus for social learning processes to take place. He described CoPs as organisms constituted by groups of professionals, informally bound together by a common purpose to share their distinctive capabilities to solve organizational problems.

Learning is the result of the interplay between competences defined in a social community and by personal experiences (Nooteboom 2006). A CoP can, then, be viewed as a social container for the heterogeneous competences that frame a learning system. There are three modes of belonging to social learning systems: (a) engagement, which implies doing things together and producing artefacts; (b) imagination (based on a cultural heredity), which implies constructing an image of ourselves (and of our community and world) in order to orient ourselves; and (c) alignment, which is the outcome of sharing experiences with others. One mode can dominate the others and give different qualities to different social structures. For example, a nation can be considered a community based mainly on historical imagination; while a CoP at work is based primarily on engagement.

A defining feature of CoPs is that they are 'self-perpetuating' (Wenger 2000), as opposed to other forms of aggregation, which are normally characterized by a group assembled to accomplish a specific task[1] and which exist only as long as the project is underway. By contrast, as Wenger and Snyder (2000) explained, CoPs last for a long time and allow social capital to sediment (Lesser 2000). This tacit, common knowledge exalts over time the CoP's potential and ability to solve problems (Lesser and Everest 2001).

CoPs can be formed by service technicians' 'reps' offering technical support (see the famous example of Xerox repair representatives in Orr 1990), by police officers (like the Dutch police force in De Laat and Broer 2004), by volunteers (such as those operating in the Royal National Lifeboat Institution in Kolbotn 2004), or by engineers working for a large oil company (see the example of the Italian oil company, Eni SpA, in Scarso *et al.* 2008).

According to Lave and Wenger's (1991) definition, one of the most important features that characterize the CoP is its organic, spontaneous and informal nature. Consistent with that perspective, they can be appropriately considered auto-generative social networks based on the principle of a 'legitimate peripheral participation'[2] (Capra 2002).

The role of territorial embeddedness in the development of CoPs has often been underestimated in the literature. Recent studies on economic geography suggest that geographical proximity is a key source for a firm's competitive advantage. Tacit knowledge exchange and frequent face-to-face interactions enhance the benefits of 'being there' (Gertler 1995). We wondered whether geographical proximity as a measure of distance is enough to explain the formation and the sustainability of CoPs. Thus our first research question (RQ1):

RQ1: Does the local territorial and social context (including shared values and common ground) have an effect on the development of CoPs? Likewise, does territorial embeddedness play a role in their development and institutionalization?

By shifting positions, it is possible to see CoPs not only as (narrowly) bounded organizations or inter-organizational phenomena (at large), but also as entities relying on shared cognitive and, more importantly, geographical space. Only a few works have attempted to explore this aspect (Benner 2003; Rama *et al.* 2003; Reinau 2007). CoPs, in fact, can enhance value not only at the organizational but also at the meso-level and can affect the performance of regional innovation systems (Teigland 2006) or clusters of small and medium enterprises (SMEs) (Mason *et al.* 2006), recently defined as learning organizations and institutions for knowledge exchange (Steiner and Hartmann 2006). SMEs involved in flexible and cooperative networking at the local level can potentiate their competitive production. CoPs work as mechanisms establishing these networks and 'unlock tacit knowing, learning by doing, and social creativity' (Amin and Roberts 2008: 28) at the meso-level.

Two streams of literature have focused on the evolution of CoPs: on the one hand, they are considered an emergent phenomenon (Brown and Duguid 1991, 2001; Lave and Wenger 1991; Wenger and Snyder 2000); on the other, they are considered a managerial tool for knowledge management (Contu and Willmott 2000; Wenger, McDermott and Snyder 2002; Wenger 2004). According to the former, the ecological dimension prevails over determinism and hierarchy. A bottom-up dynamic process, sustained by the quest for a shared identity based on common practice and self-recognition, is operating. In the second, organizations develop appropriate mechanisms to stimulate and sustain communities of workers who share knowledge. In fact, 'what becomes essential is the implementation of appropriate organizational structures, processes, and mechanisms that facilitate the sharing of experience, ideas, and suggestions among individuals' (Scarso and Bolisani 2007: 376). The management of CoPs is, nevertheless, a difficult task. Conflict and competition are still intrinsic to organizational settings, and the process of cultivating CoPs by managers can induce overwhelming activity (Thompson 2005).

Our second research question (RQ2) is concerned with this issue:

> RQ2: Are the ecological and the managerial approaches really mutually exclusive or could there be a combination of the two? We think there is a community life cycle: during the first phase the emergence and bottom-up mechanisms initially prevail, but during the second phase the need for legitimacy and stability require a more formalized structure.

As can be assumed from empirical evidence regarding CoPs, there are several more or less formal interaction modalities between people in the community. CoPs are acknowledged as social network structures focusing on: the *informal dimension*, striving to identify knowledge networks in organizations and in local production systems or on the *formal dimension*, exploring research and development agreements or co-patenting activities in high-tech sectors. Our third research question was thus formulated (RQ3):

> RQ3: Do formal and informal relationships coexist within the CoP? In other words, do people select a multiple interaction modality depending on the relationship's objective?

We argue that an integrated approach that simultaneously maps multiple networks within the same CoP is what is needed. The act of belonging to a CoP should thus entail a multidimensional engagement, depending on the reason why the individual is participating (see also Bettiol and Sedita 2011).

The literature concerning CoPs stresses the importance of relationships between members to permit knowledge creation and sharing, but it does not underline any intentionality in the act of belonging. The individual perspective has been neglected, and the focus is clearly on the meso-level, on the community as a whole. We acknowledge that a clear view on the motivation propelling an individual to be an active member of a CoP is missing. Here then is our final research question (RQ4).

> RQ4: Do persons who belong to a CoP do so simply for knowledge creation and sharing? Does competition and the local market have any effect on their decision?

We argue that CoPs can be seen as a 'coopetitive system of value creation' (Dagnino 2009) or a 'coopetition' strategy device. A coopetition strategy refers to an inter-firm strategy striving to generate economic and knowledge value (coopetitive advantage) in view of both a competitive and cooperative relationship. A member can decide to belong to a CoP not only for a cooperative reason, but also for a competitive one. We can thus distinguish between at least two forms of participation: one related to cooperation and knowledge sharing and the other to competition and project-based work.

We contend that the origin of this multidimensional engagement can be found in the influence of the market, especially with regard to professionals who compete in the same local arena. This is particularly true for designers who manoeuvre in the same local market and offer products or services for a limited pool of clients. In this perspective competition should be the rule and cooperation the exception. The incentives to cooperate and to develop a CoP are less obvious with respect to those inherent to professionals working in the same organizational context (private company or public administration). Professionals in the design sector are generally independent or work in small studios (three–four members) and are competitors. Although they do not always offer the same service, they strive to excel in the same local market and to produce work with real economic value and this affects their relationship with the other members of the community.

The research setting: designers at work

The Industrial Design Society of America (IDSA), the most important design organization in the US, defines industrial design 'as the professional service of creating and developing concepts and specifications that optimize the function, value and appearance of products and systems for the mutual benefit of both user and manufacturer'.[3] This very specific concept of design is consistent with the Anglo-Saxon pragmatist tradition. Design is both relative to the form (appearance) and the function of the product in the sense that *form* follows *function*. A broader and more holistic definition of design was outlined by the International Council of Societies of Industrial Design (ICSID): 'Design is a creative activity whose aim is to establish the multifaceted qualities of objects, processes, services and their systems in whole life-cycles. Therefore, design is the central factor of innovative humanization of technologies and the crucial factor of cultural and economic exchange.'[4]

In this perspective, design is not only an industrial process related to the development of a new product but it is also a cultural phenomenon that can potentially influence society. The differences between these two definitions reveal how design is interpreted at an international level. Acknowledging the complexity and multidimensionality of industrial design, the European Commission grouped design with creative industries in the KEA report on the economy of culture in Europe. On the basis of that definition, the report outlines that:

a) the use of creativity is essential (creative skills and creative people originating in the arts field and the field of culture) to the performances, b) activities are not necessary industrial and may be prototypes, c) outputs are based on copyright but they may include other intellectual property right inputs (trademark for instance).

(KEA European Affairs 2006: 56)

The professional practice of design is undergoing rapid evolution. The diffusion of new technologies, on the one hand, and the growing role of design in the innovation processes (Hise *et al.* 1989), on the other, are deeply affecting the designer's profession. As new specializations emerge, innovative fields are developing and designers are influencing product innovation and helping to define new cultural meanings. An example of this is 'Core77', one of the most important design webzines in the world. It has dedicated an area of the website to the job market where more than fifteen categories of design are listed: 3-D modelling and computer-aided design (CAD), advertising, architecture, design education, design management, exhibit design, fashion design, graphic design, industrial design, interaction design, interior design, product development, research and strategy, sales and marketing, and web design.

As recent literature has pointed out (Florida 2002), designers, as well as other creative professionals, tend to cluster in specific metropolitan areas where they can meet new clients and keep in touch with other professionals to foster their knowledge and skills. Milan is considered the capital of industrial design (especially of home furnishings) in Italy (Verganti 2006), because it is the epicentre of the most important event in design (the Milan Design Fair), it has a high concentration of designers residing in the city, and it is the place where clients (companies) need and want good designers.

As defined by Amin and Roberts (2008), design communities are formed by professionals who spend their energies in a highly creative activity, who handle specialized, expert knowledge and who belong to 'expert/high creativity communities' (e.g. scientists, researchers, performance artists) (Table 14.1).

As far as organizing creative projects is concerned, the typical structure producing design activity is temporary and project-based (Lundin and Söderholm 1995; Hobday 2000; Grabher 2002a; Kenis *et al.* 2009). These characteristics are considered ideal for that purpose and tend to favour temporary collaboration. In fact, the design service industry is characterized by small studios or freelance professionals who, although they are independent, tend to cooperate on a regular basis with reference to specific activities. These relationships are not stable and tend to evolve over time depending on the project at hand. Described as a latent network or ecology (Grabher 2001b), it is not just a specific market organization but is fully part of the community in the sense that it is nurtured through face-to-face interactions and knowledge sharing by its members (Bettiol and Sedita 2011).

The methodology

More than three hundred designers belong to Turn, the first Italian design community. In 2009 we asked the members of that community (119 members

Table 14.1 Characteristics of design communities

Type of knowledge	Social interaction		Temporal aspects	Nature of social ties	Innovation	Organizational dynamics
	Proximity/nature of communication					
• Specialized and expert knowledge, including standards and codes (and meta-codes) • Exist to extend knowledge base • Temporary creative coalitions; knowledge changing rapidly	• Spatial and/or relational proximity • Communication facilitated through both face-to-face and long distant interaction		• Short-lived, drawing on institutional resources from a variety of expert and creative fields	• Trust-based on reputation and expertise • Weak social ties	• High energy • Radical innovation	• Group/project managed • Open to those with a reputation in the field • Management through intermediaries and boundary objects

Source: Amin and Roberts (2008)

belonging to fifty-three studios) to fill out an online questionnaire developed in collaboration with SurveyMonkey, an American company that enables users to create their own web surveys. The questionnaire, planned after several interviews with members of the Turn CoP, was divided into three parts.

In the first part, we collected general information about the responders (concerning education, profession, etc.) and we inquired about relations between members. A list of all the CoP's members was made up and the responders were asked to give information about those they were in contact with (including the purpose of those contacts, their frequency and communication tool used). In particular, two types of relationships, considered mutually exclusive, were investigated. The first type concerned social ties based on knowledge sharing. These ties were typically constructed to discuss issues related to professional work and community building. The second type was concerned with project-based ties characterized by involvement in creative projects. We asked responders to indicate which modality of interaction (either social or project-based) was the most prevalent one. We analyzed the vitality of the contacts by asking about the average intensity of the interaction (on a daily, weekly, monthly or occasional basis), the relevance of the relationship for the responder's professional activity (none, low, high) and the means of communication (face to face, events, or information and communication technologies). We also asked the responders to indicate the number of common projects developed together over the past three years.

In the second part we explored the patterns of learning and knowledge acquisition and examined the role played by the professionals at various levels (community, local area, national and international) and their access to various information sources (Internet, specialized magazines, universities and research centres).

Finally, in the third part we investigated the quality of the responders' participation in the CoP's life, the benefits they obtained and their overall degree of satisfaction in being members of Turn. As forty-eight of the questionnaires were completed by the responders, the response ratio was considered acceptable (40 per cent).

Turn: and the birth and evolution of a CoP

Turin is a business and cultural centre located in north-west Italy. The city has more than one million residents and is home to much of the Italian automobile industry, although it is now only the headquarters of Fiat, the most important Italian car manufacturer.

Turn, the first Italian design community made up for the most part by graphic and industrial designers and architects, in 2005, just before the Winter Olympic Games and when Turin had just been nominated the First World Design Capital for 2008. These two events were a turning point for the city and laid the ground for Turn's birth. Before being nominated for the Winter Olympic Games, Turin was a declining city, hard hit by the economic decline. The Winter Olympic

Games helped to change the city's crumbling image and forced Turin to rethink itself as the capital of creative activities. During that time a group of young (under thirty) creative professionals came up with an idea to widen their network of contacts to give them more opportunities to share experiences and information with other professionals. The first step was taken in 2004 when Luca Ballarini (graphic designer and founder of Bellissimo[5]) sent an email to twelve friends and colleagues working in the Turin area (most were friends from the time he studied at the Polytechnic of Turin). The email was sent as a *call of duty* to emerging creative professionals based in Turin seeking more visibility at the local level. These professionals wanted to claim a more incisive role in the local socio-economic environment until then completely absorbed by the automotive industry. The email set off an unexpected, snowball reaction. The first twelve called other colleagues in a typical peer-to-peer process. As Marco Rainò, past president of Turin, explained,[6]

> There were frequent and informal meetings (every week), which were open to anybody who was interested in the creative field. There were twelve of us at the start, but the number quickly began to grow. There were soon forty to fifty people participating in our meetings. We could barely fit in the same room!
>
> (Our translation)

All of 2004 was dedicated to those informal, brainstorming meetings during which professionals in the area shared ideas and proposed projects. The idea of creating a community was born as the participants realized they shared a common idea and need to share/exchange information and knowledge about their trade. Soon two lines of thought became apparent: according to the first the group was to be an open but formal association of professionals who could participate freely. According to the second, the group was to be a more informal but closed net of professionals who would gain membership after a selection process. The first line of thought prevailed and the design community was formally founded at the end of 2004. With the approval of all the participants a subgroup started working on rules for managing the community. At the end of 2005 several proposals were put forward: the governance of the community would be entrusted to a board (*Direttivo*) of persons in charge of organizing and managing its activities. The board was initially composed of nine members elected every two years by all the members. The board would assist the president and the vice present (usually selected from among board members) who officially represented the community. The statute has recently been modified and now three members of the board are elected every six months to permit more people to be involved in managing the CoP's activities. The governance model is 'democratic' and is based on the election of the board by the members of the community. A statute defining rules and election modalities was also elaborated.

Turn is a cultural association striving to promote the visibility of the professionals involved and to foster knowledge sharing among its members.

Membership is open to professionals or firms working in the design field and based in the metropolitan area of Turin or within the Piedmont region. The fact that the board can admit professionals outside the Turin area is an important feature. There is an annual membership fee of €100 for every 'studio' or freelance professional who applies. It is interesting to note the type of members who can apply. Although there are numerous freelance professionals working in the design field, the 'studio' was chosen as its unit of reference, because it was considered an effective way to group these professionals in a stable way and to avoid problems related to project-based organizations, so diffuse in this field. Marco Rainò explained that choice:

> Creativity is a dynamic and instable work. You have people who get together to work on a specific project and when it's finished they split for other projects. There are also a lot of temporary collaborators who work in the studios so it is hard to keep track of the people involved in the creative work. That is why we chose to accept studios as members in order to involve the most people possible and at the same time to promote stable relationships with creative people working in the Turin area.
>
> (Our translation)

Not only the heads of the studios but also all those working at the studio even as interns or who are involved in a specific project can be members of the CoP.

The CoP was officially founded in 2005 and forty studios were enrolled. That number was relatively stable until 2008, when it doubled, reaching eighty-seven studios, partially because Turin was appointed World Design Capital. In 2009 the number fell to fifty-three studios as several studios withdrew when the initial attention subsided. Marco Rainò pointed out that 'several studios approached the community as it was a good marketing opportunity for them, but they did not really get the spirit of the community, which is more oriented to knowledge sharing. It is not a surprise that after the World Design Capital they left the community' (our translation).

Although Turn deals with different expectations, it has been coherent with its core values. The upsizing and subsequent downsizing are a demonstration of its resilience and elasticity; it has proven that it has its own centre of gravity.

A large number of creative people are externally connected to the community (mostly freelance designers) and Marco Rainò estimates that the actual number of people involved is three hundred. He explained that

> Almost every studio has collaborators, at least two to three individuals who work within the studio on a regular basis. Since the studio where they work is a member, they can participate in the activities of the community even if they cannot vote. But some of those who have worked as collaborators have eventually opened their own studios and have later became visible members of the community.
>
> (Our translation)

Although Turn seems rigidly organized, just as any normal association, its borders are blurred. In that respect Turn seems more a movement than a traditional association. It is larger than the sum of its members and its influence on the Turin's exciting design scene is very important.

Turn has had its own tough times even in connection with its role as an economic agent. This is a very important issue, especially in relation to our research question about coopetition strategy. In 2005 Turn was asked to oversee an important design contest: the marketing division of Fiat, then headed by Lapo Elkann (Gianni Agnelli's nephew), asked Turn to come up with some ideas for a new marketing campaign. That opportunity was an important recognition for Turn: Fiat is the most important company in Turin and has a high symbolic value, so it seemed that the old Turin was turning to the new one for ideas and suggestions. The board of Turn agreed to organize the contest and to collect the proposals, but the publicity went sour and several studios (members of Turn) openly criticized the board when Luca Ballarini's (Turn's acting president) presentation, was chosen by Fiat's management as the most convincing ad campaign. Several members accused the board and the president of foul play. The fact that the final choice was made by Fiat and not by the board did not rectify the matter. Most felt that there had been lack of transparency and that the competition was unfair. The episode has had a negative impact on the life of the community. As a result Turn decided explicitly not to manage creative competitions and not to be involved in activities having a direct impact on the market in which most of the members operate. Instead, it turned to pre-competitive initiatives working more on communication and promoting visibility of Turin's young creative movement. Since Turn is a registered trademark, it must adhere to a strict set of rules, in particular in connection with public contracts. Turn now organizes public campaigns and projects to promote the city's name in design and has developed special projects for the Furniture Fair (the most important design event in the world) in Milan.

The borderline between cooperation, the area in which the community has legitimacy, and competition, a banned arena, is well defined and plays an important role. The members of the CoP are, in fact, competitors: they offer almost comparable services in the same (local) market. They strive to cooperate to improve their knowledge and to exchange experiences and from this point of view the community is very important.

Descriptive statistics

According to our survey, 38.1 per cent of the responders declared that they earned less than €50k per year, 42.86 per cent declared they earned between 50k and 200k and 19.04 per cent declared they earned more than 200k, with more than 7.14 per cent earning over one million euros (Table 14.2).

With regard to the number of employees, the majority (61.7 per cent) of the responders had between two and ten employees, almost a third (29.79 per cent) are freelance professionals (with no employees) and 8.51 per cent have more than ten employees (Table 14.3).

Table 14.2 Turnover of members in 2008

Turnover (€)	Percentage
< 50k	38.10
50–100k	21.43
100–200k	21.43
200–500k	11.90
500–1000k	0.00
> 1,000k	7.14

Source: Our survey

Table 14.3 Number of employees

No. of employees	Percentage
0 (freelance)	29.79
2–4	36.17
5–10	25.53
> 10	8.51

Source: Our survey

Table 14.4 Educational background

Typology	Percentage
College	10.3
University degree	67.2
Masters or PhD	22.4

Source: Our survey

Table 14.5 Awards

Awards	Percentage
Yes	47.83
No	36.96
Never applied	15.22

Source: Our survey

The majority (67.2 per cent) of the responders had a university degree and 22.4 per cent had a masters or a PhD, while only 10.3 per cent went to college. It is interesting that 91 per cent of the members acquired their university degree in Turin while 9 per cent studied in other areas (Lisbon, Milan, New York) (see Table 14.4).

We also asked the responders if their work had ever been awarded prizes for excellence in design. Almost half of the members (47.83 per cent) had indeed won awards, 36.96 per cent had not, while 15.22 had never applied for an award (Table 14.5).

The questionnaire also assessed the sources of information used by members for their professional growth. The results indicated how different sources of information were ranked: the rating ran from nothing (no importance) to top (maximum importance). As it is evident from Table 14.6, conversations with members were by no means the most relevant (or prevalent) way of collecting valuable information but only one of many. In particular, conversations with designers (not members of Turn) living in Turin seemed to play an important role together with conversations with designers living in Italy (outside Turin area) and abroad. The relationship between the members of the community are not exclusive in terms of quality of information but are part of a more complex network of relationships within the metropolitan area (Turin) as well as outside it. The most important source of information was individual learning. It might seem a contradiction, but being constantly up to date is a necessity for a designer who needs to be aware of new aesthetic trends as well as technological innovations.

We also asked the responders about two possible relationships (social ties and project-based ties), which were considered mutually exclusive. The responders were asked to select which of the two was their prevalent interaction modality with other members of the CoP. We then mapped the two networks. In the *social network*, relationships were based on the opportunity to exchange knowledge not related to the completion of a specific task. Knowledge sharing was considered rather informal and based on general information related to the profession. In the *project network*, relationships were characterized by formal collaboration concerning the development of specific projects for clients. That network was strictly related to the market demand and information circulating within projects was not freely exchanged with the rest of the community. When a specific output was produced for the market, members were competitors because the workplace was the same local area.

The social network was formed by 211 ties (Table 14.7) and sustained by different means of communication. Face-to-face (F2F) meetings and events organized by the community were the most popular ways to exchange knowledge. About 42 per cent of ties took place through F2F meetings and about 40 per cent through events. Although the social network was dedicated primarily to knowledge sharing, a minority of those ties ended up working together on a common project (about 28 per cent). The professional relevance[7] of the ties was also assessed. About 63 per cent of the ties had low or no relevance. The frequency of social relationships was considered very strong as the vast majority of the contacts occurred on a daily base (about 68 per cent).

The project network was formed by 195 ties (Table 14.7), which were mainly sustained by F2F meetings (about 78 per cent). Almost all the ties were linked to involvement in common projects (98 per cent), and were defined frequent by many (about 44 per cent of the collaborations regarded the collaboration on more than four projects[8]). Project-based ties were considered very relevant for professional activity (about 88 per cent of the ties were considered very important), and they took place on both a daily (37 per cent) and on an irregular (39 per cent) basis.

Table 14.6 Relative importance of qualified sources of information

	Conversations with other Turners	Conversations with Turin designers	Conversations with Italian designers	Conversations with foreign designers	Conversations with academics	Individual learning	Formal training	Conferences and seminars
Nothing	10.9	0.0	4.3	15.2	19.6	0.0	19.6	0.0
Low	32.6	15.2	23.9	19.6	43.5	2.2	23.9	28.3
Average	28.3	39.1	37.0	30.4	8.7	6.5	30.4	41.3
High	23.9	41.3	28.3	32.6	23.9	76.1	21.7	28.3
Top	4.3	4.3	6.5	2.2	4.3	15.2	4.3	2.2

Source: Our survey

Table 14.7 Characteristics of social and project networks

Type	Communication means			Projects			Relevance			Frequency		
		No.	%		No.	%		No.	%		No.	%
Social	F2F	87	41.63	None	151	72.24	None	31	15.05	Daily	143	68.10
	Events	84	40.19	1–3	49	23.44	Low	99	48.05	Weekly	24	11.43
	Phone	19	9.09	+4	9	4.32	High	76	36.90	Monthly	35	16.67
	Mail	19	8.61							Scattered	8	3.80
	Blog–forum	1	0.48									
	Total	209	100.00		209	100.00		206	100.00		210	100.00
Project	F2F	151	78.24	None	4	2.05	None	1	0.52	Daily	72	36.93
	Events	6	3.10	1–3	105	53.85	Low	23	11.85	Weekly	22	11.28
	Phone	16	8.30	+4	86	44.10	High	170	87.63	Monthly	24	12.31
	Mail	20	10.36							Scattered	77	39.48
	Blog–forum	0	0.00									
	Total	193	100.00		195	100.00		194	100.00		195	100.00

Source: Bettiol and Sedita (2011)

The results presented in Table 14.7 emphasize the importance of investigating the two sub-networks separately. The social network reflects the true spirit of the CoP, which was built on shared values and common interests and was considered the preferred place to circulate knowledge and information between members (Lave and Wenger 1991). The CoP was active in planning both official (events) and informal (daily F2F meetings) occasions facilitating physical contact. It became apparent when the relevance of the knowledge shared was analyzed that the CoP was more a tool for identity building than an effective leverage for increasing professional returns. Comparing the professional relevance of the ties in the two networks, the project-based ones ranked on average much higher than the social ones.

The project network reflects the project-based nature of the activities concerned with design. The frequency of relationships is consistent with the inherent discontinuity of project organization. A large percentage of the relationships within the project network took place either on a daily or on an irregular basis. This may appear contradictory, but it is nonetheless characteristic of the typical way people work when they are committed to a project-based structure. Contacts were frequent during the stage the project was being implemented while they were latent during periods between projects (Grabher 2001a, 2002b).

Discussion and final remarks

The chapter aimed to analyze some features of a CoP and to consider important underexplored aspects that drew us to formulate our research questions: What is the relevance of territorial embeddedness in the formation and evolution of a CoP? What kind of governance does a CoP have? What types of interactions occur between its members? How does competition affect the members' behaviour?

Turn, the first Italian design community located in Turin, offered an interesting empirical illustration of the modalities by which creative output is planned and developed. The interwoven effect of territorial embeddedness, social ties and business networks in shaping creative projects within a CoP was amply examined.

That specific locality was the starting point for a CoP primarily composed of members who attended the same schools and lived in the same area. Our reference was the city of Turin struggling with an economic slump and in need of new professionals and of legitimacy. Turn affirmed itself as a point of reference for the designers in that area. Both ecological and hierarchical forms of governance typified the CoP. Its emergent nature, which characterized the first period of its life cycle, was integrated, during the second stage, with a more formalized structure, which met the needs of the market and amplified the communication potential of the individual designers searching for visibility and professional recognition. The main feature of the CoP as a place for tacit knowledge exchange among professionals who shared the same objectives and values was found to be very much alive. Its members, in fact, interact at different levels, mixing informal and formal modalities, selecting the right partners for knowledge exchange, the 'buzz' or for projects. The duality of social and project-based ties potentiated the strategic orientation of the studios belonging to the CoP. Consistent with the coopetition strategy that it chose, both cooperation and competition mechanisms distinguished the members' relationships. It could be argued, finally, that the CoP limited the members' development and expansion, but the results show that this was not the case. Designers, in fact, belonged to Turn but also collaborated with one another and with collaborators at the local, national and international levels, creating a knowledge multiplier effect. External knowledge and competences entered the community and enriched its knowledge base, keeping it alive and lively.

We are aware that our research has some limitations, mainly related to the size of the sample analyzed and its focus on a specific case study. We acknowledge the importance of comparing different design communities in order to corroborate and validate our data. The work, nevertheless, offers an interesting point of departure for further studies on the theoretical and empirical properties of CoPs. Territorial embeddedness, community governance, multiple interaction ties and coopetition strategy are all important concepts that help to clarify our understanding of how design is created and implemented.

Notes

1 We are reminded here of the team involved in enhancing the 'knowledge creating company' described by Nonaka and Konno (1998) and implied in the Japanese concept of *ba*. The concept was originally proposed by the Japanese philosophers, Nishida and (later) Shimizu. Its meaning is similar to that of the English word 'place'. It refers to organizational contexts in which individuals interact at a specific time and place over a certain period of time, a kind of shared space for emerging relationships.
2 Legitimate peripheral participation (LPP) is a conceptual framework proposed by Lave and Wenger (1991) that recognizes that each existing or potential CoP member can contribute to the learning activity of the community. Novices are welcome to join the community even if they have a peripheral position and their contribution is marginal. Over time, they integrate into the community and can become core members.
3 This definition is available on IDSA website, http://www.idsa.org/what-is-industrial-design.
4 This definition is available on ICSID website, http://www.icsid.org/about/about/articles31.htm.
5 Bellissimo is a publishing and advertising company based in Turin.
6 We personally interviewed Marco Rainò and talked to him about Turn's development.
7 The responders were asked to declare how relevant the tie had been for their professional activity.
8 Collaborating on more than four projects over a three-year period means the professional was involved in more than one project a year (on average). That level of professional involvement was considered by the responders as symptomatic of a strong tie.

References

Amin, A. and Roberts, J. (2008) *Community, Economic Creativity, and Organization*, Oxford: Oxford University Press.

Benner, C. (2003) 'Learning communities in a learning region: The soft infrastructure of cross-firm learning networks in Silicon Valley', *Environment and Planning A*, 35(10): 1809–30.

Bettiol, M. and Sedita, S.R. (2011) 'The role of community of practice in developing creative industry projects', *International Journal of Project Management*, 29(4): 468–79.

Brown, J.S. and Duguid, P. (1991) 'Organizational learning and communities of practice: Towards a unified view of working, learning, and innovation', *Organization Science*, 2(1): 40–57.

Brown, J.S. and Duguid, P. (2001) 'Knowledge and organization: A social-practice perspective', *Organization Science*, 12(2): 198–213.

Callon, M., Méadel, C. and Rabeharisoa, V. (2002) 'The economy of qualities', *Economy and Society*, 31(2): 194–217.

Capra, F. (2002) *The Hidden Connections: A Science for Sustainable Living*, New York: Random House.

Contu, A. and Willmott, H. (2000) 'Comment on Wenger and Yanow. Knowing in practice: A delicate flower in the organizational learning field', *Organization*, 7(2): 269–76.

Dagnino, G.B. (2009) 'Coopetition strategy: A new kind of interfirm dynamics for value creation', in G.B. Dagnino and E. Rocco (eds) *Coopetition Strategy: Theory Experiments and Cases*, London: Routledge, pp. 25–43.

De Laat, M.F. and Broer, W. (2004) 'CoPs for cops: Managing and creating knowledge through networked expertise', in P. Hildreth and C. Kimble (eds) *Knowledge Networks: Innovation through Communities of Practice*, London: Idea Group Publishing, pp. 58–69.

Florida, R. (2002) *The Rise of the Creative Class: And How it's Transforming Work, Leisure and Everyday Life*, New York: Basic Books.

Gertler, M. (1995) '"Being there": Proximity, organization, and culture in the development and adoption of advanced manufacturing technologies', *Economic Geography*, 71(1): 1–26.

Gertler, M. (2008) 'Buzz without being there? Communities of practice in context', in A. Amin and J. Roberts (eds) *Community, Economic Creativity, and Organization*, Oxford: Oxford University Press, pp. 203–26.

Grabher, G. (2001a) 'Locating economic action: Projects, networks, localities, institutions. Commentaries', *Environment and Planning A*, 33(8): 1329–34.

Grabher, G. (2001b) 'Ecologies of creativity: The village, the group, and the heterarchic organization of the British advertising industry', *Environment and Planning A*, 33(2): 351–74.

Grabher, G. (2002a) 'Cool projects, boring institutions: Temporary collaboration in social context', *Regional Studies*, 36(3): 205–14.

Grabher, G. (2002b) 'The project ecology of advertising: Tasks, talents and teams', *Regional Studies*, 36(3): 245–62.

Grabher, G. and Ibert, O. (2006) 'Bad company? The ambiguity of personal knowledge networks', *Journal of Economic Geography*, 6(3): 251–71.

Hise, R.T., O'Neal, L., McNeal, J.U. and Parasuraman, A. (1989) 'The effect of product design activities on commercial success levels of new industrial products', *Journal of Product Innovation Management*, 6(1): 43–50.

Ho, D.C.K., Au, K.F. and Newton, E. (2003) 'The process and consequences of supply chain virtualization', *Industrial Management and Data Systems*, 103(6): 423–33.

Hobday, M. (2000) 'The project-based organization: An ideal form for managing complex products and systems?', *Research Policy*, 29(7–8): 871–93.

KEA European Affairs (2006) *The Economy of Culture in Europe*, Brussels: European Commission Directorate, General for Education and Culture.

Kenis, P., Janowicz-Panjaitan, M.K. and Cambré, B. (2009) *Temporary Organizations*, Cheltenham: Edward Elgar.

Kolbotn, R. (2004) 'Communities of practice in the Royal National Lifeboat Institution', in P. Hildreth and C. Kimble (eds) *Knowledge Networks. Innovation through Communities of Practice*, London: Idea Group Publishing, pp. 70–8.

Lave, J. and Wenger, E.C. (1991) *Situated Learning. Legitimate Peripheral Participation*, Cambridge, UK: Cambridge University Press.

Lesser, E. (ed.) (2000) *Knowledge and Social Capital, Foundations and Applications*, Boston, MA: Butterworth Heinemann.

Lesser, E. and Everest, K. (2001) 'Using communities of practices to manage intellectual capital', *Ivey Business Journal*, 65(4): 37–41.

Lundin, R.A. and Söderholm, A. (1995) 'A theory of the temporary organization', *Scandinavian Journal of Management*, 11(4): 437–55.

Mason, C., Castleman, T. and Parker, C. (2006) 'Creating value with regional communities of SMEs', in E. Coakes and S. Clarke (eds) *Enyclopedia of Communities of Practice in Information and Knowledge Management*. London: Idea Group Publishing, pp. 115–23.

Nonaka, I. and Konno, N. (1998) 'The concept of "ba": Building a foundation for knowledge creation', *California Management Review*, 4(3): 40–54.

Nooteboom, B. (2006) 'Cognitive distance in and between CoP's and firms: Where do exploitation and exploration take place, and how are they connected?', paper presented at the DIME workshop on Communities of Practice, Durham, 27–28 October.

Orr, J. (1990) 'Sharing knowledge, celebrating identity: War stories and community memory in a service culture', in D.S. Middleton and D. Edwards (eds) *Collective Remembering: Memory in Society*, Beverly Hills, CA: Sage, pp. 169–89.

Rama, R., Ferguson, D. and Melero, A. (2003) 'Subcontracting networks in industrial districts: The electronics industries of Madrid', *Regional Studies*, 37(1): 71–88.

Reinau, K. (2007) 'Local clusters in globalized world', paper presented at the Druid Winter Conference, Aalborg, Denmark, 25–27 January.

Scarso, E. and Bolisani, E. (2007) 'Communities of practice as structures for managing knowledge in networked corporations', *Journal of Manufacturing Technology Management*, 19(3): 374–90.

Scarso, E., Bolisani, E. and Salvador, L. (2008) 'A systematic framework for analysing the critical success factors of communities of practice', *Journal of Knowledge Management*, 13(6): 431–47.

Steiner, M. and Hartmann, C. (2006) 'Organizational learning in clusters: A case study on material and immaterial dimensions of cooperation', *Regional Studies*, 40(5): 493–506.

Suchman, L. (1987) *Plans and Situated Actions: The Problem of Human-machine Communication*, New York: Cambridge University Press.

Teigland, R. (2006) 'Exploring the role of communities of practice in regional innovation systems', in E. Coakes and S. Clarke (eds) *Encyclopedia of Communities of Practice in Information and Knowledge Management*. London: Idea Group Publishing, pp. 163–5.

Thompson, M. (2005) 'Structural and epistemic parameters in communities of practice', *Organization Science*, 16(2): 151–64.

Verganti, R. (2006) 'Innovating through DESIGN', *Harvard Business Review*, 84(12): 114–22.

Wenger, E.C. (1998) *Communities of Practice. Learning, Meaning, and Identity*, Cambridge, UK: Cambridge University Press.

Wenger, E.C. (2000) 'Communities of practice and social learning systems', *Organization*, 7(2): 225–46.

Wenger, E.C. (2004) 'Knowledge management as a doughnut: Shaping your knowledge strategy through communities of practices', *Ivey Business Journal*, January–February. http://www.knowledgeboard.com/download/1890/Knowledge-management-as-a-doughnut.pdf.pdf (accessed 20 September 2011).

Wenger, E.C. and Snyder, W.M. (2000) 'Communities of practice: The organizational frontier', *Harvard Business Review*, 78(1): 139–45.

Wenger, E.C., McDermott, R.A. and Snyder, W.M. (2002) *Cultivating Communities of Practice: A Guide to Managing Knowledge*, Boston, MA: Harvard Business School Press.

15 The importance of gatekeeping processes and reputation building in the sustainability of creative milieus

Evidence from case studies in Lisbon, Barcelona and São Paulo

Pedro Costa

Introduction

Certain territories and experiences have stood out as 'creative milieus' because they offer a specific atmosphere or certain conditions required to embed and develop sustainable creative processes in cultural activities (see Camagni *et al.* 2004; Cooke and Lazzeretti 2007; Costa 2007; Costa *et al.* 2007; Lazzeretti 2009; and in a wider perspective, O'Connor and Wynne 1996; Scott 2000). Specific governance mechanisms have played a key part in most of these success cases. The aim of this chapter is to explore a specific set of conditions that fosters creative processes in these experiences, particularly those related to reputation-building mechanisms and gatekeeping processes, which are undoubtedly vital to the development and sustainability of these cultural and creative activities.

Our conceptual framework focuses on the notion of creative milieu as one that combines a specific local production/consumption system, a specific governance system and a specific collective representations system. The chapter draws on this latter aspect in particular and the first part explores the role of the construction and sustainability of symbolic aspects in the development of a creative milieu situation.

Departing from the context of 'creativity' rhetoric and the many fuzzy concepts associated with these debates in recent years (Boden 1990; Csikszentmihalyi 1996; Hall 2000; Landry 2000; Caves 2002; ERICArts 2002; Florida 2002; Healey 2004; Kunzmann 2004; Towse 2004; Scott 2006; NESTA 2008), we propose three central conceptual statements and claim there is a need to shift from a conventional cultural intermediation perspective to a more focused analysis of reputation-building mechanisms.

An empirical illustration is then made in the framework of a broader research programme (the 'Creatcity' project, studying the forms of governance associated to creative dynamics in urban areas); this covers a wide range of 'potentially creative' situations comprising ten case studies in three cities (Lisbon, Portugal; Barcelona, Spain; São Paulo, Brazil), three cultural districts (Bairro Alto and Chiado, Lisbon;

Gracia, Barcelona; Vila Madalena, São Paulo), two industrial areas either under a process of urban (re)conversion or awaiting redevelopment (22@ Barcelona, and Alcântara, Lisbon), a well-established large scale event (São Paulo Fashion Week), a multicultural-based neighbourhood (Martim Moniz, Lisbon), two particular institutional experiences (Palo Alto, Barcelona, and SESC, São Paulo) and a 'regular' quarter (Almada, Lisbon). After a brief description of the main characteristics and dynamics in each of these experiences, we summarize some key aspects in the role of gatekeeping processes and mediation mechanisms in the development of these case studies, and demonstrate the importance of symbolic aspects and reputation building to their success.

Finally, these aspects are systematized and some concluding remarks are made on policy-making orientations.

New challenges for the debate on cultural and creative industries

In recent years, there has been intense debate and ample discussion and controversy around the concepts of 'creative industries' and 'creative cities', and more generally on the role of creativity and creative activities in territorial development (Costa *et al.* 2008).

On one hand, this need of discussion and all the 'noise' around it result from the fuzziness of most of the concepts used (Kunzmann 2004); to some extent this is due to the progressive convergence of diverse interests and academic traditions, with distinct disciplinary origins, and to the cross-fertilization of theoretical and methodological perspectives, in order to fill the need to overcome unsatisfying narrow thematic approaches to real transversal phenomenon. On the other hand, the debate is politically very attractive, and these concepts and rhetoric have been appropriated in policy making, increasing its 'fuzziness'. Multidimensional development policies based on such activities and 'creativity rhetoric' are certainly welcome in times of considerable economic change and budgetary contraction: the transversal policy actions and the multiplicity of outcomes that can be achieved in these fields in terms of various sustainable development goals (from value adding and economic growth, to job creation, social inclusion, urban regeneration, or participation and identity expression of minorities) are particularly attractive in this context. Thus, 'creativity' quickly became a trendy topic.

While we acknowledge the inevitability of going beyond this 'smoke curtain' and carrying out further enquiry on these issues, this is not the place for an in-depth analysis of this matter. Here, we would just like to contribute by systematizing some key issues in these debates, which are challenging the way we look at these concepts and analyze these activities. For that, we start with some personal reflections that result from several years' work in this field, assuming a clear focus in the specific field of cultural activities.

Creativity, value creation and reputation building

Drawing on all the creativity debates over recent years in various knowledge fields (urban planning, economics, geography, sociology, psychology, artificial intelligence, cultural studies, etc.) and the accompanying controversies (e.g. Hall 2000; Healey 2004; Markusen 2006; Scott 2006; Evans 2009; Flew and Cunningham 2010), we propose three central ideas in order to shed some more light on the relation between creativity, value creation and reputation-building processes in cultural activities, which are vital to our analysis.

First, creativity should be clearly assumed as a relative concept. At the same time, it should be recognized as something that cuts across (at least potentially) *all* economic activities and social practices.

So, creativity is relative: as seen before (Costa *et al.* 2007; Costa 2008), creativity is linked to processes or artefacts that require certain characteristics (to bring novelty, innovativeness and value). Margaret Boden (1990) stated that there are different kinds of creativity (psychological versus historical) and it can be seen in different lights and at distinct levels – something creative in one context or for one person is not necessarily so for another (e.g. a child that is able to paint something for the first time, a regular painter that explores a 'secure' artistic field, or an outstanding artist that explores the boundaries and expands the established artistic field, all express different kinds of creativity). Creators can surprise us by conceiving something unusual, that we are unfamiliar with; they can do something that represents a new point of view or perspective of the same subject; or they can bring something that apparently would be impossible to conceive. In these diverse situations, Boden (1990) states we are therefore confronted with non-familiar, exploratory or transformational creativity, respectively. Just as with innovation, creativity has 'incremental' and 'fundamental' steps and as a result must be seen as relative (in terms of time, space, and the personal and social frameworks in which that creativity emerges and is experienced).

Parallel to this, the assumption that creativity is in everything (not only in cultural, but also in other activities and with different degrees of intensity and social recognition) has significant implications for the analysis of creative dynamics. In effect, creativity is in everything, and can be part of everyday life, in social practices and economic processes. We are used to seeing it in 'traditional' cultural activities, or in some parts of these clusters at least (eventually excluding the manufacture of 'supports' and so on). We are also seeing it in some components of other economic products that increasingly include cultural, symbolic or aesthetic contents[1] (e.g. through design or architecture), which gradually spread to almost all economic sectors, but we must recognize that it can even exist in other activities that are often unrelated to cultural contents,[2] which are very diverse and that are socially perceived and legitimized in very distinct ways.

The corollary of this first proposal is that cultural activities are creative and should be recognized as such (or at least in some of their components) but this should be done at diverse levels and with different degrees of intensity and recognition. One crucial factor should not be underestimated: the social valorization of creativity, and therefore the need for an in-depth understanding of the varying degrees of social legitimization in these processes and all the aspects related to individual recognition of creativity.

For our purposes, it is necessary to shift from an excessive focus on the 'novelty' issue when analyzing these subjects (the overvaluation of the 'innovative' and 'new' dimensions of creativity that have been dominating most analysis in this field) to a more conscious analysis of the mechanisms underlying social recognition and the 'value creation' in each specific circumstance.

Second, we propose the notion that value creation in cultural activities can involve several facets (related to creativity but also with various other aspects) and must also be assumed as relative and contextual. Value creation (be it economic value or social, historical or cultural value, for instance) is dependent on legitimization, in other words on social (or individual) awareness of its value. This is true both to evaluate something as 'creative' (as stated in the previous point) but also to define the strict value of each product so as to recognize its economic/social/cultural value (Throsby 2001). This value can be the result of numerous factors: the actual quality, the fact of being new or innovative, its visibility, its brand, its reputation, the social distinction it can provide, and so on. But more importantly, this value can also be assessed (and recognized) in a multiplicity of layers, in different fields, at different scales, in a way that can be more or less comprehensive, in a specific society or social segment (e.g. the value of a piece of contemporary art versus a Renaissance painting). Therefore, the recognition of this value is necessarily made by each individual (naturally embedded in specific socio-economic and material contexts[3]), considering a wide diversity of reputational contexts of that specific 'creative good' or that artist. As has been widely illustrated by diverse works from sociology of art and culture (and cultural economics), this value creation (and, thus, economic added value) is made in a complex way by a variety of agents (in different art worlds, scenes, milieus, subcultures, etc.; see Becker 1982; DiMaggio 1987; Bourdieu 1994; Throsby 2001; Caves 2002) – and where countless gatekeepers and intermediation processes play a fundamental role, legitimizing works and authors in a multiplicity of fields or layers, that each individual perceives and experiences from a particular perspective.

A corollary to this is that we believe more focus should be given in academic analysis to the reputation-building mechanisms and to the conventions' construction processes that are underneath this. In effect, these can be decisive factors when determining the value of many cultural goods, and we should acknowledge the diversity, complexity and richness of mechanisms that are underlying these processes.

Third, we propose that reputation-building mechanisms are complex and have multiple interlinking dimensions, which range from authorship to the scene in which the work is made or experienced, among many other aspects. While this is nothing new, it is generally underestimated in current debates on creative activities. Moreover, art history and contemporary empirical observation have systematically demonstrated that this occurs in at least three distinct layers:

- the reputation of the creative product itself (the creative artefact, to use Boden's term, or in other words the artwork, or the creative good/service if we assume a wider perspective);

- the reputation of the artist or creator (authorship is often more determinant than the work itself, as art history constantly shows us);[4]
- the reputation of the place(s) in which these products are created/experienced/developed or these artists move – territories, milieus, scenes, *buzzes* (e.g. the music scenes in several cities, or all the cultural quarters and creative districts) – often associated with specific aesthetic affiliations, organizational/institutional arrangements, specific governance forms, activity clusters, etc.

All three layers are fundamental not only to the creation of the value (in the various phases of the value chain) of a creative good, but also, as Scott (2000) clearly demonstrates, for the territorial organization of these activities, particularly as they are mostly project-based work. In such labour markets, the symbolic construction of the value (for artists, for scenes, for the artwork itself) is heavily dependent on the formal and informal 'contracts' and negotiations that are made (both in material and in symbolic fields) by a wide range of actors that move in these milieus, from artists, technicians, entrepreneurs, critics, professors, to other sets of gatekeepers, and they are vital to the construction and development of careers, opportunities and *buzzes* (see Scott 2000, 2006; Caves 2002).

It must be acknowledged that the symbolic construction of value (and therefore its implications in the potential for generating economic value) in these contexts is a very complex mechanism that results from the combination and interrelation of these various interlinking dimensions; it is expressed in a multiplicity of shared conventions (be they more formal or informal, comprehensive or narrow, mainstream or alternative) on the real value of that creation, combining the user's individual perception of the reputation of the artist, the place, the affiliation, and the work of art itself.

For our analytical purposes, the corollary of this is the recognition of the importance of the sustainability of these conventions, or in other words the relevance of the permanent management of the shared meaning(s) about the value(s) of these activities, persons and places; and this leads us directly to the issue of the sustainability of the 'creative dynamics' and the way it is intrinsically dependent on all those mechanisms.

From the analysis of intermediation and gatekeepers to reputation-building processes

Intermediation and gatekeeping processes are widely studied in the field of cultural and creative industries, mostly in the tradition of the sociology of art and culture (from the pioneer works of DiMaggio and Hirsch 1976, and Becker 1982) and cultural economics. In recent years, these issues have been addressed in several other approaches and debates, in fields such as geography, economics and regional science (considering creative activities as well as many others[5]), with Richard Caves' (2002) 'institutional' approach being particularly interesting in this context.

However, it can be useful to demystify the gatekeeping concept and to 'unpack' the diversity of the intermediation mechanisms and gatekeeping functions usually involved in this (also fuzzy) concept. Indeed, these gatekeepers have a multitude of functions that are very diverse, and that are being challenged very differently nowadays: gatekeepers are essential to filter information, to provide information about what and who is on, to value, to rank, and to define hierarchies about what is fundamental, in a context of great uncertainty on both the demand and supply sides (Caves 2002). They are taste makers; they can provide distribution, in a variety of channels and windows; they can assure visibility; they can define and mark the success or failure of an artwork, in each art world and specific field of legitimization (be it the market, the group of friends, or the lucky few who appreciate that artwork that no one else will ever understand). Curators, critics, editors, media channels, journalists, programmers, art dealers, public collections and many others play a set of different, sometimes interlinking roles (e.g. the same agent or another that is closely connected assuming simultaneously several of these parts) in the provision of the cultural good or in the supply of information about it to the potential consumer, and thus in the structuring of the multiple art worlds.[6]

We believe it is now important to proceed to a small shift of perspective, away from the 'gatekeeping processes' point of view, and turn to the reputation-building mechanisms (and thus value creation) within these same processes, specifically focusing on the processes of constructing and maintaining reputations, which is intrinsically linked to the building and sustainability of the conventions mentioned above.

At this point, we should not be distracted by current debates on the hypothetical disintermediation of these creative industries (mostly centred in industries like music editing, audiovisual or videogames, whose traditional intermediary roles are particularly challenged by technological changes and the digital turn). Even in these cases, the fundamental role of gatekeepers is totally intact, just changing from some agents and processes to others (notably digital gatekeepers and gatekeeping processes that are often more diffuse, based on more fluid networks of knowledge diffusion): it is true that anyone in Europe can upload their music or films on the Internet and some seconds later it can be experienced in New Zealand, on the other side of the world; however, the relevant question to be asked is what makes a person on the other side of the world (know and) want to access the content that anyone can put in the web in Europe? The important issue here is which processes and mechanisms make this information flow and the reputation about the product/creator/place sufficient for someone to access it (be it in more mainstream or from alternative/emergent fields or scenes).

In the light of this, we consider it essential to focus on the relation between these reputation-building mechanisms and territory. The creative milieu concept was a key part of the theoretical framework of the research project on which the case studies described in the next section are based. This approach, drawing on innovative milieus literature, allowed us to read the creative dynamics observed in each of these case studies as a set of three distinct layers that configured that territorial situation:

- a specific localized productive system;
- a specific governance system;
- a specific collective representations system.

This framework (and particularly the third layer) allows us to assume and understand the primary role of these reputation-building mechanisms in the development of the dynamics observed in each territorial situation. The role of the symbolic aspects in the development of each creative milieu can therefore be captured and analyzed, and an attempt made to unpack 'the black box' of the intertwined reputations of 'creations', 'creators' and 'places of creation', in each of the specific cases, and to find how this alchemy can be mobilized to make these territorial systems sustainable.[7]

Creative milieus, governance and reputation-building mechanisms: empirical evidence in ten case studies

In this section we shed some light on the results of the empirical analysis used in this chapter as material for our discussion on the importance of reputation-building mechanisms in the development and sustainability of creative milieus. It draws on a partial set of the information collected in a specific research project, conducted in three different metropolises.

The 'Creatcity' project framework

The aim of the 'Creatcity' project ('Creatcity. A Governance Culture for the Creative City: Urban Vitality and International Networks'), funded by the Portuguese Science and Technology Foundation (FCT/MCTES), was to discuss territorially based creative dynamics and their governance mechanisms in diverse urban contexts. Drawing on the 'creative cities' debates, it sought to further knowledge and to build strategic action guidelines on governance mechanisms and dynamics that promote and embed urban vitality, creativity and competitiveness. It combined a conceptual and empirical component and focused on the cities of Lisbon (Portugal), Barcelona (Spain) and São Paulo (Brazil), where ten empirical case studies were selected for in-depth analysis.

The project was based on a transversal analysis of creativity in the three cities with the aim of drawing strategic policy-acting guidelines for the Lisbon metropolitan area. It encompassed several thematic dimensions: (a) systematizing contemporary economic restructuring and territorial challenges in each metropolitan area; (b) mapping their creative activities and resources; (c) analyzing the relation of these creative dynamics with material space, urban morphology and social appropriation of urban areas; and (d) examining local policy actions for internationalization.[8]

In addition to these specific case studies, other methodologies were also applied (desk research, both empirical and conceptual, etc.). Complementary empirical analyses were made in the three cities (data series, statistical analysis, etc.) as well as extra fieldwork in some case studies (urban, functional and morphological analyses, photographic survey, image examination, etc.). But the most pertinent analysis relevant to gatekeeping processes was conducted in a methodological framework that combined two steps:

1   A set of exploratory interviews: twenty-two exploratory interviews (ten in Lisbon, six in Barcelona, six in São Paulo) with local/regional/central government in different fields from urban, cultural and economic policy areas; with experts in consultancy and the academic world; and with some prominent creative/cultural institutions.
2   A set of case studies: ten case studies in the three metropolises (using nearly seventy in-depth interviews and other methodologies), i.e. Bairro Alto, Almada, Alcântara and Martim Moniz areas in Lisbon; Gracia district, 22@ urban renewal operation, and Palo Alto Association in Barcelona; Vila Madalena district, São Paulo Fashion Week event, and SESC (Commerce Social Services) institutional activity in São Paulo.

The following section provides a brief overview of the case studies and systematizes some of the typologies obtained from this research.

An overview of the ten case studies and their governance mechanisms

The aim of the project was not to compare the three different cities. Indeed, they are quite different demographically, socially, economically and in urban dynamics, as well as in their political and institutional frameworks. Instead, the purpose was to inquire about the capacity to embed and develop creative milieus (or territorially based culture-led dynamics) in different 'urban' ambiances.

Therefore, and following our exploratory interviews, ten distinct case studies were chosen as the basis for the analysis. The selection took into account the various kinds of 'typical' culture-led territorial dynamics mapped in recent literature around the world, such as cultural quarters, brownfield areas under redevelopment, urban regeneration operations, flagship events, or multicultural and multi-ethnic situations.

A comparative approach was taken in just three of the case studies: Bairro Alto in Lisbon, Gracia in Barcelona and Vila Madalena in São Paulo, all of which are 'conventional' creative districts or cultural quarters. Despite slight differences and nuances, and quite diverse historical and institutional backgrounds and urban characteristics, they share an analogous situation: 'creative' segments of the population (artists, bohemians, cultural activities, nightlife and other conviviality and sociability nodes) were going through a process of 'taking over' traditional residential areas in the three cases. Moreover, they are now all experiencing growing gentrification processes and a sort of shift from production to consumption, or from traditional cultural activities to more commodified market-based aesthetic-driven activities (with the progressive replacement of performing and visual arts with design shops and nightlife, for instance). Like many other cultural and creative districts all over the world, there are also strong use conflicts between residents and users, night-time and daytime activities, traditional and new residents, traditional and new activities, etc.

Some of the cases studies were chosen in industrial areas under redevelopment, covering different kinds of situations. The 22@ case study in Barcelona was chosen representing a top-down perspective. It is centred in a huge urban redevelopement operation in Catalonia's, and Spain's, former biggest industrial area (Poblenou), which is going through an inevitable restructuring process due to the contemporary global socio-economic context. Mixing the attractiveness of creative activities, real estate development and deep urban change, this operation aimed to attract many creative industries, mostly in fields related to high-tech research and development (R&D) or audiovisual and multimedia, to this location.

Using a bottom-up perspective, we selected the Palo Alto Association case, also in the same Poblenou area. Here, abandoned industrial facilities are still being occupied by collectives of artists (formally or informally, with squats, rentals or temporary occupations), just as in many other brownfield areas around the world. This sheds light on the long-term institutionalization process in such cases, like this longstanding association, where these spaces go from being rented by groups of artistic and creative friends to becoming the reputable location for some of the city's best known and established designers and architects.

Alcântara in Lisbon is another similar case, albeit still in an earlier phase. It also has an abandoned industrial area, near the city centre, close to the river, in an excellent location in terms of access, which makes it very attractive for real estate development. Seven major developments are planned for the area but are still waiting for licensing (and a master plan) from the local authorities. At the same time, some signs of traditional cultural activities and mainstream nightlife in the area would bring about the existence of creative dynamics. Meanwhile, one of the real estate promoters decided to rent some of the ex-industrial facilities and pavilions for creative activities until planning permission was given; this was a huge success and rapidly generated specific creative-led territorial dynamics in that area of the city and a strong hype around that. However, it is assumed this will be short term as the five-year contracts signed with the landlords were designed to terminate once planning permission had been granted.

Another typical situation is the multicultural territory case study, in part of Lisbon's old city centre (the Martim Moniz area), where a multicultural and multi-ethnic set of communities with strongly culturally marked social and economic practices has come together. The results of this specific case were quite disappointing in terms of the strength of effective cultural cross-fertilizations and consequent 'creative productions', other than each community's particular manifestations of identity and the development of markets for specific ethnic products; however, the area undoubtedly has great potential for growing intercultural exchange and the development of specific creative mechanisms and movements based on the multiple and lively cultural expressions taking place.

Encompassing situations in the usual literature review, we also incorporated a big event, namely the São Paulo Fashion Week case study. Contrary to many other events, this very interesting experience is a long-term (privately run) operation that consistently and continuously links artistic and economic aspects, through a small permanent structure, even though it is only a twice yearly event; it links the fashion world with media, communication, textile, commerce, business services, tourism, and various other economic sectors, in a coherent and widely acknowledged manner. As the promoters assume, it is not just a fashion event, since its impact and areas of action are broadly transversal to myriad economic and cultural activities.

The São Paulo's SESC case study is a rather original and quite interesting institutional experience, in light of the most visible success cases linked to the 'creative cities' rhetoric. SESC is an institutional structure for the provision of cultural, sport and entertainment services to commerce workers and their families (though in practice extended to the whole society), managed by business associations, but funded from a percentage of the salaries of all commerce/service workers, under federal regulation. It operates all over Brazil but is particularly relevant and visible in São Paulo, as its budget in a region that represents almost a third of the country's gross national product (GNP) is significant. However, the most interesting aspect is that this structure develops site-specific projects in each neighbourhood, which resemble community centres and serve a combination of functions in the same complex;[9] they have specific characteristics that are adapted to the socio-economic profile and needs of that area of the city. It is not only this territorial specificity that is remarkable but also their aim of mixing targets and audiences by bringing together the activities and services provided under one roof (e.g. theatre, library, exhibitions, craft courses, jewellery ateliers, training, as well as dental services, gym, swimming pools, eateries). They serve a mix of populations (from the multiple cultural audiences to the students attending photo classes; from the local citizen going swimming to the children using the Internet; from the old man that goes every morning to read his paper to nearby office workers enjoying lunch at affordable prices), offering an easy, non-sacralized (and cheap) contact with cultural activity. This is assumed in the broadest sense, from generalist to specific/elitist cultural programming, including very famous artists at reasonable prices.

Finally, Almada, a consolidated city in Lisbon suburbs, was chosen as our last case study to cover our need for a 'regular' quarter, a 'normal' area with the aim of understanding the conditions that develop creative dynamics in an ordinary, everyday-life territory that literature does not usually associate with creative dynamics. Although the dynamics here were not so institutionalized or publicly acknowledged as in other cases, they were especially interesting and consistent and proved one of the biggest surprises of our study. Perhaps the area is not so 'normal' as we intended, but in fact, no territory is; moreover, the dynamics verified in Almada in diverse creative fields[10] are clearly embedded in a strong traditional associative fabric, with historical roots in this area, together with very consistent policy intervention in the cultural field. Nevertheless, the case shows us that creativity and creative dynamics can arise in many diverse contexts and situations that are far from those that are more typical.

To sum up, we can say that there was undoubtedly a diversity of situations here, reflecting the wide range of empirical situations and case studies analyzed in specialized literature in recent decades:

- Some are clearly territorial dynamics based on more or less structured local productive systems and locally rooted milieus, while others are less territorialized projects or experiences, which nonetheless have clear spatial implications.
- Some are essentially bottom-up experiences, emerging from endogenous agents and local communities, while others clearly result from top-down initiatives.
- Some depart from local or regional public initiatives and policies, others are based essentially on private initiatives, and yet others are mixed initiatives involving a wide variety of agents, with a diverse nature.
- Some are central to the city and to urban representations, while others assume more peripheral locations in the metropolitan areas of which they are a part.
- Some are essentially based on more alternative or independent cultural activities, while others cover a wide range of mainstream cultural and creative activities.
- Some are centred on dynamics based on a broad range of creativity and creative activities, while others are based on the traditional core of cultural activities.

Our analysis of these diverse situations sought to understand each of the ten case studies in the light of a specific conceptual framework (which is not the objective of this chapter to develop; for that see, for example, Costa *et al.* 2007; Costa *et al.* 2008; Seixas and Costa 2010); it is clearly centred on the notion of creative milieus and on the discussion of the governance mechanisms underlying these territorial systems, and the long-term sustainability prospects of these dynamics.

The main issues addressed in these analyses include:

1   The reasons for their development: which factors were underneath these dynamics, and why they were found there and not anywhere else; what is notable about them?
2   The identification of the main governance forms underlying these dynamics.
3   The prospects for their sustainability in the long term: were these situations likely to remain as such, and in the same part of town, or might they move elsewhere (given all the gentrification risks, conflicts and uneven power relations that marked each specific case)?
4   The policy action: could deliberate (public?) action be taken (and/or would be desirable) in order to enhance the sustainability of these areas/experiences?

What kind of governance mechanisms are at the root of these
"success" cases? Very diverse experiences: (I)

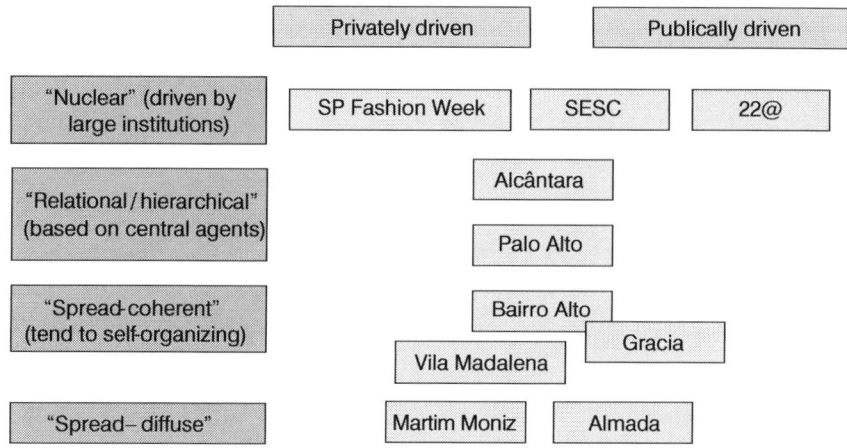

Figure 15.1 Main governance mechanisms in the 10 case studies, typology 1

Source: 'CreatCity' project, our elaboration

In the light of this framework, a set of typologies was developed for this analysis that considered their governance mechanisms and the perspectives for their sustainability, as shown in Figures 15.1 (public/private nature and the degree of diffusion/concentration of experiences) and 15.2 (degree of territorialization and the urban typological nature of experiences).

We leave the analysis of these situations to the cited papers, and focus here on underlining the variety of situations and the resulting diversity of implications in terms of need for public intervention and specific policies (which are framed in a final typology in Costa 2010). For the purposes of the analysis in this text, we just draw attention to the diversity of factors identified as critical to the sustainability of these systems, but focusing our attention on some of them.

As can be seen in Figure 15.3, the sustainability of these situations depends on many factors, some related to the evolution of the structural conditions on which the experience and its endogenous dynamics are based, others to the evolution of urban contextual conditions, and yet others related to the evolution of the external framework. As already stated, some are associated to the fields of the production of symbolic value (e.g. image, role in mediation processes, but also self-representations and common identity), and those will be addressed in the next section. However, most analyses usually underestimate two factors and, as they are also closely interrelated to the previous aspect, we would like to emphasize them here: the relevance of specific actors/individuals in these processes (which was a determinant in the genesis of several of our case studies and is often obscured by more structuralist approaches) and the management of internal use conflicts between actors, inherent to all these systems (whose regulation is vital for the long-term evolution of each case).

What kind of governance mechanisms are at the root of these
"success" cases? Very diverse experiences: (II)

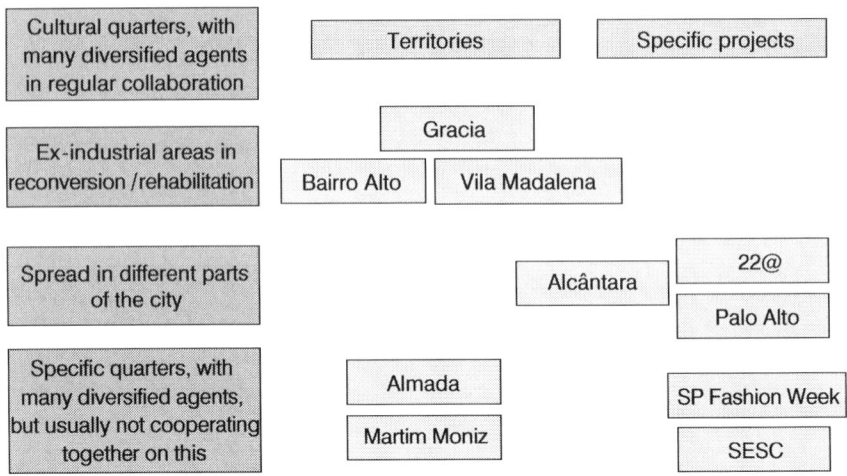

| Cultural quarters, with many diversified agents in regular collaboration | Territories | Specific projects |

Gracia

Bairro Alto | Vila Madalena

Spread in different parts of the city

Alcântara

22@

Palo Alto

Specific quarters, with many diversified agents, but usually not cooperating together on this

Almada

Martim Moniz

SP Fashion Week

SESC

Ex-industrial areas in reconversion / rehabilitation

Figure 15.2 Main governance mechanisms in the 10 case studies, typology 2

Source: 'CreatCity' project, our elaboration

A permanent management of (in)visible tensions

Evolution of structural conditions of the experience/territory (endogenous dynamics)

(e.g. density, dimension, heterogeneity, symbolic reputation, etc.)

Evolution of urban contextual conditions

(urban morphology, social, economic, etc.)

Evolution of external framework

(e.g., competition conditions, etc.)

Production of symbolic value (image, role on mediation processes, but also self-representations and common identity

Sustainability of the experience

'Individual' factors (leadership, policy, etc.)

Management of internal use - conflicts

− PERMANENT REINVENTION
− IMPORTANCE OF PUBLIC INTERVENTION (DIRECT/INDIRECT)

Figure 15.3 Crucial factors for sustainability

Source: 'CreatCity' project, our elaboration

The most important outcome to be underlined here is the need for a permanent balance and management between the multiple interests and rationales of the various agents involved in each of these systems, which is closely associated with their specific governance mechanisms (in most of the cases essentially self-regulatory ones). This leads us to postulate the need of considering the permanent (re)invention of those governance mechanisms in every situation, as well as to assume the vital importance of thinking of the relation of these systems to the various kinds of potential public intervention (direct or indirect) regarding their sustainability.

Reputation building and sustainability of the territorial systems

Reputation and symbolic aspects are essential to the development of creative milieus and territorialized creative dynamics (Costa *et al.* 2007; Costa 2008) as they play a key role in congregating specific art worlds around particular places, that distinguish themselves for polarizing labour markets, providing socialization, access to information, visibility and legitimization circuits, among other aspects.

In the framework of this project, we also strived to understand in what way they are fundamental to the sustainability of these situations, and how the management of these symbolic and reputational issues in the context of the specific governance forms of each system is critical (as the management of internal use conflicts) to their sustainability.

The diversity of mechanisms analyzed is summed up in Table 15.1, which relates these symbolic issues in each case study to their main characteristics and governance forms.

The reputation of these places as creative milieus not only depends on a wide range of factors, but more importantly is critical for the reproduction of the system itself, although not always positively. The (real or artificial) positive image of a place or situation as a 'creative experience' can sometimes even prejudice creativity.

The case of the three cultural districts is paradigmatic. As in many other creative quarters around the world, this reputation can develop and accelerate gentrification processes and the shift from production-based systems to consumption-based dynamics; for instance, local creation of performing and visual artists can be replaced by design and antique shops, art galleries or other 'creative cluster' actors, more willing to pay for the land and to benefit from more 'mainstreamed' symbolic representations of these areas, in the perceptions of both external and internal agents. This situation undoubtedly occurs in all three cases: Bairro Alto, Vila Madalena and Gracia (for details, see Costa *et al.* 2010).

Symbolic and reputational aspects are direct and also evident in the São Paulo Fashion Week case. An event like this is necessarily based on reputation, which can be explored in various ways. For now, the event's reputation has essentially positive effects; even government authorities have taken advantage of it to promote public health and environmental campaigns. In this case it is the promoting structure that most benefits and the building of reputation and conventions enlarge the field of action (and potential added value) for the event's private promoters.

Table 15.1 Case studies: governance structure and reputation-building mechanisms

Case study	Main characteristics of the case	Governance structure	Type of experience, regarding sustainability and policy action	Importance of reputation-building mechanisms
Bairro Alto (Lisbon) Gracia (Barcelona) Vila Madalena (São Paulo)	• Territorial dynamic • Cultural quarters, with many diversified agents in regular collaboration • Multiplicity of cultural activities and vital importance of sociability nodes • Strong use conflicts	• 'Spread – coherent' (tend to self-organizing)	• Decentralized, cooperative and potentially auto-sufficient (self-regulatory mechanisms versus risks associated to strong use conflicts)	• Reputation ↔ gentrification processes • Mainstreaming issues • Production → consumption based systems • Multiple use conflicts
22@ (Barcelona)	• Brownfield area in reconversion/rehabilitation • Top-down reconversion operation • Huge dimension • Importance of media, audiovisual, creative industries, R&D, etc. • Strong use conflicts	• 'Nuclear' (driven by large institutions) • Essentially publicly driven • Top-down	• Centralized, very dependent on public support or regulation (direct or indirect)	• Reputation of key agents in the 'high-tech' symbolic transformation • Gentrification and use conflicts with alternative creative segments
Palo Alto (Barcelona)	• Brownfield area in reconversion/rehabilitation • Bottom-up project (long-standing) • Long-term 'institutionalization' process • Alternative → Mainstreaming	• 'Relational/hierarchical' (based on central agents) • Bottom-up	• Based on private/associative initiative, with evolving objectives (and evolving public support)	• Symbolic visibility is essential for the sustainability with the change in governance structures – with public intervention
Alcântara (Lisboa)	• Brownfield area in reconversion/rehabilitation • Including a private-based medium-term project (Lx Factory) • Mostly creative industries	• 'Relational/hierarchical' (based on central agents)	• Based on private/associative initiative, with evolving objectives (and evolving public support)	• Symbolic visibility is essential for the sustainability with the change in objectives (and governance structures?) – with public intervention?

Case study	Main characteristics of the case	Governance structure	Type of experience, regarding sustainability and policy action	Importance of reputation-building mechanisms
São Paulo Fashion Week (São Paulo)	• Regular event (long-standing) • Non-territorialized: spread in different parts of the city • Long-term strategy • Fashion cluster and beyond	• 'Nuclear' (driven by large institutions) • Privately driven	• Market-based, but with long-term strategy and strongly defined focus of sustainability	• Reputation ↔ enlargement of fields of action • Stakeholders involved
SESC (São Paulo)	• Institution (with particular funding scheme) • Network of proximity centres spread in different parts of the city • Territorial proximity-based (neighborhood-adapted) • Diverse range of activities	• 'Nuclear' (driven by large institutions) • Indirect public support (by regulation)	• Centralized, very dependent on public support or regulation (direct or indirect)	• Symbolic capital as leverage for activities versus • Difficulties of managing different segments (distinctiveness and liminality)
Martim Moniz (Lisbon)	• Specific quarter, with many diversified agents, but usually not cooperating on this • Multicultural, multi-ethnic situation • City centre	• 'Spread – diffuse' (less cooperative)	• More 'uncertain' and 'casual' dynamics, with weaker self-identity (and dependency on public support?)	• Symbolic importance of ethnicity • Symbolic field as the main missing link to the coherence and sustainability?
Almada (Lisbon)	• Specific quarter, with many diversified agents, but usually not cooperating together on this • 'Regular' quarter • Strong associative tradition and local policy intervention • Periphery (suburban)	• 'Spread – diffuse' (partially cooperative)	• More 'uncertain' and 'casual' dynamics, with weaker self-identity (and dependency on public support?)	• Periphery image versus cultural centrality • Symbolic field as the main missing link to the coherence and sustainability?

Source: Our elaboration based on 'CreatCity' project outputs

Reputation and legitimization mechanisms are also relevant in 22@ in Barcelona. On the one hand, due to the impact that leading public bodies (universities, R&D institutions, public audiovisual sector) have in 'colonizing' the renewed spaces and in the area's 'upgraded' creative image, which can potentially attract other investors and promoters in these sectors. On the other hand, due to the use conflicts verified in the area, which are opposing two very distinct symbolic 'Poblenous'. Like the cases of creative districts, these are critical aspects to the system's sustainability, through gentrification processes and the substitution of residents and activities in this huge area, and their impacts in terms of the multitude of 'alternative' production that is still currently located there.

This situation is also being noticed in the other two brownfield areas cases: Palo Alto and Alcântara. Though at different stages of evolution, social (and political) awareness of the 'creative situation' is clearly vital for their maintenance in both situations as the original projects and the relation forces within their governance system evolve. In the Palo Alto case, the symbolic and reputational effects have been vital to the project's re-orientation and this was essential to its sustainability; the situation is potentially similar, at least in the Lx Factory case, in the Alcântara case study. This happened some years ago in the Spanish case. The reputation and visibility gained by some of its agents, notably the public acknowledgement of designer Mariscal after his link to the Olympic Games, was essential in catalyzing the public intervention that enabled the project to be maintained when the original owners wanted to sell the land. The city council bought the property as posterior rentals for the artists there; this intervention is an excellent example of how reputation can be central to the sustainability of these systems. A similar situation is now taking place in Alcântara. Naturally, the firms that rented the places to artists while waiting for permission for their real estate development will soon be returning to their original plans. But they are facing strong pressure and lobbying within the arts and creative milieus for public intervention (be it the same kind as in the Spanish case, or planning and regulation-based).

Curiously, the SESC case is the least contested and most unanimously recognized of the ten cases, and its reputational base is an important leverage for the development of all its activities (including huge promotion mechanisms and media activity). This case is marked by transversal involvement of different populations in multi-layer strategies for a variety of audiences and is therefore particularly interesting in terms of the difficulties of managing reputation and legitimizing mechanisms in the context of the tricky conciliation of different market segments (and art worlds) in their cultural provision. Inclusiveness strategies are not easy to implement when some of the agents are used to work on the basis of distinctiveness and liminality.

Finally, the two least structured systems: although they are vital, dynamic and decentralized, they are effectively less cooperative and less self-sustainable as coherent systems than the other cases. We believe that this symbolic and representational field is one of the missing links in which public action can be important in order to improve the governance mechanisms and the coherence of these systems.

Although the Martim Moniz area is largely recognized as the main multicultural and multi-ethnic place in the centre of Lisbon, in fact the multiple communities are not really connected in representations (or, to a certain extent, in real practices) nor form an effective cooperative system. Cultural expression and participation are essential to this area's vitality, and these are aspects that can still be improved in reputational terms (both quantitively and qualitatively).

Central Almada benefits from the strong reputation of some key institutions, particularly in the performing arts (internationally renowned groups, festivals, facilities) and even from the acknowledgment of the region's strong associative tradition and well-defined identity; however, it is still not seen as a coherent system, in most people's symbolic representations.[11] Action that focuses not only on territorial marketing, but on promoting real bonds and interactions amongst the existing agents could be fundamental here to the development and self-awareness of this system, thus improving its potential sustainability.

Conclusions

This chapter aimed to explore the importance of gatekeeping processes and reputation-building mechanisms in the development of creative activities and the enhancement of creative milieus.

It is necessary to go further in this field and move from the more traditional focus on the gatekeepers and intermediation analysis to a stricter analysis of the reputation-building processes and gatekeeping mechanisms required for the creation of cultural, social and economic value in these activities, and thus often vital to the sustainability of creative milieus and culture-led territorial systems.

The sustainability of these situations is therefore often closely linked to the sustainability of the diverse 'conventions' (more mainstream or alternative, universally shared or not) that people share about the value of those milieus, their artists and their creations, about the value of the 'living experiences' that can be made in such places.

While this is immediately perceptible when we think of heritage goods or most culture-led development operations linked to the identity of place, and to material and immaterial heritage, it is also valid for a broader set of experiences and cases like the ten case studies under analysis here.

This leads us to the diversity of governance mechanisms underlying these experiences (some strongly based on public interventions, others on market, many on formal and informal complex networks of interdependencies), and to the diverse needs of public intervention that are being (or could be) pursued there.

It should be noted that however well intentioned this public intervention is, it may sometimes have harmful effects, particularly in the symbolic field. As some of these case studies clearly demonstrate (notably in the three cultural districts, like in many similar cases throughout the world), these actions can be prejudicial if neither the territory nor the real governance forms sustaining the system and regulating the permanent use conflicts between their multiple agents are well understood. For instance, the institutionalization (and symbolic mainstreaming) of creative and cultural quarters often have effects in terms of gentrification processes and of mainstreaming of cultural activities that tend to push culturally creative people (at least the less prosperous or the more alternative, transgressive and really creative) away to other areas. Although more and more people may commonly perceive the neighbourhood to be creative (and it would be selling even more 'creative goods'), it may in fact become less and less creative (albeit sometimes retaining conviviality and sociability nodes for 'creative people', which is also fundamental to the development and sustainability of these clusters).

It is therefore strategically important for policy-making intervention to understand the real governance mechanisms sustaining each local system, to have the capacity to recognize and manage the use conflicts and the different agents' interests and motivations and to act very carefully when dealing with the symbolic sphere: usually, it is politically very attractive but, in the long term, its effects on the territory are not assured.

Notes

1 In other words (and regardless of all the controversy in this conceptual field) the ones that include the three characteristics Throsby relates to 'cultural goods': incorporating some form of creativity, implying the transmission of aesthetic or symbolic meaning, and potentially acknowledging authorship (see Throsby 2001).

2 And in this particular aspect, we should acknowledge Florida's (2002) contribution to the 'creative' debates, with his 'broad band' creative class.

3 As can be seen in Bourdieu's work on these issues, particularly considering the notion of 'fields', but also their potential flexibility (see Bourdieu 1994).

4 As can be clearly seen by the way careers are managed in these art worlds (on this, see Caves 2002).

5 See, for example, a special publication of *Regional Studies* on this topic (vol. 42, issue 6, July 2008).

6 Which explains that these gatekeeping processes can also be viewed many times as a source of lock in and exclusion.

7 We are considering here consistent territorialized systems, which will be quite different from examples of (almost) de-territorialized situations, such as 'temporary clusters', 'field configuring events' or 'materialization of a art field situations', as described by many authors in recent years.

8 For more information see http://creatcity.dinamia.iscte.pt.

9 Which can be an ex-industrial facility (e.g. SESC Pompeia), a corporate building like many others in the main street (Avenida Paulista) or assume other forms such as warehouses or even farms.

10 These creative fields go well beyond the well-known dynamics in performing arts for which Almada is traditionally recognized, with several companies and festivals, including the most important in Portugal in the theatrical field.

11 Even with Almada City Council actively promoting media campaigns to change the city's suburban image of the 'other side of the river' with the dominant idea that people need to go to Lisbon for all everyday-life activities (with the 'on the right side' slogan, focused on the quality of life, and cultural and other amenities provided by the city).

References

Becker, H. (1982) *Art Worlds*, Berkeley, CA: University of California Press.
Boden, M. (1990) *The Creative Mind: Myths and Mechanisms*, London: Weidenfeld and Nicolson.
Bourdieu, P. (1994) *The Field of Cultural Production*, Cambridge, UK: Polity Press.
Camagni, R., Maillat, D. and Matteacciolli, A. (eds) (2004) *Ressources naturelles et culturelles, milieux et développement local*, Neuchatel: EDES.
Caves, R. (2002) *Creative Industries: Contracts between Art and Commerce*, Cambridge, MA and London: Harvard University Press.
Cooke, P. and Lazzeretti, L. (2007) *Creative Cities, Cultural Clusters and Local Development*, Cheltenham: Edward Elgar.
Costa, P. (2007) 'Creativity, innovation and territorial agglomeration in cultural activities: The roots of the creative city', in P. Cooke and L. Lazzeretti (eds) *Creative Cities, Cultural Clusters and Local Development*, Cheltenham: Edward Elgar, pp. 183–210.
Costa, P. (2008) 'Creative milieus, gatekeepers and cultural production: Evidence from a survey to Portuguese artists', *Review of Cultural Economics*, Korea Association for Cultural Economics, 11(1): 3–31.
Costa, P. (2010) 'Creative milieus and urban governance: A typology based on 10 case studies in Lisboa, Barcelona and São Paulo', paper presented at the 16th International Conference on Cultural Economics by the ACEI, Copenhagen, Denmark, 9–12 June.
Costa, P., Vasconcelos, B. and Sugahara, G. (2007) 'O meio urbano e a génese da criatividade nas actividades culturais', in *Recriar e valorizar o território*, Actas do 13º congresso da APDR, Açores, 5–7 Julho, Coimbra: APDR.
Costa, P., Magalhães, M., Vasconcelos, B. and Sugahara, G. (2008) 'On "creative cities" governance models: A comparative approach', *The Service Industries Journal*, 28(3–4): 393–413.
Costa, P., Latoeira, C. and Lopes, R. (2010) *Apropriação, conflitos de uso e produção do espaço público em 3 bairros criativos: uma abordagem fotográfica ao Bairro Alto, Gracia e Vila Madalena*, Working Paper no. 07/10, Lisbon: DINÂMIA-CET.
Csikszentmihalyi, M. (1996) *Creativity: Flow and the Psychology of Discovery and Invention*, London: Harper Collins.
DiMaggio, P. (1987) 'Classification in art', *American Sociological Review*, 52(4): 440–55.
DiMaggio, P. and Hirsch, P. (1976) 'Production organizations in the arts', *American Behavioral Scientist*, 19(6): 735–52.
ERICArts – European Research Institute for Comparative Cultural Policy and the Arts (2002) *Creative Europe: On Governance and Management of Artistic Creativity in Europe*, Bonn: ERICArts.
Evans, G. (2009) 'Creative cities, creative spaces and urban policy', *Urban Studies*, 46(5–6): 1003–40.
Flew, T. and Cunningham, S. (2010) 'Creative industries after the first decade of debate', *The Information Society*, 26(2): 113–23.
Florida, R. (2002) *The Rise of the Creative Class: And How it's Transforming Work, Leisure and Everyday Life*, New York: Basic Books.
Hall, P. (2000) 'Creative cities and economic development', *Urban Studies*, 37(4): 639–49.
Healey, P. (2004) 'Creativity and urban governance', *DISP*, 158(3): 11–20.
Kunzmann, K. (2004) 'An agenda for creative governance in city regions', *DISP*, 158(3): 5–10.

Landry, C. (2000) *The Creative City: A Toolkit for Urban Innovators*, London: Comedia/ Earthscan.

Lazzeretti, L. (2009) 'The creative capacity of culture and the new creative milieu', in G. Becattini, M. Bellandi and L. De Propris (eds) *Handbook of Industrial Districts*, Cheltenham: Edward Elgar, pp. 281–94.

Markusen, A. (2006) 'Urban development and the politics of a creative class: Evidence from the study of artists', *Environment and Planning A*, 38(10): 1921–40.

NESTA (2008) *Beyond the Creative Industries*, Technical Report, London: NESTA.

O'Connor, J. and Wynne, D. (ed.) (1996) *From the Margins to the Centre: Cultural Production and Consumption in the Post-industrial City*, Aldershot: Arena.

Scott, A.J. (2000) *The Cultural Economy of Cities*, New Delhi, London and Thousand Oaks, CA: Sage.

Scott, A.J. (2006) 'Creative cities: Conceptual issues and policy questions', *Journal of Urban Affairs*, 28(1): 1–17.

Seixas, J. and Costa, P. (2010) 'Criatividade e governança na cidade contemporânea: a conjugação de dois conceitos poliédricos e complementares', *Cidades, Comunidades e Territórios*, 20–21: 27–41.

Throsby, D. (2001) *Economics and Culture*, Cambridge, UK: Cambridge University Press.

Towse, R. (2004) *Towards an Economics of Creativity*, RECIDA Working Paper no. 1, Rotterdam: Faculty of History and the Arts, Erasmus University Rotterdam.

Index

Printed in Great Britain
by Amazon